POLICE POWERS IN
THE EVOLUTION AN

Edited by R.C. MACLEOD and
DAVID SCHNEIDERMAN

Police Powers in Canada: The Evolution and Practice of Authority

Published in association with the Centre for Constitutional Studies,
University of Alberta, by

UNIVERSITY OF TORONTO PRESS
Toronto Buffalo London

Toronto Buffalo London
Printed in Canada

ISBN 0-8020-2863-2 (cloth)
ISBN 0-8020-7362-x (paper)

Printed on acid-free paper

Canadian Cataloguing in Publication Data

Main entry under title:

Police powers in Canada : the evolution and practice of authority

Co-published by the Centre for Constitutional Studies,
University of Alberta.
Papers presented at a conference held in Edmonton,
Oct. 18–19, 1991.
ISBN 0-8020-2863-2 (bound) ISBN 0-8020-7362-X (pbk.)

1. Police power – Canada – Congresses. 2. Police –
Canada – Congresses. I. Macleod, R.C., 1940– .
II. Schneiderman, David, 1958– . III. University
of Alberta. Centre for Constitutional Studies.

HV8157.P65 1994 363.2'0971 C94-930574-X

Contents

Contributors

Chris Braiden	Superintendent (Retired), Edmonton Police Service
Jean-Paul Brodeur	International Centre of Comparative Criminology, University of Montreal
M.L. Friedland	Faculty of Law, University of Toronto
Curt Taylor Griffiths	School of Criminology, Simon Fraser University
DeLloyd J. Guth	Faculty of Law, University of Manitoba
Harish C. Jain	Faculty of Business, McMaster University
R.C. Macleod	Department of History, University of Alberta
Greg Marquis	Department of History, Saint Mary's University
James C. Robb	Faculty of Law, University of Alberta
David Schneiderman	Centre for Constitutional Studies, University of Alberta
Roger A. Shiner	Department of Philosophy, University of Alberta
David E. Smith	Department of Political Studies, University of Saskatchewan
Philip C. Stenning	Centre of Criminology, University of Toronto
Don Stuart	Faculty of Law, Queen's University
Louise Viau	Faculty of Law, University of Montreal

Acknowledgments

We would like to acknowledge the generous financial support provided for this project by the Alberta Law Foundation. Our colleagues on the management board of the Centre for Constitutional Studies – Tim Christian, Bruce Elman, Gerald Gall, Ronald Hamowy, Anne McLellan, Peter Meekison, and Allan Tupper – were helpful and supportive throughout. We would like to thank Irene Fecycz, who helped with the editorial work. Above all we would like to express our appreciation for the efforts of Christine Urquhart, without whom nothing gets done around the Centre.

Introduction

The steady rise in crime rates, combined with dramatic media spectacles at home (Oka) and elsewhere (the Rodney King episode), have eroded public confidence in the police to a degree unprecedented in this century. At the same time the Canadian Charter of Rights and Freedoms has raised new questions about police powers, casting doubts on practices of long standing. The nineteenth-century notion of police powers in the United States concerned the ability of government to place limits on peoples' 'liberty' and 'property.' We use the term in a more modern way – to refer to the powers conferred upon the police rather than to the ability of the state to engage in economic regulation. While the courts in the United States began the process of defining police powers in this modern way even before *Miranda*, we are unaccustomed to thinking about what our police should or should not do in very precise terms. The project organized by the Centre for Constitutional Studies at the University of Alberta was intended to help initiate that process. These papers are the result.

Policing as we know it evolved in communities that were, by our standards, extraordinarily homogenous in terms of race, language, and religion. Where police existed at all before the nineteenth century, they were extensions of the King's army; their essence was force and fear. The great innovation of the new police was that the principal source of their authority lay not in numbers or firepower but in their role as delegates of the larger society. They were perceived by the generally law-abiding majority of the population as the community's representatives in the enforcement of its rules. As many historians have pointed out, there were class divisions that complicated the picture, but there is abundant evidence that the police could count on the active support of most of the people most of the time, even when it came to the unpopular duties of investigating crime and making arrests.

In the heterogeneous societies that are the norm at the end of the twentieth century, however, the old rules no longer apply. The police officer is no longer the impartial enforcer of the rules. He or she is perceived primarily as a member of a racial, ethnic group, or gender, usually the dominant one in the society. It is assumed that the officer will, consciously or unconsciously, favour members of his or her group and apply the law harshly against members of other groups. At a minimum, the effectiveness of the police is greatly reduced. Law-abiding individuals from minority groups are reluctant to cooperate with the police because they believe suspects from their community will not be treated fairly. The question of whether or not those individuals have objectively broken the law becomes secondary. At worst, all trust disappears and the police are regarded as enemies of the people; laws are seen as devices to continue the subjugation of the minority and maintain the dominance of the majority. In these circumstances the authority of the police shrinks to the area covered by the range of their weaponry. While short-term effects of the loss of trust can be immensely volatile, as in Los Angeles and Oka, its long-term effects are corrosive of civil society.

There is no shortage of proposed solutions to the dilemmas faced by the police and by those concerned with maintaining an optimum balance between order and liberty. These can be grouped loosely into four categories: *technological, managerial, political*, and *legal. Technological* solutions emanate mostly from the United States. They include the adoption of all manner of gadgets and techniques: from computers to DNA testing to sophisticated weapons, all designed to give the police an edge over criminals and, presumably, thereby to deter potential law-breakers. Demands for greater numbers of police also fall into this category. None of these technological solutions, alone or in combination, seems likely to address fundamental and systemic problems. This is not to say that there should not be adequate numbers of police, but the numbers of police per capita have not fallen in recent times; if anything they have risen in most jurisdictions. Nor is it to say they should not be well equipped, but there is no evidence that better equipment correlates with lower crime rates.

The set of policies that might be called *managerial* solutions include the recruitment of minorities, improved training, civilian review, and community policing. By now, it is taken for granted that the principal remedy for racial hostilities is to recruit members of various groups with the goal of creating a demographic analogue of the larger society. The theory, usually more of an assumption since evidence is rarely produced to support it, seems to be that once each minority achieves its proper level of representation, public confidence in the police will be restored. As a practical matter, for any police force above the level of a small town, complications multiply. Unless the ethnic pattern of the police on the street is matched to that of the population neighbourhood by neighbourhood, the overall ethnic balance remains an abstraction. Minorities are not interchangeable, as policies aimed at recruitment often seem to assume. Distrust between various minority groups may often be as important as that between minorities and the dominant society. If the moral authority of the police is somehow tied to being ethnically representative, should the legal definition of police powers follow suit? These are uncomfortable questions, but they need to be addressed if there is to be any hope of seriously attacking the problem.

Recruitment of minorities has overshadowed the importance of training programs aimed at teaching police about minority community practices and values. Where these have been undertaken, as in Metro Toronto, they have not been taken seriously enough to be useful. None the less, they seem to show considerable promise. Police forces, like most large organizations, are quite resistant to remedial work. The administrative difficulties of holding training courses are high since they involve pulling active officers off the street intermittently, while the immediate political rewards are low. Visuals of minority constables graduating or being sworn in make the newspapers and television news; training courses do not.

Much hope has been placed on civilian review of police misconduct. Proponents argue that, when it comes to investigating and then disciplining officers for acts of misconduct, there is little public confidence that police management will do so fairly and impartially. Civilian review boards have been established slowly throughout the country, but appear to have taken on a solid presence in a number of large Canadian urban police forces, provincially, and nationally in the RCMP. Even so, it is argued, public confidence in the civilian review process remains precarious, as long as front-line investigations and recommendations remain in the purview of acting police officers.

The movement to community policing seems, in many ways, the most positive of recent developments. In one sense, community policing is an effort to return to the medieval roots of the English constable. In fact, as late as the 1940s and before the widespread use of the automobile and radio communications, all policing was of necessity community policing. Technology permitted the development of large, centralized urban police forces in the last sixty years. Only recently have observers begun to notice that the advantages of centralization might be outweighed by the costs. Local knowledge and the trust of the community are not readily acquired from a patrol car.

The principal *political* solution initiated most recently involves another kind of community policing: the potential devolution of responsibility from rural police forces to local aboriginal communities. In the few places in Canada where it has been tried, results have been mixed but remain promising. The American experience suggests that positive results may grow from devolution. Clearly, some experimentation is in order. Together with initiatives designed to localize the criminal-justice process by involving Aboriginal people in the court system and in the process of deciding whether or not to undertake criminal prosecutions, Aboriginal policing may help to legitimize and humanize the criminal-justice system.

Legal solutions for what ails the police diverge into two sharply different, but related directions. The police, generally speaking, would prefer tougher criminal laws and less lenient courts. They see one of the major causes of the failure of police efforts at curbing crime to be a system that simultaneously gives wrongdoers all the breaks and police all the constraints. While there is public support for tougher penalties and less lenience, there has so far been little legislative interest except, perhaps, regarding the reform of parole and young-offenders legislation. One of the primary means of constraining police practices in the last decade has been the Charter of Rights and Freedoms. For lawyers, in contrast to the police, the Charter has been a positive development. While it has cut back significantly on the latitude formerly enjoyed by the police, both lawyers and judges have been the main beneficiaries in terms of increased jurisdiction and influence. Naturally, they see this as a good thing and tend to promote further restrictions on police powers.

The papers collected here identify and contextualize the problems that, cumulatively, have precipitated the crisis in policing. They also attempt to suggest solutions to the problems along the four axes we have identified. Their contributions are intended not only as catalysts for further thought and work, but also as concrete proposals, at a time when the question of police powers calls for urgent and pressing reform. It remains our view that the foundations of constitutional order are tied to the latent and actual exercise of power by law-enforcement agencies. If relations between the police and civil society continue to erode, the actual exercise of force will correspondingly rise, a dangerous prospect for any democratic society.

Our earliest definitions of police powers came, along with the police themselves, almost unnoticed in the political baggage of European settlement. The *maréchaussée* of New France presumably exercised the same authority as their counterparts in the France of Louis XV. They have not been much studied and some would argue that this subject does not matter for those who seek an understanding of the evolution of twentieth-century police, since the victorious British did away with them after 1760. Others have claimed that the creation of the Mounted Police in the 1870s was in some sense a revival of the French tradition.

The British replaced the *maréchaussée* of the French regime, who, as full-time employees of the state, seem to be a very modern institution, with the constable. This was, as DeLloyd Guth notes, an office of great antiquity, already eight or nine centuries old before it crossed the Atlantic to Canada. Most of the historical and criminological writing on the police has concentrated on the organizational aspects of the institution. How many police are there? Who pays them? What jurisdiction controls their daily activities? Important as these issues undoubtedly are, police powers are substantially independent of them. Guth argues that the dual character of the English constable has remained consistent since medieval times. The success and longevity of the institution are due to the fact that the constable represents both royal authority and the local community. Changes in the police force that alter this duality risk destroying police effectiveness or creating a tyranny, depending upon which way the balance shifts.

In spite of the relatively higher visibility of the RCMP and the provincial forces in Ontario and Quebec, most policing in this country, as Greg Marquis points out, has always been done by municipal police. Police culture comes out of a century and a half of urban history and local politics with profound, if largely unexplored, consequences for police powers. Peel's London model was influential but spread more slowly than might have been expected. Technology had important consequences for how police went about their work and dealt with their fellow citizens. Local parsimony meant that nineteenth-century police were almost universally pressed into performing a variety of social-service functions. These duties mitigated the coercive side of policing and strengthened the ties to the community. Beginning in the 1920s, the notion that crime-fighting was the only legitimate police activity began to make itself felt. The police worked closely with local magistrates' courts, but until the second half of the twentieth century the higher levels of the legal system hardly noticed their existence. Now that the higher courts have begun to take an active role in defining police powers, it will be important for them to recognize that they must come to terms with strongly entrenched traditions.

The general theme of police powers evolving in response to perceived administrative necessities without much reference to either legislation or case law is reiterated in R.C. Macleod's paper on the RCMP and provincial policing. Macleod has argued in earlier writings that the emergence of the RCMP as a powerful national police force was largely an unplanned response to local circumstances in Western Canada in the late nineteenth century. This paper advances the proposition that the two decades between 1920 and 1940 was a crucial period for determining the overall structure of policing in Canada in the twentieth century. After the cancellation of provincial policing contracts with Alberta and Saskatchewan during the First World War and the decline in concerns about subversion in the early 1920s, the RCMP could easily have shrunk to a vestigial remnant and left provincial policing entirely to the provinces. Instead the RCMP not only survived but returned to provincial policing on a larger scale, becoming something like a national police force by the Second World War. For the RCMP, surviving the 1920s required finding new roles. With the expansion of government, the RCMP discovered more than enough to keep them busy in carrying out non-criminal investigative work for various federal-government departments.

If the adaptability of the RCMP was challenged in the 1920s, it faces a number of equally severe tests in the 1990s. None of these challenges, as Curtis Griffith's paper makes clear, is more pressing than that of Aboriginal policing. In no other area are the solutions less obvious, not only for the RCMP but for all the police and governing bodies involved, from councils of elders in the high Arctic to inner-city forces in southern Canada. Criminologists are far from unanimous in diagnosing the extent to which deficiencies in policing contribute to the severe crime problem in most Aboriginal communities. The few experiments in Aboriginal policing undertaken so far have yielded mainly negative lessons. The more numerous royal-commission studies have yet to produce unambiguous signposts.

We have already mentioned a number of different strategies that have been invoked as a corrective to the present crisis in policing. Harish Jain discusses one of these: recruiting members of visible-minority communities. Building on earlier studies from 1985 and 1987, Jain analyses statistics regarding the representation and recruitment of visible minorities from fourteen police organizations across Canada. The study shows a steady improvement in recruitment and promotion, but numbers remain far below the representation of visible minorities in the labour markets these police forces serve. Reviewing the variety of recruitment strategies that are being employed, Jain concludes that what is now required are new and innovative recruitment strategies as well as an accompanying change of organizational culture within police forces.

Perhaps the absence of approaches for coping with such hard issues as Aboriginal policing derives from a Canadian reluctance to think of police work as a political activity. As David Smith's study reveals, Canadians have been more than content to regard the police as above politics. Canadian political scientists, in turn, have largely ignored what is in most other countries a rich field of inquiry. Some criminologists and lawyers have explored the political dimensions of policing, but their work is outside the principal frameworks of Canadian political thought such as federalism. Smith's outline of the possible directions political science research might take suggests that useful insights will result if others follow his lead.

Philip Stenning's paper demonstrates that the public and academic perceptions noted by Smith are firmly rooted in Canadian police practices. Most Canadian politicians and senior police officials have enthusiastically endorsed Lord Denning's doctrine in *Blackburn* (1968), which attempts to divorce police operations entirely from political control. Stenning believes that such efforts to separate the police from politics, however defined, are indefensible in theory and impossible in practice. He is not much more sanguine about the trend to community policing with its necessarily closer involvement of police with local politics. Stenning raises the interesting issue of the political rights of individual police officers and explores the possible directions that the Charter might take in defining those rights.

James Robb is concerned as well with the relationship between the police and politics. He highlights this relationship by discussing two recent events that compromised the cherished appearance of neutrality. The first concerns the prosecution of television journalist Doug Small and others for a budget leak in advance of the minister of finance's speech in the House of Commons. Evidence at the trial indicated that political pressure was being placed on investigating RCMP officers to lay charges, despite their considered opinions to the contrary. The second concerns a parliamentary bill to delay the investigation of Members of Parliament by the RCMP that was rushed into passage after the RCMP commissioner indicated there were fifteen MPs under investigation. The law gives Parliament extraordinary powers to intervene in criminal investigations regarding Members of Parliament and has the potential of compromising police investigations and interfering with the decision to lay charges. Each event raises the spectre of police partisanship and calls into question the myth of independence. Robb calls for a theoretical reconsideration of the role of the police with a view to breaking down the distinction between police and politics.

Discussions about the appropriate balance between police powers and citizens' rights often are reduced to conversations about 'us' (the law-abiding) versus 'them' (criminals). Roger Shiner eschews such inquiries in favour of an examination of the philosophical foundations for police powers and citizens' rights. He offers a familiar account based on John Rawls's 'original position,' where citizens design a system of criminal justice that guarantees certain basic rights, such as a right to counsel, because these would be protections that all citizen would want for themselves. By engaging in this kind of thought experiment, Shiner argues, one cannot simply equate the powers necessary for law enforcement with the rights of citizens, balancing off one against the other. Rather, police powers are derived from citizens' rights. The more reliable balance is that between the interests each of us has as autonomous persons and as equal partners in the design of a system of criminal justice. This is just the kind of balance that could be struck by citizens endeavouring to act behind a veil of ignorance in the Rawlsian original position.

According to some police accounts, the entrenchment of legal rights under the Charter has led to a dangerous erosion of the rule of law in Canada. Don Stuart examines the premise of police resistance to reform of the criminal law by reviewing Charter decisions that affect police practices. Despite claims that its decisions have been 'salutary,' the Supreme Court has been most aggressive in the exclusion of evidence in criminal trials. Consequently, the cases decided under the Charter's exclusionary rule have had the most significance in reforming police practices. While this activism, Stuart argues, is consistent with a purposive approach to Charter interpretation, the frequency and success of these applications have led to only a small minority of acquittals. While there has been a similar activism under the Charter's guarantee against unreasonable searches and seizures, for the most part, police practices in regard to matters such as random vehicle stops, the discretion to enforce the law, and the power to arrest remain largely unaffected by the Charter. Stuart concludes that not only should the police acquaint themselves willingly with these new Charter developments, they should be more open to participating in legislative reform of the criminal law than they have in the past.

Despite the myriad of recommendations for the reform of the criminal law made by the now-defunct Law Reform Commission of Canada, Parliament, for the most part, declined to act. With the advent of the Charter, the courts were able to step into the breach. How efficacious has reform under the Charter been and how preferable is reform instigated by litigation compared to parliamentary reform? Martin Friedland considers these questions with particular reference to recent Charter case law and Law Reform Commission recommendations. He begins by discussing the reasons why parliamentary reform is to be preferred over judicial reform, including reasons of accountability, coherence, interest-group participation, and cost. Reviewing specific judicial reform under the Charter in such areas as wire-taps, the right to silence, and entrapment, Friedland concludes that in each area legislative reform along the lines recommended by the Law Reform Commission would have been far preferable. He laments that, with the demise of the Commission and the multitude of court interventions, it will be difficult to reverse these trends.

The armed confrontation between members of the Mohawk communities at Kanesetake and Kahnawake and the Sûreté du Québec is the focus for Jean-Paul Brodeur and Louise Viau's case study concerning police accountability in crisis situations. The numerous complaints regarding the conduct of the police during the crisis, in addition to the storming of the barricade at Kanesetake that resulted in the death of Corporal Marcel Lemay and the dramatic escalation of the crisis, constitute the bases for their discussion of accountability. From an organizational perspective, they conclude that the Sûreté du Québec failed at all levels to adequately supervise and control their rank and file. The available mechanisms for investigating acts of police misconduct and disciplining wrong-doers, however, are inadequate to the task. These mechanisms are triggered only by external complaints and are concerned only with individual acts of misconduct, rather than organizational failures. From a legal perspective, Brodeur and Viau expose the inadequacy of legal mechanisms, such as Charter litigation, to control or correct police misconduct in times of crisis. Many of the police actions that were the subject of complaints, such as maintaining security perimeters and roadblocks, and cutting off press food supplies and communications, likely were not contrary to the Charter in any event. They conclude by recommending clarification and reform of the law to control police powers in crisis situations.

After the academics have had their say, a working police officer's point of view should provide a reality check. Chris Braiden has been a policeman in Edmonton for more than thirty years, rising from constable to superintendent. He retired from the Edmonton Police Service shortly after he wrote this paper, in part at least so that he would have more time to devote to the requests from other police forces to talk to them about Edmonton's highly successful community policing program, which he originated. Distilling the experience of three decades into a short paper is not easy, but Braiden's principal message is clear enough. The enemies of effective policing are the entrenched culture of policing and managerial complacency. The tools to overcome these defects are decentralization and a rededication to meeting the needs of neighbourhoods within the city. The problems of race and class are side issues. Changes to the ethnic and gender composition of police forces will do nothing by themselves to meet community policing needs.

PART ONE: THE HISTORY OF POLICE POWERS

1

The Traditional Common Law Constable, 1235–1829: From Bracton to the Fieldings to Canada

DELLOYD J. GUTH

Legal historians who choose to study constables usually face colleagues and readers who first want to know if you are 'for them or against them.' At the end of the twentieth century the subject can become so polarized that little high ground remains for overview and balance. The support side holds police unions, ministries of the attorney-general, the prosecutorial bar, and numerous law-and-order groups. The other attracts criminologists, civil libertarians, charitable groups, and the criminal-defence bar. Law schools, for their part, too often educate only the defence half of each neophyte criminal lawyer, avoiding direct study of police and prosecutorial perspectives. Course offerings can leave choices limited to those that focus on the defendant's position in our modern adversarial system (for instance, in courses such as civil liberties, evidence, criminal law, the Charter, and constitutional law).[1] Over on its side, police education can suffer similar myopia, by closing doors and minds to legal-judicial professionals and social-services experts who challenge rather than champion whatever current views the police have of themselves. Teaching law to new constables, and rewarding veterans enrolled in continuing-education courses, too often gets lowest priority, way behind target-shooting. Added to this adversarial, even Manichean, atmosphere is the regular media bombardment with stories of corrupt cops, victimized citizens, gruesome murders, easily exonerated police use of deadly force and high-speed chases, politically protected or targeted prosecutions, and racism in hiring, promoting, and policing practices. At the very least, this 'us versus them' polarization prevents any serious discourse about who our constables should be and what these constables are lawfully empowered to do.

The answers can only come from two sources: the present law and the constable's past. I will leave the modern law to those better able to define it. My purpose here is to retrieve exemplary evidence for the constable's historical identity. The danger in not knowing one's past is not in being doomed to repeat it but, more simply, in losing any ability to recognize repetition. And while we can learn equally from mistakes and successes, our own and others', by means of memory or evidence, that learning can only come to us once it is past and retrievable upon reflection or by research. Constables who lack or avoid an awareness of their office's past will have no sense of that office's present uniqueness or mission. Such constables merely have jobs, and hoped-for pensions, but certainly not a profession, a sworn calling. For the sake of the office of constable, and its traditions, they would best go sell ties or pluck chickens!

Professional constables need not be intimidated or bored by having to learn from their past, and legal historians owe their long-overdue attention to making that past more accessible to them. This essay offers a modest survey of primary evidence, at a time when the legal history of crime and criminal law is expanding; but, as of the 1990s, the historical identity of the constable still gets lost in the broader contexts and the modern polarization. My purpose will be to locate basic themes in the constable's historical identity that offer standards by which to measure what the constable's present identity might still be. Our time will run from medieval origins to the mid-nineteenth century; our place will begin in England and then transplant the constable into what is now Canada; and our context will be the defining nature of English common law.

To put the Canadian end before the medieval English beginning, recall that Canada uniquely possesses two police traditions. The common-law constable, my focus here, predated the Magna Carta (1215), received reinvigoration by the Fieldings five centuries later, and became the 'new police' sponsored by Sir Robert Peel and created by statute in 1829.[2] By 1900 most Canadian cities had adapted this model, or at least its common-law spirit, to their separate needs. This 'blue' tradition was common law in several senses, but originally because its constable worked directly for the magistrate and was integral to that court-based, judge-made law that is common law. These 'blues' existed in sharp contrast to the much more recent 'brown' or 'red-coat' tradition. That came to Western Canada in the 1873 statutory creation of the North-West Mounted Police,[3] modelled deliberately on the armed, mounted, and military lines of a Royal Irish Constabulary, which England had begun to design in 1786 for Dublin and then had redesigned for all of Ireland in Peel's Peace Preservation Act of 1814.[4] Re-founded in 1921 as the Royal Canadian Mounted Police, this model has developed its own history, the early history of which is best told by Professor Rod Macleod.[5]

In the beginning, even before the existence of a royal law common throughout England, there was the constable, in word and in deed. The word's history has been traced, rather unhelpfully, back to identify an employee in a stable, perhaps someone associated with the early medieval landlord's horses, possibly in charge of the stud: hence, '*comes-stabuli.*'[6] The deed's history has been offered clearer definition and identity, in the sense of what constables have been empowered to do over their ten centuries of record.[7] They originated as peace-keepers in England even before the Norman French conquest of 1066. Their millennium of service has centred on two theoretical sources of authority: local communal origins for the office itself, and executive delegation of duties, first from landlords and then from the primal landlord, the king. Thus empowered, immediately by their communities and ultimately by the crown, constables acted, or refused to act, as civilian citizens, never as military foot-soldiers. Early societies recognized, as we do, that for exercises of power to be lawful they must rest on the authority of law, not on the will or whimsy of an individual or a group. Constables have been caught historically at mid-point, with authorization coming from below, flowing upwards out of their community, while from above, flowing downwards, came the authority of common law, meaning royal law. The first made them agents of their peers, the second made them officers of the law.

In addition to community, crown, and civilian identities, there remained two further elements in the historical definition of English common-law constables. Their office located them in medieval courtrooms and their raison d'être rested on the power of arrest by which they serviced their courts. We can know this only from the legal evidence, certainly not from the more popular historical writings of the day.

What is curious about the literature of medieval times is that its authors rarely used courtrooms for their settings and constables or judges for their characters. Writers such as Chaucer and Langland wrote about common things for uncommonly literate folks, but constables were evidently too ordinary or too irrelevant to be interesting. If we locate ourselves farther back, at the round table of King Arthur, as recreated by Malory, that fanciful world needed knights not constables. Most other such medieval writings glorified saints, not sinners, and constables were supposed to be neither. Even the tale of Robin Hood, King John, and the sheriff of Nottingham, from around the year 1200, did not need to put its readers or listeners, and its many bad guys, into courtrooms and under a constable's arrest.

The first major legal text from that era, authored by Glanvill (ca. 1170), had little to say about crime and nothing about constables.[8] However, the next description of England's royal laws and legal system, authored by Bracton a few decades after Magna Carta (1215), could not be more explicit in placing the constable's identity within the courts. '[I]t is the duty of the constable to enroll everything in order, for he has record as to the things he sees; but he cannot judge, because ... the third element of a judicial proceeding is lacking, namely a judge and jurisdiction. He has record as to matters of fact, not matters of judgment and law.'[9] What better articulation of a constable's routine deeds, then and now?

First, the constable in the years after Magna Carta was to keep a 'record as to the things he sees.' Bracton presumed literacy, which probably fewer than a quarter of the adult male population had achieved. His constable had to write and read the language of royal law courts, which required at least rudimentary recognition of the Latin forms for writs and warrants, as well as the Law French vocabulary spoken in court. Any person who 'sees' a misdeed was thereby empowered to make the arrest, constable or not, which is why that power remained universally civilian and community-based. But Bracton went on to make sure his reader knew what 'things' seen by a constable needed recording for the court: 'matters of fact, not matters of judgment and law.' Constables were keepers of the court's senses. In any specific case the court deferred to its constables, who controlled by record what that court needed to know about what was seen, heard, felt, smelled, and even tasted. Such were the matters of fact for any case: what happened, when, where, who, and how? The why in any case remained a matter of judgment, reserved even then to trial juries or to summary magistrates. They decided motives and intentions, guilt or innocence, in the form of a verdict (*vere-dictum* = truth-telling) rendered after the facts were on record. Judges, of course, reserved all 'matters of judgment and law' strictly to themselves, when law had to be applied to the verdict, in the award of punishment (if a crime) or compensation (if a civil tort, that is, a trespass).

In all such medieval adjudication, the constable's role remained unmistakably clear: not just the eyes and ears of the court in each case but also its strong arm, to execute court orders and bodily arrests. 'But he cannot judge': that is, the constable must be content with evidence-finding, fact-recording, and by extension with whatever verdict and judgment the others made. Seven and one-half centuries ago, Bracton therefore had noted all that was needed to be known about English common-law constables and their deeds, at least until the time of Henry and Sir John Fielding in the 1750s.

Bracton's definition came two generations before passage of the Statute of Winchester (1285),[10] which most police histories claim as the starting-point for common-law constables. What such histories do not mention is that this statute's main purpose was to order all males between the ages of fifteen and sixty to be armed with swords, knives, bows, and arrows 'for keeping the peace.' Such universal arming of the populace must have been ordered out of royal desperation near the end of a century scarred by civil wars and local vendettas. King Edward I (1272–1307) could only hope that he was not creating motley mini-armies for his own overthrow, if hostile baronial landlords gained their control. To prevent this outcome, the crown entrusted supervisory control in each locality to its civilian constables, not to any military agent. The Statute of Winchester required that each district elect two constables to supervise this armed community and to report all offenders to royal judges when they came on circuit. If new law was needed, these judges should report to the king in Parliament 'and the king will provide a remedy therefor.' Anyone not answering the hue and cry must also 'be presented by the constables to the justices assigned, and then afterwards by them to the king as aforesaid.' Can there be clearer evidence that community and crown were the sources of the constable's authority? and that constables were in control? and that the direct chain of command was citizens to constable to judge to the crown? In this shrewd parliamentary move, the crown had pre-empted continued feudal militarization with this strictly civilian solution of putting its common-law officers and processes in charge.

After 1300 evidence survives to illustrate what constables actually did, or had done to them. In Bedfordshire, the royal Sessions of the Peace in the mid-fourteenth century heard on average that one in ten assaults made were against constables. They were all acting officially ('in executing their office as constables') and identified as crown servants ('on the part of the lord king' or 'a servant of the lord king'). In all cases the constables were making arrests, and in a few instances they had allowed appearance bonds, only to be betrayed by defaulting defendants. Evidently in the absence of a magistrate, constables could also take surety-of-the-peace bonds. In one case a constable and his wife were assaulted, while in another a defendant stood convicted of beating up a bailiff and then threatening several constables 'so that they did not dare to perform their office.'[11] Later, in an Oxfordshire Sessions of the Peace in 1398, a rebellious mob beat the constable for refusing to join their riot, shouting 'aryseth' aryseth' alle men et goth' wyth' vs et ho so wilnot gou wiht' vs (he schal be ded).'[12] For an office that paid no salary or fixed fees, and was usually held for only one year, such hazards could hardly be compensated by occasional fee-gouging and extortion.

London would produce the model for so-called new police after 1829, but it also documented 410 years earlier the old model, again well before the Fieldings. In the *Liber Albus*, or 'white book,' of London compiled in 1419, their constables acted as peace-keepers alongside and above curfew-watchers, beadles, scavagers, frank-pledgers, and ale-conners. All these other officers worked only at the ward level, while the constable enjoyed city-wide powers. Only the constable had full powers of arrest, of chase throughout the city on the hue and cry, and of search whenever an officer of a ward requested it. Constables answered directly to the mayor and aldermen, each sitting not in any political capacity but in their judicial roles as named royal commissioners of the peace within London.[13]

By 1500, the constable had a predominantly urban identity. The original distinction was between a High Constable of each hundred, as confirmed by the Statute of Winchester (1285), and the Petty Constable, charged with peace-keeping in particular towns or parishes within the High Constable's hundred. This prefigured more modern chief constables, but the actual fate of the High Constable ended formally only in 1869,[14] long after counties and cities had replaced the hundreds as royal administrative units for local government. Our first definitive source about constables, dated 1583 and written by William Lambarde, emphasized their identity based on community, crown, courts, and a civilian character. Lambarde defined a constable as 'an officer that supporteth the Queenes Maiestie in the maintenaunce of hir peace.'[15]

How did they, in theory, serve Queen Elizabeth I? Lambarde uttered the magic verb 'prevent' almost two centuries before the Fieldings. Most police historians still wrongly credit them for inventing 'prevention' in the 1750s. In Lambarde's own words, in 1583 constables had three duties: 'first in foreseeing that nothing be done that tendeth, either directlye, or by meanes, to the breach of the peace: secondly, in quiet or pacifying those that are occupied in the breach of the peace: & thirdly, in punishing such as have alreadie broken the peace.' The constable should act, first, *before* offences occur; second, *during* the offence, to restore the peace with a threat of arrest and legal process; and then, only third, *after* the offence by applying the full punitive powers of the law. Prevent, pacify, punish: that was Lambarde's order of priorities. He made clear how the constable could prevent crime: 'take (or arrest) suspected persons, which walke in the night, and sleepe in the day: or whiche do haunt any house, where is suspicion of bauderie: and they may carie them before a Iustice of the peace, to finde suerties of their good behaviour.'[16]

Who appointed and disciplined, hired and fired, the constables? Again, Lambarde wrote in 1583 that they 'be subject to the commaundements of the Iustices ... yea and to the preceptes of Coroners also.' Regarding magistrates, constables 'may not dispute whether their commaundementes be grounded upon sufficient auctoritie, or no: as knowing that ... such Officer be holden excused for executing the same, howsoever that Iustice of peace himselfe be blamed for it.' The magistrate was entirely in control of the criminal proceedings, and he then delegated full powers of arrest, but only to constables. If necessary the constable could 'iustifie the killing of such a partie, if it so bee that hee cannot otherwise take him,' when executing a magistrate's arrest warrant.[17] Extant evidence indicates that constables rarely killed during the three centuries before or after the reign of Queen Elizabeth.

Between the death of Queen Elizabeth I in 1603 and the arrival of Henry Fielding as a justice of the peace in 1748, the court-centred nature of the constable's identity did not change, but the varieties of duties multiplied like rabbits. Tudor and Stuart monarchs centralized common-law administration at the expense of the pre-Reformation church's canon law and the post-feudal landlord's customary law. Constables, and their magistrates, became the work-horses for this common-law consolidation of power. The crown cast constables in expanded roles as tax-collectors and as recruiters by force of young males for army and navy service. Because most of this royal centralization entered the common law by parliamentary statute, the constable's duties were specified in writing, no longer customary and discretionary at a magistrate's order. The list of new duties by the early 1600s was astonishing. Constables, in addition to court, arrest, and peace-keeping tasks, had to enforce price regulations in market-places and taverns, prosecute players of unlawful games (such as bowling and shove ha'penny), respond to the College of Physicians in suppressing quacks, supervise the collection of moneys to feed prisoners in local gaols, chase down defaultors on the poor tax, enforce Statutes of Labourers against the unemployed, account for fines and forfeitures used for highway maintenance, ensure that local weights and measures conformed to royal standards, and continuously prosecute owners and frequenters of bawdy-houses and gaming-clubs.[18]

All this statutory activity added up to a remarkable shift from pre-Reformation private, confessional morality to a post-Reformation public, judicialized morality increasingly defined by Parliament.[19] What had been sins, and matters of individual conscience disciplined by the church, hence mainly outside the medieval constable's mandate, were by 1600 designated crimes, or at least statutory misdemeanours, and thus very much the responsibility of seventeenth-century constables.

The expanded list of wrongdoings that constables could and should enforce appeared to have been matched by their expanded summary powers to punish. They increasingly presented offenders in local courts, with or without private or victim's informations, and then executed the assessed fine, flogging, gaoling, ducking, or pillory.[20] The constable's oath of 1620 had him swear 'to learn and understand the contents of the statute of Winchest. [1285] and divers other laws ... made for the punishment of rogues, vagabonds, and sturdie beggers, haunting and resorting within the precinct of your office, and punish the offenders accordingly,' including those who 'shal play at any unlawful games.' The oath then ended with 'You shal also have regard for the maintenance of Artillerie within your said office.'[21] That should melt any police historian's myth about traditionally unarmed constables, although the lawful circumstances under which local constables might carry firearms, not just night-sticks or batons, have yet to be documented.[22]

This entire criminal-justice system, centred on the crown's common-law magistrate and constable, careened between crises and corruption by the 1750s. Population growth after 1700, almost all of it into cities, came at a time when Parliament had gone on another binge of crime-creation. The list of human acts lengthened for which the punishment was public execution or overseas transportation, mainly for property offences such as poaching in forests. The immediate result was a corresponding increase in juries refusing to convict, especially among neighbours, because of the potential savagery of sentencing. Statutes and rules of evidence became strictly construed. Magistrates increasingly recommended pardons and reprieves of sentences. Restrictions on what the criminal-justice system could produce, by way of predictable punishments, were compounded by the limited way in which prosecutions could be initiated. There had never been a public, crown, or community prosecutor. All criminal-law enforcement had had to begin with private complaints, presumed to be from victims or their next-of-kin, even when a grand jury of indictment sat. Rarely did an individual constable lay charges directly.[23]

In the circumstances facing the Fieldings by 1750, this reliance on reluctant citizen-initiated prosecutions and vastly overburdened, unpaid constables threatened to turn towns and cities into thief-havens. Rural landlords, and to a lesser extent urban merchants, who controlled Parliament and secured their own appointments as magistrates, thereby increased their earlier grip on 'their' constables. It should not surprise us to learn that criminalizing more and more human acts produced less and less effective overall enforcement, more local jury acquittals, but also more opportunities to corrupt constables.

Knowing that common-law constables had a wholesome history before the Statute of Winchester, and that their primary duty to prevent crime existed long before the Fieldings, what did the original evidence establish as to what, if anything, the Fieldings contributed to the constable's historical identity?

Henry Fielding's life was one series of modestly successful careers as playwright, poet, journalist, novelist, lawyer, and magistrate. Each in turn left him short of money. Called to the bar at the Middle Temple in 1740, at age thirty-three, he practised sporadically for the next five years, mainly on the Summer's Western Circuit. That left him time each year to make repeated returns to journalism. In financial desperation he begged and received appointment as justice of the peace for Westminster (30 July 1748), then also for Middlesex (January 1749). In between, he moved into the residence in Bow

Street, Covent Garden, previously occupied by the magistrate Sir Thomas De Veil. Fielding held his first court there on 2 November 1748. Slightly more than a year later, on 29 January 1749/50, he launched his Bow Street Runners in the first of many raids against various break-and-enter, smash-and-grab gangs. Several were led by Thomas Pendergast, Thomas Lewis (alias Captain Flash), and – yes – one Thomas Jones (who called his real-life gang 'The Royal Family'). Fielding's novel, *Tom Jones*, had been published thirteen months before this Thomas Jones swung from Tyburn gallows, nearly a case of life imitating art. Henry Fielding fast became the scourge of petty property thieves and their financial fences, London's plurality of pawnbrokers. He also made a routine of raiding bawdy-houses, gaming-houses, and public houses, particularly those known to give comfort to London's criminals.[24]

He had his century's certitude about humanity's division into good and evil persons, as well as England's robust anti-Catholicism and anti-Semitism.[25] Reading his few surviving legal treatises reveals his firm belief that a criminal class existed and chose freely to do evil. At the same time, he asserted that social-economic circumstances predetermined the victimization of young girls into prostitution, young boys into street gangs, and the poor generally into survival thievery. His solution was to pursue criminals relentlessly within the judicial system, while raising money with admirable success to create public hostels for wayward girls, to turn street urchins into cabin boys for the royal navy, and to find domestic employment for the poor.[26] A man of ideas and empathy, Henry Fielding was first and always a publicist. An advocate by temperament and profession, he eagerly pressed ideas and causes, through personal contacts with the powerful and through journalistic ventures, on the minds of the literate public. He certainly deserves notice as the first person to master the popular media on behalf of law-and-order causes, shamelessly selling each short-lived newspaper through detailed stories of the latest outrageous crimes.

Henry Fielding served less than six years as magistrate (1748–54) out of his Bow Street residence. His half-brother, Sir John Fielding, blinded at age nineteen by a medical mistake, overlapped Henry's last three years as another Westminster-Middlesex magistrate, and then stayed on for twenty-six more years after Henry's death. Historians of the police in our century have handed along an orthodoxy about the Fieldings that tags their 'Bow Street Runners' as forerunners of the 1829 'new' police. The Fieldings have been credited with inventing 'prevention,' assigning constables to beats where they were resident, and securing paid and longer-than-one-year terms of employment. All of this would suggest origins for modern police professionalism. Little of it squares with the contemporary evidence that survives.

Any such search for origins, especially if driven by some predefined theory or present-day preference, usually fits the evidence to the theory. The general temptation among those who do legal history is that they may stand too close to the way many lawyers and judges research and reconstruct: backwards from the present and teleologically towards a purposeful proof. The orthodoxy about the Fieldings among police historians well illustrates the problem. The alternative employed in this paper is to take an old-fashioned trip into primary evidence contemporaneous to constables, whether in Bracton's day or that of the Fieldings, and then allow that evidence to shape the questions, answers, topics, and issues. What then does the extant evidence reveal about the Fieldings and their constables?

There are two overwhelming problems of evidence facing anyone researching the Fieldings and their constables. All institutional records from Bow Street, 1749–1839, went the way of all rubbish in 1881, when the present Police Office opened there, directly across from the Royal Opera House, Covent Garden.[27] Who was to blame for the burning? Probably a bureaucratic martinet with a passion for making more empty storage space for more recent records. Thus, we can never retrieve realities about the daily anecdotal and annual aggregative police business at Bow Street.

That leaves the second problem of evidence. To know the Fieldings and their constables, we are left with a few pamphlets and various newspapers, mainly their own. We cannot always pinpoint authorship, to Henry or Sir John or others. When we do, we get lots of rambling rantings against robbery and thievery in a literary style that often drips with moralizing sarcasm and satire. All of Henry's newspaper ventures failed, amounting to at least three during his last nine years.[28] Each tried to survive in large part by reporting London street crime. We can never know how much, or how much more, of such street crime actually existed, then and there, so any talk about crime rates has no evidentiary base. Thus, we can never know, except perhaps from his own ailing newspapers, whether Henry Fielding became part of the problem, fanning public flames of fear, or part of the solution, raising a 1750s version of the medieval hue and cry to help restore community control over his streets. The fact that his newspapers consecutively failed, presumably in large part for want of readers and advertisers, suggests that he had less influence either way.

What then did the Fieldings add to the office of constable, as they found it in 1748? Keep in mind that the constable had been identified for over five hundred years with community, crown, civilian, and common-law courtroom sources of power.

In articles in his newspapers that we know he authored, Henry Fielding revealed a richly moralistic view of crime, which designated the constable primarily an enforcer of public morality. In *The True Patriot*, a weekly that ran only in 1745–46, he left no doubt that criminals freely chose to do evil, so he applauded a thief's suicide and showed little sympathy for an unwed servant-mother's infanticide.[29] His next weekly newspaper, *The Jacobite's Journal*, also lasted a year (1747–48). Here he wrote strongly anti-war, anti-military, and pro-capital-punishment articles. His pen poured out stories about mob rule, followed by demands for more watchmen in the towns doing silent patrol to catch thieves in the act.[30] Three years after he became a magistrate he launched another short-lived paper, the *Covent-Garden Journal* (1752). With often biting sarcasm, he demanded strict regulation of public houses, vagrants, and 'spirituous liquors.' Fielding showed no faith in the 'common people,' labelled 'the Vulgar,' who he found lacking in public conscience, making impossible any revival of the hue and cry. Regarding prostitution, he constantly damned it as female victimization by male exploiters, demanding that its suppression be left under local magistrate control without appeal to Westminster, that bail be forbidden accused keepers of such houses, and that constables routinely make harassing raids. But crime to the Fieldings meant street thievery, and included those pawnbrokers who kept it profitable. The role of constables in all of this was on the streets, immersed first hand in community life, bribing informers, raiding suspected houses with a magistrate's warrant, and rallying victims to lay charges and to come forward as witnesses.[31]

There was little substantial difference here from the pre-Fieldings' constable. The differences were in matters of style and, especially, matters of system. The heart of the Fieldings' contribution to the constable's identity was emphasis on systematic publicity for crime itself and a high public profile for constables. That new style and system for these traditional constables urged them to:

1 create personal networks of anonymous informers, paid when necessary;
2 engage in immediate and diligent pursuit, regardless of assigned jurisdictional boundaries, no doubt on the principle that it was easier to get forgiveness than permission;
3 routinely advertise specific crimes in newspapers (owned by the Fieldings?), to encourage victims and witnesses to use the judicial process (controlled by the Fieldings?);
4 repeatedly give newspaper advice to the public on how to secure property against breaking and entering;
5 announce fixed patrol beats for constables and watchmen, and then add surprise raids;
6 send all fines and forfeitures to charitable groups that find employment for those tempted into criminal activity;

7 aid magistrates in aggressive interrogation of the accused and witnesses;
8 create a public register for all recovered stolen goods for all wanted offenders;
9 make receivers and possessors of stolen goods liable to criminal prosecution, to destroy recycled profits from crime;
10 expand the making and enforcing of licensing laws;
11 use rewards, bribes, stake-outs, criminal-identification line-ups, and recognizances to control targeted suspects; and
12 permit the use of military troops only under the command of magistrates, with the aid of their constables, to quell full-scale riots.

This list[32] did not offer individual changes to what constables had been doing previously. If anything the Fieldings could be called reactionaries, not reformers, in the sense that they only sought to make the traditional constable more effective. If there is a modern ring to this list, that can remind us of how much constables in the 1990s can still learn from their past. Certainly the modern tabloid press has learned, as the Fieldings taught, that crime sells newspapers.

From the Fieldings all of this was a mix of journalistic and judicial exhortation. At one point in 1752, Henry Fielding urged parent-readers of his newspaper to buy his pamphlet about grisly murders in order to, in his words, 'tell true murder stories to children and they will not become murderers.'[33] But when it came to making concrete reforms to what magistrates and constables did, or could lawfully do, the Fieldings promoted a 'plan' for the police that amounted to more of the same.[34]

Sir John Fielding admitted as much in his 1758 pamphlet entitled 'An Account of the Origins and Effects of a Police Set on Foot ... upon a Plan ... by the Late Henry Fielding, Esq.' With a tone of reverential urgency, he related a plan drafted in 1753 directed against 'Gangs of Housebreakers, Lead-stealers, etc. which consisted chiefly of young Fellows who were Thieves from their Cradles.' How to prevent this? Remove all petty thieves, beggars, and deserted children from the streets; but where to, we are not told. Close down public houses and 'illegal Music-Meetings.' Finally, 'prevent Street-walking, by keeping the Whores within Doors.'[35] As a prescription for class warfare one could hardly do better. What strikes clearest about this so-called plan is its utter lack of imagination and innovation, offering little more than faith that each generation simply needed to purge itself of its born criminals.

Sir John's description of results of the 'plan' were rapturously related and even less impressive, if we expected signs of profound changes in policy or in practice. Early in 1754 their constables attacked the gangs and saw that 'nine Capital Offenders were brought to Justice ... in the Space of three Months.' The blitzkrieg continued, as adult 'Shoplifters, Pilferers, and Pickpockets ... were transported,' presumably to penal colonies. The Fieldings sent two hundred boys to the royal and merchant navies as cabin boys, having successfully raised money from London merchants to clothe them adequately. Because gamblers preyed on gentle folk and the nobility, Henry Fielding sent a fancy dressed undercover constable to identify offenders and gather evidence.[36] Again, one should be impressed with the energy and system applied, but one also must concede that the entire purpose was to make the status quo work better by using law instrumentally as a purgative.

That pamphlet was the only writing about constables that the Fieldings produced. After twenty-two pages on the 'plan,' Sir John showed how conventional the constable remained in their eyes and efforts. The magistrate, he said, 'should keep the civil Power alive, that is to say, the Constables; constantly instructing them in their Duty, and paying them for extraordinary and dangerous Enterprises; and above all, promote Harmony amongst them; for when the civil Power is divided it is nothing; but when Constables are collected together, known to each other, and bound by the Connections of good Fellowship, Friendship, and the Bonds of Society, they become sensible of their Office, stand by one another, and are a formidable Body.' He then added that they were always available to victims as 'pursuers,' that 'there is always one or more orderly Men on Duty to enquire into the Truth of Informations,' presumably at Bow Street, and that 'A Register-Clerk' recorded all suspects and the goods stolen. That ended the Fieldings' system, or at least as much as Sir John wanted made known to the public.[37]

Where did all this leave the pre-Fielding constable? Basically enhanced but also unchanged, which is another way of saying that the Fieldings missed their opportunity. What the scattered evidence from them concerning constables made clear was that criminals constituted a class within society that had to be physically removed and that crime prevention meant a systematic mustering of civilian powers within the common law that put the spotlight on the criminal acts. Just weeks before he died, Henry Fielding expressed these sentiments perfectly about how one prevents the criminal act. In *A Voyage to Lisbon*, he related this anecdote: '"For it is very hard, my lord," said a convicted felon at the bar of the late excellent Judge Burnet, "to hang a poor man for stealing a horse." – "You are not to be hanged, sir," answered my ever-honoured and beloved friend, "for stealing a horse, but you are to be hanged that horses may not be stolen."'[38] For the Fieldings, law existed to sustain orderly relations between persons and their things, for property and property-owners, both male and female. Anyone disrupting those relationships was disposable. None of this should surprise us, two and a half centuries later.

What might surprise is that the Fieldings' energetic style and system for constables focused so exclusively on pursuit of the petty, not the major, crimes. While they no doubt abhorred crimes involving violence, such as homicide, rape, robbery, and wounding, their listed prescriptions for constables emphasized small-scale, mainly non-violent street offences, done by pilferers and pick-pockets. Albeit, the Fieldings were only magistrates, not high-court, assize, or gaol-delivery judges; but the sum total of the evidence around them revealed little evidence of or concern for major offences. We need recall that the 1750s approached the all-time English high point for criminalizing seemingly petty property offences that led offenders to the gallows, the colonies, or the ship's cabin. Again, the Fieldings simply sought to improve that status quo, hanging a horse-thief so 'that horses may not be stolen.' But if property crime was as rampant as the Fieldings' newspapers urged, then substantial changes to the constable, the magistrate, and the prosecutorial system could at least have been suggested by them.

The Fieldings thus left the English common-law constable's identity substantially as they had found it. All this occurred about the time when the office could transplant and grow on this side of the North Atlantic. Following the Battle of the Plains of Abraham (1759), one might expect an accelerated imposition of the English magistrate-constable criminal-justice system. The truth about that system's arrival, and about the constable in Nova Scotia and the gendarme in Lower Canada at that time, however, remains interred in undisturbed documents. We know infinitely more about police in pre-modern England and *ancien régime* France than we do for this modern country's subsequent three centuries. How much of the English common-law constable made the voyage out from old England and north of her thirteen New England colonies?

If the traditional constable outlived the Fieldings, then Canadian police history's first priority should be to locate his transplanted peer after the 1750s, when legal-judicial records from the Maritimes and Lower Canada begin to survive for systematic study. The *Loix de Police* (1782), drafted for Quebec at the request of Governor Guy Carleton, located the burden for law enforcement entirely on the community but under the actual control of the *seigneur*, usually acting as magistrate. The imposed English model was entirely medieval; Carleton clearly showed no sign of influence by the Fieldings. Aside from executing the magistrate's warrants, Quebec's police had to be fire-watchers, on patrol for loose livestock, cabaret and hotel invigilators, curfew-enforcers, custodians of local gaols, and supervisors of market-places.[39] After 1785 in the Maritimes and 1791 in the two Canadas, the evidence for the constable's identity should carry us to 1829. Unfortunately for Canadian police history, that era of origins remains a dark age, lacking even shadows of knowledge because no glimmer of research light has been systematically thrown on its constables. There are no answers because to date no one has bothered to ask the questions of origins and receptions for policing models into what becomes Canada.[40]

Back in England, the era from 1749 to 1829 also awaits more systematic police historians, but less for reasons of neglect and more because of an assumption that the Fieldings started an inevitable ball rolling towards the 1829 'new' police. If my arguments here are correct about the Fieldings, then they also explain why only the traditional magistrate-constable model appears to have made it to England's North Atlantic colonies in that 1749–1829 period.

That traditional common-law constable, as court-based and answerable directly to the magistrate, died in 1829 with enactment of Sir Robert Peel's Metropolitan Police Improvement Bill (10 George IV, c. 44).[41] It created a more permanent, paid professional constable, but transferred accountability ultimately to cabinet-level, political, executive authority at the central Home Office. Intermediate control was vested in Home Office–appointed police commissioners, the first two being Colonel Charles Rowan and Richard Mayne. The statute of 1829 had not allowed a centralized national structure, but left Metropolitan London in administrative control and, by extension, reinforced the principle of municipal-based policing. But it did potentially compromise for the future that feature of traditional constables that made them agents of the community in which they resided. By open and outside recruitment, erosion of the community principle began. What did not change, between the traditional constable and the statutory 'new' one, was the location of ultimate authority in the crown. Constables continued to act entirely on behalf of common, that is royal-central, law before and after 1829. The final traditional feature of constables was their civilian character. This feature remained for Metropolitan London and expanded by statute in the 1840s for county and municipal constabularies.[42] But the parallel military model was developing, also promoted by Sir Robert Peel – the Royal Irish Constabulary as an armed, mounted, resident-in-barracks guard that much resembled the French *gendarmerie*.

The impact of the 1829 statute in these British colonies, like the general issue of the 'reception' of policing models, also has yet to be studied. We know that the old magistrate-constable model remained the norm for various Upper Canada municipalities. After 1835, Toronto's city council began naming their half-dozen constables and such non-judicial, political appointments began to be made in other towns, at least for as long as funds for salaries existed. A mounted police force, much like the Royal Irish Constabulary, appeared by statute in Upper Canada in 1845, but failed to be extended in 1856.[43] They were intended to be centralized replacements for all municipal forces. Public outcry, stirred by local politicians, led to retention of municipally controlled police, more in the spirit of Metropolitan London's 'new' police. In 1858 Toronto created a separate police board.[44] In that year, Matthew Baillie Begbie and Chartres Brew arrived at Fort Langley, British Columbia, to recruit along the Royal Irish Constabulary model to control hordes of American gold-miners on the Fraser River.[45] But the competing municipal model would also arrive in Victoria in 1862, Winnipeg in 1874, Calgary (1885), Vancouver (1886), Edmonton (1893), and Regina (1903). With the 1873 founding of the North-West Mounted Police, the two modern English models began separate development here in what can benignly be labelled as a state of creative tension. In the 1990s this double-tracking in Canada continues to produce a polarization within the Canadian policing profession.

What then has this cursory history taught about the English common-law constable's identity? Put another way: what is left of that historical identity in Canada today? Any salvaging must begin by eliminating the RCMP, built on the military model of the Royal Irish Constabulary and not on the common-law, community, or civilian bases. By the same criteria, provincial police departments and highway patrols excluded themselves, before take-overs by the RCMP beginning in 1928 (except for Ontario and Quebec). This leaves the focus on Canada's municipal departments.

There the constables may be community-controlled but, at least in the larger cities, also usually non-resident. They swear basically the same oath to the Queen's service as the 1829 Act provided, thus continuing sole identification with the crown and with crime prevention, not just detection post facto.[46] In this sense they remain common-law constables, albeit as defined in section 2 of the Criminal Code of Canada.[47] But the big difference is as prescribed in the 1829 act: the Canadian common-law constable too is now a creature of statute, severed from the provincial magistrate, still administered by a chief constable, but accountable to a political executive, be it the municipal police commission or, ultimately, the provincial attorney-general. In court our constable becomes merely first witness for the crown. Outside, Canadian common-law constables continue to gravitate towards that military model, with its laddered ranks, heavy armament, lock-step parade marching, tactical squads, and technologically armoured patrol cars.[48]

In retrospect, then, one need not be a romantic to prefer the pre-1829 constable, but it probably helps. Nevertheless, those identifying marks of a community-, crown-, civilian-, and court-based character, along with the Fieldings' list for systematic strategies, did create a high standard that modern Canadian constables ignore at everyone's peril.

NOTES

This essay, like the project for which I wrote it, invites future researchers to join in a large, hitherto uncharted part of the Canadian past: its police, as a transplanted institution from England. My intention is to map out the traditional English model and then raise the issue of its reception into Canada, without having further space to resolve or even document the latter. For the opportunity to launch here what promises to be a much larger, longer study elsewhere, I am indebted to the patient support of Professor Rod Macleod; and for a careful reading of the penultimate draft, I gratefully acknowledge the help of Professor Clive Emsley, director of the European Centre for the Study of Policing (The Open University, Milton Keynes, UK). His recent book, *The English Police: A Political and Social History* (London: St Martin's Press 1991) offers the best survey for this essay's subject-matter.

1 Outside such doctrinal law-school curricula, modern academic writings on police are not so much polarized as divided by presumptions that each interpreter brings to and imposes on the extant evidence: for example, the *instrumentalist* presumes police to be 'tools' of a dominant group's class, race, or gender agenda; the *structuralist* studies police as an inter-relational, mechanical part of social organization, but with its own internal rules and character; the *moralist* casts police either as 'good guys' uniquely defined for the eternal struggle against 'bad guys,' or alternatively as 'bad guys' at war with libertarian values and as agents of majoritarian or state power; and the *functionalist*, akin to positivist and empiricist researchers, reconstructs past police activities, often quantitatively, in order to describe what they 'really' did and how they 'really' operated in a particular time and place.

2 10 Geo. 4, c. 44.

3 *An Act Respecting the Administration of Justice, and for the Establishment of a Police Force in the North West Territories*, S.C. 1873, c. 35.

4 *Dublin Police Act, 1786* (U.K.), 26 Geo. 3, c. 24 (Irish Statutes); and a *Peace Preservation Forces Act, 1814* (U.K.), 54 Geo. 3, c. 131, followed by an *Irish County Constabulary Act, 1822* (U.K.), 3 Geo. 4, c. 103. The topic is thoroughly studied by G. Broeker, *Rural Disorder and Police Reform in Ireland 1812–36* (Toronto: University of Toronto Press 1970), and by S.H. Palmer, *Police and Protest in England and Ireland, 1780–1850* (New York: Cambridge University Press 1988).

5 R.C. Macleod, *The North-West Mounted Police and Law Enforcement, 1873–1905* (Toronto: University of Toronto Press 1976).

6 *The Compact Edition of the Oxford English Dictionary*, vol. 1 (Oxford: Oxford University Press 1971), 871–2.

7 Two caveats, please: my focus on the English common-law constable for this

essay does not mean to suggest: (a) that constables, in a broader sense of peace or police officers, do not exist in other times and places under different titles; or (b) that in England others, particularly the more numerous watchmen, are not significant in the history of institutionalized law and order.

8 G.D.G. Hall, ed., *The Treatise on the Laws and Customs of the Realm of England Commonly Called Glanvill* (London: Thomas Nelson and Sons 1965), 171–7 ('Book XIV: Criminal Pleas').

9 G.E. Woodbine, ed., *Bracton De Legibus et Consuetudinibus Angliae (On the Laws and Customs of England)*, vol. 4, trans. S.E. Thorne (Cambridge, Mass.: The Belknap Press of Harvard University Press 1977), 136. Bracton's topic is 'Essoins' and the jurisdictional context is for the Tower of London.

10 *Statute of Winchester, 1285* (U.K.), 13 Edw. 1, c. 6: *Statutes of the Realm*, vol. 1, 96–8.

11 E.G. Kimball, ed., *Sessions of the Peace for Bedfordshire 1355–1359, 1363–1364* (London: Her Majesty's Stationery Office 1969), 25, 34, 39, 42–3, 47, 62, 73–5, 86, and 106.

12 E.G. Kimball, ed., *Oxfordshire Sessions of the Peace in the Reign of Richard II* (Oxford: Oxfordshire Record Society LIII 1983), 73.

13 H.T. Riley, ed., *Liber Albus: The White Book of the City of London, compiled A.D. 1419*, trans. H.T. Riley (London: Richard Griffin and Co. 1861), 271–4.

14 See *High Constables Act, 1869* (U.K.), 32 & 33 Vict., c. 47.

15 W. Lambarde, *The Duties of Constables, Borsholders, Tithingmen, and Such Other Low Ministers of the Peace* (London: Rafe Newberie and Henrie Middleton 1583; repr. New York: Da Capo Press 1969), 5–6.

16 Ibid., 11–12.

17 Ibid., 19–20.

18 J.R. Kent, *The English Village Constable 1580–1642* (Oxford: Clarendon Press 1986), 52–5, 187–205; C.B. Herrup, *The Common Peace: Participation and the Criminal Law in Seventeenth-Century England* (New York: Cambridge University Press 1987), 68–74; and W.J. King, 'Vagrancy and Local Law Enforcement: Why Be a Constable in Stuart Lancashire?' *The Historian* 62 (1980).

19 R.H. Helmholz, *Roman Canon Law in Reformation England* (Cambridge: Cambridge University Press 1990), 113–15.

20 W.J. King, 'Early Stuart Court Leets: Still Needful and Useful,' *Histoire Sociale/Social History* 23 (1990): 271.

21 J. Wilkinson, *A Treatise Collected out of the Statutes ... with an Easie and Plain Methode for the Keeping of a Court Leet, Court Baron, and Hundred Court* (London: Companie of Stationers 1620), 137.

22 Much later, in incidental expense accounts for the police's Public Office in Worship Street, Shoreditch, London, dated 15 April 1797, post-Fieldings but pre-Peel,

payment for thirteen pounds, sixteen shillings went 'To Wm. Parker for Pistols for 6 Constables': Public Record Office, PC1/37/115. While six pistols in one constabulary do not prove a general policy, especially between 1620 and 1797, given the growing turbulence of urban street crime, it would be the more surprising if constables remained unarmed.

23 J.M. Beattie, *Crime and the Courts in England 1660–1800* (Princeton: Princeton University Press 1986), 420–36, 631. This authoritative and comprehensive study does not focus at length on the office or activities of constables.

24 See M.C. Battestin and R.R. Battestin, *Henry Fielding: A Life* (New York: Routledge 1989), esp. 501–2 regarding Thomas Jones.

25 Ibid., 427, 528; and in Henry Fielding's weekly newspaper *The Jacobite's Journal*, published only in 1747–8.

26 These themes repeat throughout Henry Fielding's columns in his newspapers between 1745 and his death on 8 October 1854 in Lisbon; see notes 28–33 below.

27 P. Pringle, 'Introduction,' in H. Goddard, *Memoirs of a Bow Street Runner* (London: Museum Press 1956), ix.

28 *The True Patriot* (5 Nov. 1745 to 17 June 1746); *The Jacobite's Journal* (5 Dec. 1747 to 5 Nov. 1748); *The Covent-Garden Journal* (4 Jan. 1752 to 25 Nov. 1752); and numerous contributions to *The Public Advertiser*, especially by Sir John Fielding after his half-brother's death.

29 See the issues dated 10 Dec. 1745 and 18 Feb. 1746 and an annotated edition by M.A. Locke, ed., *Henry Fielding, The True Patriot: And the History of Our Own Times* (New York: Haskell House Publishers 1975).

30 See the issues dated 26 Dec. 1747, 20 Feb. 1748, and 16 July 1748; the modern edition is by W.B. Coley, ed., *The Jacobite's Journal and Related Writings* (Middletown, Conn.: Wesleyan University Press 1975).

31 See such issues as 11 Jan. 1752, 25 Jan. 1752, 10 March 1752, and 30 May 1752; the modern edition is by G.E. Jensen, ed., *The Covent-Garden Journal*, vols. 1 and 2 (New Haven: Yale University Press 1915).

32 These twelve points are synthesized from Henry Fielding's three newspapers and from Sir John Fielding's writings in *The Public Advertiser* (1752–81).

33 See the *Covent-Garden Journal*, 14 Apr. 1752.

34 One seeks signs of any reformist plan in vain throughout H. Fielding, *An Enquiry into the Causes of the Late Increase of Robbers, and Related Writings*, ed. M.R. Zirker (Oxford: Clarendon Press 1988). This is the only pamphlet published in his lifetime that offers a systematic analysis; but it does not get beyond a diatribe against the criminal decadence of his times and a description of the procedural difficulties in obtaining successful prosecutions. Equal disappointment awaits anyone who can find Sir John Fielding's *Extracts from such of the Penal Laws,*

as particularly relate to the Peace and Good Order of this Metropolis (London: 1761), which includes the text attributed to Henry Fielding entitled 'A Treatise on the Office of Constable.'

35 Sir J. Fielding, *An Account of the Origins and Effects of a Police Set on Foot ... Upon a Plan ... by the Late Henry Fielding, Esq.* (London: A. Millar 1758) [hereinafter *An Account*]. This is the best summary of the Fieldings' special philosophy, including a section entitled 'A Plan for Preserving those deserted Girls in this Town, who become Prostitutes from Necessity.' There is a strong, consistently pro-feminist side to Henry Fielding's writings, both in his novels and earliest pamphleteering; for example, in *The Champion; or, British Mercury*, issue dated 1 Jan. 1739/40, 146–50, and in *The Champion; or, Evening Advertiser*, issue dated 15 May 1740, 213–19, where he urges full gender equality: both newspapers were collected and published 25 June 1741 in two volumes by J. Huggonson, ed. (London: Ludgate Hill 1741).

36 *An Account*, 17–22.

37 Ibid., 37–8.

38 H. Fielding, *Jonathan Wild* [*and*] *The Journal of a Voyage to Lisbon*, ed. A.R. Humphreys and D. Brooks (New York: Dutton Everyman's Library 1973), 195.

39 *An Abstract of the Loix de Police; or, Public Regulations for the Establishment of Peace and Good Order, that were of Force in the Province of Quebec, in the Time of the French Government* (London: Charles Eyre and William Strahan 1772).

40 The only person to make the attempt provides a succinct, accurate start: P.C. Stenning, *Legal Status of the Police* (Ottawa: Law Reform Commission of Canada 1982), 35–55 [hereinafter *Legal Status*]. One mid-nineteenth-century starting-point could be Judge Gowan's *The Canadian Constables' Assistant*, ed. J. Patton (Barrie, Ont.: J.W. Young 1852). I am grateful to Professor Rod Macleod for bringing this to my attention. For studies on later nineteenth century and more recent policing in British North America, see *Urban History Review* 19 1990.

41 From Sir John Fielding's death in 1781 to *Peel's Act* of 1829, a full history exists outside this brief essay. A series of police 'public offices' were created by statutes, beginning in 1792. If the Fieldings were consolidators rather than innovators, the person closer to earning credit for conceptual changes before 1829 was P. Colquhoun, *A Treatise on the Police of the Metropolis* (London: 1795).

42 Beginning with *An Act for the Establishment of County and District Constables by the Authority of Justices of the Peace, 27 August 1839* (U.K.), 2 & 3 Vict., c. 93; a series of *Parish Constables Acts*, beginning in 1842, 5 & 6 Vict., c. 109; and then the *County and Borough Police Act, 1856* (U.K.), 19 & 20 Vict., c. 69.

One useful survey of these developments is in F.W. Maitland, *Justice and Police* (London: Macmillan and Co. 1885), 105–17.

43 First statutory mention of constables in Upper Canada is in the *Second Session of the First Parliament, 1793* (U.K.), 33 Geo. 3, c. 2, s.10, where the oath shows no sign of reception from anywhere, simply requiring that 'you shall well and truly serve our sovereign lord the King, in the office of [constable] ... according to the best of your skill and knowledge'; see J. Nickalls, ed., *The Statutes of the Province of Upper Canada* (Kingston: Francis M. Hill 1831), 37. And see *Legal Status* (n. 40, above) 42–3.

44 *Legal Status*, 51.

45 G.P.V. Akrigg and H.B. Akrigg, *British Columbia Chronicle 1847–1871: Gold and Colonists* (Vancouver: Discovery Press 1977), 134, 139.

46 Comparing the different oaths that Canadian municipal constables swear with that of the RCMP is most revealing: the common-law constable, for example in British Columbia's twelve municipal police departments, swears to the Crown to serve 'according to law,' to 'cause the peace to be kept and preserved, and will prevent all offences against the persons and properties of Her Majesty's subjects'; whereas the RCMP oath is strictly one of obedience to the internal command structure, to 'faithfully, diligently and impartially execute and perform the duties required of me ..., and will well and truly obey and perform all lawful orders and instructions that I receive.' (R.S.C., c. R-10, s. 14.2, schedule section 14, p. 62). The common-law constable's oath exists verbatim in the *Irish Constabulary Act, 1822*, (n. 4, above).

47 R.S.C. 1991, c. C-46, s. 2, where there is no use of the title 'constable' by itself but only under the generic title 'peace officer,' along with at least twenty-one other types. See also ss. 25–33 (Protection of Persons Administering and Enforcing the Law, and Suppression of Riots) and then Part IV, ss. 118–49 (Offences Against the Administration of Law and Justice); the former creates lawful immunities and defences for constables, among others, while the latter defines liabilities and offences for the same officers.

48 In the essays in this volume following this one, particularly by Dr Greg Marquis, Professor Rod Macleod, and Dr Philip Stenning, these historical themes and changes are carefully expanded for the post-Confederation era.

2

Power from the Street: The Canadian Municipal Police

GREG MARQUIS

The municipal police department is a relic of an earlier century. Today almost three-fifths of Canada's 55,000 public police officers work for municipal or regional departments. Close to 10,000 belong to the Metropolitan Toronto Police Force and the Montreal Urban Community Police Service. Social, technological, and organizational changes have transformed aspects of policing in the twentieth century. The urban police have never been so well trained and equipped. Police agencies now include more women, university graduates, and members of visible and ethnic minorities. The current ratio of sworn municipal officers to civilian personnel (support and clerical staff) is three to one.[1]

Civilianization, patrol cars, and computers notwithstanding, fundamental continuities remain between today's modernized, post–Charter of Rights professionals and their Victorian predecessors. The basic continuity, of course, rests on the ultimately coercive nature of the state and its local agents, which is the basic characteristic of police occupational culture.

Police history is not synonymous with legal history. Historically, police powers such as questioning, search, and seizure have been less a product of formal law than of political culture, day-to-day police routine, and the social origins of personnel. Recent public-opinion polls confirm a historic fact: most Canadians support their police. From the mid-nineteenth until the mid-twentieth century, public expectations, the professional aspirations of senior officers, the streetwise style of the rank and file, and the stunted development of criminal justice institutions and social welfare proved conducive to 'crime control.' This style of policing paid little attention to the suspect's rights and often discredited the concept of 'British justice' central to Canadian political culture.[2] From their inception in the middle of the nineteenth century, the urban political increased their formal and informal powers over common offenders and fringe elements. In return, they were expected to 'fill the gaps' in municipal and social-welfare administration. The following overview of the period 1830 to 1980 suggests that structural factors explain why both police and public came to share such an open-ended view of police powers.[3]

ORIGINS

Innumerable historians, amateur and professional, have attributed the appearance of the 'new police' in the nineteenth century Anglo-American world to the success of the London Metropolitan Police of 1829. This link tends to be assumed rather than illustrated with hard evidence.[4] Similarly, earlier police chroniclers automatically listed fear of crime as a major causal factor in police reform; this now seems less plausible.[5] Older Whiggish explanations saw the police as an inevitable and humane institution of local reform. This view of police as guardians permeates in-house histories and reflects popular tastes that are based more on myth. Social scientists and social historians, by contrast, particularly those trained in the 1960s and 1970s, tend to situate police reform in the context of class relations.[6] The transition from commercial to industrial capitalism, according to social historians, was accompanied by changes in the institutional superstructure: new laws and new institutions of control such as police, penitentiaries, and schools. Crime was a crude form of social protest. These 'revisionists' agree with the earlier liberal historians that the police were organized to contain disorder, but stress the class instrumentality of the police mandate. The new police, in other words, were an intrusive arm of the capitalist state and, along with the justice system's other components, attempted to discipline and criminalize elements of the working class.[7]

This Marxist-based paradigm is attractive for four reasons: (1) The police and other new institutions of social control appeared with the Industrial Revolution. (2) The new police came under the direct or indirect supervision of the new middle class of professionals and capitalists. Traditional order-keepers, magistrates and constables, represented an earlier paternalistic social order. Under its new masters, the police institution was used to break strikes, enforce 'middle-class' liquor regulations, and monitor socialists and unemployed organizations. (3) Resistance to the new police was strongest in plebeian quarters. (4) Police and court records and press accounts suggest that the bulk of arrests, prosecutions, and convictions came from the working class. The revisionist approach, although rooted in a more realistic social analysis, is as flawed as the Whiggish interpretation, as it is equally deterministic.[8]

The first wave of Canadian police reform began early in the reign of Queen Victoria. By the 1840s British North America was a sparsely settled rural and small-town society with a handful of major urban centres: Montreal, Quebec,

Toronto, Halifax, and Saint John. Two decades after Confederation this pattern began to change. New towns were founded in the West, Ontario's urban network flourished, and greater Montreal expanded through suburbanization and industrialization. By 1921 federal census officials reported that one-half of the population lived in urban settings. According to the Dominion Bureau of Statistics, 125 cities and towns with populations of over 4000 employed roughly 3900 police officers (the recently reorganized RCMP totalled about 1700). Montreal and Toronto maintained police departments of several hundred each, but most municipal forces were small, half ranging from two to five men, another third from six to twenty. Below the 125 reporting to the DBS were scores of even smaller local 'departments' of one or two men. Ottawa and the provinces, other than providing legislation affecting enforcement (such as the 1892 Criminal Code and provincial liquor laws) were not involved in urban law enforcement. The results of such decentralization were wide differences in styles of management, working conditions, and pay.[9]

Municipal autonomy was the chief structural characteristic of urban policing until the post–Second World War era. The first 'police' had been night or seasonal watchmen employed by town councils to assist magistrates and constables in preserving the peace (towns continued to appoint watchmen after establishing police forces). Permanent police forces, along with changes in petty justice, usually accompanied advances in municipal administration. The police, in other words, were central to the municipal revolution of the mid-nineteenth century that brought responsible government and local control to urban ratepayers. British North American constabularies – with the exception of Newfoundland, which had a weak municipal tradition – had more in common with English borough forces, supervised by watch committees, than with the London Metropolitan Police, which reported to the Home Secretary. Municipal autonomy had a profound impact on Canada's police 'system.'[10]

The following table, indicating the pattern of police diffusion across British North America, should be approached with caution as it is not complete. Furthermore, in most centres police reform was a gradual and uneven process, subject to local political, fiscal, and social conditions. The political and ethnic situation in 1830s Lower Canada, for example, almost resulted in an Irish-modelled constabulary in Montreal, Quebec, and the rural areas (gendarmeries were established on a temporary basis when the Lower Canadian constitution was suspended). Exactly when a force of watchmen became a 'modern' centralized police force is open to debate.[11] Yet police reform did represent a significant extension of the local state, however tentative, over the individual. The police quickly became the most important branch of civic administration, and a whipping boy in local politics.[12]

Police reform: British North America

Place	Year	Control
Toronto	1835	city council/police commission
Montreal	1833	city council[a]
Quebec	1833	city council[a]
Halifax	1841	city council[c]
Hamilton	1847	city council/police commission
Kingston	1846	city council/police commission
Saint John	1849	city council[b]
Charlottetown	1855	city council
Ottawa	1866	city council/police commission
Victoria	1862	city council[d]
St John's	1872	government[e]
Winnipeg	1874	city council/police commission
Vancouver	1886	city council/police commission

a Initially no full-time police; police under government control, 1838–43
b Chief nominated by provincial government
c Day police and nightwatch joined 1864
d Under government control to 1862
e 'Police' evident before 1872 legislation

SOURCE: Greg Marquis, *Policing Canada's Century: A History of the Canadian Association of Chiefs of Police* (Toronto: University of Toronto Press 1993), chap. 1.

ACCOUNTABILITY

Accountability has become a major issue in late-twentieth-century policing, at least in non-police circles. Civilian review boards, codification of police powers, and other measures have been suggested to limit abuses of police authority. Victorian police managers were circumscribed by taxation-conscious civic politicians, requests from the civic élite and other special interests, and an often uncooperative local press. Personnel policy – recruitment, wages, promotion, and dismissal – was never beyond such local influence as sectarianism, even with reforms such as Ontario's creation of police commissions. Inspired by American practice, in 1858 Upper Canada enacted legislation, first applicable to Toronto, introducing boards of police commissioners, special-purpose bodies consisting of two judicial officials and the local mayor. The two provincial appointees, the majority, were supposed to be 'above politics' (something of a rarity in a nineteenth-century Canadian judge). Eventually the police-commission system spread throughout Ontario and parts of the West; it was insignificant in Quebec and the Maritimes where direct political control was the norm.[13] Whatever the form of governance, its impact was more on the style of policing than its content. Arrest patterns, for example, do not seem to have been affected significantly by the presence of a board of police commissioners as opposed to a town-council police committee (although further research may modify this hypothesis).

At present, it is impossible to generalize about the degree of autonomy enjoyed by municipal chief constables. Brian Grosman, in a 1974 report on police services in Prince Edward Island, described what historical research may well prove to be the Canadian norm, a policing style that was 'for the most part subjective, outside public scrutiny, not generally subject to review, and based on standards which are never explained.'[14] Yet most chief constables in the early twentieth century believed themselves hemmed in by local 'politics.' The minutes of the Toronto and Vancouver boards of police commissioners indicate that police chiefs often were guided on specific policies such as vice enforcement. Municipal policing was a favourite target of politicians and would-be politicians such as Gerry McGeer of Vancouver, William Howland and Arthur Roebuck of Toronto, and Jean Drapeau of Montreal (two more recent police critics are John Sewell and Jean Doré). A 'law and order' campaign in municipal politics could also support the police, as in 1920s Toronto. Direct political supervision of law enforcement was the very antithesis of Canadian police professionalism according to the Chief Constables' Association of Canada (organized in 1905) and subsequent provincial and regional police lobbies (all dominated by municipal chiefs). Turnover at the executive level was a sign of political interference, which is why, in the police world, dour 'Toronto the Good.' with only six chief constables in the period 1886–1962, ranked far ahead of Montreal or Vancouver (the latter with twenty chiefs in the same period). There were, despite the popular view of the Canadian police as disciplined and incorruptible, a number of scandals in various urban centres, most of them having to do with liquor, vice regulation, and petty graft. Four public inquiries involving police administration were convened in Montreal between 1894 and 1924, a similar number in Toronto from 1918 to 1936, two in Vancouver before the Second World War, and two in Winnipeg from 1900 to 1940.[15]

Overall, the authorities subscribed to the theory that the police, in the best traditions of British justice, were accountable to the rule of law. Police critics, therefore, were challenging the political and social order itself, and deserved few courtesies. Citizens and their lawyers did complain to governing authorities about the actions of individual policemen. Town-council committees or boards of police commissioners could be meddlesome, but they also served as a buffer between police and critics. The courts were lenient towards officers who employed deadly force against escaping suspects, even those wanted for minor infractions. Furthermore, the police discouraged civilian complaints by threatening to lay charges against would-be critics. The most common reason for dismissal was not for dishonesty, partisanship, or excessive use of force but intemperance, which was more of an internal disciplinary infraction.[16]

The most sustained attack on the municipal police was launched in the years 1900–20, a period in which public debate on social conditions was dominated by the 'Social Gospel.' The initial strength of this critique, and its ultimate demise, explains why police officials viewed civilian police reformers as short-sighted and partisan. Social Gospellers, including the Protestant and Catholic clergy, journalists, women's groups, temperance advocates, and sabbatarians, subjected the police in most urban centres to close scrutiny. Moral and social reform committees, Local Councils of Women, the Women's Christian Temperance Union, the Lord's Day Alliance, and other groups held meetings, wrote letters, and sent delegations to city hall and the provincial legislature. Their chief grievance was that the police and courts were not sufficiently aggressive against prostitution, gambling, and illegal drinking. The issue of Prohibition, the litmus test of 'political correctness' during the Progressive age, was particularly worrisome to police officials.[17] It was during this period that the police were forced to deal with juvenile courts and a greater use of suspended sentences and probation. The larger departments, under pressure from women's groups, hired a few policewomen who were not well integrated into operations but served as matrons, roving welfare workers, morality and detective department operatives, or clerks. The moral-reform aspect of the Social Gospel went into decline during the late 1920s. Conditions during the 1920s and 1930s allowed the police to project a professional image as crime-fighters, thus undercutting residual moral-reform criticism.

PUBLIC ORDER

Among the anticipated functions of the new police, three were prominent. The first was order-keeping. The police enjoyed a legitimate monopoly of force in service of the state. The British North American policeman inherited the constable's dual role – protector of the King's Peace and officer of the local court.[18] The history of police reform in cities such as Saint John, Montreal, Quebec, and Toronto conforms to a pattern evident in Britain and the United States, where violence arising from ethnic, sectarian, political, and class conflicts threatened to overwhelm traditional mechanisms of social control. A decade of piecemeal police reform in Saint John, a major port of entry for Irish immigrants, ended dramatically with a 12 July 1849 riot that took over one dozen lives. The prevention and dispersal by civil police of riots and other 'affrays' was designed to lessen reliance on the more deadly British military and the unpredictable combination of militia and special constables. Riots had not vanished by the late nineteenth century, but social violence in Canadian urban centres, generally, had subsided. One important legacy of the crowd-control responsibilities of the police was an obsession with physical prowess and military drill. Once established with uniforms, lock-ups, truncheons and in some cases swords and pistols, the municipal police set out to 'pacify' the streets. Their proactive patrols encountered much resistance and ridicule in the 1830s to 1850s, but by the Confederation period the urban police had established themselves as an institution of considerable power.

Records and press reports indicate that most arrests were responses to public-order violations such as drunkenness and disturbing the peace. The connection between police reform, police courts, municipal by-laws, and lock-ups is a practical example of criminology's 'labelling theory.' The five-fold rise in criminal convictions between the 1870s and the 1920s had much to do with an increase in legislated social controls and an augmented police presence. Before the organization of a police force and lock-up under its 1855 charter, for example, there were few arrests for public drunkenness in Charlottetown. By the early twentieth century a number of the larger departments had acquired patrol wagons and electric signal systems that facilitated urban surveillance (and surveillance of the police worker by management). Mounted units, retained in the larger centres, proved useful in containing public demonstrations, strikes, and illegal parades.[19]

CRIME FIGHTERS?

The second anticipated police duty was crime control and detection. Short-term panics over theft and arson had led to the deployment of night-watchmen or special constables in late-eighteenth and early-nineteenth-century British North American seaports. By mid-century police on the beat and specialized detectives (employed only in the larger towns) were expected to know local criminals, chiefly thieves, burglars, fraud artists, prostitutes and fences, by name and reputation. They were also instructed to ascertain *likely* criminals – strangers – by their appearance, acquaintances, and circumstances. The career cop learned that crime was an attitude and lifestyle, not simply an action or series of actions. This occupational skill, a rejection of the legal doctrine 'innocent until proven guilty,' had, as a number of historians point out, a profound legacy for the twentieth century. The vagrancy charge, meant to lessen the potential burden on local charity, became a major police tool in dealing with 'likely' criminals. Detectives were concerned primarily with stolen goods. The police did not regard perpetrators of interpersonal acts of violence or participants in weekend drinking sprees as criminals. Yet these offenders, including a lumpenproletariat of jailbirds, were the grist of the petty-justice mill. Force, or the threat of force, was the most effective response to known criminals and unruly youths. Cries of official brutality were rare; citizens were more apt to applaud than condemn police aggression.[20] Revolvers, which some departments issued for night duty in the early decades of municipal policing, no doubt were useful in winning respect.

Unlike twentieth-century social scientists, the police have had few difficulties with defining crime, the treatment of which became central to an emergent sense of professionalism. The municipal police believed that they, not the glamorized RCMP, were Canada's 'real' police. As far as chief constables were concerned, the police and criminals were in a state of war, a sort of criminological Social Darwinism. This adversarial relationship easily spilled over into an occupational distrust of socialists and other radicals dedicated to undermining authority structures. From the 1920s to the 1950s, Communism, in the opinion of the police, was tantamount to criminality. Ritualistic crime-fighting rhetoric was repeated so often that the police themselves, despite the more complex nature of their duties, came to believe it. The theory that criminality was not a specific act so much as a lifestyle fuelled police advocacy of an expanded legal basis for criminal identification (fingerprinting), the preventative detention of habitual offenders, and the denial of parole to violent or career criminals. It also explains the special emphasis given by detectives to hotels, boarding houses, pawnshops, pool halls, cafés, licenced premises, and dancehalls. The urban cop, although cognizant of the influences of an evil environment, attributed crime to individual pathology and moral responsibility. As late as 1970, according to a University of Toronto Centre of Criminology study, most Canadians shared this assessment of criminal causation.[21]

SERVICE FUNCTION

Third came the service/regulatory function, reflecting the original meaning of the word police. To understand the totality of police authority we must consider the evolving 'catch-all' role of the police in small towns and large cities alike. Historian John Weaver calls this process 'community entanglement.'[22] Not every town organized a constabulary because of riots, street violence, or outbreaks of larceny – in many cases a police department was simply the administrative arm of a newly incorporated municipality, such as Charlottetown in 1855. Hamilton's first chief constable was also the inspector of streets. The Vancouver police inspected bakeries. The Toronto police commission regulated the street economy through licencing powers under the *Municipal Act*. The service function detracted, in terms of human resources, from crime-fighting, but without it most police departments would have been largely idle, and subsequently pared down or even dismantled. Many police chiefs, like other public administrators, became adept at compiling self-serving reports to justify annual budgetary requests. If this entailed counting the number of unlicenced dogs and unlit street lamps, so be it. The records suggest that the typical policeman in the period 1850–1920 spent little time 'fighting' crime and almost no time detecting it.

Given the unsophisticated state of urban bureaucracy, civic authorities faced with new regulatory or welfare problems passed them on to their police. From the mid-nineteenth to the early-twentieth century police departments faced mounting demands from municipal government, private agencies, and individuals of all classes. Police stations were used to shelter the respectable transient on his way through the Maritimes or Ontario in search of work. The Montreal police sheltered nearly 300,000 during the Great Depression. Lost children were provided for; domestic quarrels were settled; the injured and sick were transported in police ambulances; patrolmen secured the unlocked doors of business premises and checked on temporarily vacant private residences. Early in this century a number of municipal forces assumed responsibility for the rudiments of traffic engineering, down to painting crosswalks. The police station was the community welfare/emergency centre whose duty officer was an important arbiter of urban life. The expansion of the regulatory welfare state after the Second World War gradually countered, but did not eradicate, this trend. Although radio-equipped cars continued to respond to citizen-initiated calls, in the postwar years the police station itself became somewhat remote from the community, associated more with the perpetrators than the victims of crime. In larger centres they became imposing and somewhat inaccessible edifices having more in common with corporate offices than old-style station houses. The service role had allowed police departments to collect more and more information, a commodity essential to any bureaucracy, and bought the institution political support.[23] The tradition survives in smaller police departments with low arrest rates, limited technology, and informal operational styles.[24]

TECHNOLOGY

On the operational side of policing, technology has been as significant as criminal law. Telephones, typewriters, Bertillon anthropometric measurements of criminals, and photography had arrived by the 1890s. By the First World War motorcycles were replacing horses. One of the more profound unanticipated duties was traffic regulation in the age of the automobile. The car revolutionized urban and rural life and changed the very shape of cities. By the 1920s Canadians had become obsessed by the automobile, a trend slowed only by the 1930s Depression and the Second World War. By 1960 there was a registered motor vehicle for every 3.4 Canadians. The automobile, once institutionalized, affected all aspects of policing. Urban-traffic and highway-safety infractions, generally under municipal and provincial jurisdiction, became the bread and butter of the postwar police. Traffic cases clogged the lower courts, generating revenues for the provinces and municipalities and paperwork for the police. Traffic regulation fostered a new area of professional expertise and specialization, with the appointment of traffic officers, squads, or divisions, depending on the size of the department. The democratic nature of the automotive revolution meant that citizens of all classes were potential prey of the traffic cop, a fact not lost upon police managers seeking to explain a decline in police popularity after the Second World War. By the mid-1970s 80 per cent of persons being processed by the police (municipal, provincial, and federal) were charged with driving offences, most of them summary-conviction infractions.[25]

The automobile, fitted with two-way radios, altered the organization of police work and redefined the framework of relations with the community. One of the strengths of policing's first century was the beat system, which made constables not only highly visible, but also well informed on persons and activities in specific neighbourhoods. Radio cars were first introduced in the 1930s. Dispatchers, answering citizen complaints on the telephone and intra-departmental communications, came to play a key role. Before the Second World War the Vancouver Police Department already had more men assigned to vehicles than to regular beats. The police chief's 1938 report suggested that patrol cars and motorcycles, although taking men off the street, were perpetuating the service function of the beat, albeit in reactive fashion. That year motorized patrols responded to over 41,000 calls involving 'crime, domestic troubles, landlord and tenant troubles, fires, inhalation cases, automobile accidents, industrial incidents, sudden deaths and missing persons.'[26] The natural habitat of the radio car were the suburban residential and commercial areas that began to proliferate after the Second World War.

By the early 1950s there was a motor vehicle for every six or seven officers in Canada's 240 largest municipal departments. The deployment of radio cars was delayed in smaller communities until the 1960s, but within a generation the police had become wedded to the automobile. There is no hard evidence to prove that random motorized patrols have an appreciable effect on crime, but as the 1939 Vancouver report suggested, they did allow police to respond quickly to citizen-initiated requests. Higher-quality frequency-modulation technology (allowing car-to-car communications) was installed beginning in the

1940s. The 1950s and 1960s saw radio cars reach the small towns, although foot patrols and call-box systems remained in metropolitan core areas. Telex, or teletype printers, and mechanical sorter and keypunch equipment further modernized communications and records. By the mid-1970s urban patrols, through radio contact with headquarters, which in turn contacted Ottawa by telex, were able to tap the computerized files of CPIC, the Canadian Police Information Centre. The next technological innovation was the individual computer terminal, allowing patrol officers direct access to CPIC files. Successive generations of technology were adapted to traditional police needs. The CPIC terminal of today's police cruiser, despite its impressive capabilities, is merely an updated version of the late-nineteenth century 'rogue's gallery.'

SOCIAL CHANGE, 1945–1980

The postwar process of 'metropolitanization' accelerated a trend towards police amalgamation. Urban growth was accompanied by a major influx of immigrants – continental Europeans in the 1940s and 1950s, and Asians, Africans, and West Indians in the 1960s and 1970s. By 1961 one-third of the populace lived in the five largest cities; almost half of the population designated 'urban' was in fact suburban. Social and economic change brought the maturation of the social-service state. The criminal-justice system underwent expansion and centralization, with significant increases in personnel and operating expenditures. Between 1963 and 1976 the number of municipal police departments reporting to the Dominion Bureau of Statistics Uniform Crime Reporting program dropped from 710 to 466. The creation of the Metropolitan Toronto Police Force in the late 1950s and the Montreal Urban Community Police Service and Ontario's regional police in the early 1970s reflected the proliferation of the metropolitan area, defined as 'a complex of closely related centres of population located within daily commuting distance to the central city, or urban core.'[27] These amalgamations, which involved centralizing command and communications, as well as meeting the expectations of inner-city, suburban, and in some instances rural dwellers, were resented in some circles. Ontario's regional police were modelled on recent English precedent, where the Home Office had encouraged amalgamation in the interest of efficiency. By the mid-1970s the York, Niagara, Hamilton-Wentworth, Waterloo, Peel, Sudbury, Durham, and Halton regional forces ranged in size from 250–700 officers.[28]

PROVINCIAL INTERVENTION

Modernizers within municipal police institutions, town councils, governing authorities, and provincial governments faced a dilemma. How could standardization and efficiency be reconciled with local control? Operationally, as police chiefs and civil servants had pointed out since the early 1900s, police departments shared common characteristics and concerns. Yet they also varied in terms of size, training, discipline, record-keeping and bureaucratization, relations with civic authorities and the press, and so on. Indeed, some differences may have been so great as to obstruct the historical analysis of crime conditions, as statistics were not always comparable from town to town or region to region. During the 1920s, 1930s, and 1940s a number of leading police administrators were attracted to 'national policing,' a Canadian version of the English system, with financial, training, pension, and inspection services provided by the central government. The RCMP, one possible agent of standardization, did expand into rural contract policing in several provinces in the period 1928–1950. The Mounties, one of the more powerful instruments of the central government, even took over the policing of a number of small municipalities. Yet municipal autonomy, enshrined in the *BNA Act* and a century of custom, accompanied by a backlash against Ottawa's aggrandizing tendencies in the period 1939–1945, precluded police centralization on a national scale.

After the Second World War, the provinces launched their own administrative and public-finance revolution, competing with and at times complementing the federal government's growing social presence. The growth of the welfare and regulatory state on the provincial level impinged on the structure of municipal autonomy. The modern state could no longer tolerate police localism. Ontario led the way with its 1946 *Police Act*, which set the standard for provincial regulation of local policing. Ontario's second innovation was a provincial police commission, formed in 1962 ostensibly to counter organized crime. These new mechanisms involved financial assistance, province-wide training, the regulation of labour relations and disciplinary appeals, and research and planning. Other provinces, to varying degrees, followed. Many, supported by police administrators if not police associations, extended the board of police commissioners system in an attempt to depoliticize administration. In 1971 legislation required British Columbia's twelve remaining municipal forces to come under boards of commissioners. The 1974 Nova Scotia *Police Act* did the same for municipalities with independent police forces and populations of at least 1500. Yet provincial intervention, which affected all spheres of municipal affairs after the Second World War, did not create provincial policing 'systems.' Despite provincial regulation, standardization, and assistance with training and finances, municipal departments are still motivated by community concerns. Municipal police managers, for example, feel that certain reform suggestions emanating from the provincial and federal levels (such as the

Solicitor General Canada 1991 document *Police Challenge 2000*) are unrealistic for the average department with limited resources.

In 1976 the twelve major metropolitan areas employed 60 per cent of municipal police personnel and recorded 44 per cent of Criminal Code offences 'known to the police.'[29] The first stirrings of public debate on the police question in the late 1960s and early 1970s invariably took place in one of the metropolitan zones: Halifax, Quebec, Montreal, Ottawa, Toronto, Hamilton, London, Windsor, Winnipeg, Calgary, Edmonton, and Vancouver. Only in these centres were populations sufficiently diverse to produce articulated critiques of law-enforcement policies and practices that went beyond the usual minor complaints. Contemporary American urban upheavals, a fear of street crime, and more liberal views on personal lifestyle, especially drug use, affected attitudes in Canada. Together with the RCMP, the Ontario Provincial Police, and la Sûreté du Quebec, police departments in these centres, and about one dozen others, were setting the police agenda by the 1970s. The larger police organizations on the one hand were more powerful, but on the other delivered a service that was 'less personal and informal than that of the small or medium-sized department.'[30]

By the 1970s, urban police administrators were facing two challenges, one external, the other from within. The first was criminal-justice reform, including not only criminal law but also institutional reforms in corrections and the rehabilitation of offenders. As the service state advanced, reclamation and treatment, not retribution and deterrence, became the goals of legal and penal reformers established in the social-service, university, and voluntary sectors. To these reformers the police were not guardians but coercive state agents who perpetuated inequities in the areas of arrest, trial, sentencing, and rehabilitation. The preventive and remedial approach to criminal justice evident in the 1938 federal Archambault Report on the penitentiaries dominated provincial studies such as the 1946 Commission to Investigate the Penal System of Saskatchewan and Quebec's Prevost Commission of the late 1960s, the 1955 Fauteux Report on corrections, and the 1969 report of the Canadian Committee on Corrections. The establishment in the early 1970s of the Law Reform Commission of Canada was viewed by the police as another challenge to their authority. The legal-rights sections of the new Canadian Charter of Rights and Freedoms, for the police, were the culmination of an academic/bureaucratic threat that had been building since the 1960s. The second challenge was internal: police unions. Unlike the RCMP, the municipal and provincial police by the 1960s had acquired the right to organize and bargain collectively. The Montreal police strike of 1969 was a sobering reminder to both management and public that the rank and file could no longer be taken for granted. The unions, according to some observers, are a potential impediment to modernization and innovation, and their concerns extend far beyond matters such as pay, benefits, and working conditions.[31]

WHO ARE THE POLICE?

In the nineteenth century, and until quite recently, the urban police were recruited not for their education, understanding of legal concepts, or sensitivity to minorities and social questions. Constables were hired for their size and physical capabilities. If they were Orangemen, Freemasons, British immigrants, or ex-soldiers, so much the better. Police chiefs in Hamilton, Toronto, and Saint John recruited from beyond their locality on the presumption that local candidates would be less amenable to discipline. The sons of farmers and tradesmen were preferred, as were Anglo-Celtic immigrants. The Hamilton police department was dominated by Protestants (as was the city), and prior to 1914 contained a large minority of British immigrants. Montreal and Quebec City had to take into account the French-speaking majority. The Montreal recruit of the 1890s had to be a British subject, literate, healthy, lead a 'regular life,' and have a working knowledge of French and English. The Winnipeg police, for its first several decades, exhibited a fondness for Scots. The Maritime urban centres, situated in a region of net emigration since the 1860s, have recruited locally. Revisionist accounts of the police suggest that they were anti–working class because they were employed in strikebreaking and in enforcing temperance laws. Yet the police, including most senior officers, were quite similar – in terms of origins, education, conjugal condition, income, religious activities, and leisure pursuits – to the average white, British or Canadian-born working man.[32]

The police themselves take umbrage at the adjective 'working-class,' by which historians and sociologists characterize traditional police work culture. As would-be professionals municipal police officers prefer to be regarded as middle-class. In terms of educational background, admittedly an arbitrary measure, until quite recently most municipal policemen were recruited from the working or lower middle class. Completion of high school was an exception, not the norm, among small-town cops. And until the 1960s and 1970s most urban policemen were not well paid, although year-round employment and service pensions, where they existed, gave them a distinct advantage over labourers, clerks, and tradesmen. In recent years hiring practices and social change have produced a new generation of community-college and university-educated officers. Yet anti-intellectualism has not disappeared, and veteran officers are unconvinced of the benefits of university education for operational policing.[33]

Historically, police departments, like other public institutions, have not reflected urban ethnic, racial, and gender realities. Like the justice system as a whole, the police institution was, and is, dominated by white males. The few policewomen attached to departments from 1912 onward were more of a novelty. Their duties, reflecting the priorities of the maternal feminists who had lobbied for their employment, were directed towards the moral protection of women and children. Greater attention to juvenile work during the 1950s saved policewomen from extinction, but a decade later they were still outnumbered by police horses. As late as 1970 Vancouver police, with a total staff of over nine hundred, had ten policewomen. Other underepresented groups were ethnic and visible minorities. Although big-city departments employed interpreters and ethnic 'operatives,' by and large the rank and file was homogeneous (with the exception of Montreal and Quebec). Recruitment practices, municipal patronage (in the hands of the largest ethnic groups), departmental tradition, and resistance from within minority communities themselves all played a part in this phenomenon, the results of which now appear in the news media on a weekly basis.[34]

POLICE AND THE COURTS

Crown Prosecutor: 'Did you warn the prisoner before he made this statement to you?'

Police Constable Gillis: 'Well, I told him to throw up his hands.'[35]

This courtroom exchange from 1914, involving a burglary prosecution, suggests the traditional street cop's understanding of the rights of the accused. The lower courts are fundamental to understanding the development of policing. The police are part of a system that commences with an arrest and ends, in many cases, with incarceration, release, and rehabilitation. The importance of the police-court link is prominent in American literature. Seventy years ago Raymond B. Fosdick's *American Police Systems* described prosecution, trial, and sentencing practices as serious impediments to effective policing. The American police, Fosdick lamented, were frustrated by legal technicalities, political interference, liberal judges, and soft juries. Yet in Canadian eyes the American police were not overly restrained by legal norms. The situation, they believed, was different in the 'Peaceable Kingdom.' In 1964 James Cramer, in *The World's Police*, portrayed Canadian police as tightly controlled by law and public opinion: 'Police action,' he explained, 'is subject to scrutiny by press as well as the courts. The results of police investigations are ventilated in open courts and their methods revealed for all to see.'[36]

Canadian police practices may have been enlightened in 1964 relative to other countries, but it would be interesting to know the degree to which the police themselves, rather than being regulated by the courts, shaped the climate and procedure of the lower courts. In this century the rise of the provincial attorneys-general and their agents, the development of provincial court systems, and the growth of the defence bar have significantly affected police authority in the courts. Yet for many decades urban 'police courts' in large towns and cities operated as judicial assembly lines. Administered by mayors and aldermen (ex officio justices of the peace) and, later, stipendiary magistrates appointed by the province, these institutions became clearing-houses for urban misbehaviour, ranging from fines for minor infractions to the preliminary examination of murder suspects. British justice rhetoric notwithstanding, the final product usually was the guilty offender. The police, as a result of their nineteenth-century background, came to view magistrates' courts not as autonomous criminal-justice institutions giving equal treatment to police and the accused, but as administrative extensions of the police establishment. Legal technicalities and defence counsel were frowned upon, particularly when employed by persons 'known to the police.' The fact that stipendiary or provincial magistrates played no small role in police affairs lessened, in practice, the formal distinctions between police and police court. The courts and police headquarters often were located in the same building. A 1960s study of pre-trial detention practices in Toronto suggested that police authority in bail and other matters had serious consequences for offenders held on remand. By the 1960s and 1970s this occupational attitude, encouraged by governing authorities and senior officers, had a pedigree of over a century.[37]

CONCLUSION

The Canadian municipal police department, despite its critics,[38] is not likely to disappear in our lifetime. And neither – despite the Charter of Rights, Criminal Law Review, and improved recruitment and training practices – will traditional police attitudes. This paper argues that police actions arise out of society, not police 'deviance.' Historically, our political culture was prepared to allow the police a relatively free hand. In the last three decades specific individuals and groups have challenged this legitimacy. So have the courts. But the crime-fighting image is one readily accepted by the general public, which regards organized police critics such as women's groups, visible minorities, and civil-liberties advocates as special interests. Social change and legal reform have produced and will continue to produce important changes in law enforcement. The creation of metropolitan and regional police agencies has altered the scale of the institution and its relations with the community. Yet the municipal police department remains an essentially nineteenth-century bureaucracy based on coercion, militaristic discipline, information-gathering, and community service.

NOTES

This is a revised version of a paper prepared for the Police Powers Symposium, Edmonton, 18–19 October 1991.

1 Solicitor General Canada, *A Vision of the Future of Policing in Canada: Police Challenge 2000 Background Document* (Ottawa: Solicitor General Canada 1990), 11. The police-civilian employee ratio for municipal departments reporting to the Dominion Bureau of Statistics was 13–1 in 1952 and 8–1 in 1972; see *Police Administration Statistics*, 1952–72.

2 G. Marquis, 'Doing Justice to "British Justice": Law, Ideology and Canadian Historiography,' in W.W. Pue and B. Wright, eds, *Canadian Perspectives on Law and Society: Issues in Legal History* (Ottawa: Carleton University Press 1988), 43. One study defines British crime control as a prosecution style 'which emphasizes factual over legal guilt and will examine each case on its merits, concerned with innocence or guilt but not constitutional issues.' See I.K. MacKenzie and G.P. Gallagher, *Behind the Uniform: Policing in Britain and America* (New York: St Martin's Press 1989), 48.

3 This paper deals principally with independent municipal and regional police forces, not the significant number of RCMP municipal contract detachments, although their roles are almost identical.

4 See, for example, J. Sewell, *Police: Urban Policing in Canada* (Toronto: Lorimer 1985), chap. 1.

5 C. Emsley, *Policing and Its Context 1750–1870* (London: MacMillan Press 1983); S.H. Palmer, *Police and Protest in England and Ireland, 1780–1850* (New York: Cambridge University Press 1988); E. Monkkonen, *Police in Urban America, 1860–1920* (Cambridge: Harvard University Press 1981). There is as yet no equivalent work on nineteenth-century British North America, although volume 19 of the *Urban History Review* (1990) is a useful police history issue. See also C.K. Talbot, C.H.S. Jayewardene, and T.J. Juliani, *Canada's Constables: The Historical Development of Policing in Canada* (Ottawa: Crimecare Inc. 1986).

6 An approach pioneered in Canada by H. Clare Pentland's 1960 doctoral thesis, later published as H.C. Pentland, *Labour and Capital in Canada, 1650–1860* (Toronto: Lorimer 1981).

7 M. Cross, '"The Laws Are Like Cobwebs": Popular Resistance to Authority in Mid-Nineteenth Century British North America,' in P.B. Waite, S. Oxner, and T. Barnes, eds, *Law in a Colonial Society: The Nova Scotia Experience* (Toronto:

Carswell 1987), 105; N. Rogers, 'Serving Toronto the Good: The Development of the City Police Force, 1834–1884' in V. Russell, ed., *Forging a Consensus: Historical Essays on Toronto* (Toronto: University of Toronto Press 1984), 116. The class interpretation is carried to extremes in S. Harring, *Policing a Class Society: The Experience of American Cities, 1865–1915* (New Brunswick, NJ: Rutgers University Press 1983).

8 For a critique of both liberal and revisionist police historiography, see R. Reiner, *The Politics of the Police* (New York: St Martin's Press 1985), chap. 1.

9 Dominion Bureau of Statistics, *Criminal Statistics for the Year Ending September 31, 1921* (Ottawa: Dominion Bureau of Statistics 1922), table X, Police Statistics.

10 G. Marquis, 'The Contours of Canadian Urban Justice, 1830–1875,' *Urban History Review* 15 (1987): 269.

11 E.K. Senior, 'The Influence of the British Garrison on the Development of the Montreal Police, 1832–1853,' in R.C. Macleod, ed., *Lawful Authority: Readings in the History of Criminal Justice in Canada* (Toronto: Copp, Clark and Pittman 1988), 85; A. Greer, 'The Birth of the Police in Canada,' in A. Greer and I. Radforth, eds, *Colonial Leviathan: State Formation in Mid-Nineteenth Century Canada* (Toronto: University of Toronto Press 1992), 17.

12 G. Marquis, '"A Machine of Oppression under the Guise of the Law": The Saint John Police Establishment, 1860–1890,' *Acadiensis* 16 (1986): 58.

13 P. Stenning, *Police Commissions and Boards in Canada* (Toronto: Centre of Criminology, University of Toronto 1981).

14 B.A. Grosman, *Report on Policing Province of Prince Edward Island* (Charlottetown: typescript, 1974), 18.

15 J.P. Brodeur, *La délinquence de l'ordre: Recherches sur les commissions d'enquête I* (LaSalle: Editions Hurtubise 1984); J. Swan, *A Century of Service: The Vancouver Police, 1886–1986* (Vancouver: Vancouver Police Historical Society and Centennial Museum 1986). This popular view has much to do with the mythic image of the early RCMP. See K. Walden, *Visions of Order* (Toronto: University of Toronto Press 1980).

16 P. McGahan, *Crime and Policing in Maritime Canada: Chapters from the Urban Records* (Fredericton: Goose Land Editions 1988), 53–4, 146–9.

17 G. Marquis, 'The Canadian Police and Prohibition, 1890–1930' (1991) [unpublished].

18 C. Emsley, 'Community Regulation and Imperial Regulation: Peasants, Gendarmes and State Formulation' (1991), 14 [unpublished].

19 Royal Commission, *Report of the Royal Commission Concerning Jails in the Province of Nova Scotia* (Halifax: 1933), 96–7; R. Hutchinson, *A Century of Service: A History of the Winnipeg Police Force, 1874–1974* (Winnipeg: City of Winnipeg Police Force 1974), 39.

20 J. Fingard, *The Dark Side of Life in Victorian Halifax* (Porters Lake: Pottersfield Press 1989); Ontario Prison Reform Commission, *Report of the Commissioners Appointed to Enquire into the Prison and Reformatory System of Ontario* (Toronto: Warwick & Sons 1891), 340; D.R. Johnson, *Policing the Urban Underworld: The Impact of Crime on the Development of American Policing, 1800–1887* (Philadelphia: Temple University Press 1979), 185.

21 G. Marquis, 'Practical Criminology: The Early Years of the Chief Constables' Association of Canada' (1990) [unpublished]; M.C. Courtis, *Attitudes on Crime and the Police in Toronto: A Report on Some Survey Findings* (Toronto: University of Toronto Centre of Criminology 1970), 133–4.

22 J. Weaver, 'Social Control, Martial Conformity and Community Entanglement: The Varied Beats of the Hamilton Police, 1895–1920' *Urban History Review* 19 (1990): 113.

23 Monkonnen, n. 5, above; G. Marquis, 'The Police as a Social Service in Twentieth Century Toronto' (1990) [unpublished] 'Enforcing the Law: The Charlottetown Police Force,' in D. Baldwin and T. Spira, eds, *Gaslights, Epidemics and Vagabond Cows: Charlottetown in the Victorian Age* (Charlottetown: Ragweed Press 1988), 86; 'The History of Policing in the Maritimes: Themes and Prospects,' *Urban History Review* 19 (1990): 86.

24 C. Murphy, 'The Social and Formal Organization of Small Town Policing: A Comparative Analysis of RCMP and Municipal Policing,' Ph.D. thesis, University of Toronto, 1986.

25 Dominion Bureau of Statistics, *The Motor Vehicle, 1960* (Ottawa: Section, Vital Statistics 1961); Statistics Canada, *Canada Year Book, 1980–81* (Ottawa: Statistics Canada 1982), 55–6.

26 Vancouver City Police Department, *Annual Report* (Vancouver: Vancouver City Police Department 1938).

27 I.M. Robinson, *Canadian Urban Growth Trends* (Vancouver: University of British Columbia 1981), 28; Dominion Bureau of Statistics, *Police Administration Statistics, 1965* (Ottawa: Statistics Canada 1966).

28 Royal Commission, *Report of the Royal Commission on Metropolitan Toronto* (Toronto: The Commission 1965), 60.

29 Statistics Canada, *Crime and Traffic Enforcement Statistics, 1976* (Ottawa: Statistics Canada 1977); Statistics Canada, *Police Administration Statistics, 1975 and 1976* (Ottawa: Statistics Canada 1977).

30 Royal Commission on the Donald Marshall Jr. Prosecution, *Discrimination Against Blacks in Nova Scotia: The Criminal Justice System* (Study) by W. Head and D. Clairmont (Halifax: The Commission 1989), 26.

31 A. Parizeau and D. Szabo, *The Canadian Criminal Justice System* (Toronto: Lexington Books 1977); G. Marquis, 'Canadian Police Chiefs and Law Reform:

The Historical Perspective,' *Canadian Journal of Criminology* 23 (1991): 385.

32 G. Marquis, 'Working Men in Uniform: The Early Twentieth Century Toronto Police,' *Histoire sociale/Social History* 20 (1987): 259; M. McCulloch, 'Most Assuredly Perpetual Motion: Police and Policing in Quebec City, 1838–1858,' *Urban History Review* 19 (1990): 100; R. Dandurand and C. Lanctot, *Manuel de police à l'usage de la police du Montréal* (Montreal: La Compagnie d'Imprimerie Perrault 1893), 20–1. The ethnic diversity of the Victorian Montreal department contrasts with its present overwhelmingly francophone nature.

33 Marquis, 'Working Men'; Weaver, 'Social Control' (n. 22).

34 For insights into the culture of the contemporary police see C. Vincent, *Police Officer* (Ottawa: Carleton University Press 1990).

35 *Vancouver Province*, 7 March 1914.

36 R.B. Fosdick, *American Police Systems* (New York: The Century Co. 1921); J. Cramer, *The World's Police* (London: Cassell and Co. 1964), 63.

37 Marquis, 'Contours of Canadian Urban Justice' (n. 10); Grosman, '*Report on Policing* (n. 14, 53–5); M. Friedland, *Detention before Trial: A Study of Criminal Cases Tried in the Toronto Magistrates' Courts* (Toronto: University of Toronto Press 1965); G. Homel, 'Denison's Law: Criminal Justice and the Police Court in Toronto, 1877–1921,' in Macleod, ed., *Lawful Authority*, 167.

38 A. Grant, *Policing Arrangements in New Brunswick with Particular Reference to the Highway Patrol Function* (Toronto: Osgoode Hall Law School 1988). Grant's report recommends the abolition of local departments. Given the current crisis in public finance and a possible decentralization in federal-provincial relations, senior levels of government will be unwilling or unable to exert a greater influence in urban policing, other than the traditional avenue of criminal law.

3

The RCMP and the Evolution of Provincial Policing

R.C. MACLEOD

Canada has in the RCMP a highly respected national police force. Their existence has unquestionably, if informally, strengthened the powers of the police in Canada generally throughout the twentieth century. The emergence of the RCMP as the dominant police organization in the country was largely unplanned. On two occasions there was a very definite possibility that the Mounted Police might retreat into the remote frontier regions of northern Canada, leaving the field open for the development of provincial police in all provinces. I have discussed the first of these critical periods for the survival of the Mounted Police in earlier writings.[1] This paper is mainly concerned with the decade of the 1920s, when the RCMP again faced the possibility of disbandment, only to emerge triumphant by the mid-1930s as the provincial police force for a majority of the provinces. The survival of the RCMP in this period has usually been interpreted as resulting from federal government concerns about subversion. A close examination of events fails to sustain such a view. There were no signs of concern about subversion on the part of the Liberal governments of the 1920s that made the crucial decisions. Mackenzie King, in fact, categorically ruled out the use of the RCMP for anti-subversive purposes. Less colourful but ultimately much more powerful forces were at work.

Let me briefly review the early development of provincial policing in Canada. Before the 1870s there were no police forces outside the largest cities. British Columbia, Quebec, and Ontario created embryonic provincial police force in the decade after Confederation, but they remained rather insignificant organizations until well into the twentieth century. The real innovation began in 1873 when the federal government created the North-West Mounted Police, whose jurisdiction covered the area that later became Alberta and Saskatchewan. In 1905, with the creation of the new provinces, the Mounted Police took over provincial policing under contract, a development forced on the federal government by public opinion in the West. The contracts lasted little more than a decade, but the Alberta and Saskatchewan provincial police created after the contracts ended were modelled closely on the Mounted Police and manned by former members of the NWMP.[2] More significant still, the RCMP resumed provincial policing in Saskatchewan in 1928 and in Alberta in 1932, and extended its operations to Manitoba and the Atlantic provinces in the latter year. Newfoundland made the same arrangement upon joining Confederation in 1949, and the following year British Columbia gave up its provincial police, leaving only Ontario and Quebec with independent provincial forces.

It has always intrigued me that Canadians were so willing to depart from the British and American models of very decentralized police organization. In many respects, although by no means all, our approach to policing resembles more closely that of the continental European countries, not only in its greater centralization but in a willingness to grant more power and authority to the police.[3] Some outside observers of Canadian society have seen this approach arising from a generalized deference to authority in the Canadian national character. I think it can be more convincingly explained by an examination of how our police institutions came into existence.

The pattern that has existed for most of the twentieth century took on its definitive form in the 1920s, but it was by no means a foregone conclusion that it would develop as it did. We are so accustomed to the way things have been since 1932 that it is hard to imagine how different it might have been with ten separate provincial police forces and the RCMP confined entirely to federal duties. Historians have almost ignored the fact that there were serious attempts to abolish the RCMP in 1922 and 1923. Successive federal governments between 1920 and 1932 paid lip service to the provinces' constitutional responsibility for policing, while moving steadily in the opposite direction. Not only did the Mounted Police survive to resume provincial policing on a country-wide scale, but their administrative role expanded enormously in this period.

The decision to create the Royal Canadian Mounted Police in 1920 through a merger of the Dominion Police and the Royal North-West Mounted Police was due primarily to the atmosphere of crisis created by the Winnipeg General Strike.[4] The Borden government saw the future of the Mounted Police as an anti-subversive force that would keep suspect organizations under surveillance and act as a mobile reserve to reinforce local authorities throughout the country if necessary. The debate in the House of Commons on the reorganization produced some opposition, led by MPs from the Atlantic provinces. The bluntest denunciation of the plan came from Robert H. Butts (Cape Breton South): 'I have been magistrate, sometimes I have been called judge, of a town of between 9,000 and 10,000 people. We never had need of Mounted Police down there, and we have no need of them now ... Do not send hayseeds from away across the plains down to Nova Scotia ... I say that it is dangerous to send them there. I speak for 73,000 people in Cape Breton, and I can say that they will not appreciate any such intrusion.'[5] Another Nova Scotia representative, J.H. Sinclair, added: 'The Federal Government are assuming a duty that they do not require to assume; that the provinces are not asking them to assume; that the provinces themselves are well able to take care of.'[6]

What is interesting about this debate is that there was almost no opposition from Ontario or Quebec, the provinces that might have been expected to be most jealous of provincial rights. The reason appears to be that the Atlantic provinces were the only part of Canada still without provincial police. Resistance to the introduction of modern police forces was an almost universal experience in Western Europe and North America during the nineteenth century. Police usurped the dispute-settling functions of local élites, who naturally resented this diminution of their power.[7] The language used by the maritimers who opposed the extension of RCMP services to their region leaves no doubt that this was the basis of their antagonism. But given the realities of Canadian politics, resistance from the Atlantic region alone would not be enough to deflect the government.

The first postwar election brought an entirely new set of political circumstances, with a Liberal minority government dependent for its survival on the votes of the new Progressive party, a radical farmers organization with ties to urban labour and socialist groups. The new prime minister, Mackenzie King, had no particular interest in the RCMP and was intent on forging an alliance with the Progressives. Labour unrest subsided in the wake of the Winnipeg General Strike, and the necessity for surveillance of radical organizations seemed less pressing. The government's lack of a clear policy on the future of the RCMP surfaced when the minister of defence, George Graham, announced that the police would be transferred from Justice to his department. The move would have made a good deal of sense if the RCMP were to act primarily as a backup for local forces in cases of civil unrest, a role previously performed by the militia.[8] Arthur Meighen, Hugh Guthrie, and other former Conservative cabinet ministers attacked the proposal, arguing that it was a dangerous militarization of what had always been a civilian body.[9]

Mackenzie King, in an apparent effort to head off this assault from an unexpected quarter, announced that his government was unwilling to use the RCMP in labour disputes. Municipal authorities should continue to use the militia in times of trouble.[10] But if this was the case, why bother with the Mounted Police at all? The Progressive leader, T.A. Crerar, immediately recognized the illogicality of the government's position and called for the operations of the force to be confined to the Yukon and the Northwest Territories. If there was ever a serious possibility that the Mounted Police might be reduced to insignificance, this was the moment. The government was dependent upon the votes of the Progressives to stay in power. Crerar's arguments that such a move would save money and remove a constitutional anomaly had broad appeal to members of all parties. George Graham's response indicates how flustered the government was: 'I agree that constitutionally my hon. friend is absolutely right, but in working out the affairs, particularly of a new country, we are not always safe in adhering to the letter of the constitution. Sometimes we have to violate almost the letter of the law, in order to be practical.'[11]

Ironically, what saved the Mounted Police was that the role of principal critic was taken over by J.S. Woodsworth, the Labour member for Winnipeg Centre, who was already emerging as the principal voice of the Left in Canadian politics. It was Woodsworth who moved a resolution calling for RCMP operations to be restricted to the northern territories. His reasons for doing so were ideological rather than constitutional. The Mounted Police, he said, had acted as spies and agents provocateurs during the Winnipeg General Strike and were continuing to do so. He wanted it stopped.[12] Unfortunately for Woodsworth, half the Progressive members, all but a handful of Liberals, and all the Conservatives thought that this kind of security and intelligence work was essential. The resolution lost 108–47 (see table 1).

The anomalies of the situation were not lost on Mackenzie King, who commented in his diary: 'On abolishing the Royal Mounted Police from the provinces I was able to point out the resol'n wd. abolish Dominion police as well & thereby without taking sides, vote against it on good grounds. A curious division 100 to 40 or thereabouts, I voting with Meighen & others all mixed up.'[13] King's discomfort with a situation that allied him with his arch-enemy Meighen was not lost on Woodsworth either. The following year he introduced a modified resolution calling for a splitting of the RCMP back into its two original components, the Dominion Police and the Royal North-West Mounted Police, with the latter to be excluded from the provinces.[14] King retreated into silence while the minister of justice, Sir Lomer Gouin, defended the existing system on the grounds of administrative efficiency. Support for the resolution dropped to half the level of the previous year, with half the Progressives and all but two Liberals deserting the cause (see table 2).

The question raised by this episode is why King came down in favour of the RCMP when to go back to the old system had clear political attractions. It also constituted a direct contradiction of King's position on the constitutional relationship with provincial governments. In a speech to the Ontario Liberal party in August 1922, King criticized the previous government for its willingness to

TABLE 1
1922 vote on restricting RCMP to Territories

	BC	Alta.	Sask.	Man.	Ont.	Que.	NB	NS	PEI	Total
Liberal				1		12				13
Conservative										
Progressive	2	7	3	9	9		1			31
Labour		2		1						3
Total	2	9	3	11	9	12	1			47

SOURCE: House of Commons, *Debates*, 1922, 843–4

TABLE 2
1923 vote on splitting RCMP and restricting operations to Territories

	BC	Alta.	Sask.	Man.	Ont.	Que.	NB	NS	PEI	Total
Liberal						2				2
Conservative										
Progressuve	2	3	3	4	6					18
Labour		2		1						3
Total	2	5	3	5	6	2				23

SOURCE: House of Commons, *Debates*, 1923, 1152

send in the army in cases of labour unrest. 'As I see the division of functioning and power under our constitution in all these problems which affect local liberties and local interests and in a larger way provincial liberties and provincial interests, it is not for the federal government to usurp the rights and powers reserved by the constitution to localities and provinces, nor for the localities and provinces to shift their problems for solution into the federal arena.'[15] The minister in charge of the Mounted Police, in this case Minister of Justice Gouin, must have made it clear to King that he considered it essential to retain the force. Speaking in the 1923 debate, Gouin specifically mentioned three kinds of duties the RCMP were carrying out that he considered vital: enforcing the Inland Revenue Act and the narcotics laws and looking after Indian reserves.[16]

This statement was true as far as it went, but it was not the whole story or perhaps even the most important part of it. In their brief existence the RCMP had acquired responsibility for investigating violations of more than thirty federal statutes, from the *Air Board Act* to the *Weights and Measures Act*. The Dominion Police had done some of this work before 1920, and some departments had hired private agencies like Pinkerton's when the necessity arose. For the most part, however, the work had not been undertaken in any systematic way at all. Suddenly, government departments had at their disposal a nation-wide body of well-trained men with not that much to do. The number of investigations undertaken by the RCMP to enforce federal statutes rose from 2068 during their first year of operation to 4173 in 1925 and 8353 in 1932.[17] In the early 1920s about half of these investigations involved narcotics cases or hunting for illegal stills – activities that were almost indistinguishable from the Criminal Code cases that constituted the day-to-day work of other police forces. But the increases in the number of cases through the decade did not come in these categories. The number of drug cases remained fairly steady, while bootlegging declined a little with the gradual movement away from Prohibition in most parts of the country. The bulk of the increase was in work that was more administrative than criminal.

This trend showed itself in even more striking fashion in the expansion of a category of activity the RCMP called 'assistance to other departments.' These were investigations requested by other government departments that did not fall directly under one of the statutes that were the formal responsibility of the police. In the early 1920s, for example, one of the largest groups of investigations under this category consisted of background checks on applications for citizenship by immigrants. This particular activity declined as immigration ebbed in the late 1920s and almost ceased in the 1930s, but there was no slow-down in the general growth of administrative work. The number of investigations for other departments went from 8500 in 1921 to 21,743 in 1925 to 83,216 in 1932.[18] Even after the RCMP took over provincial policing in Alberta, Saskatchewan, Manitoba, New Brunswick, Nova Scotia, and Prince Edward Island, the number of administrative investigations far exceeded criminal cases. In 1932 Criminal Code investigations amounted to only 17,469 of a total of 119,825.[19]

The RCMP were an important element in the great expansion of the Canadian state in the early twentieth century. Governments all over the Western world were regulating the lives of their citizens and providing services in ways that were unheard of before the First World War. To do either effectively required the kind of capacity for research and investigation that the Mounted Police were supplying. The alternative was for each government agency to establish its own police or investigative agency, as was happening in the United States in this period.[20] Ambitious bureaucrats might like to have their own police, but in a country the size of Canada, this was a very expensive luxury. The Mounted Police were well trained, they were stationed throughout the country, and their services cost other departments nothing. It was all very well to insist on the constitutional niceties while in opposition, but the practical problems of governing created their own imperatives. Hence the following exchange in 1925 between Arthur Meighen and Minister of Justice Lapointe:

Mr. MEIGHEN: How many provinces are the police used in now?
Mr. LAPOINTE: In all the provinces.
Mr. MEIGHEN: The government has seen a new light on that subject.
Mr. LAPOINTE: I do not know whether I should say it, but I am free to admit I have come to learn that they are doing a splendid work.[21]

Bureaucrats with limited budgets naturally made extensive use of the RCMP and were responsible for the growth of this work even during the Depression. In 1932 the commissioner of the RCMP commented: 'The practice of employing this force as a species of handmaiden has grown up almost entirely since the reorganization of 1920. Many departments have interests in various parts of the country which require attention and if it were not for the services which we render, they would be obliged either to maintain a force of "field agents," to use an American term, or to neglect them; and so it is of advantage to be able to call upon the services of a force, the members of which have long experience and for the most part are able to unite authority with tact and judgment in discharging the duties arising out of this class of work.[22]

The rather patronizing tone of this excerpt reflects the fact that by 1932 the RCMP had returned to provincial policing in six of the nine provinces. It was, however, its work for other government departments that ensured the survival of the force in the late 1920s. The initiative for the RCMP's revival of its role as a provincial police force came not from Ottawa but from the government of Saskatchewan. In November 1926 the new premier of the province, James G. Gardiner, wrote to Lapointe to request a meeting to discuss the question of police. 'The policing of this Province is rapidly developing into a condition which is likely to bring the whole matter into the field of political controversy. The main reason for this, to my mind, is that we are very much over policed. We have a condition which developed during the war, which leaves us with virtually three police forces, the R.C.M.P., the Provincial Police and the Municipal Police. The result is that there is overlapping, local friction, disagreement between different organizations, the appearance of too many uniformed men at every public gathering, – (giving the appearance of a military occupation) and cost which, if continued will develop a first class political issue.'[23] He suggested three possible ways to remedy the situation: return to the pre-1917 situation with the RCMP carrying out provincial policing, have the provincial police take over federal duties, or have the RCMP operate only along the U.S. border and in the North.

Ottawa agreed to put the matter on the agenda of a planned federal-provincial conference in 1927, but for reasons that are not clear that plan was dropped. The most probable explanation is that none of the other provinces showed much interest. That Saskatchewan continued to push the question was due to a number of circumstances. Regina was a small city that harboured not only the headquarters of the provincial police but also the RCMP Training Depot. Police uniforms were undoubtedly more numerous and visible there than anywhere else in the country. The Saskatchewan Liberal party had remained in power continuously since 1905 by maintaining an extremely efficient political organization that relied heavily on the active participation of government employees, including the police. But Gardiner was beginning to have doubts about the efficacy, if not the propriety, of basing a political organization on public employees.[24] He was also aware of the unpopularity of the enforcement of liquor laws, and may have considered it desirable that public hostility focus on the federal government. At any rate, enforcement of the liquor laws was specifically included in the list of responsibilities the province expected the RCMP to handle that was put forward by the Saskatchewan government.[25]

Commissioner Starnes of the RCMP prepared a secret report for the minister of justice in response to the Saskatchewan initiative. This document presented a number of powerful arguments for having the RCMP return to provincial policing in Saskatchewan and against the other alternatives suggested by the province. It is worth looking at these in some detail since they establish a rationale for federal policing that remains essentially unchanged down to the present. Starnes began by asserting that even if all provinces established provincial forces and took over federal duties, Ottawa would still have to maintain a force of about four hundred to look after the Yukon and Northwest Territories along with duties formerly handled by the Dominion Police. But, he continued, there were other considerations:

1 Few of the Provinces show any inclination to perform Federal work. Saskatchewan and Alberta are the only ones which have given any sign of thinking of such a proposal. British Columbia, Manitoba, Ontario and New Brunswick have small Provincial Forces and have made no suggestion of any desire to assume new duties. Quebec, Nova Scotia and Prince Edward Island have no Provincial Forces.
2 The Royal Canadian Mounted Police perform duties in the Provinces, both eastern and western, of a scope and volume seldom realized. To undertake them on the scale now prevailing would mean a great increase of strength of existing Provincial Forces, apart from the case of Provinces which do not possess such forces.[26]

The report discussed the kind of administrative duties carried out for government departments in some detail, and Starnes then gave half a dozen reasons why the RCMP was the agency best suited to carry out these duties.

1 It would be one thing for a Federal Department to ask aid of a Force with headquarters in Ottawa, and with a Dominion-wide system, and another to correspond with police headquarters in the several Provincial capitals, which have no powers or agencies outside their Provincial boundaries.
2 Cases often have ramifications from one Province to another; a few recent examples are ...
3 Again, the Royal Canadian Mounted Police enjoy peculiar facilities for dealing with the Indian population. It is work which is traditional with the Force; and which it claims to discharge with efficiency and sympathy. The Indian population presents marked general characteristics, and it is convenient to deal with it, in police matters, on a common system.
4 Under the present arrangement the Government may add to the duties of the Royal Canadian Mounted Police at will, they being under its control; whereas if it is to be served by a Provincial Police under an agreement, each additional type of duty required would be the subject of negotiation.
5 The Royal Canadian Mounted Police have the advantage – a most important one – of a reserve of strength ...
6 Finally, there is the security service maintained to keep the Government acquainted with the progress and importance of revolutionary societies, subversive movements, etc.; it is submitted that this can only be done by officials of the Dominion government, involving as it does highly confidential correspondence with other parts of the Empire, and dealing with conspiracies spread over several Provinces, which can be understood when viewed as a whole.[27]

The report estimates that because of the existing RCMP detachments in the province, taking over provincial policing would require an additional seventy men. The Saskatchewan Provincial Police numbered 140 at the time and cost the province about $500,000 a year. The new arrangement would cost Saskatchewan about $200,000 annually.

Starnes's report was an extraordinarily able document. It addressed the different interests of two levels of government and offered both a convincing choice between service, efficiency, and savings with the RCMP or expense, inefficiency, and potential conflict without it. With this powerful ammunition in hand it was easy to resolve the issue. Lapointe simply sent a copy to Regina and the provincial government wrote back almost by return mail offering to disband their provincial police and renegotiate the pre-1917 contract with the

RCMP.[28] Gardiner and his attorney-general, T.C. Davis, travelled to Ottawa in January 1928 to work out the details with Lapointe and Starnes. Here a hitch developed over the most potentially troublesome part of the agreement; just how the provincial attorney-general was to exercise control in matters affecting provincial jurisdiction. The former arrangements with Alberta and Saskatchewan had broken down when police in the two provinces had received conflicting orders over the enforcement of Prohibition.[29] Davis and Gardiner tried to get around this difficulty by inserting a clause in the draft agreement giving the attorney-general the right to approve appointments to senior RCMP positions in the province.[30] Lapointe refused, and Gardiner and Davis returned home without an agreement.

After a flurry of telegrams, the Saskatchewan government agreed to accept federal assurances that they would be consulted informally on appointments.[31] A second meeting in March brought final agreement, and on 1 June 1928 the RCMP returned to provincial policing. The agreement, momentous as it was for the future of policing in Canada, aroused no political interest whatever in Ottawa. Cabinet approved it without hesitation, and when Lapointe announced it in the House of Commons during the discussion of the RCMP estimates, not a single question was asked.[32]

If King and Lapointe were prepared to encourage a drift in the direction of police centralization, the Conservative government of R.B. Bennett elected in 1930 adopted a much more aggressive policy. In 1932 the RCMP absorbed the last sizeable independent federal law-enforcement agency, the 600–man preventive service of the Department of National Revenue. At the same time all the provinces were offered the services of the RCMP for provincial policing on the same basis as Saskatchewan. The annual cost would be $1000 for each man stationed in the province, a figure that was well below the cost of maintaining a provincial police (the pay of an Alberta Provincial Police constable, for example, was $1680).[33] Even though a sizeable number of those officers stationed in a province would be doing federal-government work, this was a bargain. Five of the remaining provinces signed contracts with the federal government that year, including two that had never had provincial police of their own.

There was, of course, a cost involved in terms of giving up a substantial degree of control over an area that belonged to the provinces by right. Thus, the three largest and wealthiest provinces – Quebec, Ontario, and British Columbia – turned down the offer. Thus also, Prime Minister Bennett tried to disguise the extent of the federal subsidy. Asked in the House of Commons if the rate of $1000 per man meant that the provinces were paying the full costs of contract policing, Bennett replied: 'It is based on the assumption that it will cover the cost.'[34] This was at best misleading and was the kind of information that a determined opponent could easily check.

Bennett and his minister of justice, Hugh Guthrie, were spared the necessity of defending their policy by the intervention of J.S. Woodsworth. As he had done a decade earlier, Woodsworth launched a vigorous attack on the anti-subversive activities of the RCMP.[35] In a virtual replay of the 1922 situation, the House immediately abandoned constitutional considerations for the pleasures of ideological debate. In the tense circumstances of the 1930s, fears of class warfare were enhanced and Woodsworth's eloquence failed to attract even the handful of supporters of his previous attacks. When Woodsworth read an excerpt from a Toronto speech by Commissioner J.H. MacBrien suggesting that all foreign-born Communists should be deported, many MP's applauded. Back in power after 1935, the Liberals consistently defended the expansion that had taken place under Bennett. It was Liberal governments that added Newfoundland to the system in 1949 and British Columbia in 1950.

What emerges from the decade of the 1920s and remains essentially unchanged for the last sixty years is the curious, but very Canadian, situation of a single integrated federal-provincial police force for the periphery with two 'distinct societies' at the centre. In theory this should be an inherently unstable situation, yet it shows little sign of developing cracks. The move to greater provincial power over the last two decades has not resulted in demands for provincial forces. Alberta, arguably the most aggressive proponent of provincial rights in this period, has recently concluded a new contract. In all the discussions about the Constitution leading up to the referendum, the police were the subject only in connection with native control of law enforcement.

From one perspective, the RCMP seem to be an extraordinarily powerful organization. They cover the country from sea to sea to sea and have a range of duties more extensive by far than any other North American law-enforcement agency. This remains so even with the loss of their security-and-intelligence functions to CSIS. The relationship that has evolved between provincial and federal policing, however, works in the direction of limiting the power of the RCMP. They operate as provincial police entirely at the discretion of provincial governments and cannot afford to antagonize them. The possibility clearly existed in the 1930s that the movement to contract policing might expand to what some people at the time regarded as its logical conclusion, the inclusion of all the provinces. This would certainly have been administratively and constitutionally tidy, but would also have removed the most important check on the powers of the RCMP.

NOTES

1 R.C. Macleod, *The North West Mounted Police and Law Enforcement, 1873–1905* (Toronto: University of Toronto Press 1976).
2 D.F. Robertson, 'The Saskatchewan Provincial Police, 1917–1919,' *Saskatchewan History* 30 (1978); J. Villa-Arce, 'The Alberta Provincial Police,' *Alberta History* 21 (1973); C. Stewart and L. Hudson, *Mahony's Minute Men: The Saga of the Saskatchewan Provincial Police 1917–1928* (Saskatoon: Modern Press 1978).
3 For an extraordinarily able comparison of the evolution of police forces in France, England, Germany, and the United States, see C. Emsley, *Policing and Its Context 1750–1870* (New York: Schocken Books 1983). The argument about the Canadian character has been put forward most forcefully in E.Z. Friedenberg, *Deference to Authority: The Case of Canada* (New York: Random House 1980).
4 S.W. Horrall, 'The Royal North West Mounted Police and Labour Unrest in Western Canada, 1919,' *Canadian Historical Review* 61 (1980).
5 House of Commons, *Debates*, 1920, 3198–9.
6 Ibid., 3211.
7 W.J. Lowe, 'The Lancashire Constabulary, 1845–1870: The Social and Occupational Function of a Victorian Police Force,' *Criminal Justice History: An International Annual* 3 (1983): 41; R.W. England, Jr, 'Investigating Homicides in Northern England, 1800–1824,' *Criminal Justice History* 5 (1985): 105.
8 L.W. Bentley, 'Aid of the Civil Power: Social and Political Aspects, 1904–1924,' *Canadian Defence Quarterly* 7 (1978); D. MacGillivray, 'Military Aid to the Civil Power: The Cape Breton Experience in the 1920s,' *Acadiensis* 3 (1974); D. Morton, 'Aid to the Civil Power: The Canadian Militia in Support of Social Order, 1867–1914,' *Canadian Historical Review* 50 (1970).
9 House of Commons, *Debates*, 1922, 660–6.
10 Ibid., 667.
11 Ibid., 831.
12 Ibid., 675.
13 W.L.M. King, *The Mackenzie King Diaries, 1893–1931* (Toronto: University of Toronto Press 1973), 10 April 1922.
14 House of Commons, *Debates*, 1923, 816.
15 Ottawa *Citizen*, 31 Aug. 1922.
16 *Debates*, 1923, 1147.
17 Royal Canadian Mounted Police, *Annual Report*, 1921, 1925, 1932.
18 RCMP, *Annual Report*, 1921, 1925, 1932.
19 RCMP, *Annual Report*, 1932, 15.

20 This was by no means confined to the federal government or even to the principal state administrative agencies. For example, the Long Island State Park Commission in the 1920s had its own police force and squad of investigators. R.A. Caro, *The Power Broker: Robert Moses and the Fall of New York* (New York: Knopf 1974), 13–14.

21 House of Commons, *Debates*, 1925, 5041.

22 RCMP, *Annual Report*, 1932, 19.

23 National Archives of Canada, RG 14 D 2, vol. 198, Unpublished Sessional Papers 1929, no. 190, p. 3, Gardiner to Lapointe, 30 Nov. 1926.

24 N. Ward and D. Smith, *Jimmy Gardiner: Relentless Liberal* (Toronto: University of Toronto Press 1990), 80.

25 NAC, RG 14 D 2, Unpublished Sessional Papers, 1929, no. 190, T.C. Davis, Attorney-General of Saskatchewan, to Ernest Lapointe, 11 Jan. 1926.

26 NAC, RG 14 D 2, Unpublished Sessional Papers, 1929, no. 190, 'Dominion-Provincial Conference, 1927: Policing of Provinces,' 2.

27 Ibid., 5.

28 NAC, RG 14 D 2, Unpublished Sessional Papers, 1929, no. 190, T.C. Davis to Ernest Lapointe, 17 Dec. 1927.

29 S. Moir, 'The Alberta Provincial Police,' M.A. thesis, University of Alberta, 1992, 48–53.

30 NAC, RG 14 D 2, Unpublished Sessional Papers, 1929, no. 190, Davis to Lapointe, 11 Jan. 1928.

31 Ibid., telegram, Davis to Lapointe, 4 Feb. 1928.

32 House of Commons, *Debates*, 1928, 4067.

33 Moir, 'Alberta Provincial Police,' 54.

34 House of Commons, *Debates*, 1932, 1774.

35 Ibid., 2591–3.

PART TWO: POLICE POWERS AND CITIZENS' RIGHTS

4

Citizens' Rights and Police Powers

ROGER A. SHINER

THE ORIGINAL POSITION

In this discussion of the philosophical basis for police powers and citizens' rights, I shall not advance any remarkable or novel theses. It has been said that one important task of philosophy is to remind us of the familiar when we lose our way amid it.[1] My remarks will consist largely of reminders about the familiar.

I note one complication first and then pass on. My title speaks of 'citizens' rights'; yet many people think of the rights under discussion as human rights. The notions are different in their philosophical resonances. Human rights we have in the state of nature, and they are candidates for powerful side constraints on any possible civil society. Citizens' rights we have only in civil society, and we are stuck if society is not so civil. The notions of 'citizens' rights' and 'human rights' are connected this way. If a human right is to have any meaning in civil society, it must be concretized or given a determination by the positive law of that society. Citizens' rights – the rights possessed by the citizens of a particular political system – are the form that determinations of human rights take in that system. Thus, in Canada, the right that is given all inhabitants of Canada by s.10(b) of the Charter,[2] the right to retain and instruct counsel without delay and to be informed of that right, is a determination of some general human right to a part of fundamental criminal justice, in this case procedural justice. We may continue to talk of 'citizens' rights'; but we should not forget their status as determinations of human rights.

In a modern liberal-democratic state such as Canada, the powers of the police to achieve the ends for which that institution is designed are not unlimited. They are limited by law in many ways[3] – by the formal provisions of statute or code,[4] by traditional common-law provisions,[5] by the provisions of a constitution or charter.[6] Anecdotally, limitations of this kind are often experienced by the police themselves and by their political supporters as undue interference with their task of the efficient dispatch of villains behind bars where such villains belong. It is a statistical commonplace that in countries such as Canada, the United States, and the United Kingdom members of minorities are represented in those countries' jail population out of all proportion to the percentage of their representation in the population as a whole. It is often extremely difficult to persuade members of predominantly white suburbia, for whom crime is something that takes place in literally another place and metaphorically another world, that they, the law-abiding, have an interest in a system of citizens' rights that gives to the lawbreaking procedural and substantive limitations on police powers. I want to begin this paper by conducting a thought experiment to try to reveal how that interest comes about.

Imagine a group of individuals[7] faced with the task of determining the fundamental principles for the design of social institutions – in this case, the principles for the definition and limitation of police powers. Rawls refers to the situation in which such a group find themselves as 'the original position': the position is not intended as a historical reality, but as a hypothesis whose implications are to be considered for their analytical power. Rawls is concerned to use the device of the original position to say something about justice, and that is my concern here, too, specifically about criminal justice. To this end, Rawls continues: 'Among the essential features of [the original position] is that no one knows [their] place in society, [their] class position or social status, nor does anyone know [their] fortune in the distribution of natural assets and abilities, [their] intelligence, strength, and the like.[8] ... The principles of justice are chosen behind a veil of ignorance. '[9] If we are to understand why principles of fundamental justice require the limitation of police powers by citizens' rights, we must similarly imagine ourselves behind a 'veil of ignorance' faced with a task of institutional design. We have to ask ourselves: What principles for the design of institutions of law enforcement would we want to adopt if we did not know whether we are male or female, streetsmart or naïve, young or old, poor or rich, black or white, native or Caucasian, and so forth.

It is all too easy to regard limitations on police powers in the name of citizens' rights as giving too much protection to the wrong people, because one (understandably enough) cannot imagine oneself in one's actual historical position ever needing the protection of those limitations. Nor, I think, does it in the end help for a person like myself, for instance, to try straightforwardly to imagine what it would be like to be a black hassled on the streets of Montreal or Halifax, a native hassled on the streets of Winnipeg, or a woman trying to cope with the practical consequences of reporting a sexual assault to the police. With the best will in the world I cannot imagine what it is like, for relatively little in my own experience of life has been at all comparable. The issue is not, What kind of principles of criminal justice would I want to have if I were black, or a woman, in contemporary Canada? The issue is, What kind of principles of criminal justice would I want to have if I were ignorant of all those things of which Rawls's people in the original position are ignorant; if I did not know my race, my gender, my talents?

There are two quite distinct ways of thinking about citizens' rights. Looked at one way, a criminal-justice right such as that specified in s.10(b) of the Charter is an instrumental device for the securing of some valued social goal – securing most-favoured-nation trading status, perhaps, or readmission to membership in the United Nations. As part of international political bargaining, a rich democracy may say to a poor one-party state, 'We will not sell you grain/build you power stations unless you show more respect for human rights.' The poor country agrees, not because its leaders value human rights, but because they need the grain/the power station. The danger of course is that, if the instrumental realities count against such a right, it will be abandoned. As soon as the poor country needs no more grain, away goes the 'respect' for human rights.

There is a quite different way of thinking about the right to retain and instruct counsel, as follows. One may think of sufficient respect for the right as an antecedent side constraint of any possible appeal to instrumental considerations in the design of institutions. By 'antecedent side constraint,' I mean that the substantive demands of the constraint must be met before any further questions of institutional design are taken up. When a country such as Canada entrenches such a right in its constitution, it is in essence thinking about the right in this second way. The question is, How may one go about justifying thinking about such a right in the second way, rather than the first way? How can we justify thinking of citizens' rights as side constraints on the institution of law enforcement, rather than as considerations to be weighed in the balance of instrumentalities in the face of the goals of law enforcement?

My suggestion is that my thought experiment of designing social institutions in an original position provides the way. Somehow, the move has to be made from thinking of limitations on police power in the name of citizens' rights as protecting the wrong people – Them, whoever they are – to thinking of those rights as a protection to which any citizen is entitled just by virtue of their citizenship. By thinking of a right such as that given by s.10(b) of the Charter as a right that a person would choose to include in the basic design of law-enforcement institutions in the original position, one expresses what is meant by a right that any citizen would want to be able, if necessary, to enjoy.

One expresses, furthermore, what it is for such a right to be one to which any citizen is entitled. Perhaps the availability of the s.10(b) right is not one that answers to any immediate and concrete interest of mine. Concretely, I might be much more interested in the right of entry in s.6(1), which would ensure I can get back home after I go to the United States for a meeting later this month; or the mobility right of s.6(2)(a), if I were contemplating a change of job. To make me realize my interest in the s.10(b) right to counsel, you might say to me: 'But can't you see that you would have an interest in s.10(b) if you were to be arrested by the police and detained?' I might reply: 'Yes, I can see that I would have an interest in the circumstances you describe.' But that interest assumes a hypothetical. Hypothetical interests of this kind – interests attached hypothetically, not (so it seems) really, to concrete individuals – seem to be poor grounds for fundamental rights of criminal justice. Such hypothetical interests do not seem to be able to serve as side constraints in institutional design. Real interests seem to be required.

We therefore need to have a way of grasping the character of a citizen's right when thought of as a side constraint that preserves its nature as an abstract, background right, and yet that makes it real and not merely hypothetical. The thought experiment does this. It shows us how our interest in a structure of citizens' rights as limitations on police powers is one that is linked to the very idea of civil society, an association of persons established willingly by them for their self-realization and flourishing. What legally underwrites a right such as that given by s.10(b) is the fact that it appears in a properly pedigreed legal document. What philosophically underwrites such a right is that it is one any person contemplating the design of law-enforcement institutions in the original position would want to include in the list of citizens' rights, because it is a right the protection of which any person would want to have. Its character as a fundamental right is brought out in this way, but is disguised by the suggestion that it is a right that I, as a concrete individual, would only want hypothetically.

There are further reasons why any person would want to have such a right; these reasons, however, lie more deeply in the background theory of political morality than it would be proper or possible to go here. The underlying reasons have to do with the classical liberal view of a person as fundamentally deserving of respect, of a person as a member of the kingdom of ends. Persons are most saliently free and autonomous choosers. The way to show persons respect for their personhood is to show respect for their capacity for choice. One way to do that, at the most abstract and general level, is to constrain the design of actual social institutions by principles to which any person so understood would consent behind the veil of ignorance in the original position. More concretely, many of the limitations on police powers in democratic countries are designed to respect the capacity of citizens to make autonomous choices, and to restrict their liberty only in ways that respect and respond to choice.

THE BALANCING METAPHOR

The Law Reform Commission of Canada, in Working Paper 30, speaks of a 'balance between police powers and individual rights.'[10] In their later *Report 33*, the wording is varied; they describe their project as one of 'a careful endeavour to balance the liberty of the person against the obligation of the state to provide protection to its citizens.'[11] I want in this section of my paper to probe some of the implications of this 'balancing' metaphor and of the differences in connotation of the LRC's two versions of the metaphor.[12]

In their general 'philosophical' document on criminal procedure, *Report 32*,[13] the LRC make the valuable point that regulation of police powers, a major component of criminal procedure, does not merely have the negative sense of 'limitations' on police powers. It also has the positive sense of 'authorization' of certain actions on the part of peace officers. A legal 'power' as conceived by classical jurisprudence[14] is an ability conferred upon a person by law to alter, by their own will directed to that end, the rights, duties, liabilities, or other legal relations, either of their own or of other persons. Its jural correlative – what some person B has with respect to a given action, for example, if some person A has a power with respect to that action – is a liability. Its jural opposite – what some person A has with respect to some given action, for example, if A has no power with respect to that action – is a disability. A justice who grants a search warrant confers by law an ability upon a peace officer to alter by their own will the liability of an owner of property to trespass upon and/or confiscate that property. Without such legal authority a peace officer who enters a house and takes away goods has a disability with respect to such actions; the rightful owner has no liability to such a seizure but rather a legal immunity. Police powers *stricto sensu* are thus legal abilities to perform actions that would otherwise be legally forbidden; they are not duties to perform actions to which the law would otherwise be indifferent. Analogously, s.8 of the Charter does not itself provide the authorization the police or other governmental agencies require; rather, 'it is a limitation upon the powers they derive from other sources.'[15]

These facts about police powers and citizens' constitutional rights contribute to the intuitive attractiveness of the balancing metaphor. We have the picture of two things, each of which considered independently is a positive good, but which under the complex conditions of modern society conflict. Individual liberty is a good, but so also is the authority to perform given actions for valued social ends. The goal of human flourishing thus requires, or so it seems, a striking of an appropriate balance between these two goods. This intuitively attractive picture is, however, a misleading oversimplification. It is a powerful philosophical picture, but it is only that. It may or may not represent reality. We must not be held captive by its power, but must compare it with the reality it purports to picture. I shall embark on such a comparison.

The LRC also say in R32 that: 'the repression of crime cannot be viewed as an ultimate, self sustaining goal, an end in itself. Rather it is only one method for pursuing the higher goal of maximizing freedom in a democratic state.'[16] I shall begin with the first of these two sentences, though we will come eventually to the second. The police power of search and seizure, for instance, is, I say again, an ability given to the police by law to perform an action that would otherwise be unlawful. The actions a peace officer performs in exercise of that authority are not just in themselves, but just only because of the lawful authority with which they are performed.[17] At a certain level of abstraction, the relation between the citizenry and the police is no different from that between the citizenry and a large variety of other organizations that the citizens of a state choose to create by mutual association and agreement for the furtherance of their welfare. I have in mind here not only governmental organizations such as social-services departments, environmental-protection agencies, national-defence forces, and the like, but also private-sector organizations such as multinational oil companies, professional sports leagues, trade unions, and the like. Organization theory[18] postulates that, while organizations are properly instruments for the securing of social goals, organizational actions and decisions are frequently better understood by imputing to the organization self-serving or 'reflexive' goals. Organizations tend to suffer 'goal displacement'; they have a propensity to deviate from the pursuit of their stated goals. Their instrumentality is 'recalcitrant.' Well-known features of organizations contribute to this dysfunction – an organization's temporal independence of the set of persons that at any given time make up the organization; the definition of its individual character as a structure of impersonal roles, rules, and offices; in the case of governmental agencies in particular, the liability to 'agency capture,' a drift away from service of the interests of the citizens in regulation to service of the interests of the entities regulated. At one level, when law-enforcement agencies view the repression of crime as 'an ultimate, self sustaining goal,' they are doing no more than exhibit the characteristic dysfunctionality to which any organization is vulnerable.[19]

The implication of the balancing metaphor, and of talk about achieving a balance between police powers and citizens' rights, is that law enforcement is a legitimate goal in itself. As a legitimate goal, it has attached to it rights to the pursuit of that goal. These rights are independently existing rights that must be balanced against the equally independent right to liberty of citizens. But the transition in the implication is spurious, and the balancing metaphor dangerously misleading. For there simply are no such independent rights attached to the pursuit of law enforcement. The perception that there are such rights arises out of goal displacement on the part of the institution of law enforcement. Law-enforcement agencies do have rights, as I have indicated. But those rights do not belong to them *ab initio*. They have those rights as a result of the just grant to them by the citizenry of certain powers and of authority.

Much rethinking is needed of the balancing metaphor. If two things are to be weighed in a balance, then the two things must be commensurable. It's often said that apples cannot be compared with oranges. But they can be compared in a balance. I can check that I have apples and oranges in the proportion of two to one by weight that I need for my recipe because apples and oranges each have mass and we have a well-understood technique for measuring mass. But it is not immediately obvious how citizens' rights and police powers can be directly measured against each other in the same way. For, if the classical definition of a power is correct, then citizens' rights must be more fundamental than police powers. Police have the powers that they have only by virtue of the exercise by citizens of their right or liberty to authorize, if they choose to do so, interferences with that liberty under specified circumstances. Police powers are of a different order of political being than citizens' rights. It is a mistake at the foundation of criminal justice to think the former can, let alone 'should,' be directly balanced against the latter.

We have, though, not yet finished exploring all the possibilities for unpacking the balancing metaphor. We need to consider seriously why it is that the citizens of a state might wish to delegate to police the powers that the police do have. Let us remind ourselves of the second formulation by the LRC. They speak of 'the obligation of a state to protect its citizens,' and of 'the higher goal of maximizing freedom in a democratic state.' Let us consider the obligation of a state to protect its citizens. Clearly, this is, if understood aright, a major value underlying the reasons for the award of police powers. Liberal political morality is classically thought to have as one of its founding principles the famous Harm Principle of John Stuart Mill – the principle that 'the sole end for which mankind are warranted, individually or collectively, in interfering with the liberty of action of any of their number, is self protection. That the only purpose for which power can be rightfully exercised over any member of a civilized community, against [their] will, is to prevent harm to others.'[20] We the people grant powers to police to interfere with the liberty of others to prevent those others from causing harm to yet others.[21] The underlying reason why this ground for interference with liberty is acceptable and why no other is acceptable is given by the LRC. The restriction of the liberty of some must in the end be justified on, and only on, the grounds that it maximizes liberty for all. The obligation the state has to protect its citizens arises in the end out of the Harm Principle or something very much like it. Given a society of sufficient complexity, a system of self-protection pure and simple is impossible. Part of the public good of the rule of law is that the protective task is handed over to a specified agency that is none the less subject to law. The obligation of the state to protect its citizens is no more fundamental, and so no more fit to be balanced directly against citizens' rights, than the powers that the state's law-enforcement agencies have in order to be able to discharge said obligation.

Compare here the different formulations of the balancing metaphor by Prowse J.A. and Dickson J. (as he then was) in the two hearings of *Hunter* v. *Southam*. Dickson contrasts 'the governmental interest in carrying out a given search' with 'the individual['s interest] in resisting the governmental intrusion upon [their] privacy.'[22] Prowse J.A. contrasts 'the public's need for effective law enforcement' with 'the individual's right to be secure against unreasonable search and seizure.'[23] Prowse J.A.'s wording does not reify the government or the state into an entity with respectworthy interests independently of the public in whose name and in whose interests the government operates. Likewise, L'Heureux-Dubé J. in *Cloutier* speaks of 'reconcil[ing] the public's interest in the effective and safe enforcement of the law on the one hand, and on the other its [sc. the public's] interest in ensuring the freedom and dignity of individuals.'[24] We are 'the public': both what goes into the law-enforcement side of the balance and the weight assigned to it must be responsive to our interests, and not to those of a self-subsistent agency.

All that can be balanced in the cause of just institutional design is liberty – the liberty of some against the liberty of others. According to Rawls, the first and overriding principle for the establishment of a state with just institutions has to be the principle that 'each person is to have an equal right to the most extensive basic liberty compatible with a similar liberty for others.'[25] This is Rawls's Liberty Principle, as much a part of the canon of contemporary political theory as the Harm Principle. No institution can be adopted that results in the assignment of less-extensive basic liberty to some than to others, nor one that results in less-extensive liberty for all in the name of some value other than liberty. The notion of 'basic liberty' is important. Clearly, systems of criminal justice do at some point assign differences of liberty – some folks go to jail and some folks don't. But the system can still be just – can still conform to the Liberty Principle, can still assign equal basic liberty – if the definitions of the circumstances under which the liberty is restricted by the criminal-justice system – the substantive definitions of offences and the procedures for arrest, indictment, and trial – themselves conform to the Liberty Principle. The LRC's criterion, that a criminal code of offences and procedures maximize citizens' liberty, is best construed as their (scarcely less abstract) version of what it would be to meet the extremely abstract condition specified by Rawls.

The balancing metaphor can be made sense of in, and only in, the following way. Prior to the whole balancing exercise is the fundamental liberty of each person as an autonomous chooser. This liberty also constrains the choice of what may be balanced, and what may count as a proper balance, by the requirement that this liberty be maximized. In one scale of the balance lie the benefits to be gained to all from adoption of a system that licenses the interference with liberty under defined circumstances. In the other scale lies the costs of such losses of liberty. Fundamentally, the citizen's right to liberty is not in one scale of the balance with something else – the proper powers of the police – opposed to it. We can only begin to discuss meaningfully the issue of the proper extent of police powers after we have first arrived at some criterion or principle for determining when a balance of the above costs and benefits has been struck. The LRC's maximizing criterion is one such, and a very attractive, principle.

FLESH ON CONCEPTUAL SKELETONS

This paper so far has exhibited the stock-in-trade of the philosopher, conceptual argument. The law can be very concrete. *R.* v. *Berger*[26] stands for the proposition that information from unnamed confidential sources is not a sufficient basis for issuing a search warrant where there was no evidence to substantiate the veracity of the informers, no information as to how the informers acquired this knowledge, and no independent evidence to support the story of the informers. *R.* v. *B (JE)*[27] settles that a police officer may have the assistance of persons who are neither named in the warrant nor peace officers, provided that the police officer remains in control of and accountable for the search. The distance from such propositions to, for example, Rawls's Liberty Principle or Mill's Harm Principle is large.[28] But something can be done to bridge the gap. In the case of the issuance of search warrants, two more specific principles are relied on, the principles of judiciality and particularity. The issuing of a search warrant is a judicial act, and is therefore subject to general constraints of what makes an act judicial, as opposed to administrative, executive, or whatever. Justice is independent and impartial. Sections 10(1) and (3) of the Combines Act[29] make the Director of Investigation and Research of the Combines Investigation Branch both the person who authorizes search and seizure under the act and the person who carries out the investigation of which the search and seizure forms part. Thus, the authorizer of the warrant is not acting impartially, and thus not judicially. The provisions of the act therefore offend against judiciality, and so are unreasonable under s.8 of the Charter (as in *Hunter*). Particularity requires that the premises to be searched, the things expecting to be found, and the offence in relation to which the search is conducted all be specified.[30] It is not difficult to see that these principles have their roots in due deference to individual liberty, so that interferences with liberty are minimized, together with due deference to the public's interest in effective law enforcement, which underwrites the very notion of a search warrant itself.

The LRC in its most general musings about criminal procedure, R32, lists seven principles of fundamental criminal justice in relation to procedure – fairness, efficiency, clarity, restraint, accountability, participation, and protection. These principles also provide some content to the middle ground between the specifics of particular rules and regulations and very general principles of political morality. A major and substantive work on the theory of criminal procedure – which the present paper is clearly not – would attempt to trace the connections between the most general principles, the intermediate principles, and the black-letter law with which courts and the police actually have to work, with the aim of assessing the degree to which the law as it stands can be brought into coherent equilibrium with fundamental principle.[31] It is then the task of law reformers, legislators, courts themselves, and the like to decide what to do if there is inconsistency.

I would like to give one, too brief, example of the style of jurisprudential analysis I have in mind, by putting in a theoretical context L'Heureux-Dubé J.'s analysis in *Cloutier* of the principles on which she bases her decision.[32] She is concerned initially with the preservation of the integrity of the criminal-justice system. This goal, she says, requires 'safe and effective' law enforcement by the police. Such law enforcement, given the overall goal, implies two further things – 'the process of arrest must be capable of ensuring that those arrested will come before the court,' and 'the process of arrest must ensure that evidence found on the accused and in [their] immediate surroundings is preserved.' The former of this pair implies authorization to conduct a search for 'weapons or other dangerous articles ... to preclude the possibility of their use against the police, the nearby public or the accused [themselves].' The latter implies a power on the part of the police 'to collect evidence that can be used in establishing the guilt of a suspect beyond a reasonable doubt.' Thus, she implicitly concludes,without a power of some sort to search and seize incidental upon arrest, 'the legitimacy of the justice system would be a mere illusion.' Against this background, the court makes the quite specific ruling that

Police officers have the power to search an accused as an incident to a lawful arrest and to seize anything in his possession or immediate surroundings to guarantee the safety of the police and the accused, prevent the accused's escape or provide evidence against him. The existence of reasonable and probable grounds to believe that the accused is in possession of weapons or evidence is not a prerequisite to the existence of the power to search, provided however that the search is for a valid objective and not unrelated to the objectives of the proper administration of justice. Further, the search must not be conducted in an abusive fashion and the use of physical or psychological constraints should be proportionate to the objective sought and the other circumstances of the situation.[33]

To see the connection of her reasoning with the grand issues of a few paragraphs above, we must ask why her general conclusion is correct. In the end, it is because our sense of justice underwrites the following view. Suppose a system of criminal justice in which there was no authorization of search and seizure incidental to arrest. As a result, the persons themselves often escaped. They rarely appeared before courts for trial; were rarely convicted and sentenced. We would readily regard such a system as a system of criminal injustice. Why is that? Because, for an institution to be a criminal-justice system, it must respect the value of protecting the individual from harm by others. A system with the flaws described here would not do that. Essentially the same reasoning applies to the preservation of evidence for trial purposes. Given the propriety of the goal of protection from harm, a system in which, because there was no authorization of search and seizure incidental to arrest, evidence relevant to the establishment of guilt was rarely available for presentation to courts would likewise be a system of criminal injustice.

On the other hand, the arrested person has all those individual rights that they had prior to their arrest and that derive from citizenship. Thus, any search must not be wrongful in the sense of a violation of those rights. 'A search will not be wrongful if it is authorized by law, if the law itself is reasonable and if the search is conducted in a reasonable manner.'[34] Issues of 'authorization by law' will involve both judiciality and partiality, as well as the validity of any controlling legal norms – the latter, together with the issue of the reasonableness of the law, being matters of wide range. L'Heureux-Dubé J.'s main task is to address the third issue. The kind of 'frisk' search at issue in *Cloutier* she concludes to be reasonable because it is a 'minimal intrusion ... necessary to ensure that criminal justice is properly administered.'[35] It also satisfies two other criteria she lays down: 'the purpose of the search must not be unrelated to the objectives of the proper administration of justice' – intimidating, ridiculing, or pressuring the accused in order to obtain admissions would not meet this 'relatedness' requirement; and 'the search must not be conducted in an abusive fashion and, in particular, the use of physical or psychological constraint should be proportionate to the objectives sought and the other circumstances of the situation.' It should be clear that the imposition of these constraints on search and seizure incidental to arrest is intended to serve the value of respect for the liberty of the arrested individual. Physical and psychological constraint, intimidation, ridicule, and bodily searches of one kind or another are all violations of the dignity and the liberty of the person on whom they are inflicted.[36]

There is clearly room for debate about the appropriateness of the standard chosen in *Cloutier*. A 'minimally necessary intrusion' standard is stronger than a 'proportionality' standard. A 'not unrelated to objectives' standard is a weaker standard than a 'carefully designed, or rationally connected to' standard.[37] Defenders of civil liberties will argue that respect for individual liberty implies the stronger standards. In the end, we have to ask ourselves which of the standards we would want to incorporate into the design of the criminal-justice system, if we were designing in an original position behind a veil of ignorance. There is no straightforward answer to that question, and no answer will be offered here. Yet that is the question.

In my remarks about the balancing metaphor, I have been insisting that we must see the balance as needing to be struck between two different interests each of us has as an autonomous and free person. We must not picture the balance as between the interests of each of us as individuals and the interests of some alien entity – the government or the state and its agents the police. The image of the original position expresses precisely this point. The persons in the original position are aware that each of them individually has a fundamental interest in liberty. They realize also two further things. The design of institutions must therefore be such as to protect liberty by some perimeter fence within which it can be exercised free of unjustified interference.[38] On the other hand, the design of institutions must embody some notion of justified interference with the liberty of those who would harm their fellow persons. The question of the appropriate balance between these two elements will be settled in a way that itself maximally respects liberty if we enquire how that balance would be struck by a group of autonomous choosers who were ignorant of their likelihood of being among the harmers or the harmed, the restrictors or the restricted. For we concrete actual persons to design our actual public institutions, and specifically the rules and regulations of police powers, in a way that maximally respects our liberty, we must try, in the assessment of the actual institutions we now have, to mimic the thought processes of our hypothetical colleagues in the original position behind their veil of ignorance. In that way we shall best ensure that our actual institutions conform to the respect for liberty that is so fundamental to us all.[39]

NOTES

1 See especially the later work of Ludwig Wittgenstein and John Wisdom; for example, L. Wittgenstein, 'Preface,' in L. Wittgenstein, *Philosophical Investigations* (Oxford: Blackwell 1958), and J. Wisdom, *Philosophy and Psychoanalysis* (Oxford: Blackwell 1957), chaps 4, 6, 7. See also my essay 'From Epistemology to Romance via Wisdom,' in I. Dilman, ed., *Philosophy and Life: Essays on John Wisdom* (The Hague: Nijhoff 1984), 291.
2 *Canadian Charter of Rights and Freedoms*, Part I of the *Constitution Act, 1982*, being Schedule B of the *Canada Act 1982* (U.K.), 1982, c. 11.
3 They are also, of course, limited in many other ways that it is the job of sociology, psychology, political science, and so forth to explore. I do not address such matters here.
4 Sections 487–491.2 of the Criminal Code, R.S.C. 1985, c. C-46, lay out various conditions for the obtaining of search warrants, the return of material seized, and so forth.
5 *Cloutier* v. *Langlois* (1990), 53 C.C.C. (3d) 257 (S.C.C.) affirms that the police have at common law a power to search a lawfully arrested person subject to conditions spelt out in the opinion.
6 Section 8 of the Charter and the Fourth Amendment to the U.S. Constitution both grant protection against unreasonable search and seizure.
7 Political theorists will immediately recognize the indebtedness of the following to J. Rawls, *A Theory of Justice* (Cambridge, Mass.: Harvard University Press 1971). Insofar as I deploy this Rawlsian device, I situate myself within the Western liberal tradition of political thought.
8 Gender and race are clearly *ejusdem generis* here.
9 Rawls, *Theory of Justice*, 12.
10 Law Reform Commission of Canada, *Police Powers – Search and Seizure in Criminal Law Enforcement* (Working Paper 30) (Ottawa: Law Reform Commission of Canada 1983), 80 [hereinafter *WP30*].
11 Law Reform Commission of Canada, *Report 33: Recodifying Criminal Procedure*, vol. 1 (Ottawa: Law Reform Commission of Canada 1991), 3.
12 The balancing metaphor is not, of course, confined to the ivory tower; it is oft found on the bench. See, for example, *Lindley* v. *Rutter*, [1981] QB 128 at 134, Donaldson L.J.; *Southam Inc.* v. *Hunter* (1983), 3 C.C.C. (3d) 497 at 503 (Alta. C.A.), Prowse J.A.; *Hunter* v. *Southam* (1984), 14 C.C.C. (3d) 97 at 109 (S.C.C.), Dickson J.; *Cloutier*, (n. 5, above), 274, L'Heureux-Dubé J.

13 Law Reform Commission of Canada, *Report 32: Our Criminal Procedure* (Ottawa: Law Reform Commission of Canada 1988).
14 See, for example, W. Hohfeld, *Fundamental Legal Conceptions* (New Haven: Yale University Press 1934); P.J. Fitzgerald, ed., *Salmond on Jurisprudence*, 12th ed. (London: Sweet and Maxwell 1966,) 228ff.
15 See *Southam Inc.* (n. 12, above), 503, Prowse J.A. The sentiment is repeated with approval by Dickson J. (as he then was) in *Hunter* (n. 12, above), 106.
16 LRC, *Report 32*, 11.
17 I leave further unspecified the concept of 'lawful authority.' But see the text associated with note 14, and also R.A. Shiner, 'Law and Authority,' *Canadian Journal of Law and Jurisprudence* 2 (1989): 3.
18 I here summarize remarks made by Meir Dan-Cohen in chapter 2 of *Rights, Persons and Organizations* (Berkeley and Los Angeles: University of California Press 1986), a passage that is itself already a summary of a large body of literature.
19 A different kind of dysfunctionality is, with respect, represented by L'Heureux-Dubé J. in *Cloutier* (at 275) when she asserts that the basis and 'primary purpose' of criminal justice is 'the punishment of conduct that is contrary to the fundamental values of society.' The use of punishment may be essential to the proper functioning of a criminal-justice system. But to elevate punishment to the status of the goal of a criminal-justice system, against which the rival goal of individuality must be balanced, is a mistake. Though I disagree with her on this point, there is much in L'Heureux-Dubé J.'s theoretical analysis in *Cloutier* that is valuable.
20 From the essay by J.S. Mill, 'On Liberty,' in M. Lerner, ed., *Essential Works of John Stuart Mill* (New York: Bantam Books 1965), 263.
21 I duck here an important issue raised by the Law Reform Commission of Canada in *WP30* – of the difference between preventive and responsive policing and police powers. The LRC asserts that Canada has historically been willing to accept a far greater extent of preventive police powers than other comparable countries. There clearly is here a real substantive question of institutional design, and one about which defenders of civil liberties will have strong views. Classic doctrines of civil liberty firmly repudiate any form of 'prior restraint,' such as when a controversial figure is forbidden to express his or her views on the grounds that public safety would be imperilled. I express no opinion here on the relative merits of preventive and responsive police powers.
22 At 109 (my emphasis).
23 At 503 (my emphasis).
24 At 278 (see n. 5). Cf. here Joseph Raz's basis for the justification of political authority, his 'service' conception of authority, and his 'normal justification thesis.' According to the service conception of authority, the role and primary

function of authorities is to serve the governed by mediating between people and the right reasons that apply to them (J. Raz, *The Morality of Freedom* [Oxford: Clarendon Press 1986], 41-2]. 'The normal way to establish that a person has authority over another person involves showing that the alleged subject is likely better to comply with reasons that apply to [them] (other than the alleged authoritative directives) if [they] accept the directives of the alleged authority as authoritatively binding and tr[y] to follow them, rather than by trying to follow the reasons which apply to [them] directly' (Raz, p. 53).

25 *Theory of Justice*, 61.

26 (1989), 48 C.C.C. (3d) 185 (Sask. C.A.).

27 (1989), 52 C.C.C. (3d) 224 (N.S.C.A.).

28 As also may be the gap between those propositions themselves and the particular fact-situation in some instant case – if a person not a peace officer behaves thus and so, and a peace officer behaves thus and so, does that count as 'the peace officer remaining in control of and accountable for the search'? In the end, gaps of this kind are bridged only by the direct application of a predicate to a case. See R.A. Shiner, 'Ethical Justification and Case-By-Case Reasoning,' in D. Odegard, ed., *Ethics and Justification* (Edmonton: Academic Printing and Publishing 1988), 91.

29 *Combines Investigation Act*, R.S.C. 1970, c. C-23.

30 Although, according to Justice Moshansky, 'clearly there is a half-way point between the requirements of precise enumeration of documents expected to be seized and what becomes in effect a carte blanche in the hands of the seizing officer.' See *Re Alder and the Queen* (1977), 37 C.C.C. (2d) 234 at 240 (Alta. S.C., T.D.).

31 An important first step in this mammoth project is D. Stuart, *Charter Justice in Canadian Criminal Law* (Scarborough: Carswell 1991). The book gives a synoptic overview of the cases decided under the Charter to do with criminal justice, and makes a number of general assertions about their relation to principle. None the less, the focus of the research is primarily descriptive (what the courts have said) rather than analytical or philosophical.

32 At 275–8.

33 Holding as summarized by *Martin's Annual Criminal Code 1993* (Toronto: Canada Law Book Co. 1992), CH/25.

34 A principle laid down in *R.* v. *Collins* (1987), 33 C.C.C. (3d) 1 at 14–15 (S.C.C.); *R.* v. *Debot* (1989), 52 C.C.C. (3d) 193 at 200 and 209 (S.C.C.), and reaffirmed in *Cloutier*.

35 Being a minimal intrusion is offered only as a sufficient condition of reasonableness, not a necessary condition. What other characteristics of searches are sufficient for reasonableness are not specified.

36 Cf. also *R.* v. *Greffe* (1990), 75 C.R. (3d) 257 at 269 (S.C.C.), Lamer J., holding that a rectal examination by a doctor using a sigmoidoscope was an extremely serious violation of the accused's Charter rights where the accused had been ostensibly arrested for outstanding traffic warrants, absent any evidence on the record of reasonable and probable grounds for believing the accused was in the possession of heroin. Such an intrusive rectal search and considerations of human and bodily integrity demanded the highest standard of justification before such a search could be reasonable.

37 One of the controlling standards for the interpretation of s.1 of the Charter, as laid down in *R.* v. *Oakes* (1986), 24 C.C.C. (3d) 321 (S.C.C.).

38 'The rights guaranteed in the Charter erect around each individual, metaphorically speaking, an invisible fence over which the state will not be allowed to trespass. The role of the courts is to map out, piece by piece, the parameters of the fence' [*Morgentaler, Smoling and Scott* v. *R.* (1988), 31 C.R.R. 1 at 81, (S.C.C.), Wilson J.]. The image is not original to Wilson J.: cf. H.L.A. Hart's discussion of legal rights as a 'protective perimeter' around fundamental liberty in *Essays on Bentham* (Oxford: Clarendon Press 1983), 171ff.

39 I am grateful to Janet Sisson for comments on an earlier draft of these remarks.

5

Policing under the Charter

DON STUART

THE POLICE CHIEFS' RULE OF LAW AND CONCERN AT THE LRC'S BIAS

In 1984 the Canadian Association of Chiefs of Police submitted a brief[1] to the Law Reform Commission of Canada highly critical of the commission's efforts to reform the criminal-justice system. The Chiefs asserted that the Commission did not understand the changing needs of modern Canadian society:

> The Criminal Justice System does require reform, however the LRC has failed to grasp the essential reform that is needed. Liberalization of homicide laws, decriminalization of property offences, expansion of the possible defences to criminal liability and the codification of inflexible, and indeed debilitating, controls on police investigative techniques are NOT required. What IS required is the streamlining of the pre-trial and court system, the strengthening of sentencing procedures, the recognition of the plight of the victim of crime and the re-introduction into our society of an essential respect for the rule of law and an understanding that it is NOT acceptable to infringe on other people's rights.[2]

According to the chiefs, our society had to return to the belief that each individual had to have respect for the rights of others. There had been a 'very dangerous erosion' of the 'rule of law' in Canada. Too many people felt that it was acceptable to do whatever they wanted to do regardless of the effect of their conduct on others. To reverse this trend towards 'societal breakdown' and to return to a respect for the 'rule of law,' people should be made personally accountable and the criminal law had to be strong. The chiefs bluntly rejected the commission's work on police powers. The problem was the bias in the commission's philosophy that favoured the rights of the suspect every time over the interests of effective law enforcement. The chiefs were blunt in rejecting the commission's call for codification of police powers:

> The LRC has decided that complete codification of police powers and procedures is necessary in order to prevent potential police abuse of a suspect's legal rights. Yet the LRC has failed to produce empirical data supporting its contention that there is an entrenched police abuse of suspects' rights. The LRC is proceeding on a perceived potentiality; an academic exercise of hypothetical arguments over problems far more imagined than real. Besides the obvious insult to the police, the extreme bias resulting from such a theoretically conjectural viewpoint also leads to the possibility of the elimination of the Common Law from the Canadian Criminal Justice System ... The Common Law allows for flexibility within our legal process; a flexibility that, while maintaining general rules of conduct, will allow for acceptable deviance when to do so would serve the ends of equity and justice.[3]

MR JUSTICE SOPINKA: EXCLUSION UNDER CHARTER IS SALUTARY AND THE COURT HAS STRUCK A PROPER BALANCE

On 28 June 1990, Mr Justice Sopinka of the Supreme Court of Canada gave an address to the RCMP Inspectors' Orientation and Development Course in Ottawa, entitled 'Eight Years Under the Charter.' His Lordship acknowledged that the area most altered by the Charter of rights and Freedoms has been criminal law and procedure and that it is difficult for courts to balance the rights of an accused against the interests of society in effective law enforcement. He emphasized that our system of criminal justice is based on the precept that 'it is better that guilty persons should go free than one innocent person be punished.' According to Justice Sopinka, one of the most 'substantial and salutary changes' brought about by the Charter is the possibility that evidence obtained in violation of Charter rights can be excluded. Section 24(2) provides that evidence obtained in violation of the Charter must be excluded if it is established that admission would bring the administration of justice into disrepute. Prior to the Charter, illegally obtained evidence was nevertheless admitted in criminal trials if relevant to guilt.

His Lordship reviewed a number of recent Supreme Court of Canada judgments bearing directly on the law-enforcement function and suggested that some will make the lives of policemen easier and some more difficult. He suggested that the Court is not unmindful of problems facing police officers and that the Court has tried to arrive at a fair balance: 'I think it is fair to say that the Court has tried to balance the vitally important state interest in the prevention and detection of crime against the equally important public interest in the rule of law and the protection of individual rights. Law enforcement agencies no doubt think we have gone too far in the direction of protecting individual rights while civil libertarians take the opposite view. Wherever the line is drawn, it will leave some disappointed. I can assure you, however, that both interests receive careful and anxious consideration by the Court.'[4]

FOCUS OF THIS PAPER

I have recently completed a book[5] attempting a detailed assessment of the impact of the Charter on almost every aspect of the Canadian criminal-justice system. The focus here will be on broad policy issues respecting Charter implications for the police. The paper assesses whether the exclusion of evidence under the Charter has indeed been 'salutary' and whether emerging Charter standards on the essential police powers to exercise discretion, stop, search, arrest, and interrogate are achieving a proper balance. Finally, suggestions will be offered as to the appropriate police response to the Charter and to attempts to reform the law relating to police powers. I first need to declare my own biases.

ASSUMPTIONS ABOUT POLICE WORK

My direct knowledge about policing is limited and derived from a number of very different experiences. In 1969–70, I undertook a records survey and participant observation in three rural, city, and metropolitan police forces in England. It is only at such close quarters that one comes to appreciate how vital police forces are to communities and how much they are relied upon for so much more than crime control. There are the separate worlds of the detective and the uniformed officer. Being a good detective requires sharp intelligence and dogged perseverance. One detective chose to interrogate me about the utility of my thesis work in a far more effective way than any university examiner subsequently achieved! I came to appreciate the street savvy of some uniformed officers, who had an almost magical knack of calming down ugly street scenes. I formed the impression that the larger the police force the lower the police morale because of a more taxing aggregation of social problems and the anonymity of fellow officers. Whatever the force, there was always a pivotal officer who set the tone for the particular division or precinct.

In the early 1970s, when I was teaching law in Edmonton, various visits with students to the police station and chances to ride in patrol cars led me to empathize with lowly constables who, at that time, resented an instruction from on high that they should get out of their patrol vehicles and on foot. Several officers observed that those giving the orders had never had the opportunity to patrol Jasper Avenue in Edmonton in the middle of the night in subzero conditions.

In 1988–9, I was a full-time prosecutor in the City of Toronto. The experience of prosecuting some twelve cases a day for four months in the trial courts left me with a great respect for the professionalism and integrity of most police officers. I say 'most' because there were a few occasions when, in examination-in-chief of a police witness, I experienced police officers lying on the stand in an obvious attempt to please the Crown and ensure a conviction. On more than one occasion, on a *voir dire* on the right to counsel, an officer testified how far he had gone in reading the accused his rights and that the accused had indicated he understood them and did not want a lawyer. Yet, nothing to this effect appeared in the officer's notebook. Once again, I became impressed by the dedication and bravery of officers in dealing with scenes of violence, which gave no time for reflection. I was particularly impressed by the standards and professionalism of officers dealing with the distressingly frequent and violent incidents of domestic assault. This brief Crown experience also emphasized the reality that it is police officers who bear the responsibility for trying to get all witnesses and victims to Court. The platitude is often mouthed that the outcome of the criminal trial is of no concern to police officers. This is hard to believe. Officers have the prime responsibility of explaining negative outcomes to witnesses and victims. Especially if the officer was the investigating officer in a lengthy investigation, it would be impossible not to internalize an acquittal or a stay resulting from a Charter breach.

It seems self-evident that police discretion is inevitable and necessary because no criminal code has yet been able to demarcate all criminal conduct without ambiguity at some point; because there are simply insufficient resources to enforce all laws; and because there will always be an infinite variety of special circumstances in the interactions between officer and citizen. In the American context, Justice Breitel has put this very well: 'If every policeman, every prosecutor, every court and every post-sentence agency performed his or its responsibility in strict accordance with the rules of law, precisely and narrowly laid down, the criminal law would be ordered but intolerable. Living would be a sterile compliance with self-killing rules and taboos. By comparison, primitive society would seem free indeed.'[6]

It seems equally self-evident that external legal controls must be placed on police discretion. It is the very essence of democracy and the rule of law that state power not be autocratic. The trouble with the perspective in the brief of the chiefs of police is that their concept of the rule of law seems to be the minimalist one of their power to enforce any law at will and in any way. The rule of law means the rule of law with liberal values. This entails restraint on the powers of agents of the state and remedies where there is abuse. Their brief also seems to validate the hypothesis of a leading scholar on policing, Jerome Skolnick,[7] that police are too often committed to an alienated bureaucracy that, obsessed by danger and authority, demands order, efficiency, and initiative in enforcing the law.

Of course legal controls are by no means the only way of influencing police conduct. The best hope for professionalism amongst police forces no doubt still lies in better recruitment and training. Given hierarchical rank structure and occupational solidarity, police most likely are influenced to act in one way or another by the messages and standards of the highest ranks. Other influences can be police commissions and civilian review boards, which markedly vary across the country in terms of structure and power.

There is, indeed, nothing novel in the notion that legal restraints should be declared and imposed on the police. What is distinctive about emerging Charter standards is that they are entrenched and not easy to change. Is there, then, a fair balance between the interests of law enforcement and the rights of the accused, as Mr Justice Sopinka suggests? Or has the Charter unduly handcuffed the police and privileged those who do not respect the law, with undue costs to society and to victims in particular? We turn first to Canada's ten-year experience in excluding evidence obtained in violation of the Charter.

IS EXCLUSION OF EVIDENCE 'SALUTARY'?

Unlike the Canadian Bill of Rights, or the United States Constitution, the Canadian Charter of Rights and Freedoms entrenches remedial powers for breaches. Under section 24(2), there is an express power to exclude evidence where it is established that admission would bring the administration of justice into disrepute: 'Where ... a Court concludes that evidence was obtained in a manner that infringed or denied any rights or freedoms guaranteed by this Charter, the evidence shall be excluded if it is established that, having regard to all the circumstances, the admission of it in the proceedings would bring the administration of justice into disrepute.'

1. Some Judges Prefer Exclusion To Be Rare

This point of view is best expressed in the eloquent dissenting judgment of Mr Justice Zuber in the decision of the Ontario Court of Appeal in *Duguay* (1985).[8] Experienced police officers arrested three youths on suspicion that they were involved in a residential burglary. The victims of the theft had noticed three young men in their neighbours' backyard the evening of the break-in. One of the young men asked the victims as they left whether it was their custom to put their dogs in the garage. Descriptions of these young men were provided to the police. The neighbour was able to identify one of the young men as M. The neighbour telephoned M and asked him to come over with his friends of the night before. When they arrived, the victims recognized M and S. At this point the police placed them under arrest. The trial judge found that the police officers had neither reasonable and probable grounds for an arrest nor an honest belief that they had the necessary grounds. Associate Chief Justice MacKinnon for the majority of the Court of Appeal, with Mr Justice Martin concurring, held that, on the facts found by the trial judge, the arrest had been arbitrary since it was for the improper purpose of assisting in the investigation. A 'hunch' of an experienced detective had to have some reasonable basis and could not be an excuse for 'irrational and high-handed actions.' The majority decided to exclude the incriminating statements given to the police, the stereo set recovered as a result of one of the statements, and evidence of fingerprints. According to the majority, 'If the Court should turn a blind eye to this kind of conduct, then the police may assume that they have the court's tacit approval of it. I do not view the exclusion of the evidence as a punishment of the police for their conduct, although it is to be hoped that it will act as a future deterrent. It is rather an affirmation of fundamental values of our society, and the only means in this case of ensuring that the individual's Charter rights are not illusory.'[9]

In his vigorous dissent Mr Justice Zuber doubted whether there had been a Charter violation and held that, even if there had, the evidence should not have been excluded. Relying in part on views previously expressed by members of the British Columbia Court of Appeal,[10] he suggested a number of principles that should be considered under s. 24(2):

1. The compromise of s. 24(2) 'tilts the balance in favour of truth, so that evidence, even though obtained as a result of constitutional violation, is *prima facie* admissible.'[11]
2. It is not necessary for courts to turn a blind eye to Charter violations by admitting the evidence since they have a wide range of other remedies.
3. Canadian courts should be wary of moving in the direction of the American exclusionary rule.
4. The reliability of the evidence cannot defeat the effect of s. 24(2) but is an important consideration.

'The question becomes whether the admission of the truth (albeit discovered as a result of a Charter violation) will bring the administration of justice into disrepute. The converse question is: What will the suppression of the truth do to the repute of the administration of justice?'[12]

5 The criminal-justice system until 1982 regularly admitted evidence despite the fact that it was illegally obtained and was held in high regard.

'Granted that the Charter has changed the law but it has not overnight transformed the healthy repute of the administration of justice into a fragile flower ready to wilt because of the admission of evidence obtained as a result of a violation of the Charter rights of an accused. The regard of the Canadian public for the administration of justice prior to the Charter, despite the fact that evidence illegally obtained was admitted as a matter of course, was, in my view, very high. The repute of the administration of justice has not now suddenly become highly vulnerable.'[13]

6 Exclusion of evidence to control the police has no place under s. 24(2) and has not been proved to be an effective remedy.
7 Disrepute must rest on the view of the whole community rather than of the few 'no matter how knowledgeable or expert.'
8 Evidence should be excluded in 'highly exceptional cases.'

'Frequent resort to the exclusion of evidence will create a perception by the public that the criminal justice system is a sort of legalistic game in which a misstep by the police confers immunity upon the accused. This perception will most certainly bring the administration of justice into disrepute.'[14]

2. *Supreme Court's Interventionist Perspective*

The Supreme Court of Canada however soon made it clear that exclusion of evidence was *not* to be rare. In *Therens* (1985),[15] the majority excluded breathalyser evidence obtained after a violation of the right to counsel, despite good-faith reliance by the police on prior jurisprudence in the Supreme Court that persons subjected to breathalyser demands were *not* detained and therefore *not* entitled to counsel. In *Clarkson* (1986),[16] the Supreme Court upheld the acquittal of an accused charged with murdering her husband. The accused had been advised of her right to counsel at the scene, but had indicated that there was 'no point' in having counsel. The interrogation continued in spite of the efforts of an aunt to have it postponed and to convince the accused to stop talking until counsel was present. For the Court on this point, Madam Justice Wilson held that the accused's confession had been obtained in violation of a right to counsel and should be excluded under s. 24(2). The police interrogation had clearly been aimed to extract a confession from someone they feared would not confess when she later sobered up and appreciated the need for counsel. In surprisingly terse reasons, given the enormity of the result, the Court held that this 'flagrant exploitation' by the police of the fact that the accused was in no condition to insist on her rights had to be the kind of violation giving rise to the remedy of exclusion.

It was only in *Collins* (1987)[17] that the Supreme Court, through a majority judgment of Mr Justice Lamer (now Chief Justice), carefully articulated an approach to s. 24(2), which it has asserted ever since. Lamer J. accepts that s. 24(2) adopts an 'intermediate' position between the American rule excluding all unconstitutionally obtained evidence and the common-law rule admitting all evidence irrespective of police methods. His Lordship very clearly states that s. 24(2) cannot be used by Canadian courts to exclude evidence to discipline the police and is not a remedy for police misconduct. The section could have been drafted in that way, but it instead focused on whether the admission of evidence would, in the long term, bring the administration of justice into disrepute. However, Lamer J. later seems to contradict himself in his express recognition that exclusion might occur where judges wish not to condone police or prosecutorial misconduct.

The double-speak evident in *Collins* on this point has continued in later decisions. According to Chief Justice Dickson in *Genest* (1989): 'While the purpose of s. 24(2) is not to deter police misconduct, the Court should be reluctant to admit evidence that shows the signs of being obtained by an abuse of common law and Charter rights by the Police.'[18] Similarly, Mr Justice Sopinka, for the majority in *Kokesch* (1991),[19] writes: 'This Court must not be seen to condone deliberate unlawful conduct designed to subvert both the legal and constitutional limits of police power to intrude on individual privacy.[20]

Lamer J. in *Collins* determined that the key question of whether the admission of evidence would bring the administration of justice into disrepute is a question of law to be determined by Courts without evidence, such as opinion-poll data on the actual effect of exclusion on public opinion. Mr Justice Lamer reasoned that the public only become conscious of the importance of Charter rights where they are in some way brought closer to the system personally or through the experience of friends or family. As Lamer J. bluntly put it: 'The Charter is designed to protect the accused from the majority, so the enforcement of the Charter must not be left to that majority.'[21] The Court adopted the reasonable-person test[22] of 'would the admission of the evidence bring the administration of justice into disrepute in the eyes of a reasonable man, dispassionate and fully apprised of the circumstances of the case?' However, His Lordship added that the reasonable person is 'usually the average person in the community, but only when that community's current mood is reasonable.'[23]

This aspect of the *Collins* approach has been vehemently criticized by Professor David Paciocco as an unjustifiable resort by the courts to the expediency of exclusion despite the language of s. 24(2) and irrespective of what the public might think about it.[24] On the other hand, Professor Jobson has supported the approach on the basis that s. 24(2) requires a professional understanding of our complex system of criminal justice and the democratic ideals of the Charter.[25] Ordinary citizens may too easily sacrifice long-term goals 'for a felt need to stamp out crime and support police illegality.'[26]

A final blow to the argument that exclusion of evidence should be rare lies in the further holding in *Collins* that the availability of other remedies was simply 'irrelevant' to the question of whether to exclude under s. 24(2).[27]

In *Collins* Mr Justice Lamer, in considering how the judge was to 'consider all the circumstances' under s. 24(2), found it as 'a matter of personal preference' useful to group the factors according to the way in which they affected the repute of the administration of justice.[28] This aspect of *Collins* has ever since been the pivotal consideration under s. 24(2). His personal approach has been applied like a boiler-plate. A clear summary of *Collins* by Chief Justice Dickson for the majority in *Jacoy* (1988)[29] is frequently relied upon:

> First, the court must consider whether the admission of evidence will affect the fairness of the trial. If this inquiry is answered affirmatively, 'the admission of evidence would *tend* to bring the administration of justice into disrepute and, subject to a consideration of other factors, the evidence generally should be excluded' ... One of the factors relevant to this determination is the nature of the evidence; if the evidence is real evidence that existed irrespective of the *Charter* violation, its admission will rarely render the trial unfair.
>
> The second set of factors concerns the seriousness of the violation. Relevant to this group is whether the violation was committed in good faith, whether it was inadvertent or of a merely technical nature, whether it was motivated by urgency or to prevent the loss of evidence, and whether the evidence could have been obtained without *Charter* violation.
>
> Finally, the court must look at factors relating to the effect of excluding the evidence. The administration of justice may be brought into disrepute by excluding evidence essential to substantiate the charge where the breach of the *Charter* was trivial. While this consideration is particularly important where the offence is serious, if the admission of the evidence would result in an unfair trial, the seriousness of the offence would not render the evidence admissible.[30]

This approach distinguishes between evidence that affects the fairness of the trial, in the sense that the accused is conscripted against himself, and evidence that does not, such as tangible evidence of a weapon or a drug that the police find without the help of the accused. On the *Collins* approach, if the evidence does affect the fairness of a trial, there is in effect a presumption that the evidence should be excluded under s. 24(2). In the case of other types of evidence, the presumption is that the evidence should normally *not* be excluded.

In *Strachen* (1988)[31] Chief Justice Dickson for the Court clearly set out to reject a commonly asserted view since *Therens* and *Collins* that evidence obtained in violation of the Charter that went to the fairness of the trial, typically confessions following a violation of the right to counsel, was to be automatically excluded. Chief Justice Dickson could not have been clearer: 'Routine exclusion of evidence necessary to substantiate charges may itself bring the administration of justice into disrepute. Any denial of a Charter right is serious, but s. 24(2) is not an automatic exclusionary rule. Not every breach of the right to counsel will result in the exclusion of evidence.'[32]

Chief Justice Dickson asserted an equally important corrective against the trend not to exclude real evidence in *Genest* (1989).[33] Writing for the Court, he held that consideration of the impact of exclusion in the particular case should not be determinative, otherwise exclusion of evidence under s. 24(2) would be 'very rare': 'While the purpose of the rule is not to allow an accused to escape conviction, neither should it be interpreted as available only in those cases where it has no effect at all on the result of the trial. Consideration whether to exclude evidence should not be so closely tied to the ultimate result in a particular case. Justice Lamer for the majority in *Collins* held that a court should consider the effect on the administration of justice of excluding evidence but that factor alone should not decide the case.'[34]

Judging by reported case law, it still appears true that evidence is more likely to be excluded if it is characterized as affecting the fairness of the trial. But, the record is quite clear that exclusion is discretionary. The Supreme Court itself has admitted incriminating evidence going to the fairness of the trial[35] and has, by contrast, on occasion moved to exclude real evidence obtained in violation of the Charter.[36]

Lower courts, too, now regularly emphasize that exclusion under s. 24(2) is not automatic. Thus, the Ontario Court of Appeal has held that the violation of the accused's right to consult counsel in private will not in every case require the exclusion of evidence obtained thereafter.[37] On the other hand, the Saskatchewan Court of Appeal has rejected the view that exclusion of real evidence obtained in violation of the Charter should be rare.[38]

In their decisions as to whether to exclude, courts now dutifully apply the *Collins* approach of first considering whether the evidence goes to the fairness of the trial, then whether the Charter violation is serious, and then the effect of exclusion on the repute of the justice system. One often gets the impression that consideration of the third group of factors is largely formalistic. Once a court reaches the third group, the decision to include or exclude seems already to have been made. Reference to the repute occurring from inclusion or exclusion bolsters that opinion. If this is true, it is ironic. Only the third group of factors concern the issue of 'disrepute,' which is what s. 24(2) is expressed to be about. Especially in those cases of real evidence not emanating from the accused, the key determination seems to be how the court views the seriousness of the violation. Evidence will only be excluded if the court is prepared to brand the police conduct in terms such as 'deliberate,' 'flagrant,' or 'blatant.'

This is well demonstrated by the split decision of the Supreme Court in *Greffe* (1990).[39] Relying on 'confidential information received and background investigation' that the accused was importing drugs, police alerted airport customs officials. Those officials detained him at the airport and subjected him to a strip-search without informing him of the reason for the detention or his right to counsel under ss. 10(a) and 10(b). The police then arrested him, providing, the trial judge found, the spurious reason of outstanding traffic warrants. He was told he would be the subject of a body search at hospital. The hospital sigmoidoscope examination recovered two condoms of heroin of a street value of approximately $225,000.

Mr Justice Lamer, for the majority,[40] held that real evidence of heroin found by rectal search had to be excluded under s. 24(2) given the seriousness of a cumulative effect of Charter violations. According to Lamer J., the trial judge had erred by concluding through *ex post facto* reasoning that the police had reasonable and probable grounds because drugs had been found. The record revealed no evidence to support the existence of such grounds. The premise, therefore, had to be that the search had proceeded as incidental to an arrest for outstanding traffic warrants and not on the basis of reasonable and probable grounds for belief that the accused was in possession of heroin. The violations of the accused's rights under s. 10 by the customs inspectors went to the very reasonableness of the subsequent search by the police. The fact that the rectal examination was conducted as incidental to an arrest for traffic warrants, absent any evidence on the record of reasonable and probable grounds for the belief that the accused was in possession of heroin, made the unreasonable search an extremely serious violation of the accused's Charter rights. On the assumption that the police were acting on suspicion, the Court had to disassociate itself from the police conduct given the flagrant and serious violation of the rights of the accused. The Charter breaches were not isolated errors of judgments but, rather, part of a larger pattern of disregard.[41]

In marked contrast, Chief Justice Dickson for the minority[42] would *not* have excluded the evidence. The Charter violations were technical in nature and an example of 'minor police stupidity.' The failure to arrest for the proper offence had been a trivial violation of the accused's Charter rights. The finding of the trial judge that the police had reasonable and probable grounds should not be reversed. Nor should there be any inference drawn that the police had acted in bad faith in arresting the accused for outstanding traffic violations. There was no evidence of malice on the part of the authorities towards the accused and no evidence of mistreatment.[43]

One of the factors in the determination of the seriousness of the violation is the question of police 'good faith.' This factor usually is indirectly addressed, as is the case whenever a court decides that a breach by the police was flagrant. The Supreme Court seems to have been quite inconsistent in its decisions. On occasion, the evidence has not been excluded on the consideration that police had in good faith relied on statutory search powers subsequently declared unconstitutional, as in the case of writs of assistance[44] and consensual electronic surveillance without prior judicial authorization.[45] On the other hand, the Court has been unsympathetic to the police where they have been relying on previous case law that is now being changed, as we have already seen in the decision of *Therens*. In *Hebert* (1990),[46] police had placed an informer in a cell, relying on a clear authorization to do so in a pre-Charter ruling of the Supreme Court. All courts of appeal had ruled subsequently that to do so would not violate the Charter. The Supreme Court, however, found that there was a new pre-trial right to silence under s. 7 and went on to exclude the confession. For the Court on this point, Madam Justice McLachlin flatly rejected the good-faith argument on the basis that 'ignorance of the effect of the Charter does not preclude application of s. 24(2) of the Charter (*Therens*) nor does it cure an unfair trial.'[47]

The latest decision on the issue of good-faith reliance, *Kokesch* (1991),[48] produced an interesting difference of opinion. Mr Justice Sopinka, for the majority,[49] determined that evidence of marijuana discovered in the search of a residence pursuant to a search warrant should be excluded since the evidence had been obtained as a result of an unconstitutional perimeter search of the building on mere suspicion. Good faith was here not capable of mitigating the seriousness of the s. 8 violation. On the evidence, the police knew they had insufficient grounds either to search without a warrant or to obtain a search warrant under the Narcotic Control Act. Even if the officers had honestly but mistakenly believed that they had the power to search, they could not be said to have been proceeding in 'good faith' as that term was understood under s. 24(2). Either they knew they were trespassing 'or they ought to have known.' Sopinka J. did not wish to be seen as imposing upon the police a burden of 'instant interpretation of court decisions' and left open the question of the length of time after a judgment that ought to be permitted to pass before knowledge was 'attributed to the police for the purposes of assessing good faith.'

In contrast, Chief Justice Dickson in dissent[50] would not have excluded the evidence and found that there was evidence of good faith on the part of the authorities. The police officers' error as to the scope of authority to engage in the perimeter search was not unreasonable. An opinion that such a search would not offend the Charter had been shared by the British Columbia Court of Appeal. Here, the police motivation was to obtain evidence in a situation where other avenues appeared to have been foreclosed. They had obtained a search warrant prior to the actual search of the dwelling house.

3. Critique of the Supreme Court's Approach

Professor David Paciocco[51] has attacked the Supreme Court for fashioning an 'extremely aggressive exclusionary remedy' involving a departure from the words and intent of s. 24(2). He suggests that exclusion should be rare and that 'the exclusionary philosophy of the Court is not driven a wit by what are almost certainly the views of the average Canadian on the matter.'[52]

The most careful attempt to ascertain what the public would think of exclusion of evidence under the Charter is found in a study conducted by Professors Bryant and others.[53] Groups of citizens were confronted with detailed vignettes, mostly based on actual Supreme Court decisions, such as the one in *Therens*. While the social research documented a gap between public and social opinion in a number of contexts, notably in the case of drinking and driving and the right to counsel, the researchers are guarded in their conclusions. They suggest it is not at all clear that the gap will remain fixed and that the relationship between public opinion and moral legitimacy of the system is complex. It was premature to conclude that the apparent gap between judicial and public opinion endangers public confidence in our justice system.

Even if it were to be definitively established that the public care far less about the rights of the accused than do judges, surely our conception of a justice system is not one of trial by plebiscite. Given the history and wording of s. 24(2), the Supreme Court's approach *has* been expansive. However, it is difficult to see why, given its overall purposive approach to the entrenched Charter, the Supreme Court was somehow restricted or did wrong in trying to make the remedy of exclusion under s. 24(2) meaningful in the hope that Charter rights, in the context of the criminal-justice system, would not be mere rhetoric.

The power of the exclusionary remedy in place should not be exaggerated. Unlike the automatic exclusionary rule in the United States, the Canadian remedy clearly involves a balancing of all factors. While there is no empirical data as to the exact impact of the Charter on the criminal-justice system, some assessment can be based on the ten years of written reasons in criminal trials across Canada, both reported and unreported. It seems quite clear that criminal trials in Canada are often no longer just concerned with guilt. The frequency and success of Charter arguments based on police conduct show that the legitimacy of police power and action is now being repeatedly questioned in trials before judges. The Law Reform Commission has been proved correct, rather than biased, in their assertion of the need to review police powers and conduct. There is a serious problem that is not academic navel-gazing. Before the Charter, too much faith was placed in the efficacy of civil action against peace officers,[54] although the record actually demonstrated that few such civil suits were pursued and few were successful.[55]

Notwithstanding the success of Charter arguments, it is still clear that, with or without the Charter, a very small minority of accused are acquitted.[56] Clearly, though, the Courts are sometimes prepared to exclude evidence and acquit accused, some even of very serious offences indeed. In spite of heartbreak for particular victims in such cases, in my view it is a good thing the Courts are now in a position and are prepared to insist on fairer standards of law enforcement (and prosecution). Although the stated rationale of exclusion is to preserve the integrity of the criminal-justice system, it seems quite clear that the hope is that, in future cases, fairer standards will be followed so that evidence will not have to be excluded. On this view, the real question is whether the Charter standards for agents of the state are providing sufficient or too much protection for the accused. We turn now to consider some of the major new standards affecting policing.

NEW CHARTER STANDARDS FOR POLICING

1. Discretion to Enforce

Criminal courts have been most reluctant to review the exercise of discretion by a police officer (or a prosecutor). The reluctance has been based on a notion of separation of powers and a concern that the administration of criminal justice would be jeopardized by endless applications for review and the transfer of too much discretion to judges. Since the Charter, review of the exercise of discretion of police, prosecutors, or an attorney-general can no longer be resisted on the basis of a separation-of-powers doctrine. In *Operation Dismantle* (1985),[57] the Supreme Court held that decisions of the executive branch of government, including Cabinet decisions, *are* subject to Charter review by the courts. Courts have held that it is not contrary to principles of fundamental justice for police and prosecutors to have discretionary powers, but have accepted that the exercise of power in a particular case might give rise to a Charter remedy.

In the case of reviewing police discretion, *Beare* (1988)[58] is the leading authority. The Saskatchewan Court of Appeal had struck down the Criminal Code fingerprinting powers in cases where police have reasonable and probable grounds to believe that the person has committed an indictable offence. The Saskatchewan Court held there was too much discretion for police officers and the provision should require an officer to show reasonable and probable grounds for believing fingerprinting was necessary. The Supreme Court, through La Forest J., disagreed and reversed:

> The existence of the discretion conferred by the statutory provisions does not, in my view, offend principles of fundamental justice. Discretion is an essential feature of the criminal justice system. A system that attempted to eliminate discretion would be unworkably complex and rigid. Police necessarily exercise discretion in deciding when to lay charges, to arrest and to conduct incidental searches, as prosecutors do in deciding whether or not to withdraw a charge, enter a stay, consent to an adjournment, proceed by way of indictment or summary conviction, launch an appeal and so on.
>
> The Criminal Code provides no guidelines for the exercise of discretion in any of these areas. The day-to-day operation of law enforcement and the criminal justice system nonetheless depends upon the exercise of that discretion.[59]

The Court added, however, that there would be a remedy under s. 24 of the Charter where it was established in a particular case that police (or prosecutorial) discretion had been exercised 'for improper or arbitrary motives.'[60]

The power to intervene in the case of particular conduct by a police officer (or prosecutor) is now generally litigated under an application to stay as an abuse of process and, less often, as a denial of equality before the law under s. 15 of the Charter. In both cases, such challenges face an uphill battle. In the former case, the Supreme Court now clearly recognizes[61] that a judicial stay should be granted where 'compelling an accused to stand trial would violate those fundamental principles of justice which underlie the community's sense of fair play and decency' or where the proceedings are 'oppressive and/or vexatious.' However, the Supreme Court and courts of appeal have insisted that the power should be exercised only in the 'clearest of cases,' and very rarely grant such a stay. In the case of s. 15 challenges to the exercise of discretion by a particular officer, it is now clear that there will have to be more than evidence of regional disparity in the application of the law.[62] There will have to be clear evidence of discrimination.[63] The lack of success of such claims thus far[64] suggests that criminal courts will continue to be an inadequate forum for consideration of such serious but difficult to substantiate charges as racism.[65]

2. *Random Vehicle Stops*

In a series of decisions the Supreme Court of Canada has established that the police have very wide powers to stop motor vehicles. Motorists thus have very little protection under the Charter. The Court has held that powers to stop vehicles at random that exist under express provisions of highway traffic acts,[66] or even are implied from a power to request a motorist to stop and surrender his licence on demand,[67] do result in detentions that are arbitrary given that there are no criteria as to which motorists can be stopped. However, the Court found that these arbitrary detention powers were demonstrably justified in a free and democratic society under s. 1.

In *Hufsky* (1988),[68] a unanimous Court stressed the importance of highway safety and the role to be played by random stops in detecting motor-vehicle offences, many of which could not be detected by mere observation of driving. The stop in question had the dual purpose of checking for both the driving papers and the sobriety of drivers. The only guideline had been that at least one marked police vehicle had to be present. There were no criteria to determine which vehicle should be stopped. This was at the sole discretion of the officer. The officer who stopped the accused was in uniform but in an unmarked car. There had been nothing unusual about the accused's driving. The court concluded its brief reasons as follows:

> The nature and degree of the intrusion of a random stop for the purposes of the spot check procedure in the present case, remembering that the driving of a motor vehicle is a licensed activity subject to regulation and control in the interests of safety, is proportionate to the purpose to be served. If the stopping of motor vehicles for such purposes is not to be seriously inhibited, it should not, in my respectful opinion, be subjected to the kinds of conditions or restrictions reflected in the American jurisprudence,[69] which would appear seriously to undermine its effectiveness while not significantly reducing its intrusiveness. As for publicity, which was referred to in

Dedman, supra, in connection with common law authority for a random stop for the purposes contemplated by the R.I.D.E. program, I think it may be taken now that the public is well aware of random stop authority because of both its frequent and widespread exercise and its recognition by legislatures.[70]

Some commentators,[71] and even the Saskatchewan Court of Appeal,[72] attempted to distinguish *Hufsky* in the case of random roving stops, which were seen to be more arbitrary and more intrusive than a checkpoint stop. However, a five-to-four majority of the Supreme Court in *Ladouceur* (1990)[73] held that there was to be no such distinction and that such random stops also were demonstrably justified as reasonable limits on arbitrary detention under s. 1 of the Charter. For the majority, Mr Justice Cory[74] noted that stopping vehicles was the only way of checking a driver's licence and insurance, the mechanical fitness of a vehicle, and the sobriety of the driver. Random stops supplied the only effective deterrent. Furthermore, effective organized programs were an impossibility in rural areas and generally difficult to establish owing to physical constraints and shortages of personnel. The stops were of relatively short duration, requiring the production of only a few documents, and caused minimal inconvenience to the driver.[75]

Mr Justice Sopinka for the minority[76] would have read the power down, as had the Ontario Court of Appeal: 'This case may be viewed as the last straw. If sanctioned, we will be agreeing that a police officer can stop any vehicle at any time, in any place, without having any reason to do so. For the motorist, this means a total negation of the freedom from arbitrary detention guaranteed by s. 9 of the Charter. This is something that would not be tolerated with respect to pedestrians in their use of the public streets and walkways.'[77] This roving, random stop infringed the right far more than the organized random stops at predetermined locations authorized by *Hufsky* and had the potential for abuse.[78]

The Supreme Court in *Hufsky* and *Ladouceur* has, then, recognized an extraordinarily wide power for police to stop motorists at random. Mr Justice Cory in *Ladouceur* did identify some limits. He suggested that 'intrusive searches' of the driver or the vehicle would 'probably be subject to challenge as infringing s. 8 of the Charter.'[79] His Lordship also seems to suggest that the stop powers have to be exercised in relation to driving offences: 'Officers can stop persons only for legal reasons, in this case reasons related to driving a car such as checking the driver's licence and insurance, the sobriety of the driver and the mechanical fitness of the vehicle. Once stopped the only questions that may justifiably be asked are those related to driving offences. Any further, more intrusive procedures could only be undertaken based upon reasonable and probable grounds. Where a stop is found to be unlawful, the evidence from the stop could well be excluded under s. 24(2) of the Charter.'[80] It will remain to be seen to what extent the Court will be prepared to exclude evidence of other offences found after a random vehicle stop.

3. Search and Seizure

One of the most expansive interpretations of the Charter has occurred in the case of the protection available under section 8 which provides that everyone has the 'right to be secure against unreasonable search or seizure.' In a series of decisions, beginning with its landmark decision in *Hunter* v. *Southam* (1984),[81] the Supreme Court has established a number of minimum constitutional standards for search or seizure in the case of the investigations of crimes (including drug offences). Although the jurisprudence is exceedingly complex, it would appear that a section 8 challenge to a search or seizure will succeed if:

1 it was illegal;[82]
2 there was no warrant where it was feasible to get one;
3 there was no neutral and impartial review of the warrant by one capable of acting judicially or there was no reasonable grounds established upon oath;
4 there was mere suspicion rather than reasonable belief; or
5 the search or seizure was conducted in an unreasonable manner.

There can be little doubt that the assertion of these standards in numerous cases has reduced police powers to search or seize. The commitment to protect privacy by requiring a warrant where practical led to the striking down of the power to conduct a warrantless search of even dwelling houses under writs of assistance[83] and of the Criminal Code power, under what is now section 184(2)(a), to electronically intercept communication on mere consent of one party to the communication.[84]

It is not yet clear how far powers to search or seize will be curtailed, as the Supreme Court has not yet fully determined the applicability of the standards to contentious areas such as searches of vehicles or searches of the person. In the case of searches of the person, of particular interest to police officers is the constitutionality of their common-law power to search automatically as an incident on arrest, either for weapons or for further evidence. A quick reading of *Cloutier* v. *Langois* (1990)[85] suggests that such an unrestricted right has survived the Charter. However, the Supreme Court through Madam Justice L'Heureux-Dubé speaks with a forked tongue. Although it holds that the police need not have reasonable grounds, the Court determines that the power is not unlimited and can be exercised only where the police have acted with discretion, have a valid objective in pursuit of the ends of criminal justice, and have not been abusive. The search was a mere 'frisk' or 'pat down' search, and *Cloutier* may well not have addressed the constitutionality of more intrusive types of personal searches.[86]

The Supreme Court's determination that an illegal search is necessarily unconstitutional should concern the police. Despite a huge array of statutory powers to search in Canada and some common-law powers, there are still large areas of particular importance to police that are still highly disputed. Given that police officers are often called upon to act on the spur of the moment in many varied and often dangerous situations, this lack of clarity cannot be satisfactory. It is, for example, quite extraordinary that the power of a police officer to enter a dwelling house in Canada in volatile cases of domestic violence is not clear. Another troubling example is the lack of power to obtain bodily samples from accused in custody for forensic testing, especially given that there is at present no legal possibility of obtaining a search warrant for these purposes.

4. Arrest

Powers to arrest on reasonable grounds have been largely unaffected by imposition of Charter standards. Some lower courts have held that a blanket arrest policy contrary to Criminal Code appearance notice requirements is arbitrary detention contrary to section 9.[87] Thus far, this is the minority view[88] and the Supreme Court has not agreed to hear further appeals on the issue.

The Supreme Court has held that the true reasons for an arrest must be given to comply with the dictates of s. 10(a) of the Charter,[89] although it has recently shown some flexibility.[90]

5. Police Questioning and Interrogation

In the Supreme Court's many interpretations of the right to counsel on arrest or detention and in its creation of a pre-trial right to silence under s. 7 in *Hebert* (1990),[91] new constitutional limits have been placed on police powers to question and interrogate. However, in both cases, the Supreme Court has indeed been most mindful of law-enforcement interests. Indeed, the Supreme Court has given surprisingly mixed messages to police officers.

The right to counsel is triggered by arrest or detention. Although the Supreme Court has determined that detention includes psychological compulsion by police,[92] it has not yet reversed lower-court decisions that police interrogations of a suspect in his or her home or at a police station do not amount to detention.

Under s. 10(b) there is not only a right to counsel but a right to be informed of that right. One might have expected the Supreme Court to interpret this right to require that the police make sure that the accused has understood what the right entails. However, thus far the Supreme Court has only held that there has been a violation of the right to inform where the accused has indicated that he did not understand.[93] In its leading decision in *Manninen* (1987)[94] the Supreme Court declared that s. 10(b) imposed correlative duties on the police to afford a reasonable opportunity to exercise the right and to refrain from questioning or attempting to elicit evidence until such reasonable opportunity had been provided. On the other hand, the Court has repeatedly made it clear that such duties only arise where the accused asserts his or her right to counsel. This assertion, surprisingly, offers the best protection to the knowledgeable accused at the expense of those who are ignorant and thus more vulnerable. The Supreme Court has further insisted that the duties will be 'suspended' if the accused does not exercise his or her rights with reasonable diligence.[95] This latter requirement has led to a series of inconsistent rulings.[96]

Perhaps the best example of a mixed message – or is this merely proper balancing according to Sopinka J. – is *Hebert*. Madam Justice McLachlin for the Supreme Court spends an elaborate part of the judgment justifying a new constitutional pre-trial right to silence, which had been violated when the police placed an undercover officer in the cell after the accused had indicated he did not wish to speak to the police. However, the Court also pragmatically imposes four limits to this newly recognized constitutional right to silence. The police are authorized to question the accused in the absence of counsel after the accused has retained counsel. The right to silence applies only after detention. It does not affect voluntary statements to a cell-mate not acting as an agent of the state. Finally, it is not violated where an undercover officer merely observes the suspect and does not actively elicit the information. The latter seems to be a most difficult distinction to draw in practice and provides little clarity, as desperately required by undercover agents. It seems surprising that the Supreme Court did not also require that police officers warn detainees of the new right to silence and also simply asserted that the doctrine of waiver here had no application.

HAS THE SUPREME COURT STRUCK A PROPER BALANCE?

Mr Justice Sopinka may well be correct in suggesting that these emerging constitutional standards will probably satisfy neither the police nor civil libertarians.

It seems quite clear that the Charter is not a panacea. It will, on present interpretation, be an inadequate remedy for reviewing charges of racial discrimination in law enforcement. There is clearly no constitutional protection against abuse of police power in random vehicle stops.

From the police point of view, there have been severe restrictions placed on powers to search and seize, and there are too many ambiguities in the law relating to police questioning and interrogation.

HOW SHOULD THE POLICE RESPOND TO THE CHARTER AND LAW REFORM?

It seems clear that all police officers have an obligation to respect the Charter and the standards set by the Supreme Court. This is also true of judges. Recently in *Fowler* (1990),[97] Mr Justice Lyon of the Manitoba Court of Appeal, a signatory to the Charter as premier of Manitoba, suggested that excluding truthful evidence under s. 24(2) of the Charter was not one of the major purposes of the drafters of the Charter and should be rare. His position was a minority one, and a colleague on the Manitoba Court of Appeal, O'Sullivan J.A., was justified in his strong rebuke: 'Truth is one of the grand objectives of the criminal justice system; it is not the only objective. The common law has recognized over the ages that truth may come at too great a price to warrant its reception into evidence. That is the reason why we have rules of evidence ... [In] applying the Charter we are bound by the interpretations given to it not by its framers, but by the majority of the Supreme Court of Canada. We may have a duty, as we certainly have the right, to subject the Supreme Court's views to vigorous criticism, but in the end, if the rule of law and hierarchy of courts is to prevail, we are bound by the guidelines set by that court.[98]

In the case of the police, the risk of not learning and following emerging Charter standards is that important criminal cases will be lost owing to exclusion of evidence. The message surely is that the best protection against the Charter is to learn its standards, and follow them, so that evidence will never have to be excluded. It seems quite clear that several Charter standards do adequately, and indeed more than adequately, accommodate considerations of law-enforcement expediency.

One would have thought that police groups, rather than opposing attempts by the Law Reform Commission of Canada and others to clarify police powers, would instead have been supportive. This is especially true in the area of search and seizure, as these powers are in sore need of clarification. Of course, the difficulty is that any proposal may become so complicated and so detailed that the police rightly feel hamstrung. On the other hand, if the police leave the courts to develop Charter standards, experience thus far is that the direction will be often itself confused and complex. The Courts are now the protectors of minimum standards of civil liberties as they see it. This does not mean that sensible and practical law reform through legislative initiative should cease. For example, the power to obtain bodily samples respecting new D.N.A. printing procedures could be clarified. Here, as elsewhere, law reform can play a useful role in articulating more clearly the appropriate balance between the demands of law enforcement and a proper regard for *Charter* rights.

NOTES

1 The Canadian Association of Chiefs of Police, *The Law Reform Commission. A Police Perspective* (Ottawa: Law Reform Commission of Canada, November 1984).
2 Ibid., 3.
3 Ibid., 14–15.
4 'Eight Years Under the Charter,' 13–14.
5 D. Stuart, *Charter Justice in Canadian Criminal Law* (Toronto: Carswell 1991).
6 J. Breitel, 'Controls in Criminal Enforcement,' *University of Chicago Law Review* 27 (1960): 427.
7 J.H. Skolnick, *Justice Without Trial: Law Enforcement in Democratic Society* (New York: J. Wiley 1966).
8 *R.* v. *Duguay* (1985), 45 C.R. (3d) 140 (Ont. C.A.).
9 Ibid., 152.
10 See especially Seaton J.A. in *R.* v. *Collins* (1983), 33 C.R. (3d) 130 (B.C.C.A.) and Esson J.A. (as he then was) in *R.* v. *Hamill* (1984), 41 C.R. (3d) 123 (B.C.C.A.).
11 His Lordship here adopted the words of now Mr Justice Ewaschuk in *R.* v. *Gibson* (1984), 37 C.R. (3d) 175 (Ont. H.C.) at 185.
12 *Duguay* (n. 8, above), at 157.
13 Ibid., at 158.
14 Ibid., at 159.
15 *R.* v. *Therens* (1985), 45 C.R. (3d) 97 (S.C.C.).
16 *Clarkson* v. *R.* (1986), 50 C.R. (3d) 289 (S.C.C.).
17 *Collins* v. *R.* (1987), 56 C.R. (3d) 193 (S.C.C.).
18 *R.* v. *Genest* (1989), 45 C.C.C. (3d) 385 at 409 (S.C.C.).
19 *R.* v. *Kokesch* (1991), 1 C.R. (4th) 62 (S.C.C.). See also text associated with notes 50–2.
20 Ibid., at 73–4.
21 *Collins*, at 209.

22 The Court adopted the views of Professor Morissette, 'The Exclusion of Evidence Under the Canadian Charter of Rights and Freedoms: What To Do and What Not To Do,' *McGill Law Journal* 29 (1984): 538.
23 *Collins*, at 209.
24 D. Paciocco, 'The Judicial Repeal of s. 24(2) and the Development of the Canadian Exclusionary Rule,' *Criminal Law Quarterly* 32 (1990): 326.
25 W.H.R. Charles et al., *Evidence and the Charter of Rights and Freedoms* (Toronto: Butterworths Canada 1989), chap. 3.
26 Ibid., 273.
27 *Collins*, at 204.
28 Ibid., at 211.
29 *R.* v. *Jacoy* (1988), 66 C.R. (3d) 336 (S.C.C.).
30 Ibid., at 344–5.
31 *R.* v. *Strachen* (1988), 67 C.R. (3d) 87 (S.C.C.). *Strachen* is also most important for its ruling that the words 'obtained in a manner' do *not* require a strict causal connection between the violation and the evidence. This ruling is another one encouraging rather than restricting the remedy of exclusion.
32 Ibid., at 109. Since this paper was written a new line of authority has emerged from the Supreme Court culminating in *R.* v. *Mellenthin* (1993), 16 C.R. (4th) 273 (S.C.C.) to the effect that evidence affecting the fairness of the trial *must* be excluded without consideration of the second and third factors in *Collins*. See critical comment by R.J. Delisle, 'Mellenthin: Changing the Collins Test' (1993) 16 C.R. (4th) 286.
33 See n. 18, above.
34 Ibid., at 403.
35 See, for example, *Tremblay* v. *R.* (1987), 60 C.R. (3d) 59 (S.C.C.) ('impaired driver violent, vulgar and obnoxious') and *Mohl* v. *R.* (1989), 69 C.R. (3d) 399 (S.C.C.) (impaired driver too drunk to understand right to counsel).
36 See, for example, *Genest* (n. 18, above) and *Kokesch* (n. 19).
37 *R.* v. *Olak* (1990), 55 C.C.C. (3d) 257 (Ont. C.A.).
38 See, for example, *R.* v. *Baylis* (1988), 65 C.R. (3d) 62 (Sask. C.A.).
39 *R.* v. *Greffe* (1990), 75 C.R. (3d) 257 (S.C.C.).
40 Justices La Forest, Wilson, and Gonthier concurred.
41 *Greffe*, at 285–92.
42 Justices L'Heureux-Dubé and Cory concurred.
43 *Greffe*, at 264–8.
44 *R.* v. *Hamill* (1987), 56 C.R. (3d) 220 (S.C.C.); *R.* v. *Sieben* (1987), 56 C.R. (3d) 225 (S.C.C.).
45 *R.* v. *Duarte (Sanelli)* (1990), 74 C.R. (3d) 281 (S.C.C.).
46 *R.* v. *Hebert* (1990), 77 C.R. (3d) 145 (S.C.C.).

47 Ibid., at 193.
48 See n. 19, above. The decision in *Kokesch* to exclude was distinguished by a differently composed majority in *R.* v. *Wise* (1992), 11 C.R. (4th) 253 (S.C.C.).
49 Justices Wilson, LaForest, and McLachlin concurred.
50 Justices L'Heureux-Dubé and Cory concurred.
51 'The Judicial Repeal of s. 24(2)' (see n. 24).
52 Ibid., 365.
53 A.W. Bryant et al., 'Public Attitudes Towards the Exclusion of Evidence,' *Canadian Bar Review* 69 (1990): 1.
54 G.A. Martin, 'The Exclusionary Rule Under Foreign Law,' *Journal of Criminal Law, Criminology and Political Science* 52 (1961): 271.
55 See L.P. Katz, 'Reflections on Search and Seizure and Illegally Obtained Evidence in Canada and the United States,' *Canada-U.S. Law Journal* 3 (1980): 128–9.
56 The most dramatic impact of the Charter has been thousands of stays of proceedings in Ontario for breach of the right to be tried within a reasonable time under s. 11(b), following the Supreme Court's ruling in *R.* v. *Askov* (1990), 79 C.R. (3d) 273 (S.C.C.). This issue of court delay is crucial but not the concern of this paper.
57 *Operation Dismantle* v. *The Queen* [1985], 1 S.C.R. 441.
58 *Beare* v. *R.* (1988), 66 C.R. (3d) 97 (S.C.C.).
59 Ibid., at 116.
60 Ibid.
61 *R.* v. *Jewitt* (1985), 47 C.R. (3d) 193 (S.C.C.). See too *R.* v. *Mack* (1988), 67 C.R. (3d) 2 (S.C.C.) [entrapment].
62 *R.* v. *Turpin* (1989), 69 C.R. (3d) 97 (S.C.C.); *R.* v. *S.(S.)* (1990), 77 C.R. (3d) 272 (S.C.C.).
63 *R.* v. *Andrews*, [1989] 1 S.C.R. 143.
64 See, for example, *R.* v. *Paul Magder Furs Ltd.* (1989), 49 C.C.C. (3d) 267 (Ont. C.A.) and *R.* v. *Smith* (1993), 23 C.R. (4th) 164 (N.S.C.A.).
65 Compare the process of Manitoba's Aboriginal Justice Inquiry, which took three years and cost $3 million. See Manitoba, *Public Inquiry into the Administration of Justice and Aboriginal Peoples, Report of the Aboriginal Justice Inquiry of Manitoba* (Winnipeg: The Inquiry 1991).
66 *Highway Traffic Act*, R.S.O. 1990, c. H.8, s. 189(a)(1) – upheld in *R.* v. *Hufsky* (1988), 63 C.R. (3d) 14 (S.C.C.) and *R.* v. *Ladouceur* (1990), 77 C.R. (3d) 110 (S.C.C.).
67 *Highway Traffic Act*, R.S.A. 1980, c. H-7, s. 119 – upheld in *R.* v. *Wilson* (1990), 76 C.R. (3d) 137 (S.C.C.).
68 See n. 66.

69 Under U.S. jurisprudence permanent checkpoints are more likely to be constitutional than temporary, roving patrols; see T.E.K. Fitzgerald, 'Random Vehicle Stops After Hufsky: Two Critical Views' (1988) 63 C.R. (3d) at 31–2.
70 *Hufsky*, at 25–6.
71 E.g., Fitzgerald.
72 *R.* v. *Emke* (1989), 70 C.R. (3d) 347 (Sask. C.A.).
73 See n. 66, above.
74 Justices Lamer, L'Heureux-Dubé, Gonthier, and McLachlin concurred.
75 *Ladouceur*, at 132–5.
76 Justices Dickson C.J., Wilson, and LaForest concurred. The minority concurred in the result as it would not have excluded the evidence in the circumstances.
77 *Ladouceur*, at 118. Compare the view of J. Falconer, 'Hufsky v. The Queen and Leave in Ladouceur: What's Left?' *Criminal Law Quarterly* 30 (1988): 474–5 that it was not the Court's role to redraft legislation.
78 *Ladouceur*, at 119.
79 Ibid., at 135. In *Mellenthin* (see n. 32, above), Cory J. for a unanimous Court holds that a vehicle search following a random stop must be based on reasonable grounds.
80 Ibid.
81 (1984), 41 C.R. (3d) 97 (S.C.C.). See too, especially, *Collins* (n. 17, above) and *Kokesch* (n. 19).
82 *Kokesch*.
83 *R.* v. *Noble* (1984), 42 C.R. (3d) 209 (Ont. C.A.). Leave to appeal to the Supreme Court was refused.
84 *Duarte* (see n. 45, above).
85 (1990), 74 C.R. (3d) 316 (S.C.C.).
86 Compare, for example, *Greffe* (n. 39, above).
87 *R.* v. *Pithart* (1987), 57 C.R. (3d) 144 (B.C.C.C.).
88 See, for example, *R.* v. *Cayer* (1988), 66 C.R. (3d) 30 (Ont. C.A.).
89 See, for example, *Greffe*.
90 *R.* v. *Evans* (1991), 4 C.R. (4th) 8 (S.C.C.).
91 See n. 46, above.
92 See *Therens* (n. 15, above).
93 See *Evans* (n. 90, above); *R.* v. *Brydges* (1990), 74 C.R. (3d) 129 (S.C.C.).
94 *R.* v. *Manninen* (1987), 58 C.R. (3d) 97 (S.C.C.).
95 *R.* v. *Baig* (1987), 61 C.R. (3d) 97 (S.C.C.); *R.* v. *LeClair* (1989), 67 C.R. (3d) 209 (S.C.C.).
96 Compare, for example, *LeClair* and *R.* v. *Smith* (1989), 71 C.R. (3d) 129 (S.C.C.).
97 *R.* v. *Fowler* (1991), 3 C.R. (4th) 225 (Man. C.A.).
98 Ibid., at 236.

6

Reforming Police Powers: Who's in Charge?

M.L. FRIEDLAND

When the Law Reform Commission of Canada was established in 1971,[1] it was thought that, within the then foreseeable future, Canada would have a new Criminal Code covering criminal law and procedure. The minister of justice, John Turner, stated in the House when the bill was under consideration that 'the Commission should have a complete rewriting of the criminal law as one of its first projects.'[2] The original commission – and I should declare that I was one of the original commissioners – contemplated a new Code of Criminal Law and Procedure in its first research program, commencing with procedure: 'The Commission will undertake a study into the process of the criminal law from pre-trial stages, including police investigations and the law of arrest, to post conviction remedies with a view to drafting a comprehensive Code of Criminal Procedure.'[3]

As the end of that decade approached, progress had been relatively slow and a renewed push was made to get a new code. This was to be a 'comprehensive and accelerated review,'[4] with a cooperative effort amongst the Law Reform Commission of Canada, the Department of Justice, and the Department of the Solicitor General. Then, midway through the 1980s, the talk was that there might be a new code in 1992 on the centenary of the enactment of the 1892 code.

As of today – over twenty years after the establishment of the Law Reform Commission – the process of legislative criminal-law reform is continuing. A new code has not been enacted. Indeed, it is not even close to being enacted. A subcommittee of the Standing Committee on Justice and the Solicitor General is now conducting hearings on the general part of the code.[5] There is still a long way to go, however, before even that part of the code is enacted. Very little has yet come before Parliament dealing with criminal procedure, or, more particularly for this project, police powers.

Both the Law Reform Commission and the Government can be faulted for the pace of the progress, but at least progress was being made. Unfortunately, the Law Reform Commission of Canada, which had been working on the subject of police powers, was abolished in late February 1992. The federal minister of finance – not the minister of justice – announced in his budget speech that the Law Reform Commission, along with a number of other federal agencies, would be eliminated for financial reasons. I knew they were serious when about a month later a courier delivered my picture, which had been hanging on the wall at the Commission in Ottawa.

Let us hope that this is a temporary situation and that the Government will find another vehicle, still somewhat removed from day-to-day politics, to monitor and advise on criminal justice. Perhaps the Government should consider implementing the law-reform recommendations of the 1969 *Report of the Canadian Committee on Corrections* (the Ouimet Report),[6] a first-class document. The committee recommended that the Government set up a non-governmental committee or council, advisory to the executive branch of government, rather than to any one department. They envisaged a permanent secretariat, a research budget, and interdisciplinary committees on continuing law reform, law enforcement, and corrections. It could also be the body to handle some of the tasks envisaged for the permanent sentencing commission recommended in 1987 by the Canadian Sentencing Commission.[7]

As I have argued elsewhere,[8] criminal-law reform is almost always a slow process, with lots of mine traps along the way. The United States started to develop a new Federal Criminal Code in 1966[9] and, to this date, nothing has been enacted. England started the process in 1968[10] and a government bill is still floundering in Parliament. In a study of codification in the nineteenth century I concluded that 'law reform is affected by a great number of factors apart from the merits of the proposals. Then, as now, a combination of politics, personalities and pressure groups affected the outcome. The crucial events seem, in retrospect, largely unplotted and accidental.'[11] One very crucial event in the present context was the introduction of the Canadian Charter of Rights and Freedoms in 1982.[12]

At the same time that criminal-law reform was becoming bogged down through the parliamentary process, it started to flourish in the Supreme Court of Canada. The vacuum created by the slow process of reform in Parliament was being filled by the courts. Perhaps the Supreme Court was being pushed in this direction by former members of the Law Reform Commission of Canada who had been appointed to the Supreme Court.

As we know, the Supreme Court of Canada has used the Charter as the basis for its activism. The Court used vague words without clear meanings as the justification for its reforms. What is the natural meaning of 'fundamental justice' (s. 7), 'unreasonable search or seizure' (s. 8), 'arbitrarily detained' (s. 9), 'reasonable time' (s. 11), 'reasonable limits' (s. 1)? The courts could pour almost whatever content they wanted into the relatively empty concepts. Of course, they had real cases before them and had to make some judgment. They could not give the decision a 'six-month hoist,' as Parliament can. But, was it desirable for the Supreme Court to be such an activist court and give such expansive judgments? Did it spur the overall reform of the criminal law or slow it down? Did it make the task of legislative law reform more difficult? Will we wake up to discover that major legislative criminal-law reform in Canada is now dead?

I do not think that very many of us would have predicted ten years ago that the Charter would have had such a profound effect on our criminal jurisprudence. We knew that there would be a change with respect to an accused being told on detention that he or she had a right to counsel. This was one of the very few changes that were deliberately made by the Charter and I believe it has been proper for the courts to give this provision (s.10(b)) as wide a meaning as they have. Another area where it was anticipated that the courts would develop the law is with respect to section 24(2), the exclusion of evidence.[13] But few expected as much change in other areas of the criminal law. We were wrong.

Back in 1983 I counted (or, I should say, a research assistant counted) the number of cases cited in *Canadian Criminal Cases* in the year and a half following the introduction of the Bill of Rights in 1960[14] that cited the Bill of Rights and compared that with citation of Charter cases in the first year and a half of the Charter.[15] There were only about a dozen Bill of Rights cases reported in the first year and a half following the Bill of Rights, but over 125 Charter cases reported in its first year and a half. Over 25 per cent of the cases reported in the first five volumes of *Canadian Criminal Cases* in 1983 were Charter cases. Since then, the percentage of Charter cases has doubled. In the twelve volumes of *Canadian Criminal Cases* (volumes 51–62) reported in 1990 and part of 1991, over 50 per cent of the cases were Charter cases, and in the Supreme Court of Canada over 70 per cent of the criminal cases involved the Charter.[16] So, the Charter has become a major ingredient in the working of the criminal law.

One of the reasons that the United States Supreme Court was so active in the 1960s and 1970s was to set uniform minimum standards for the administration of criminal justice across the United States. This could only be achieved through the Supreme Court because criminal law and procedure is a matter for each state. So the Court used the 'due process' clause of the 14th Amendment to set standards for the police and state legislatures. In Canada, criminal law and procedure are matters for the federal government, and so it has not been as imperative for the courts to set uniform standards. They can be set by federal legislation.

PARLIAMENT OR THE COURTS?

What is the better way of reforming criminal law and procedure: Parliament or the Courts? In my view, Parliament is the better vehicle. I have recently been studying the New York Criminal Procedure Law[17] in connection with a project that I have undertaken with two colleagues (Kent Roach and Michael Code) into a comparison of the administration of criminal justice in Niagara Falls, New York, and Niagara Falls, Ontario. The more I look at the New York Criminal Procedure Law, the more impressed I am with its structure and the ease with which it can be used.

There are several reasons why I think legislation is preferable. Parliament can integrate the various parts of a code better than the courts, which are usually dealing with one accused and one provision of the law. The overview of the entire process can be lost in looking at the single case.

Further, Parliament speaks with one voice in a legislative enactment. The courts often give us a variety of different and lengthy judgments and it is often difficult to know what a decision actually means. Court judgments are usually relatively inaccessible to everyone except lawyers – and they are often very difficult for lawyers to understand. *Swain* (1991),[18] for example, covers over seventy-seven pages in four judgments in *Canadian Criminal Cases*, plus eleven pages for the headnote. And *Mills* (1986)[19] covers eighty-one pages in four judgments, plus nine pages for the headnote, to give just two examples.

I agree with the following comment by the Law Reform Commission of Canada in their report *Our Criminal Procedure* (1987): 'Clear rules of procedure within the criminal process establish the parameters of permissible behaviour, not only for the individual, but for state officials as well. Both the citizen and the police officer benefit from a clearer understanding of their respective rights, responsibilities and obligations in any official encounter. Clarity defines and protects the interests of all parties to the process.'[20] Clarity is usually easier to achieve through legislation than court cases.

Not only is legislative law reform normally clearer, but it is easier to change if it is shown to be wrong or undesirable. Constitutionalizing criminal procedure makes the law difficult to remake. As the Law Reform Commission of Canada rightly stated: 'Unlike constitutional protections, which suggest concepts of immutability, ordinary legislation is subject to revision by debate and action in the Houses of Parliament.'[21] As we know, Parliament or the legislatures can override a judicial decision under section 33 of the Charter, but it is politically difficult for a legislative body to do so, and it must face the harsh music of re-enactment every five years (s.33(2)). Moreover, under the Government's proposed Charlottetown constitutional proposals,[22] which were not accepted, the override would have required a 60 per cent majority to be effective. (Note that the provision referred to '60 percent of the members of Parliament or the provincial legislature' and not just to members voting. Again, this would have made the override even more difficult to achieve.)

Another major reason for favouring the legislative process over the judicial process is that the voices of pressure groups can more easily be heard through the legislative process.[23] Persons or groups with a point of view can make their voices heard in responding to requests for submissions with respect to a study paper, a working paper, a report, a legislative bill, a legislative committee hearing, and a Senate study. Further, the provincial voice can more easily be heard by the legislative process through the work of the Uniformity Commissioners and federal/provincial meetings. Of course, there are potential drawbacks: the impact of the pressure groups can be so strong that the whole train of reform goes off the rails.

The courts rarely hear more than the occasional pressure group. Although the practice for the past twenty years is liberally to grant intervenor standing to pressure groups, I note from the reports that relatively few have actually taken the opportunity to appear and submit briefs. So, for example, in the wire-tapping case of *Duarte* (1990),[24] no non-governmental intervenor appeared. And in the *Hebert* (1990)[25] case, dealing with statements to cell-mates who are undercover officers, no one apart from the Crown and the defence appeared. Amazingly, the same is true in the *Askov* (1990) delay case.[26] By contrast, in the *Beare* (1988)[27] case, dealing with fingerprinting under the Identification of Criminals Act, the Canadian Association of Chiefs of Police submitted a brief supporting the use of fingerprinting. The result of the Supreme Court decision in that case was one that the police liked.

Perhaps one of the main reasons for the relative paucity of applications for intervenor status is the cost of applying for standing and of appearing. With the decrease in government funding to many groups it is likely that pressure groups will continue to be a scarce commodity before the Supreme Court of Canada. If we are going to continue to rely mainly on the Supreme Court of Canada to reform the criminal law – and I do not think we should – we should consider new institutional structures to ensure that the courts, particularly the Supreme Court of Canada, have the full range of policy arguments before them.

Moreover, the Court should have the means of obtaining access to reliable statistics. In the *Askov* case, for example, the Court obtained on its own initiative information on the practice respecting delay in Quebec[28] and, in part, based its decision on that information. The information turned out to be wrong.[29]

A further reason for favouring legislative law reform is that Acts of Parliament are almost invariably prospective, that is, they only operate in future cases. This is the way statutes are normally interpreted. (Indeed, section 11(g) of the Charter now specifically prevents the creation of offences with retroactive effects.) Court judgments, by contrast, operate both prospectively and retrospectively.[30] Thus, any interpretation of the Supreme Court of Canada will operate on all those who will be tried in the future, but also on those who have already been tried.

American courts consciously decide whether a change in the law will be given retrospective effect. In some cases, such as in *Gideon* v. *Wainright* (1963),[31] setting out the right to counsel in serious cases, the U.S. Supreme Court gave the judgment full retroactive effect because of the possible substantial effect that not having counsel would have had on the trial process. But in other cases, such as those involving new rules on line-ups,[32] they have given only prospective effect to the judgment, that is, to line-ups taking place after the judgment. The actual cut-off point varies from case to case and is determined in subsequent cases, not in the landmark case itself. *Miranda* v. *Arizona* (1966),[33] dealing with police interrogation, applied only to cases in which the trial was commenced after *Miranda*. *Mapp* v. *Ohio* (1961),[34] the search-and-seizure case, applied to all cases still on direct appeal. It should be noted, however, that the courts always give the accused who is responsible for the change in the law the benefit of the new law as a reward for appealing.

Our courts have been reluctant to use the technique of prospective lawmaking. This is because they do not want openly to declare that they are making new law. They wish to give the appearance that they are simply declaring the law – or interpreting the Charter – and if one is declaring or interpreting the law, then it should apply to past cases as well as future cases. The only criminal cases thus far where the judgment was prospective only were the *Brydges* case in 1990,[35] *Swain* in 1991,[36] and *Bain* in 1992.[37]

In *Brydges* the Supreme Court of Canada decided that the police had to do more than tell an accused that he or she had the right to counsel; they also had to say that legal aid was available. Without an extensive discussion of prospective lawmaking, Lamer C.J. stated for the Court: 'Before concluding, it is my view that in light of the imposition of the additional duty on the police as part of the information component of the s.10(b) caution, a transition period is appropriate. This transition period is needed to enable the police to properly discharge their new burden, more specifically to take into account the reality that police officers often use printed cards from which they read the caution given to detainees. In my view, a period of 30 days from the date of this judgment is sufficient time for the police forces to react, and to prepare new cautions.'[38]

Presumably this means that anyone already tried could not base an appeal on *Brydges*; nor could those awaiting trial or those arrested within the next thirty days after the *Brydges* decision. Any other result would undercut the thirty-day time period the Court gave the police. Note, however, that Brydges was able to take advantage of the new rule, in part as his reward for making new law.

Another case in which there was a transitional period is *Swain*, where the Supreme Court struck down the provision in the Code (section 542(2)) which provided that an accused found not guilty by reason of insanity is to be ordered to be kept in strict custody until the pleasure of the lieutenant-governor of the province is known. The Court held that the section would continue to be valid for a further six months, but in a modified form. Similarly, in *Bain*, the Court gave the Government six months to bring in new jury-selection procedures.

There are other techniques our courts use to make cases somewhat prospective only. One that has been used is to limit the change to cases decided after the Charter was enacted.[39] But because the Charter has now been in operation for almost ten years, limiting the effect of changes by this device does not have much effect. Another technique is to refuse to grant leave to appeal to persons who have already been through the appeal process or when the time for appeal has gone by. This time period is usually sufficiently short that this technique can significantly control the number of persons who can take advantage of a judgment. Finally, when the violation results in the exclusion of evidence the courts must determine under section 24(2) of the Charter whether 'the admission of it in the proceedings would bring the administration of justice into disrepute.' The fact that the police relied on the previous state of the law is a relevant consideration in admitting the evidence in applying s.24(2),[40] although it does not necessarily follow that the evidence will be admitted in these cases.[41]

If courts are going to continue to remake the criminal law, they must be prepared to give more thought to prospective lawmaking in their decision-making. A further approach is to develop the law through rule-making outside court cases, which would not only make the rules prospective but would also permit consultation on the draft rules before they are finalized.[42] The Supreme Court could, for example, supply model cautions for police forces and model charges to judges.

Another point that is worth remembering in weighing judicial and legislative lawmaking is that judicial lawmaking is not without financial cost: there is court time at all levels, the cost of government lawyers and legal aid, and so on. How much research by a law-reform commission could have been undertaken for the cost of, say, the perhaps twenty or thirty reverse-onus cases that have ended up with full argument in the Supreme Court of Canada?

Finally, I would mention the obvious and important point that parliamentarians are accountable to the electorate in ways that judges are not. Parliament and the executive branch can be faulted, of course, for not moving as quickly as they should have to reform the criminal law, but I believe they should have been given a greater opportunity to do so before the Supreme Court seized the initiative.

Let us look at a few Supreme Court of Canada cases.

Duarte

In *Duarte* (1990)[43] the Supreme Court of Canada, in my opinion, went much further than they should have in remaking the law with respect to consent wire-tapping. Parliament had enacted a very detailed and sophisticated scheme to control wire-tapping in 1970.[44] The legislation did not, however, require a warrant when either the originator of the private communication or the person intended by the originator to receive it consented to a wire-tap.[45] So, a police informer could, without a warrant, obtain evidence against a suspect by means of an electronic body pack. A person who was part of a plot to murder could make a deal with the police and record, at the request of the police, what his or her accomplices had said in person or on the telephone.

Moreover, the Law Reform Commission of Canada had produced a working paper on electronic surveillance in 1986 and approved of the exemption. The commission, relying in part on a report by the Australian Law Reform Commission on privacy, concluded that 'the law must be maintained essentially as it is now ... We believe that any attempt to regulate consent interceptions would be introducing an unnecessary complexity without any real gains in terms of accuracy of fact-finding or protection of legitimate privacy interests.'[46] It should also be noted that the United States Supreme Court[47] had upheld under the U.S. Constitution a similar exemption. Only Mr Justice Lamer would have upheld the exemption. All six other members of the Court sitting on the case held that a warrant was necessary. La Forest J., giving the judgment of the Court, expressed a very strong opinion that body packs should not be used without a warrant: 'if the state were free, at its sole discretion, to make permanent electronic recordings of our private communications, there would be no meaningful residuum to our lives free from surveillance.'[48]

The result is that warrants are now required for all wire-taps. But this raises a host of questions. Is a warrant required when the police wish to record obscene calls? Can statements by an accused to the police in a police station be secretly recorded? Can an undercover officer have his or her conversations with dangerous persons monitored by radio transmission to protect the officer's safety? Can Parliament change the warrant requirement so that a justice of the peace can give these types of warrants? Can it eliminate the requirement that 'other investigative methods have been tried and have failed?'[49] Will the addition of cases of consensual wire-taps to the statistical reports cloud and mask the extent of the more serious non-consensual taps?[50]

Hunter v. *Southam*

In *Hunter* v. *Southam* (1984)[51] the Supreme Court of Canada held that the 'search or seizure' section of the Charter, section 8, required a warrant. The Supreme Court of Canada in one of its first major Charter decision in the field of criminal law adopted the American law of search and seizure.[52] Section 8, stated Dickson J., 'requires a means of *preventing* unjustified searches before they happen, not simply of determining, after the fact, whether they ought to have occurred in the first place. This, in my view, can only be accomplished by a system of prior authorization, not one of *subsequent validation*.'[53] Surely this is not the *only* way of preventing unjustified searches. Will the Supreme Court of Canada take the same approach to *arrests* without a warrant and require prior authorization? I doubt it.[54]

The Law Reform Commission at about this time, following an extensive working paper on the subject,[55] produced a well-thought-out report on search and seizure.[56] They would also require 'as a general rule the principle that police powers of search and seizure in law enforcement should be authorized by judicial warrant.'[57] But they carefully specify the cases where a warrantless search is permitted. Many of these cases will probably be decided in the same way by the Supreme Court of Canada, but one cannot be sure until the case gets to the Supreme Court. The Law Reform Commission, for example, would allow a search without a warrant when a person has been arrested 'when the search is reasonably prudent in the circumstances.'[58] The Supreme Court in *Cloutier* v. *Langlois* (1990)[59] also permits a frisk search on arrest where it is done 'for a valid objective in pursuit of the ends of criminal justice, such as the discovery of an object that may be a threat to the safety of the police, the accused or the public, or that may facilitate escape or act as evidence against the accused.'[60] The Law Reform Commission specifically says that a valid search without warrant would also include 'the spaces within the person's reach at the time of the arrest.'[61] No doubt the Supreme Court would arrive at a similar result. And the Law Reform Commission permits a 'plain view' search: 'where a peace officer in the course of a lawful search or otherwise lawfully situated discovers objects of seizure in plain view, he may seize them without a warrant.'[62] Will the Supreme Court establish a similar rule? Probably,[63] but we will have to wait and see. Further, the Law Reform Commission permits the police to search without a warrant a vehicle when the officer 'believes on reasonable grounds that: (i) an object of seizure is to be found in the vehicle; and (ii) the delay necessary to obtain a warrant would result in the loss or destruction of the object of seizure.'[64] Again, will the Supreme Court accept this rule?

It is understandable that the Supreme Court entered the field to give some content to the words 'unreasonable search and seizure.' But surely it would have been better for Parliament to have enacted the rules, which could have covered a range of problems, and could at the same time have added some safeguards that a court might not. For example, the Law Reform Commission proposed that a post-seizure report be prepared and given when a search has been conducted without a warrant.[65]

Hunter v. *Southam* may have been too ambitious. It tried to cover too much of the law. Note the distinctions the court made in later cases, distinguishing in *Thomson Newspapers* (1990)[66] between searches and seizures and in *McKinlay Transport* (1990)[67] suggesting that seizures in the quasi-criminal context may require a lesser standard than set out in *Hunter* v. *Southam*.

When Parliament enacts the rules, they can be changed. Even the warrant requirement recommended by the Law Reform Commission could have been modified, which now cannot easily be done after *Hunter* v. *Southam*. Further studies[68] might have shown, for example, that having a justice of the peace – a relatively minor official – issue a warrant is not a great safeguard to our liberty and that scrutiny after the event by someone like an ombudsman or by the court when evidence is introduced might have been a better safeguard. Having a justice of the peace issue a warrant tends to insulate the officer from responsibility and the court from determining whether there were reasonable and probable grounds for the search. Will the Supreme Court of Canada follow *U.S.* v. *Leon* (1984)[69] where it was held that 'evidence seized unreasonably but in reasonable reliance on a judicial warrant should not be excluded'?

The Court has foreclosed experimentation on techniques of compliance by seizing on the warrant requirement as the key. Perhaps it would be better for the Court to do as the U.S. Supreme Court does under the 14th Amendment and impose standards unless other effective ones are devised to handle the matter. So, for example, in *Miranda* v. *Arizona* (1966)[70] the Court stated that 'unless other fully effective means are devised to inform accused persons of their right of silence and to assure a continuous opportunity to exercise it, the following measures are required.'[71] The *Miranda* rules are then set out. Some potential experimentation is, therefore, left to the states to meet the *Miranda* requirement. The Supreme Court of Canada could have taken a similar approach to 'unreasonable search or seizure.'

Hebert

The Supreme Court of Canada in *Hebert* (1990)[72] found that the right to silence is a principle of fundamental justice under section 7 of the Charter. The Court adopted what Cory J.A. had stated in the Ontario Court of Appeal in *Woolley* (1988): 'The right to remain silent is a well-settled principle that has for generations been part of the basic tenets of our law.'[73] I have no complaint about the actual decisions in those cases, but wonder whether a right to silence should be given so definite and expansive a meaning as the Supreme Court found. In England, for example, a judge (although not counsel) is entitled to comment on the failure of the accused to enter the witness box.[74] Would that now be possible in Canada? It is of course possible that, if such a rule were proposed for Canada and the Supreme Court wished to uphold it, they could confine *Hebert* to the pretrial stage.

I think that a proposal that the Law Reform Commission tentatively made in the early 1970s makes good sense, but now probably is not possible because of *Hebert*. In their proposal, *all* statements made by an accused to the police would be excluded. Only statements made to an independent, objective person out of the control of the police would be admitted. As a quid pro quo the trier of fact would be entitled to know whether the accused declined to make a statement. The proposal did not get very far because the defence bar hated it as much as the police did. But that may have been a positive sign that it was a good idea. I still think it would be an improvement on the present system, but would be hard to get by the present interpretation of the Charter.

The Law Reform Commission has a report on *Questioning Suspects* (1984)[75] that arrived at the same conclusions as the Supreme Court. They would require the police to warn the person that 'you have a right to remain silent and you are free to exercise that right at any time.' They provide a rule similar to the majority in *Hebert* by saying that a warning is not required 'where the police officer is acting under cover and the suspect is not under arrest or detention.'

Note that in their working paper on questioning suspects the Law Reform Commission had recommended that questioning in police stations and prisons 'be electronically recorded wherever feasible.'[76] They departed from this sound recommendation in their Report on the same subject, although they stated: 'we remain convinced that such recordings will provide the best possible means of reconstructing and thus accounting for the questioning of a suspect.'[77] They said that they saw 'no need to legislate at this time the means of obtaining that evidence.' But they went on to state: 'If in our opinion the police are not providing the courts with the best possible record of questioning, we may in the future recommend that Parliament demand an improvement in the quality of evidence by enacting a requirement for electronic recording.'

Section 7 has been given a very expanded meaning, more expanded than I believe the drafters contemplated. The key case was, of course, the *B.C. Motor Vehicle* case in 1985,[78] taking us into substantive, and not just procedural, areas. It has remade the law of murder,[79] struck down the abortion law,[80] introduced a doctrine against vagueness,[81] required pre-trial disclosure,[82] and, as just noted, has introduced an expanded rule against self-incrimination. At the same time, however, in the important *Irwin Toy* case in 1989,[83] it has limited the application of section 7 to real persons. Corporations need not apply. I wonder how the Supreme Court is going to deal in the future with vagueness and lack of disclosure in relation to statutes directed at corporations.

Askov

Note that the Law Reform Commission said that they may 'in the future' make a recommendation for electronic recordings of questioning by police. One wonders why that type of tentative, suggestive approach was not adopted in the well-known section 11(d) delay case of *Askov* (1990).[84] Again, I have no complaint that Askov had his case stayed. There was unreasonable delay in that case. I am concerned about the expansive nature of the judgment. Many turned Cory J.'s remark – 'a period of delay in a range of some six to eight months between committal and trial might be deemed to be outside the limit of what is reasonable' – into a statute. Did Cory J. intend that interpretation? We know that Mr Justice Cory himself expressed some extrajudicial surprise at the aftermath. In the subsequent Supreme Court of Canada case of *Morin*,[85] the Court modified its approach and upheld a delay of over fourteen months in an impaired-driving case.

Is this not a case where Parliament should have enacted speedy trial laws as was attempted without success in 1984?[86] Most American jurisdictions have time limits that, with good cause, can be departed from.[87] Setting fixed limits is the job of Parliament. Judges and courts are not equipped to do it. If this had been a bill declaring that six months was unreasonable, there would have been time to test the data and determine whether the period was a good one. Moreover, Parliament might not have said that a stay was the only remedy available, as the Supreme Court has done.[88] Perhaps such a dire judicial remedy is all right in the United States, where the period of delay held to be prohibited under the Constitution is very substantial before a stay will be granted. But to have a complete stay after six months gives the accused too great an advantage. There are other remedies. The judge could, for example, ensure that the accused is not kept in custody and could order the trial to be expedited. The delay could even be reflected in the penalty imposed. A comprehensive legislative scheme would secure compliance in advance by a whole series of intermediary events and orders, prospectively preventing delay long before the point of time was reached for the draconian retrospective stay of proceedings after the breach had already occurred.

The Ontario Court of Appeal had been more tentative in trying to get the government to supply greater resources to the administration of justice.[89] The Supreme Court should have continued the suggestive dialogue instead of coming down so hard without sufficient warning.[90] Perhaps this would have been a good place to use prospective lawmaking by saying that in future cases a certain period of delay after committal for trial will prima facie be deemed to be unreasonable.[91] At least, then, the prosecutors and the police could more easily have taken some steps to correct the situation. Still, it has to be acknowledged that the judgment has produced a major response by the government of Ontario to provide greater resources to the judicial system.[92]

Mack and *Barnes*

The final area that I will deal with is entrapment. Here, the Supreme Court of Canada, unlike in the other areas discussed in this paper, has not yet constitutionalized the law of entrapment. It handled the issue under the abuse-of-process doctrine developed in the *Jewitt* case.[93] A similar non-Charter approach to developing, for example, double-jeopardy standards should also be adopted.[94] In my view, the more that concepts can be handled by criminal-law doctrines outside the Charter the easier it will be for there to be a cooperative partnership between the courts and Parliament. Note that, while a wide right to disclosure before trial had been adopted by the Supreme Court in *M.H.C.* v. *The Queen* (1991)[95] through common-law principles without resort to the Charter, in *Stinchcombe* (1991)[96] the issue of disclosure was turned into a constitutional issue under section 7.

The problem with the recent Supreme Court of Canada entrapment cases of *Mack* (1988)[97] and *Barnes* (1991)[98] is that they are difficult cases to read and digest. I wonder how many police officials have read the judgments. Again, I am not complaining about the law contained in the cases. Chief Justice Lamer gets it about right on the facts of those cases. This was a proper judicial development of the law. The combining of an objective and a subjective approach is, in my opinion, the right approach.

But surely it would now be better to have a legislative solution[99] and to adopt the view of the Royal Commission on the RCMP (the McDonald Commission), which provided a simple test that would be put to the jury in each case: 'The accused should be acquitted if it is established that the conduct of a member or agent of a police force in instigating the crime has gone substantially beyond what is justifiable having regard to all the circumstances, including the nature of the crime, whether the accused had a pre-existing intent, and the nature and extent of the involvement of the police.'[100]

Chief Justice Lamer leaves the issue to the judge to be dealt with as a question of law. I personally think it would be better to leave it to the triers of fact with a general test for them to follow. When it is a question of law, then one has to analyse earlier cases and draw fine distinctions. The law once did this with negligence in the civil law. By treating negligence as a question of law – we called it proximate cause – the law attempted to draw distinctions that were almost impossible to make. We now have a general test for negligence in tort law and leave it to the trier of fact to apply the law to the facts. Perhaps one reason why Lamer C.J. wanted entrapment dealt with as a legal exemption is because the onus could be placed on the accused, something that would be difficult for the Court to require in other cases.[101]

CONCLUSION

My overall conclusion is that the Supreme Court of Canada should have been somewhat more deferential to the legislative process in terms of criminal-law reform. They could have nudged, threatened, and suggested more than they have done. They should have established more of a dialogue with Parliament and the Law Reform Commission of Canada. By trying to remake too much of the law themselves they have taken some of the impetus for reform away from Parliament, and by constitutionalizing much of the criminal law they have made legislative criminal-law reform more difficult.

But Parliament and the late Law Reform Commission of Canada can be equally, if not more strongly, criticized for not moving as quickly as they should have in bringing forward reform legislation. There was a vacuum created that many wanted to see filled, and at the same time many did not have great confidence that Parliament would move to enact a new Criminal Code.

The hearings that are taking place on the general part of the code before the parliamentary subcommittee are therefore very important. If they recommend that the efforts to produce a code continue and if there is a clear demonstration by the Government that reform is going to take place legislatively, the Supreme Court might be more content to let Parliament be primarily in charge of the continuing reform of the criminal law. This is particularly so now that the Supreme Court of Canada has taken many of the blatantly rough edges off the criminal law. It is time for Parliament to take back the major initiative for criminal-law reform.

NOTES

I would like to thank my colleagues Michael Code, Kent Roach, Robert Sharpe, and Stephen Waddams for their very helpful comments on an earlier draft of the paper. The present version was completed in February 1993. It is a somewhat revised version of the paper originally presented in October 1991.

1 R.S.C. 1970, c. 23.
2 Parliament, House of Commons, *Debates: Official Report* (Ottawa: Queen's Printer, 23 Feb. 1970), 3963.
3 Law Reform Commission of Canada, *First Research Program of the Law Reform Commission of Canada* (Ottawa: Information Canada, March 1972), 14.
4 See Law Reform Commission of Canada, *Tenth Annual Report 1980–81* (Ottawa: Minister of Supply and Services 1982), 13.
5 See Parliament, *Minutes of Proceedings and Evidence of the Sub-Committee of the Standing Committee on Justice and the Solicitor General on the Recodification of the General Part of the Criminal Code* (Ottawa: Minister of Supply and Services, 12 May 1992).
6 (Ottawa: 1969), 430–1.
7 Canadian Sentencing Commission, *Sentencing Reform: A Canadian Approach* (Ottawa: Minister of Supply and Services 1987), 437.
8 M.L. Friedland, 'Codification in the Commonwealth: Earlier Efforts,' *Criminal Law Forum* 2 (1990): 145; 'R.S. Wright's Model Criminal Code: A Forgotten Chapter in the History of the Criminal Law,' in M.L. Friedland, *A Century of Criminal Justice: Perspectives on the Development of Canadian Law* (Toronto: Carswell 1984), 1 [hereinafter *A Century of Criminal Justice*].
9 See, generally, R. Schwartz, 'Reform of the Federal Criminal Laws,' *Duke Law Journal* 1977, 171; R. Drinan, M.E. Ward, and D.W. Beier, 'The Federal Criminal Code: The Houses Are Divided,' *American Criminal Law Review* 18 (1981): 509; M. Gainer, 'Report to the Attorney General on Federal Criminal Code Reform,' *Criminal Law Forum* 1 (1989): 99.
10 See Law Commission, *Report 15: Third Annual Report, 1967–68* (1968).

11 'R.S. Wright's Model Criminal Code,' 44.
12 Set out in Part I of the *Constitution Act, 1982*, being Schedule B of the *Canada Act 1982* (U.K.), 1982, c. 11.
13 Section 24 was designed to create a position somewhere midway between the American exclusionary rule and the former Anglo-Canadian rule admitting illegally obtained evidence. The courts have, however, taken a relatively straightforward test and made it exceedingly complex and in some respects more exclusionary than the American rule; see R. Harvie and H. Foster, 'Different Drummers, Different Drums: The Supreme Court of Canada, American Jurisprudence and the Continuing Revision of Criminal Law under the Charter,' *Ottawa Law Review* 24 (1992): 39, at 49ff., and 61.
14 S.C. 1960, c. 44.
15 Friedland, 'Criminal Justice and the Charter,' in *A Century of Criminal Justice*, 205.
16 I am indebted to Alan Baldachin, now in his third year in the Faculty of Law, for his assistance with this task.
17 Criminal Procedure Law, Laws of 1970, Chapter 996.
18 *R.* v. *Swain* (1991), 63 C.C.C. (3d) 481 (S.C.C.).
19 *R.* v. *Mills* (1986), 26 C.C.C. (3d) 481 (S.C.C.).
20 Law Reform Commission of Canada, *Report 32: Our Criminal Procedure* (Ottawa: Law Reform Commission of Canada 1988), 25.
21 Law Reform Commission of Canada, *Report 23: Questioning Suspects* (Ottawa: Law Reform Commission of Canada 1984), 9 [hereinafter *Report 23*].
22 *Shaping Canada's Future Together* (Ottawa: Minister of Supply and Services 1991), 4.
23 See, generally, M.L. Friedland, 'Pressure Groups and the Development of the Criminal Law,' in *A Century of Criminal Justice*, 67.
24 *R.* v. *Duarte* (1990), 53 C.C.C. (3d) 1 (S.C.C.).
25 *R.* v. *Hebert* (1990), 57 C.C.C. (3d) 1 (S.C.C.).
26 *R.* v. *Askov* (1990), 59 C.C.C. (3d) 449 (S.C.C.).
27 *R.* v. *Beare* (1988), 45 C.C.C. (3d) 57 (S.C.C.).
28 See n. 26, above, at 489–90.
29 See M.A. Code, *Trial Within a Reasonable Time* (Toronto: Carswell 1992).
30 See, generally, M.L. Friedland, 'Prospective and Retrospective Judicial Lawmaking,' *University of Toronto Law Journal* 24 (1974): 170.
31 (1963), 372 U.S. 335.
32 See *Stovall* v. *Denno* (1967), 388 U.S. 293, interpreting the retroactive effect of *U.S.* v. *Wade* (1967), 388 U.S. 218 and *Gilbert* v. *California* (1967), 388 U.S. 263.
33 (1966), 384 U.S. 436.

34 (1961), 367 U.S. 643.
35 *R.* v. *Brydges* (1990), 53 C.C.C. (3d) 330 (S.C.C.). See also *Reference Re Language Rights Under the Manitoba Act, 1870*, [1985] S.C.R. 721, allowing a transition period for translation, re-enactment, printing, and publishing of previously unilingual legislation.
36 See n. 18, above.
37 (1992), 69 C.C.C. (3d) 481.
38 *Brydges*, 351.
39 *R.* v. *Stevens* (1988), 41 C.C.C. (3d) 193 (S.C.C.).
40 See, e.g., *Duarte* (n. 24, above); *R.* v. *Hamill* (1987), 33 C.C.C. (3d) 110 (S.C.C.).
41 See *R.* v. *Therens* (1985), 18 C.C.C. (3d) 481 (S.C.C.); *Hebert* (n. 25, above); *Brydges* (n. 35).
42 See Friedland, 'Prospective and Retrospective Judicial Lawmaking,' 185–90.
43 See n. 24, above.
44 *Protection of Privacy Act*, S.C. 1973–74, c.50, s.2 (now Part VI of the *Criminal Code*).
45 *Criminal Code*, R.S.C. 1985, c. C-46, s. 184 (2)(a).
46 Law Reform Commission of Canada, *Electronic Surveillance* (Working Paper 47) (Ottawa: Law Reform Commission of Canada 1986), 27–8.
47 *U.S.* v. *White* (1971), 401 U.S. 743.
48 *Duarte*, at 11.
49 *Criminal Code*, s. 185 (1)(h).
50 A bill has recently been introduced in Parliament to deal with some of these questions; see Toronto *Globe and Mail*, 12 Dec. 1992.
51 (1984), 14 C.C.C. (3d) 97 (S.C.C.).
52 See the criticism of this approach in D.V. Macdougall, 'Canadian Legal Identity and American Influences,' *Law Society Gazette* 25 (1991): 107.
53 *Southam*, at 109.
54 See, for example, *R.* v. *Storrey* (1990), 53 C.C.C. (3d) 316 (S.C.C.).
55 Law Reform Commission of Canada, *Police Powers: Search and Seizure in Criminal Law Enforcement* (Working Paper 30) (Ottawa: Law Reform Commission of Canada 1983).
56 Law Reform Commission of Canada, *Report 24: Search and Seizure* (Ottawa: Law Reform Commission of Canada 1984) [hereinafter *Report 24*].
57 Ibid., 9.
58 Ibid., 35, s. 19(1).
59 (1990), 53 C.C.C. (3d) 257 (S.C.C.).
60 Ibid., 278.
61 *Report 24*, 36, s. 19(2).

62 Ibid., 42, s. 25.
63 See *R.* v. *Mellenthin* (1992), 76 C.C.C. (3d) 481 (S.C.C.).
64 *Report 24*, 38, s. 22.
65 Ibid., 39, s. 23.
66 (1990), 54 C.C.C. (3d) 417 (S.C.C.).
67 *R.* v. *McKinlay Transport Ltd.* (1990), 55 C.C.C. (3d) 530 (S.C.C.).
68 See R.V. Ericson, *Making Crime: A Study of Detective Work* (Toronto: Butterworths 1981), 152. See also A. Doob, P. Baranek, and S. Addario, *Understanding Justices* (Toronto: Centre of Criminology 1991).
69 (1984), 468 U.S. 897.
70 (1966), 384 U.S. 436.
71 Ibid., at 444.
72 See n. 25, above.
73 *R.* v. *Woolley* (1988), 40 C.C.C. (3d) 531 at 539 (Ont. C.A.).
74 See R. Cross, *Cross on Evidence,* 7th ed. by R. Cross and C. Tapper (London: Butterworths 1990), 384.
75 *Report 23* (see n. 21, above).
76 Law Reform Commission of Canada, *Questioning Suspects* (Working Paper 32) (Ottawa: Law Reform Commission of Canada 1984), 58.
77 *Report 23*, 18.
78 *Reference Re Section 94(2) of the Motor Vehicle Act* (1985), 23 C.C.C. (3d) 289 (S.C.C.).
79 *R.* v. *Vaillancourt* (1987), 39 C.C.C. (3d) 118 (S.C.C.): *R.* v. *Martineau* (1990), 58 C.C.C. (3d) 353 (S.C.C.).
80 *Morgentaler, Smoling and Scott* v. *R.* (1988), 37 C.C.C. (3d) 449 (S.C.C).
81 *R.* v. *Morales* (1992), 77 C.C.C. (3d) 91 (S.C.C.); *R.* v. *Nova Scotia Pharmaceutical Society* (1992), 74 C.C.C. (3d) 289 (S.C.C.).
82 *R.* v. *Stinchcombe* (1991), 68 C.C.C. (3d) 1 (S.C.C.).
83 *Irwin Toy Ltd.* v. *Quebec (Attorney General),* [1989] 1 S.C.R. 927.
84 *Askov*, see n. 26, above.
85 *R.* v. *Morin* (1992), 71 C.C.C. (3d) 1 (S.C.C.).
86 Bill C-19, *Criminal Law Reform Act,* 1984, died on the order paper when Parliament was dissolved that year. See generally, M. Code, 'A Comparative Study of the Impact of Constitutional Instruments on the American and Canadian Criminal Justice Systems: Procedure Governing Constitutional Hearings and Trial Within a Reasonable Time,' LL.M. thesis, University of Toronto, 1991.
87 See, generally, Code, *Trial Within a Reasonable Time.*
88 *Re Rahey and The Queen* (1987), 33 C.C.C. (3d) 289 (S.C.C).
89 Grange J.A. stated for the Ontario Court of Appeal in *R.* v. *Askov* (1987), 37 C.C.C. (3d) 289 at 297 (Ont. C.A.): 'Inadequacy of facilities ... probably is to be

weighed in the balance against the Crown, perhaps not quite so much now as later after governments have been given the opportunity to take corrective measures.'

90 Lamer J. had stated in *Mills* (see n. 19, above), at 550, that '[t]here must ... be some limit to which inadequate resources can be used to excuse delay and impair the interest of the individual.' See also pp. 561–2 providing for a transitional period. However, this was in a dissenting judgment. Cory J. refers to Lamer J.'s views on a transitional period in *Askov* (n. 26, above), at 490–1, stating '[t]his case has long since passed by that cut-off point.' There is another reference to a transitional period at 483 with reference to institutional delays: 'There may be a transitional period to allow for a temporary period of lenient treatment or systemic delay.' This sentence is lost, however, in Cory's lengthy judgment and is undermined by his later discussion at 490–1.

91 Note that in the post-*Askov* case of *R.* v. *G.C.M.* (1991), 65 C.C.C. (3d) 232 (Ont. C.A.), dealing with delay with respect to young offenders, the Ontario Court of Appeal set out guidelines for the speedy trial of young offenders and stated at 246: 'These are administrative guidelines only. They should be applied prospectively. Cases in the system should be exposed to less rigorous scrutiny on the basis of a careful balancing of the factors referred to in *Askov*.'

92 See Toronto *Globe and Mail*, 9 Oct. 1991, A9.

93 *R.* v. *Jewitt* (1985), 21 C.C.C. (3d) 7 (S.C.C.).

94 See Law Reform Commission of Canada, *Double Jeopardy, Pleas and Verdicts* (Working Paper 63) (Ottawa: Law Reform Commission of Canada 1991).

95 *M.H.C.* v. *The Queen* (1991), 63 C.C.C. (3d) 385 (S.C.C.).

96 *Stinchcombe*, n. 82, above.

97 *R.* v. *Mack* (1988), 44 C.C.C. (3d) 513 (S.C.C.).

98 *R.* v. *Barnes* (1991), 63 C.C.C. (3d) 1 (S.C.C.).

99 See, generally, M.L. Friedland, 'Controlling Entrapment,' in *A Century of Criminal Justice*, 171.

100 Commission of Inquiry Concerning Certain Activities of the Royal Canadian Mounted Police, *Freedom and Security Under the Law* (Ottawa: The Commission of Inquiry 1981) (Chair: D.C. McDonald), 1053.

101 See, for example, *R.* v. *Oakes* (1986), 24 C.C.C. (3d) 321 (S.C.C.).

PART THREE: POLICE ORGANIZATION AND MINORITY REPRESENTATION

7

Policing Aboriginal Peoples: The Challenge of Change

CURT TAYLOR GRIFFITHS

Recent years have witnessed an increasing focus of attention on Aboriginal peoples and the Canadian criminal-justice system. Aboriginal political and community leaders have expressed concern over the overrepresentation of Aboriginal persons at all stages of the criminal-justice system from arrest to incarceration in many jurisdictions. A growing number of research studies, task forces, and commissions of inquiry have documented the conflict that Aboriginal peoples often experience with the law. Federal, provincial, and territorial governments have been under mounting pressure to address what are perceived to be serious inequities in the administration of justice to Aboriginal people and to explore ways to devolve the delivery of justice services to Aboriginal bands and communities.

The delivery of police services has occupied a predominant place in most investigations of Aboriginal peoples and the administration of justice, and a considerable amount of criticism has been directed towards the RCMP, provincial, and municipal police forces. A royal commission inquiry (Hickman 1989) into the wrongful conviction and incarceration of Donald Marshall, a Micmac from Nova Scotia, placed a considerable portion of the blame on the police (see Harris 1986), as did the investigation into the shooting of J.J. Harper, an Aboriginal man, by a City of Winnipeg police officer (Hamilton and Sinclair 1991b).

Discussions and debates about Aboriginal policing are taking place against a backdrop of the political, cultural, and community revitalization of Aboriginal peoples (Nielsen 1992). As a recent report of the Corrections Service Division in the Northwest Territories (1991: 14) noted: 'local control of justice related matters is often perceived by national and community leaders as the jewel in the self-determination crown.' There has also been an escalation in the number and severity of confrontations between government authorities (generally represented by the police) and Aboriginal groups, including the crisis at Oka, Quebec, and the blockades of logging roads in British Columbia in an attempt to halt clear-cutting on disputed lands (see York and Pindera 1991; Goddard 1991).

However, contradictory positions are often adopted by Aboriginal communities in terms of desiring more resources from the existing justice system, such as more police officers, more frequent visits by the circuit courts, and more accessibility to legal services, while at the same time seeking more localized programs and services. As a recent report of the Government of the Northwest Territories (1991: 6) noted: 'This is a society in transition, and one of the manifestations of that are what appear to be contradictory demands. More RCMP and better access to lawyers are wanted, at the same time as the authority of the Canadian criminal justice system, and the basis for Canadian laws, are questioned. This is a natural consequence of a system having been imposed and administered by outsiders to the community for most of the lifetime of most of those alive today.'

As Aboriginal peoples seek greater control over their affairs in the quest for self-determination, it is likely that there will be increasing pressures on the federal and provincial/territorial governments to transfer the delivery of justice services, including policing, to Aboriginal bands and communities. This paper reviews several of the issues surrounding police-Aboriginal relations, the initiatives undertaken by police organizations in an attempt to improve the delivery of police services to Aboriginal communities, and the development of Aboriginal-controlled police services. Key issues confronting both police organizations and Aboriginal bands and communities are identified and addressed.

POLICING ABORIGINAL PEOPLES: THE HISTORICAL AND CONTEMPORARY CONTEXT

Any discussion of Aboriginal peoples and the police must consider the subordinate political and socio-economic position of Aboriginal people in Canadian society, a consequence of their colonization by Europeans and of Canadian government policies that have exerted control over virtually every aspect of Aboriginal life (Berger 1991; Cole and Chaikin 1990; Dickason 1992; Dyck 1991). In the process of colonization, the legitimacy of Aboriginal cultural practices, including traditional methods of social control, was rejected and replaced by Euro-Canadian law (see Harring 1989; Morse 1983; Moyles 1989).

A predominant role in the colonization of Aboriginal peoples was played by the RCMP, who were utilized as an instrument of national policy to establish sovereignty over vast areas in the western and northern regions of the country (see MacLeod 1976a, 1976b; Morrison 1974, 1985; Stone 1979, 1989). Loree (1985: 1) notes that 'the R.C.M.P., in particular, have long been among the most, if not *the* most, visible and obviously powerful manifestation of a dominant Euro-Canadian society, its institutions, customs, and laws.'

A consistent finding of many commissions of inquiry and research studies over the past two decades is that the relations between the police and Aboriginal peoples, in rural and urban areas, are often characterized by mutual hostility and distrust (Sunahara 1992). Depicting police-Aboriginal relations in Manitoba as 'seriously deficient,' the Manitoba Aboriginal Justice Inquiry (Hamilton and Sinclair 1991a: 610) noted: 'There are strong feelings of mistrust, if not hatred, directed towards RCMP members in some areas. Many officers are seen as being arbitrary and antagonistic toward Aboriginal people.'

There are a number of reasons why these patterns of interaction occur, including the manner in which police services are delivered and the perceptions that Aboriginal people have of the criminal-justice system generally and police officers in particular. Loree (1985: 8) notes that police officers in Aboriginal communities are 'a readily available and highly visible symbol of government failures, misunderstandings and broken promises.' Loree further argues that in policing Aboriginal communities 'the police can often find themselves caught in a three jawed vice: between the political, economic, and social realities of Native communities, an external society's concept of law and law enforcement, and the needs and demands of the police organization *per se*' (80).

This role conflict is often compounded by the fact that many police officers have little knowledge of the culture and community being policed. Individual officers may enter communities unprepared by their respective organizations to serve the needs of residents adequately. In a survey of RCMP members, Loree (1985) found that a significant number described themselves as having only a 'fair' level of general knowledge about Aboriginal peoples. Most of the information the officers did have was acquired *after* arriving in the community. This lack of understanding may contribute to a lack of communication and to misunderstandings between the police and Aboriginal residents. Among the findings of an inquiry into policing the Blood Tribe in Alberta (Rolf 1991) was that, while RCMP officers had not demonstrated any *conscious* bias in their interactions with band members, their behaviour was often *perceived* as insensitive and disrespectful.

From a survey of non-Aboriginal RCMP line-level personnel, Head (1989: 87) found 'some rather remarkable misunderstandings of the Treaty Rights, the hunting rights and the Income Tax exemptions that exist for some Native

Canadians.' Head (1989: 88) attributed much of this to the fact that only four hours of recruit training at the RCMP Depot was allotted to materials on Aboriginal peoples and that many senior training personnel 'have not had the opportunity to serve among Native Canadians or if they did have that opportunity, it is so long in the past that the experience is now quite worthless.'

Once posted to a community, officers are generally required by organizational policy to apply an incident-driven, crime-control model of policing rather than a community-policing model that would emphasize crime prevention and the provision of community-oriented policing services. A major complaint of Aboriginal persons in several Yukon communities surveyed by Parnell (1979) was that the crime-control, enforcement orientation of police officers was inappropriate for addressing community needs and was not conducive to the development of positive police-community relations.

Among Parnell's (1979: 42) recommendations were that there be a change in the criteria for evaluating and promoting RCMP officers, particularly officers policing northern communities, and that the criteria 'should involve more stress on qualities favouring education and communication skills and the ability to develop positive working relationships with the public.' The transfer policy of the RCMP, which results in officers being shifted between postings as often as once every two or three years, was also found to inhibit the development and maintenance of positive police-community relations.

There is also evidence that some police officers hold stereotypical and racist views of Aboriginal peoples. In its investigation into the circumstances surrounding the shooting death of J.J. Harper by a City of Winnipeg police officer, and the subsequent mishandling of the investigation by the department, the Manitoba Aboriginal Justice Inquiry (Hamilton and Sinclair 1991b: 93) concluded that 'racism played a part in the shooting death of J.J. Harper and the events that followed.'

Compounding the difficulties that police officers experience is a lack of information among many Aboriginal peoples about their legal rights and about the criminal-justice system. Testimony presented to the Manitoba Aboriginal Justice Inquiry (Hamilton and Sinclair 1991a: 610) indicated that, because of difficulties with the English language, many Aboriginal accused did not understand their rights and often admitted guilt so as to 'get out and away from a frightening situation they do not understand.'

Caution should be exercised in extrapolating the findings of a task force or commission of inquiry carried out in one jurisdiction to all regions of the country. There have been few field research studies on police-Aboriginal relations that would provide data on the activities of police officers in Aboriginal communities, the patterns of police-Aboriginal interaction, and on the perceptions of both police officers and community residents about the state of Aboriginal-police relations. Among the small number that have been carried out are a study of Aboriginal-police relations in the Yukon, conducted over a decade ago by Parnell (1979), and two, more recent investigations, one in Cree communities in Quebec (LaPrairie 1991) and the other in the Baffin Region, NWT (Griffiths et al. 1992). At present, there are insufficient research data to ascertain fully the factors that contribute to poor, as well as positive, police-Aboriginal relations, the relevance and effectiveness of various policing 'styles' in Aboriginal communities, and the perceptions of both the police and the policed as to the remedies required to improve police-community relations.

It is also important to note that discussions have generally focused on the delivery of policing services to Aboriginal reserves. Little attention has been given to the issues surrounding policing and Aboriginal peoples in urban centres. The investigation by the Manitoba Aboriginal Justice Inquiry (Hamilton and Sinclair 1991b) into the death of J.J. Harper in Winnipeg served to highlight the conflict that often surrounds police-Aboriginal relations in urban areas. Urban police forces have been singularly unsuccessful in recruiting Aboriginal members, although some initiatives have been undertaken to improve relations between the police and the Aboriginal community (see Griffiths and Verdun-Jones 1993)

THE CHALLENGES OF THE ABORIGINAL POLICING ENVIRONMENT

The delivery of policing services to Aboriginal peoples occurs in a diversity of settings, ranging from the southern, urban centres of Vancouver and Winnipeg, to remote communities in the northern portions of the provinces and the territories. Many of the communities in which policing services are delivered are experiencing pervasive poverty, high rates of unemployment and reliance upon public assistance, high death rates from accidents and violence, and other manifestations of the breakdown of cultures, communities and families (see Canada 1989; Krotz 1990; Shkilnyk 1985; Wolff 1991; York 1990).

Several investigators have examined the patterns of crime in Aboriginal communities (see Auger et al. 1992; LaPrairie 1991; Wood 1992). There have also been several research studies which have examined the attributes of Aboriginal persons who become involved in the criminal-justice system (See McCaskill 1985; Moyer et al. 1985). The most extensive materials on Aboriginal crime and the involvement of Aboriginal people in the criminal-justice system have been have been gathered by several task forces and commissions of inquiry (see Hamilton and Sinclair 1991a, 1991b; Linn 1992a,

1992b; Rolf 1991). These studies have produced valuable insights into the nature and extent of Aboriginal crime that have direct implications for the delivery of policing services.

Taken together, these materials suggest several *general* attributes of crime in Aboriginal communities:

1 *Many Aboriginal communities are afflicted by high rates of violent and property crime and other forms of 'trouble,' including alcohol and drug abuse, and suicide.* Even allowing for the inaccuracy of official statistics, the crime rate among Aboriginal peoples in many jurisdictions is several times that of non-Aboriginals. The violent crime rate for Aboriginal bands, for example, is three and one-half times that of the national rate. In Saskatchewan, violent crime made up 25 per cent of all Criminal Code offences committed on the reserves, while the figure was less than 10 per cent for other communities in the province (Wolff 1991).

2 *In many Aboriginal communities, there are high rates of violence and abuse directed towards women and children.* Materials presented to the Manitoba Aboriginal Justice Inquiry (Hamilton and Sinclair 1991a) suggested that one in three Aboriginal women in that province had been abused by their partners, leading the commissioners to conclude that 'Violence and abuse in Aboriginal communities has reached epidemic proportions' (481).

3 *There is often considerable variation in the patterns of crime across Aboriginal communities, even within the same region.* The variability in crime across Aboriginal communities has been documented in studies conducted in Nishnawbe-Aski communities in Ontario (Auger et al. 1992), in northern Quebec (LaPrairie 1991), and in the Eastern Arctic (Wood 1992). Among the factors that may be related to the crime rate are the enforcement practices of the police, the extent to which community residents and crime victims report offences, and the attributes of individual communities, including their leadership, the persistence of culture and traditions, and the degree to which the community has assumed responsibility for addressing its problems.

It may be unrealistic to expect that any criminal-justice function, whether government-sponsored or Aboriginal-controlled, can effectively address the myriad of difficulties that afflict many Aboriginal communities. Crime and other types of trouble, including suicides, alcohol and solvent abuse, and violence, are, in many instances, symptoms of much deeper problems that have their roots in the historical and contemporary circumstances of communities. As LaPrairie (1992: 56) notes, 'Substantive community problems ... must be overcome before real progress is made in reducing the numbers of Aboriginal people involved in the criminal justice, child welfare and youth justice systems.'

In considering Aboriginal crime, however, it is important that a focus on community attributes not obscure the responsibility of community residents for their behaviour. McCaskill (1985: 62) has argued: 'For some Native offenders being Native may be almost irrelevant to their criminal activity.' And Benson (1991: 42–3), in a discussion of crime-prevention strategies for Aboriginal communities, states: 'Although many current social problems may result from the influences of non-Aboriginal culture and historical events, it would be wrong to suggest that these are the cause of all criminal activity of Aboriginal people. This is supported by views in most Aboriginal communities which consider anti-social behaviour (crime) as a choice made by individuals and that the individual and not society are responsible for their actions.' It is against this backdrop that the development of government-sponsored and Aboriginal-controlled policing services must be considered.

POLICE ORGANIZATIONS IN A TIME OF CHANGE

Despite an increase in the number of Aboriginal-controlled police services (to be discussed below), it is likely that the RCMP, the two provincial police forces, and municipally operated police agencies will continue to be involved in policing Aboriginal peoples, even if such contact is restricted to off-reserve and urban areas. This likelihood requires a consideration of the initiatives that have been undertaken by police forces in an attempt to improve the delivery of policing services to Aboriginal people. To understand the response of Canadian police organizations to the challenges presented by Aboriginal policing, it is necessary to consider, albeit briefly, how police forces have typically reacted to critical events arising in their jurisdictions.

The path of development of systems of criminal justice has been one of an increasing centralization of power in both the policy-making and program-delivery areas. It has also, many would argue, been one of rising costs, decreasing effectiveness in crime prevention and control, and an increasing alienation of communities and their citizens from the criminal-justice system (Griffiths 1988). Police organizations have also exhibited a reluctance to significantly alter their organizational structure and the way in which policing services are delivered, even when confronted by changes in the larger socio-political environment.

The multicultural fabric of Canadian society is widely acknowledged to be one of the greatest challenges facing police organizations, and it would seem that the principles of community policing would provide a model for improving the delivery of police services in rural and urban areas of the country (Law Reform Commission of Canada 1991). Yet the conflicts that continue to exist between cultural and ethnic minorities (including Aboriginal peoples) and the police suggest that the full potential of community-based policing has not yet been realized.

Police organizations have steadfastly maintained ownership over the setting of policing priorities and the manner in which resources and personnel are allocated (Hastings and Melchers 1990). It has only been within the past decade or so that the police (to a much greater extent than their judicial and corrections counterparts) have made a deliberate effort to increase public awareness and involvement in crime-prevention initiatives and the apprehension of offenders.

Evaluative research, however, has failed to confirm the viability of 'community policing' initiatives such as Crime Stoppers, Neighborhood Watch, and Operation Identification (see Rosenbaum 1986, 1987; Carriere 1987). The actual role of the community in the delivery of police services has remained vague and undefined. Public participation has generally been limited to crime-prevention activities, with little or no provision for increasing citizen involvement in other facets of policing, including determining priorities for allocating resources or evaluating police effectiveness.

The experience to date suggests that it is not sufficient merely to append community-oriented programs onto the traditional police organizational structure. There was a similar response of policing organizations to pressures to address the issues surrounding the delivery of police services to Aboriginal peoples and, as the following discussion will reveal, it created additional difficulties for both the police and Aboriginal peoples.

RESPONDING TO THE CHALLENGE: GOVERNMENT-SPONSORED ABORIGINAL POLICING PROGRAMS

The development of Aboriginal policing programs by the RCMP and the provincial police forces was strongly influenced by the reluctance of the federal government to allow the creation of autonomous, Aboriginal-controlled police forces. Several early reports (Canadian Corrections Association 1967; Task Force on Policing on Reserves 1973) recommended the creation of an Aboriginal policing function *within* existing provincial police forces. The RCMP subsequently established the Indian Special Constable program. Similar initiatives were undertaken by the provincial police in Ontario and Quebec. Aboriginal persons were recruited and trained by the RCMP, OPP, and the QPF and deployed to detachments to assist in policing Aboriginal communities and reserves.

The RCMP Indian Special Constable program was terminated in 1990, having experienced numerous operational difficulties, including (1) a lack of input from Aboriginal communities into the recruitment and deployment of ISCs; (2) the failure of the RCMP to identify clearly the role of the ISCs, which resulted in uncertainty among ISCs and wide discrepancies between individual detachments in how ISCs were utilized; and (3) a reluctance on the part of many Aboriginal people to become, or remain, ISCs owing to hostility from the community and the social isolation that they and their families experienced (Griffiths and Yerbury 1984). In 1990, the RCMP ISC program was replaced by the Aboriginal Constable Development Program, which is designed to increase the number of Aboriginal persons eligible to become regular RCMP members (see Jarvis 1992a). In 1992, the First Nations Policing program operated by the Ontario Provincial Police was transferred to Aboriginal control under a self-government agreement.

There is in the failure of the RCMP ISC program a number of lessons that should guide future Aboriginal policing policy. First, the 'solution' to the problems surrounding Aboriginal relations with the police will not be found in inserting an Aboriginal police component into the organizational structure. Second, it is critical that Aboriginal communities be directly involved in the development and implementation of Aboriginal policing policies. In developing Aboriginal policing policy, little attention was given to the cultural and political diversity among Canada's Aboriginal peoples. Rather, generic 'Aboriginal' programs were created with little consultation with Aboriginal leaders and communities. As Head (1989: 59) notes: 'The theme "Understanding Through Communication" has often been cited as being the key-note to Native-Police relationships. Unfortunately, some of our personnel have taken this to mean that we (the Force) do the talking and they (the Natives) do the listening.'

Third, there may be limits to 'indigenizing' police forces that continue to operate under traditional police policies and practices (see Havemann 1989). And, finally, police officers may have only a limited impact on the high levels of crime and trouble that afflict many Aboriginal communities or on the numbers of Aboriginal persons becoming involved in the criminal justice system. Effective interventions will require the development of collaborative initiatives involving the community and other criminal-justice and social-service agencies and a focus on the etiology of crime and trouble, rather than merely formulating responses to it.

It appears that Canadian police organizations have acknowledged the failure of previous policies and altered their approach to Aboriginal policing. There is among police forces a greater willingness to consult and collaborate with Aboriginal communities and bands to improve the delivery of police services. The RCMP have established a national Aboriginal Advisory Committee, made up of Aboriginal elders, which meets twice a year to discuss and provide input into policing issues. In conjunction with the adoption of a community-based approach to policing, Community Advisory Committees have been established in the majority of communities policed by RCMP detachments.

The new 'attitude' of the RCMP is reflected in a number of initiatives (see Benson 1991; Jarvis 1992b). In the Yukon, for example, a Territorial/First Nations Committee on First Nations Policing has been created. The committee is composed of chiefs from four Yukon First Nations, representatives from the Yukon Department of Justice, and the community policing specialist from RCMP Division Headquarters in Whitehorse. The purpose of the committee is to analyse policing options available to Yukon First Nations and to consult with First Nation communities to document their justice-related concerns. These consultations are intended to provide an opportunity for First Nations communities to define their justice problems and to find practical solutions to them (Territorial/First Nations Committee on First Nations Policing 1992).

There are three different options for community policing being examined by the committee: (1) creating independent First Nations police forces in accordance with the Federal Solicitor General's First Nations Policy (Solicitor General of Canada 1992); (2) enhancing the services provided by the RCMP to Aboriginal peoples; and (3) maintaining current RCMP services. Each Yukon First Nation will ultimately decide which option to pursue.

The RCMP, however, continues to train and deploy officers within a generalist framework – a 'McPolicing' model in which line-level officers, communities, and policing strategies are viewed as interchangeable. Officers are to be equally at home working in Igloolik, NWT, Burnaby, BC, or undercover in Toronto. Such an approach ignores the unique requirements of Aboriginal policing, particularly in remote areas of the country.

It is important to point out, however, that Canadian police organizations, particularly those policing Aboriginal communities, operate in a highly political environment. They have little control over the demands that are placed on them and have had only a limited influence in defining the legislative role they are to play. Police officers are most often in a reactive role, responding to calls for service and to events in their policing environment. Officers may have little control over the dynamics of community life or the behaviour of individuals that result in police-citizen encounters. For example, while high arrest rates in Aboriginal communities are often ascribed to discriminatory actions on the part of police officers, such rates may be due to the prevalence of serious behaviour in the community and to the demands for service by community residents.

As the most visible (and, in many remote communities, the only) representatives of the criminal-justice system, the police are often the recipients of Aboriginal frustrations and criticisms about the justice system over which they have little control (see Benson 1991). It is perhaps unrealistic to expect that the police can address the historical and contemporary factors that have contributed to the high rates of crime and trouble in many Aboriginal communities.

THE DEVELOPMENT OF ABORIGINAL-CONTROLLED POLICE FORCES

It is in the area of policing that Aboriginal peoples have assumed the greatest control over the delivery of justice services. This is perhaps appropriate, given the conflicts that have occurred between the police and Aboriginal peoples historically and during contemporary times. Establishing autonomous police forces also provides an opportunity for Aboriginal bands to assume control over one of the most significant components of the criminal-justice system and to create a foundation for the further development of reserve-based criminal-justice systems.

Given the reluctance of the federal government to grant authority to all reserve-based Aboriginal groups to establish autonomous programs and services, the development of Aboriginal police forces across the country has been uneven. The Amerindian Police Service in Quebec and the First Nations Policing program in Ontario are the largest Aboriginal-controlled policing services, although there are smaller reserve-based forces in other jurisdictions. There is some evidence that reserve communities policed by Aboriginal police forces have experienced an improvement in police-community relations and, in some instances, a reduction in the number of arrests for certain types of offences.

There have also, however, been numerous obstacles to the development of effective Aboriginal police services (see Brodeur 1991). There is often in Aboriginal communities (as in non-Aboriginal communities) no consensus among community leaders and residents on the most appropriate course of action for the prevention and control of crime. As Benson (1991: 44) notes: 'In some Aboriginal communities, the views of different leaders conflict, primarily traditional and progressive individuals with different views of how the community should evolve. Proponents of opposite views may also disagree as to how the community should approach a problem, and whether efforts should emphasize social, economic, or political problems. Often, these disagreements may impair the effectiveness of all the leaders in a community.'

Aboriginal communities also differ in the 'personal' and 'community' resources that they can mobilize in formulating responses to crime. For example, while some Aboriginal communities have an infrastructure of strong leadership, a persistence of traditional cultural practices, and the involvement of elders, others do not. The availability of these resources will have a significant impact on the ability of the community to establish and maintain local justice initiatives.

There have also been situations involving political interference in the operation of Aboriginal policing services. Aboriginal-controlled police forces can be 'caught in the middle' between the aspirations of the band leadership and federal and provincial legislation and policy (see Brodeur 1991; Rolf 1991). This is illustrated by an incident involving the Dakota-Ojibway Tribal Police (disbanded in 1993) that occurred on the Roseau River Indian Reserve in Manitoba.

In January 1993, members of the Dakota-Ojibway Tribal Police were evicted by the band council of Roseau River after members of the tribal police force assisted the RCMP in a raid on the reserve during which video-lottery terminals, blackjack tables, and other gambling equipment were seized (Roberts 1993). The DOTC members were replaced by members of the Young Warrior Society. These events occurred against the backdrop of ongoing attempts by the Roseau River Indian Band to establish gambling on their reserve despite opposition from provincial and federal officials. The chief and council of the band have argued that the issue is one of territorial and cultural sovereignty, while the provincial government contends that all gambling in the province falls under the purview of the Manitoba Lotteries Commission.

This case illustrates the potential conflicts of interest that a reserved-based Aboriginal police force may encounter. It also raises questions about the control and accountability of other 'police' groups like the Young Warriors, who may be called upon to assume policing responsibilities in times of crisis and who may be used to replace either the RCMP or a duly established tribal police force.

Another issue surrounding Aboriginal police forces is one that has been raised generally in relation to the devolution of criminal-justice services to the community level (see Schwartz 1990). There are concerns about the ability of community-justice initiatives, including reserve-based police forces, to protect individuals who are vulnerable to victimization. Aboriginal women, in particular, have voiced concerns about the high rates of sexual and physical abuse in communities and questioned whether local justice initiatives can provide adequate protection for the victims of violence and abuse and whether appropriate sanctions can be imposed on offenders. In many Aboriginal communities, there is a reluctance to become involved in what are perceived to be the private matters of others (see Brodeur 1991; Ross 1992).

KEY ISSUES IN ABORIGINAL POLICING

The increased emphasis on Aboriginal policing by the RCMP, provincial, and municipal police forces, as well as the development of Aboriginal-controlled police services raises a myriad of questions, including, but not limited to, the following:

- What are the standards (and who should set them) that are to be used in recruiting and training Aboriginal police officers?
- What is the jurisdictional authority of Aboriginal police officers?
- What are the most appropriate models of police-service delivery to Aboriginal communities by Aboriginal and non-Aboriginal police forces?
- How are structures to ensure the accountability of Aboriginal police officers to be established?
- What system of checks and balances can be put into place to ensure that Aboriginal police forces remain as free as possible from political interference?
- What are the potential implications of Aboriginal officers policing their home communities, particularly when these communities are small and close-knit?
- What provisions, if any, can be established to provide an interface between the Aboriginal police force and the federal, provincial, and municipal police forces?
- What is the potential for developing Aboriginal-controlled police forces in off-reserve communities and in urban centres?

SUMMARY

Canadian police organizations are at a critical juncture, one that will demand of them significant structural changes, an increased decentralization of authority, the devolution of 'ownership' for strategies and programs to line-level officers and community residents, and an increased awareness of the changing policing environment in Canada. This is nowhere more evident than in the issues surrounding Aboriginal policing.

The delivery of policing services to Aboriginal peoples in Canada is a multidimensional topic, involving the organization and delivery of policing services by the RCMP and by provincial and municipal police forces, the increasing movement towards self-government and self-determination by Canada's Aboriginal peoples, and issues relating to the jurisdiction and accountability of Aboriginal and non-Aboriginal police forces. At this juncture, it is uncertain what specific models of Aboriginal policing will emerge over the next decade. There are, however, a variety of political forces at work that have the potential to alter radically the current arrangements for the delivery of police services, particularly in off-reserve communities and urban centres. These issues will pose challenges to federal, provincial, and municipal police agencies, as well as to Aboriginal bands and communities.

REFERENCES

Auger, D.J., A.N. Doob, and P. Driben. 1992. 'Crime and Control in Three Nishnawbe-Aski Nation Communities: An Exploratory Investigation.' *Canadian Journal of Criminology* 34: 317.

Benson, G.F. 1991. *Developing Crime Prevention Strategies in Aboriginal Communities*. Ottawa: Solicitor General of Canada.

Berger, T.R. 1991. *A Long and Terrible Shadow: White Values, Native Rights in the Americas, 1492–1992*. Vancouver: Douglas and McIntyre.

Brodeur, J-P. 1991. *Justice for the Cree: Policing and Alternative Dispute Resolution*. James Bay, Que.: Grand Council of the Crees.

Canada. 1989. *Basic Departmental Data*. Ottawa: Indian and Northern Affairs.

Canadian Corrections Association. 1967. *Indians and the Law: A Survey Prepared for the Honourable Arthur Laing*. Ottawa: Queen's Printer.

Carriere, K.D. 1987. 'Crime Stoppers Critically Considered.' *Canadian Criminology Forum* 8: 104.

Cawsey, Mr Justice R.A. (Chairman). 1991. *Justice on Trial. Report of the Task Force on the Criminal Justice System and Its Impact on the Indian and Metis People of Alberta*. Vol. 1 (Main Report). Edmonton: Attorney General and Solicitor General of Alberta.

Clark, S. 1992. 'Crime and Community: Issues and Directions in Aboriginal Justice.' *Canadian Journal of Criminology* 34: 513.

Cole, D., and I. Chaikin. 1990. *An Iron Hand Upon the People: The Law Against the Potlatch on the Northwest Coast*. Vancouver: Douglas and McIntyre.

Corrections Service Division, G.N.W.T. 1991. *Community Justice Initiatives: A Discussion Paper*. Yellowknife: Department of Social Services.

Depew, R. 1992. 'Policing Native Communities: Some Principles and Issues in Organizational Theory.' *Canadian Journal of Criminology* 34: 461.

Dickason, O.P. 1992. *Canada's First Nations: A History of Founding Peoples from Earliest Times*. Toronto: McClelland and Stewart.

Dyck, N. 1991. *What's the Indian 'Problem': Tutelage and Resistance in Canadian Indian Administration*. St John's, Nfld.: Institute for Social and Economic Research Memorial University.

Goddard, J. 1991. *Last Stand of the Lubicon Cree*. Vancouver: Douglas and McIntyre.

Government of the Northwest Territories. 1991. *Community Justice Initiatives: A Discussion Paper*. Yellowknife: Department of Social Services, Corrections Service Branch.

Griffiths, C.T. 1988. 'Community Corrections for Young Offenders: Proposal for a "Localized" Corrections.' *International Journal of Comparative and Applied Criminal Justice* 12: 219.

Griffiths, C.T., and J.C. Yerbury. 1984. 'Natives and Criminal Justice Policy: The Case of Native Policing.' *Canadian Journal of Criminology* 26: 147.

Griffiths, C.T., G.J. Saville, D.S. Wood, and E. Zellerer. 1992. *Crime, Law and Justice Among Inuit in the Baffin Region, Northwest Territories, Canada: Project Progress Report Number 4*. Burnaby: Criminology Research Centre, Simon Fraser University.

Griffiths, C.T., and S.N. Verdun-Jones. 1993. *Canadian Criminal Justice*. 2nd ed. Toronto: Harcourt Brace.

Hamilton, Associate Chief Justice A.C., and Associate Chief Justice C.M. Sinclair. 1991a. *Report of the Aboriginal Justice Inquiry of Manitoba. The Justice System and Aboriginal People*. Vol. 1. Winnipeg: Queen's Printer.

– 1991b. *Report of the Aboriginal Justice Inquiry of Manitoba. The Deaths of Helen Betty Osborne and John Joseph Harper*. Vol. 2. Winnipeg: Queen's Printer.

Harring, S.L. 1989. 'Rich Men of the Country: Canadian Law in the Land of the Copper Inuit, 1914–1930.' *Ottawa Law Review* 21: 1.

Harris, M. 1986. *Justice Denied: The Law Versus Donald Marshall*. Toronto: Macmillan.

Hastings, R., and R. Melchers. 1990. 'Municipal Government Involvement in Crime Prevention in Canada.' *Canadian Journal of Criminology* 31: 433.

Havemann, P. 1989. 'Law, State, and Canada's Indigenous People: Pacification by Coercion and Consent.' In T.C. Caputo, M.C. Kennedy, C.E. Reasons, and A. Brannigan, eds, *Law and Society: A Critical Perspective*, 54. Toronto: Harcourt, Brace, Jovanovich.

Head, R.H.D. 1989. *Policing for Aboriginal Canadians: The R.C.M.P. Role*. Ottawa: Royal Canadian Mounted Police.

Hickman, T.A. (Chair). 1989. *Royal Commission on the Donald Marshall, Jr. Prosecution*. Halifax: Province of Nova Scotia.

Jarvis, J. 1992a. *Inventory of Aboriginal Policing Programs in Canada. Part I. Aboriginal Police Officer Development and Policing*. Ottawa: Solicitor General of Canada.

– 1992b. *Inventory of Aboriginal Policing Programs in Canada. Part II. Aboriginal Cultural Awareness*. Ottawa: Solicitor General of Canada.

Krotz, L. 1990. *Indian Country: Inside Another Canada*. Toronto: McClelland and Stewart.

LaPrairie, C. 1991. *Justice for the Cree: Community, Crime, and Order*. James Bay, Que.: Grand Council of the Crees.
– 1992. *Exploring the Boundaries of Justice: Aboriginal Justice in the Yukon*. Ottawa: Department of Justice.
Law Reform Commission of Canada. 1991. *Aboriginal Peoples and Criminal Justice Report*. Ottawa: Law Reform Commission of Canada.
Linn, Judge P. (Chair). 1992a. *Report of the Saskatchewan Indian Justice Review Committee*. Regina: Government of Saskatchewan.
– 1992b. *Report of the Saskatchewan Metis Justice Review Committee*. Regina: Government of Saskatchewan.
Loree, D.J. 1985. *Policing Native Communities*. Ottawa: Canadian Police College.
McCaskill, D. 1985. *Patterns of Criminality and Correction Among Native Offenders in Manitoba: A Longitudinal Analysis*. Saskatoon: Prairie Region, Correctional Service of Canada.
MacLeod, R.C. 1976a. *The North-West Mounted Police and Law Enforcement, 1873–1905*. Toronto: University of Toronto Press.
– 1976b. 'Canadianizing the West: The North-West Mounted Police as Agents of National Policy, 1873–1905.' In L.H. Thomas, ed., *Essays in Western History*, 101. Edmonton: University of Alberta Press.
Morrison, W.R. 1974. 'The North-West Mounted Police and the Klondike Gold Rush.' *Journal of Contemporary History* 9: 93.
– 1985. *Showing the Flag: The Mounted Police and Canadian Sovereignty in the North, 1884–1925*. Vancouver: University of British Columbia Press.
Morse, B.W. 1983. 'Indigenous Law and State Legal Systems: Conflict and Compatibility.' In H.W. Finkler, ed., *Proceedings of the XIth International Congress of Anthropological and Ethnological Sciences, Commission on Folk Law and Legal Pluralism*, 381. Ottawa: Indian and Northern Affairs.
Moyer, S., F. Kopelman, C. LaPrairie, and B. Billingsley. 1985. *Native and Non-Native Admissions to Provincial and Territorial Correctional Institutions*. Ottawa: Solicitor General of Canada.
Moyles, R.G. 1989. *British Law and Arctic Men*. Vancouver: Northern Justice Society, Simon Fraser University.
Nielsen, M.O. 1992. 'Criminal Justice and Native Self-Government.' In R.A. Silverman and M.O. Nielsen, eds, *Aboriginal Peoples and the Criminal Justice System*, 243. Toronto: Butterworths.
Parnell, T. 1979. *We Mean No Harm – Yukon Indian-Police Relations: A Preliminary Study of Attitudes*. Whitehorse: Yukon Association of Non-Status Indians.
Roberts, D. 1993. 'Manitoba Natives evict police to keep gambling on reserve.' Toronto *Globe and Mail*, 22 January.
Rolf, Assistant Chief Judge C.H. (Commissioner). 1991. *Policing in Relation to the*

Blood Tribe, Report of a Public Inquiry, Volume 1, Findings and Recommendations. Edmonton: Lieutenant Governor in Council, Province of Alberta.

Rosenbaum, D.P. 1986. *Community Crime Prevention? Does It Work?* Beverly Hills, Calif.: Sage Publications.

– 1987. 'The Theory and Research Behind Neighborhood Watch: Is It a Sound Fear and Crime Reduction Strategy?' *Crime and Delinquency* 33: 103.

Ross, R. 1992. *Dancing with a Ghost: Exploring Indian Reality*. Toronto: Octopus Publishing Group.

Schwartz, B. 1990. 'A Separate Aboriginal Justice System?' *Manitoba Law Journal* 19: 77.

Shkilnyk, A. 1985. *A Poison Stronger Than Love*. New Haven: Yale University Press.

Silverman, R.A., and M.O. Nielsen. 1992. *Aboriginal Peoples and Canadian Criminal Justice*. Toronto: Butterworths.

Solicitor General of Canada. 1992. *First Nations Policing Policy*. Ottawa: Minister of Supply and Services Canada.

Stone, T. 1979. 'The Mounties as Vigilantes: Perceptions of Community and the Transformation of Law in the Yukon, 1885–1897.' *Law and Society Review* 14: 83.

– 1989. 'Urbanism, Law and Public Order: A View from the Klondike.' In K.S. Coates and W.R. Morrison, eds, *For Purposes of Dominion: Essays in Honour of Morris Zaslow*, 87. North York, Ont.: Captus University Publications.

Sunahara, D.F. 1992. 'Public Inquiries into Policing.' *Canadian Police College Journal* 16: 135.

Task Force on Policing on Reserves. 1973. *Report*. Ottawa: Indian and Northern Affairs.

Territorial/First Nations Committee on First Nations Policing. 1992. *A Policy Framework for the Development of a First Nations Policing Service, Yukon Territory*. Whitehorse: Yukon Department of Justice.

Wolff, L. 1991. *Crime in Aboriginal Communities, Saskatchewan 1989*. Ottawa: Canadian Centre for Justice Statistics.

Wood, D. 1992. 'Demographic Change, Relocation, and Patterns of Crime in the Baffin Region, Northwest Territories, Canada.' Burnaby: Criminology Research Centre, Simon Fraser University. Unpublished.

York, G. 1990. *The Dispossessed: Life and Death in Native Canada*. London: Vintage U.K.

York, G., and L. Pindera. 1991. *People of the Pines: The Warriors and the Legacy of Oka*. Toronto: Little, Brown and Co.

8

An Assessment of Strategies of Recruiting Visible-Minority Police Officers in Canada: 1985–1990

HARISH C. JAIN

Relations between the police and racial minorities[1] have reached crisis dimensions in major urban centres across Canada. A number of official inquiries have all served to highlight this problem. The 1989 and the 1992 Ontario Race Relations and Policing Task Force reports (Lewis 1989, 1992); the 1988 Quebec Human Rights Commission Report (Bellemare 1988), and the 1993 Task Force (Corbo) Report (Oziewicz 1993) dealt with problems in relations between police and visible minorities; the fact that the latter task forces (1992 and 1993 in Ontario and Quebec, respectively) were struck so soon after the original task-force reports points to the continuing tense relations between the police and the visible-minority communities. As well, testimony from provincial justice inquiries in Nova Scotia (Hickman 1989), Manitoba (Hamilton and Sinclair 1991), and Alberta (Rolf 1991; Cawsey 1991), and the racial-violence incidents in Toronto, Halifax, and Oka highlight the strained relations between police and racial minorities. Indeed, RCMP Commissioner Norman Inkster, participating in the recent National Conference on Racial Equality at McMaster University stated that 'Canada will face violence and social unrest unless it learns to accept an increasingly multiracial society ... If we are incapable of preparing the way for a better understanding and mutual respect ... whatever the colour of one's skin – then violence in some form is inevitable' (Inkster 1991; Marron 1990).

Visible minorities comprised 6.3 per cent of the labour force in Canada in 1986. They constituted more than 16 per cent of the labour force in Toronto and Vancouver, close to or more than 8 per cent of the workforce in Edmonton, Calgary, Winnipeg, and Ottawa-Carleton, and 6.5 per cent in Montreal. It is estimated that visible-minority Canadians will constitute almost 18 per cent of the population by the year 2000 (Picton 1992). A recent report by the federal Ministry of the Solicitor General, entitled *A Vision of the Future of Policing in*

Canada (Normandeau and Leighton 1990), noted that 'the statistical risk of racial tension and conflict increases in proportion to the representation of visible minority groups within the large metropolitan areas.' Given that the visible-minority population is growing, the authors of the report argued that 'improving police-race relations will be a continuing concern for at least the next decade.' In effect, the report suggested that police forces needed to recruit racial minorities in response to the need to enhance police-minority relations and to meet increasing demands for police services in other languages, and that they would have to recruit in an increasingly competitive labour-market environment owing to an aging population and the scarcity of qualified young people applying for police officer positions.

Based on the testimony at the Quebec Human Rights Commission inquiry into relations between the police and ethnic and visible minorities, Normandeau (1990) suggests, in regard to the Montreal police department, that (1) some citizens viewed the police as being unwelcoming to minorities, thereby having a dissuasive effect; (2) low representation of visible and other minorities helped perpetuate white police officers' prejudices against minorities, created a climate of harassment for the few 'ethnic' police officers, and hindered the professional mobility of minority police officers; and (3) the low representation failed to provide young people from the minorities with 'role models' with whom they could identify.

Normandeau (1990) goes on to point out that the inquiry committee's study analysed the Montreal police department's selection process in detail. A review of the success rate for each stage of the process – such as the selection interview and the psychological, physical, and medical examinations – and the entire selection process showed that the success rate of visible-minority (VM) applicants was three times lower than for the majority group and the ethnic minorities. The Ontario Task Force report also indicated that the success rates in recruitment and promotion were skewed heavily in favour of white males (Lewis 1990).

At the other end of the spectrum, some police representatives and others have suggested that VM perceptions regarding the role of police in society reinforce the gap between the two groups (Lunney 1985; Fleras et al. 1989). Some of these perceptions include the following: (1) new immigrants from dictatorial or repressive regimes may possess negative attitudes about the police (Fleras et al. 1989); (2) VMs may not consider law enforcement as a respectable profession (Jayewardene and Talbot 1990); and (3) a police officer's job ma be viewed as a dead end in career development (Ibid.).

It has been suggested that, owing to these and other perceptions and distrust of the police, VMs do not wish to apply and even want to be police officers.

The Ontario Task Force (1989) concluded that their review of VM application statistics and promotional patterns did not support the arguments above, and recommended an employment-equity (EE) policy for increasing the representation of VMs in Ontario police organizations. This recommendation was adopted in the *Police Services Act* of 1990 and the EE regulation issued by the Solicitor General in April 1991.

Several reports released in 1992 and early 1993 have found a prevalence of prejudicial attitudes in police organizations and have recommended better race-relations training, improvement in police culture and structure, and affirmative-action hiring (Oziewicz 1993; Abbate 1992; Small 1992). The need for greater racial minority (VM) representation in police forces and affirmative action hiring has also been echoed by the previous commissions and task forces (Hickman 1989; Lewis 1989, 1992; Bellemare 1988).

It has been argued that the community should be policed not only according to the wishes of the community but also by representatives of that community, and that police recruitment of VMs, resulting in the ethnic make-up of the police force reflecting the composition of the community, would correct police bias towards minorities and improve police-minority relations by providing a link between the police and minority communities (Jayewardene and Talbot 1990).

Thus, in order to avert the risk of racial tensions, to meet the demand by new immigrants for services in other languages, to improve police-minority relations, to provide role models for minority youths, and to reflect the ethno-cultural make-up of the communities they serve, it is critical that police forces increase the representation of VM police officers. Moreover, competition in the labour market may compel police forces to hire women and minorities in any event because of an aging population and a scarcity of qualified young people applying for police-officer jobs.

OUTLINE AND METHODOLOGY

This paper is divided into several parts. The first part highlights the representation of VMs as police officers in selected police departments compared to their representation in the external labour force. The second part, outlines and analyses the recruitment sources for police officers utilized by police organizations, proactive strategies to attract VM candidates, perceived barriers in attracting VM candidates, perceived measures of success in recruiting VM candidates, and related issues. In the third part, selection standards and employment-equity programs of police organizations are described. In the fourth part, the relative success of the recruitment strategies and the information and communication gaps in these strategies are assessed. In the final part, several recommendations to improve the recruitment and selection of VM candidates as police officers are provided.

The study on which this paper is based investigated and analysed the recruitment strategies of selected representative Canadian police forces to attract and recruit visible minorities as police officers. Wherever possible, an update of the 1985 and 1987 studies by the author is provided. (The earlier studies on the recruitment and selection of VMs in selected police departments were sponsored by the Canadian Association of Chiefs of Police (CACP) and funded by Multiculturalism and Citizenship Canada.) The participating police organizations were the Royal Canadian Mounted Police (RCMP), Vancouver Police Department, Edmonton Police Department, Calgary Police Department, Regina Police Service, City of Winnipeg Police, Metropolitan Toronto Police, Ottawa Police Force, Ontario Provincial Police (OPP), Montreal Urban Community (MUC), Quebec Police Force (QPF), St Hubert Police, Moncton Police Force, and the Halifax Police Department. These police departments also participated in the 1985 and 1987 studies.

The methodology consisted of a written questionnaire and field interviews of police-agency officials. The fourteen police organizations in the study completed a questionnaire that was sent in August 1990. In addition, field interviews were conducted with several police forces, including the RCMP, the QPF, and the Vancouver, Edmonton, Calgary, Metropolitan Toronto, Ottawa, Montreal, and Halifax police departments.

REPRESENTATION OF VISIBLE-MINORITY OFFICERS IN CANADIAN POLICE ORGANIZATIONS

As indicated in table 1, only one police department in the study did not have any VM officers in 1990. In the remaining (92 per cent) police organizations, VM police officers ranged from 0.05 per cent, in QPF, to 4.7 per cent, in the Metropolitan Toronto force. A majority of police departments had increased the number and per centage of VM officers in 1990. These organizations included Vancouver, Edmonton, Calgary, Winnipeg, Toronto, Ottawa, Montreal, and Halifax.

A majority of police organizations in 1990 had VM officers above the rank of constable, compared to only four in 1987. The Metropolitan Toronto Police had the following breakdown of VM to non-VM officers in 1990: constables, 231 to 3983; sergeant and staff sergeants, 25 to 1196; and inspectors and staff inspectors, 4 to 93. The remaining ranks were cadets and cadets in training, 34 to 146, and superintendent and Chief, 0 to 32. The RCMP had constables, 113 to 9554; corporals, 9 to 2460; sergeants, 3 to 1566; staff sergeants, 1 to 748;

TABLE 1

Visible-minority representation in police organizations (1985, 1987, and 1990) and availability of visible minorities in the labour market (aged 15 years and over)

Police organization	Visible minorities 1985 % Men	1985 % Women	1985 % Total	1987 % Men	1987 % Women	1987 % Total	1990 % Men	1990 % Women	1990 % Total	Area	VM % in Labour market (1986 Census)
RCMP	N/A	N/A	N/A	N/A	N/A	N/A	0.8	N/A	0.8	Canada	6.3
Vancouver	1.9	0.3	2.2	2.3	0.3	2.6	3.1	0.7	3.8	Vancouver	16.2
Edmonton	N/A	N/A	N/A	0.7	N/A	0.7	1.6	0.4	2.0	Edmonton	8.4
Calgary	0.7	0.1	0.8	0.4	0.2	0.6	Men & Women		1.5	Calgary	9.5
Regina	N/A	N/A	N/A	0.6	N/A	0.6	0.6	0	0.6	Regina	4.2
Winnipeg	1.3	0	1.3	1.8	0.1	1.9	3.0	0.2	3.2	Winnipeg	8.0
Toronto	Men & Women		2.7	3.0	0.4	3.4	4.3	0.4	4.7	Toronto	16.5
Ottawa	0.3	0	0.3	0.3	0	0.3	2.3	0	2.3	Ottawa/Hull	6.0
OPP	N/A	N/A	N/A	N/A	N/A	N/A	1.4	0.02	1.4	Ontario	8.5
Montreal	0.1	0	0.1	0.3	N/A	0.3	0.5	0.02	0.5	Montreal	6.7
QPF	N/A	N/A	N/A	N/A	N/A	N/A	0.02	0.02	0.05	Quebec	3.4
Halifax	1.9	0	1.9	1.9	0	1.9	Men & Women		4.5	Nova Scotia	4.5
Moncton	N/A	N/A	N/A	0.8	N/A	0.8	0.8	0	0.8	New Brusnwick	0.6
St Hubert	0	0	0	0	0	0	0	0	0	St Hubert	N/A

N/A = Not available (in most cases owing to lack of self-identification data); in some cases, data were not available by visible-minority sex breakdown.

and corporal sergeant major and sergeant major, 1 to 1. The OPP had sergeants and staff sergeants, 4 to 990. The Edmonton police had sergeants, 2 to 279. The Vancouver police had sergeants, 2 to 29. The Ottawa police had sergeants, 1 to 141. The Montreal police had sergeants, 1 to 988. The Winnipeg police had sergeants, 1 to 283. A majority of VM police officers were males.

Thus, while there is a steady improvement in both the recruitment and promotion of VMs in a majority of police organizations, almost all police organizations have some distance to travel before they approach the representation of VMs in the labour markets of the communities they serve.

RECRUITMENT

Recruitment is designed to locate, identify, and attract individuals who have the basic skills, personal characteristics, and motivation to become successful employees. Effective recruitment programs ensure a pool of potential employees in order to meet an organization's requirements. In recent years, societal pressures and human-rights legislation have affected the recruitment process, with the result that employers have to go out and actively seek job applicants from groups of people, such as racial minorities, who might not otherwise apply for certain employment because they have been denied it in the past. For instance, organizations cannot fill their recruiting needs solely through walk-in candidates or word-of-mouth referrals by friends or relatives on staff. Such a practice can result in systemic discrimination. Even if the employers do not intend to discriminate in recruiting, their personnel practices (recruiting by word-of-mouth) can result in an adverse impact on visible minorities and others, because all-white or all-male groups tend to perpetuate themselves.

RECRUITMENT SOURCES FOR ALL POLICE OFFICERS

As table 2 indicates, 71 to 86 per cent (10 to 12) of the 14 police departments used four predominant recruitment sources for attracting new candidates. These were newspapers, recruitment brochures, posters, and so on; employee referrals; walk-ins and personal contact; and high school. A comparison with previous years suggests that there has been little change in these recruiting sources from 1985 to 1990 (Jain 1988, 1987).

Table 3 indicates that employee referrals and personal contacts were listed among the top recruiting sources for generating VM and other candidates by one-half of the police departments in the study. Other top recruiting sources included universities and colleges (by 43 per cent), followed by VM role models, VM and mainstream media, and walk-ins (by 36 per cent each).

TABLE 2
Recruitment practices of selected Canadian police organizations, 1985–90 ($N = 14$)

	1985		1987		1990	
Source	No.	%	No.	%	No.	%
Newspapers, recruitment Brochures, etc.	10	71	10	71	11	79
Employee referral	9	64	9	64	10	71
Walk-ins and personal contact	11	79	11	79	11	79
High school	13	93	11	79	12	86

TABLE 3
Top five recruitment sources generating most candidates according to police organizations ($N = 14$)

Sources	No.	%
Employee referrals	7	50
Personal contacts	7	50
Universities and colleges	6	43
VM role models	5	36
VM and mainstream media	5	36
Walk-ins	5	36
Community outreach	4	29
Educational career fairs	3	21
Presentations in VM communities	2	14
Contact with minority agencies	2	14
Utilizing other police agencies	2	14
Newspapers	2	14
Multicultural unit	1	7
Human justice program	1	7

STRATEGIES TO RECRUIT VISIBLE MINORITY POLICE OFFICERS

As indicated in table 4, more than 90 per cent (12) of the 14 police agencies used two particular VM recruiting strategies in 1990, compared to 50 per cent and less in 1987 and fewer still in 1985. These strategies were: (1) involving police officers who had personal contact with the VM community in the recruitment effort and (2) using qualified and trained recruiters who could relate to VM applicants.

TABLE 4
Strategies used by police organizations to recruit visible-minority police officers, 1985–90 (N = 14)

Strategy	1985 No.	1985 %	1987 No.	1987 %	1990 No.	1990 %
Police officers with contacts	6	43	7	50	13	93
Qualified and trained recruiters	4	29	6	43	13	93
VM community group presentations	6	43	7	50	12	86
High school presentations featuring VM role models	4	29	4	29	12	86
Meeting high school teachers and administrators	1	7	3	21	12	86
VM constables	–	–	–	–	12	86
Consultation with VM organizations	–	–	–	–	12	86
Advertising in VM media	–	–	–	–	12	86
Special police recruit team	–	–	–	–	10	71
VM role models	3	21	6	43	10	71
Upgrading VM civilian staff	–	–	–	–	8	57

Three other proactive strategies were being utilized by more police organizations than ever before. A great majority (86 per cent) of police organizations in 1990 deployed VM community group presentations; made high school presentations featuring VM role models; and met with high school administrators and teachers to help identify VM candidates. The use of these techniques has grown considerably from 50 per cent and less to a predominant majority of the police organizations from 1985 to 1990.

Several other recruiting initiatives had also been adopted by a great majority of police agencies by 1990. These included using VM constables in recruiting VMs; consulting with the representatives of VM organizations; advertising in the VM media; employing special police recruiting teams that include VM officers; using VM role models; and mentoring and upgrading VM civilian staff to permit entry to the force as a police constable. Additional recruitment strategies adopted by several police organizations included (1) conducting regular recruitment workshops and ride-along programs for ethnic leaders; (2) hiring VM students during the summer to interest them in police careers after graduation; (3) placing yellow-page recruitment messages in several languages; (4) providing police personnel departments with VM officers and a multicultural service unit; (5) establishing a scholarship fund to assist VM candidates

TABLE 5
Barriers in attracting visible-minority candidates as identified by police organizations ($N = 14$)

Barriers	No.	%
Home-country perceptions of police	12	86
Distrust of police	12	86
Policing not an 'honourable profession'	12	86
VMs not welcomed in police force	8	57
Policing as dangerous	7	50
Better pportunities elsewhere	7	50
Lack of advancement opportunities	5	36

with a strong interest in a policing career, to overcome deficiencies such as lack of language proficiency, education, or job-related training; (6) making multilingual recruitment messages in the ethnic media; and (8) issuing new recruitment brochures portraying VMs as police officers.

BARRIERS IN ATTRACTING VM CANDIDATES

Police organizations were asked about the barriers they face in attracting VM candidates for police-officer positions. As is apparent in table 5, a great majority (12, or 86 per cent) of police agencies felt that VMs did not apply for the police-officer position because their home-country perceptions of police, distrust of police, and perception of policing as not an 'honourable profession.' Other reasons cited, in descending order, were VMs' perception of not being welcomed by police forces (57 per cent); VMs' perception of police work as being dangerous and the existence of better opportunities elsewhere (50 per cent); and VMs' perception that opportunities for advancement were not good with the police (36 per cent).

MEASURES OF SUCCESS OF VM RECRUITMENT DRIVE BY POLICE ORGANIZATIONS

As shown in table 6, in assessing the chief indicators of a successful recruitment drive, a great majority of police agencies (86 per cent) noted a high number of inquiries by VMs, a yearly increase in VM recruiting, a high number of VM applicants, and an increase in requests for police speakers. Other indicators of success were police attendance at community events (79 per cent), an increase in the ratio of qualified to unqualified VM applicants, and good media coverage (71 per cent each).

TABLE 6
Police measurement of the success of visible-minority recruitment drive ($N = 14$)

Indicators of success	No.	%
High number of inquiries	12	86
Yearly increase in VM recruiting	12	86
High number of VM applications	12	86
Increase in requests for		
– speakers to VM groups	12	86
– attendance at community events	11	79
– visiting churches, temples	9	64
Good media coverage	10	71
Increase in ratio of qualified/unqualified VM applicants	10	71
Decline in cost per VM application	4	29
Reduction in recruiting costs	3	21
Reduction in VM recruiting time	3	21

TRACKING RECRUITMENT AND SELECTION SOURCES

Tracking the sources or methods of recruitment and selection that are used by each police department to obtain VM and non-VM officers, by keeping statistical records, can be helpful in the following ways. Tracking provides information on

- the number of applicants from each source;
- the contribution of each source to the ratio of qualified to unqualified candidates;
- the ratio of VM to non-VM candidates;
- the contribution of each source to the number hired;
- the ratio of VM and non-VM hired, in order to determine adverse impact; and
- the influence of each source on subsequent job turnover and job performance.

The employment equity (EE) regulation issued by the solicitor general under the Ontario *Police Services Act* of 1990 requires that each police service in Ontario shall 'establish a system for determining the number of members of each prescribed group who apply for employment with the police force and for *tracking those applicants through the recruitment and selection process*' (emphasis added; see O. Reg. 153/91, s. 8(5)).

In this study, one-half of police organizations kept records of hiring by either recruiting source or the selection process, or both. These police departments included Vancouver, Edmonton, Calgary, Toronto, Ottawa, Montreal, and the Quebec Police Force. The Metropolitan Toronto Police organization, according to Superintendent Shaw, has been tracking some applicants and mentoring them, by following up at each stage of recruitment and selection, to keep them interested in joining the police force. However, he also stated that it was difficult to provide a breakdown of all VM applicants by each recruitment source since more than one source was frequently cited by the applicants.

Based on the statistical information supplied by the Edmonton and Calgary police departments in 1990–1, and the Montreal police department earlier, these organizations were keeping data by designated groups and others through each stage of the selection process. For instance, Calgary kept data broken down into the following categories: the numbers of applications received, active applications, and applicants hired; the number of temporary and permanent rejections on the basis of minimum requirements; the results of examinations and interviews and medical, fitness, driving, and polygraph tests; the results of field-board and personnel-committee examinations; and the number of withdrawals and no-shows during the recuitment process.

RESOURCES DEVOTED TO RECRUITING

Most police organizations (79 per cent) were recruiting police officers in 1990. It was therefore relevant to inquire about the resources they were devoting to recruiting VMs. A majority of police agencies incurred additional costs in recruiting VMs. At least four organizations listed some of these costs, which included advertisements in ethnic media and open houses, (QPF); establishment of a nine-member recruiting unit and equipment and operating costs (Metropolitan Toronto Police); a new position for a VM sergeant in the personnel department, the production of new posters and brochures, and extra person-hours spent on presentations and talks (Ottawa Police); and the allocation of significant funds for VM recruitment (Calgary Police).

A number of police departments had assigned both full- and part-time police officers to VM recruitment. Several had allocated advertising budgets for VM recruitment and set aside significant funds for the entire recruitment drive.

SELECTION STANDARDS

Fair selection standards that are valid and do not result in an adverse impact on visible-minority applicants can facilitate non-discriminatory hiring. By contrast, selection standards and devices such as job interviews and testing that lack validation or have adverse impact can discourage visible-minority applicants from applying for police-officer positions; and the problem can be made more difficult when VM applicants hear from others that they will never make it through the selection process. Unfair selection standards, combined with the barriers that police organizations face in attracting VM applicants, can serve to compound the problems of VM officer recruitment. Among the selection policies and methods that can act as job barriers are (1) dress-code regulations; (2) job-interview assessments; (3) lack of validation and adverse impact of selection methods.

1. Dress-Code Regulations

Dress-code regulations, such as those applying to beards and turbans in the case of baptized Sikhs, constitute a barrier to VM recruitment. A majority (57 per cent) of police forces allowed the wearing of turbans and beards, and one additional police organization was considering regulation changes.

At the time of the first study, in 1985, only one police force could accommodate baptized Sikhs as police officers (Jain 1988, 1987). In 1987, three police organizations changed their policy in this regard. In 1990, as noted above, a majority had changed their dress-code regulations.

2. Selection Interviews

Selection interviews can pose serious impediments in the hiring of visible minorities. For instance, several studies have found that job applicants are more likely to be hired if they look straight ahead rather than down. People who look the interviewer straight in the eye are rated as being confident, and responsible and having more initiative (Amalfitano and Kalt 1977). As well, applicants who demonstrate greater amounts of eye contact, head-moving, smiling, and other non-verbal behaviours are rated higher than applicants who do not (Young and Bier 1977). Each of the factors in non-verbal communication – such as facial expression, body gesture, eye contact, manual gesture, and such things as hesitations in speech and the tone and volume of the voice – is culturally determined. Therefore, these findings have severe implications for visible-minority men and women, especially recent immigrants from Third World countries.

Moreover, interviews have serous shortcomings. Several reviews of the literature on job interviews have revealed that the job interviews have relatively low reliability (that is, different interviewers come to quite disparate conclusions) and low validity (that is, interview ratings and job-performance scores

TABLE 7
Type and characteristics of interview used in selection of police officers

Police department	Type of interview	Interview scored	Interview scored by VMs	Interview scored by others	Interview weight	Number of interviews	Number of VM interviewers	Who interviews
RCMP	Other*	Yes	No	No	N/A	1	1	Non-commissioned personnel officer
Edmonton	Structured	Yes	No	No	40%	3	0	Recruiting-unit member
Calgary	Structured	No	No	No	30%	2	0	Staff sergeant detectives, constables
Vancouver	Structured	No	No	No	N/A	2	2	Recruiting sergeant or detective
Montreal	Structured	No	No	No	80%	2	0	Civilian and police professionals
Toronto	N/A	N/A	N/A	N/A	N/A	N/A	N/A	N/A
Ottawa	Structured	No	No	No	40%	3	1	Recruiting officer + 3 senior officers on recruiting board
OPP	Structured	Yes	No	No	100%	1	3	Trained uniform recruiting officer
St Hubert	Structured	Yes	No	No	100%	1	N/A	Police inspector + 2 lieutenants
QPF	Structured	Yes	N/A	N/A	100%	1	1	Civil and police employees, retirees
Regina	Structured	No	No	No	100%	2	0	Recruiting officer, chief, superintendent
Winnipeg	Structured	Yes	No	No	100%	3	1	City & policy recruiting officers, personnel & training inspector
Halifax	Structured	Yes	No	No	100%	2	0	Personnel and board of senior officers
Moncton	Unstructured	Yes	No	No	60%	1	0	Director of management services

*Combination of structured and unstructured

are not closely related). This is especially true of unstructured interviews. Structured interviews, however, can improve predictive validity (Wiesner and Cronshaw 1988).

One of the main recommendations made by the Quebec Human Rights Commission's inquiry into relations between the police and ethnic and visible minorities (Normandeau 1990; investigation, November 1988) was that 'the selection interview be structured so as to diminish the risk of subjectivity.' The inquiry committee also recommended that, in order to increase the reliability of the selection interview, the selection boards should comprise three members, and that one of the members should be a member of a visible or ethnic minority.

Performance in selection interviews was considered to be extremely important for job applicants by police organizations, as shown in table 7. Close to one-half (43 per cent) of police organizations gave job interviews 100 per cent weight,[2] one police force gave it 80 per cent weight, and an additional four forces gave it between 30 and 60 per cent weight. Thus, the selection interview could be an important roadblock in hiring visible minorities. Almost all police organizations conducted some form of structured interviews. However, fewer than one-half of the police forces had a visible-minority interviewer.

3. Validation and Adverse Impact

Too often, police organizations fail to implement procedures to check recruitment methods and practices for their negative consequences on VM recruitment. Selection standards may lack validity because they do not relate to success in on-the-job performance, and other recruitment methods may have an adverse, or unintended, affect on the number of VMs recruited. By reviewing recruitment policies for their lack of validation and for their adverse impact, police organizations can recruit more effectively. As table 8 indicates, only four police organizations conducted validation studies and only one carried out adverse-impact analysis for VMs. One positive note is that several police agencies were reviewing their selection systems and undertaking validation and adverse-impact studies. For instance, at the time of this study, the Metropolitan Toronto Police force was updating the psychological-testing process and had an on-going committee to review and revise the interview process.

EMPLOYMENT EQUITY

Employment equity (EE) plans have a direct impact on the recruitment of visible minorities and other designated groups as police officers. EE involves proactive, outreach recruiting in order to increase the number of racial minori-

TABLE 8
Validation and adverse-impact analysis of psychological tests used

		Adverse impact analysis	
Police department	Validation[1]	By VM	By Sex
RCMP	Yes	No	Yes
Edmonton	Yes	Yes	Yes
Vancouver	No	No	No
Calgary	Yes	No	No
Ottawa	Yes	No	No
OPP	No	No	No
Montreal	No	No	No
Regina	No	No	No
St Hubert	No	No	No
Toronto	N/A	N/A	N/A
Winnipeg	No[2]	No	No
Halifax	No	No	No
QPF	N/A	N/A	N/A
Moncton	No	No	No

[1]Validation here means relating selection scores with job performance or content validation
[2]Study to be implemented

ties, Aboriginal persons, women, and persons with disabilities in police services. It requires the elimination of systemic barriers pertaining to such factors as height, weight, and age, the implementation of special measures such as outreach recruitment, and the setting up of plans with specific numerical goals and timetables to increase the representation of visible minorities and other prescribed groups.

Ontario is the only jurisdiction where EE is mandatory under the *Police Services Act*. According to the EE regulation introduced by the solicitor general in the Ontario legislature on 10 April 1991, all 118 provincial police organizations, who administer 21,000 employees, were required to submit their first eighteen-month EE plan by 1 May 1992 (Appleby 1991). The results on police-force composition required submission by 1 March 1993 and every year thereafter (*Laypersons' Guide to Regulation*, undated). The EE regulation committed every police force to the ultimate goal of reflecting the make-up of society at large, by the equitable representation of the designated groups throughout its workforce in proportion to the community it serves.[3] There were no deadlines, however, for achieving this ultimate goal. The regulation required each police service to submit plans, with goals to be undertaken within a two-year time frame; however, the results were to be submitted to the Ontario government on a yearly basis. The progress was to be monitored by the Ontario Ministry of the Solicitor General.[4]

If targets were not met, sanctions (specified in the *Police Services Act*) could be applied, ranging from the appointment of an independent EE administrator to the suspension or firing of the police chief or members of the police service boards. However, no sanctions were to be applied in cases where the chief of police had made every effort to meet the goals and timetables contained in the EE plan (*News Release* 1991).

Individual police outreach recruitment efforts were to be assisted by the creation of a central inventory of applicants from designated groups, to be maintained by the Ministry of the Solicitor General. The purpose was to alleviate shortages by drawing from applicants elsewhere who might be willing to move (Appleby 1991).

As indicated in table 9, more than one-half of the police organizations in the study had EE programs. Several police departments had voluntarily adopted EE programs as of 1990. These included the RCMP, the OPP, and the Edmonton, Calgary, Montreal, Metropolitan Toronto police forces.[5] These organizations had set numerical goals and timetables for recruiting VM police officers and had also undertaken other proactive measures. The Quebec Police Force (QPF) was in the process of developing an EE plan; it had already appointed a coordinator for EE programs. The Moncton and St Hubert police forces did not appear to have an EE plan to recruit VMs as police officers. Regina is in the process of preparing an EE plan (in 1991).

The Vancouver, Ottawa, Winnipeg, and Halifax police departments had proactive VM recruitment programs, but no formal EE plans with numerical goals and timetables, as of 1990. For instance, the Vancouver police department has had a very successful intercultural training program for a number of years. The program has involved both police officers from all ranks and VM community leaders over the years. This initiative has helped in VM recruitment by providing close contact with community leaders and by building confidence and trust in the Vancouver police. In addition, the Vancouver police, along with several other municipal police departments, has been sending its recruits to the police academy at the BC Justice Institute. The recruits attend assessment centres that have been organized by the academy for some time. Assessment centres are used to identify the best candidates through a series of exercises, interviews, and tests. In 1989/90, 10 per cent of the academy's enrolment was made up of VM candidates. Assessment centres are the last, or last but one, step before hiring a candidate as a police officer (BC Police Academy 1989/90). Hence, assessment-centre technique was another method being used by the Vancouver police department, among other BC municipal police forces, to hire VMs.

TABLE 9

Employment equity programs in police agencies

Police department	Employment Equity program	Employment Equity recruiting goals	Employment Equity recruiting timetables	1990 goals	Future goals	Visible-minority liaison officers	Advisory committees with VM members	VM community involvement in recruiting VM applicants
RCMP	Yes	Yes	Yes	37	50[1]	No	Yes	Yes
Edmonton	Yes	Yes	Yes	5	10[2]	Yes	Yes	Yes
Calgary	Yes	Yes	Yes	Yes	Yes[3]	Yes	Yes	Yes
Vancouver	No	No	No	N/A	N/A	Yes	Yes	Yes
Montreal	Yes	Yes	Yes	Yes	171[4]	Yes	Yes	Yes
Ottawa	Yes	No	No	N/A	N/A	Yes	Yes	Yes
OPP	Yes	Yes	Yes	N/A	N/A[5]	Yes	Yes	Yes
Regina	No	N/A	N/A	N/A	N/A	Yes	No	No
St Hubert	No	No	No	0	0	N/A	N/A	N/A
Winnipeg	Yes	No	No	N/A	N/A	Yes	Yes	Yes
Toronto	Yes	Yes[7]	Yes	Yes	Yes	Yes	Yes	Yes
Halifax	Yes	Yes	Yes	N/A	N/A[6]	Yes	Yes	Yes
QPF	No[8]	No[8]	No[8]	N/A	N/A	No	No[9]	Yes
Moncton	No	No	No	N/A	N/A	No	No	No

1 Goal is 6.3% by year 2003.
2 Goal is 7% or 75 members by 1995; this includes Aboriginal persons.
3 Goal is 25 females, 20 Aboriginals, and 10 visible-minority persons by 1993.
4 Goal is 5.8% by 2001.
5 Goal is 3.5% by 1992.
6 Plan to attract visible minorities in 1991.
7 Toronto sets goals every year.
8 QPF is in the process of preparing an EE plan.
9 Consultation formats are being studied.

ASSESSMENT OF THE RELATIVE SUCCESS OF THE RECRUITMENT STRATEGIES

As far as it could be determined, there are no objective data available on the relative success of each type of outreach recruitment strategy. To some extent, recruitment strategies may have to be devised to suit the police–minority relations in a particular community; the concentration of VM communities within the area served by the police force; a need for experimentation with the types of strategies that work and the ones that do not; and other specific circumstances.

For instance, the Vancouver police department felt that its intercultural training effort involving the entire police force and numerous VM community leaders provided useful contacts and helped in the recruitment of VM candidates; an additional method that has removed systemic discrimination in selection has been the use of the assessment-centre technique at the police academy before candidates are hired as police officers. The Metropolitan Toronto Police felt that the mentoring of VM candidates, aggressive marketing, and adapting recruitment to the cultural norms and expectations of some VM communities (such as pitching recruitment messages at the parents and family as well as the candidate, in the case of Chinese Canadians) have been quite successful in attracting VM candidates. The Ottawa Police suggested that the scholarship and summer-student programs have met with some success. The RCMP felt that its VM advisory committee and special recruiting team have helped generate VM recruits. The Edmonton and the Calgary police have been experimenting with regular recruitment workshops and ride-along programs for ethnic leaders, as well as recruitment messages in several languages. They felt that it was too early to assess the success of these outreach efforts.

These are useful examples. However, without documentation it is not possible to isolate the effect of these strategies from numerous other outreach efforts that these and other police departments have been and are continuing to engage in. For instance, the Metropolitan Toronto Police have a nine-member recruitment team, a sizeable amount of funds for the development of recruitment material directed to VM and other underrepresented groups, a program of conducting workshops and seminars for community members, a citizens' recruitment advisory committee, in-house videos, an in-house training program, a continuing examination of all employment systems to eliminate bias (such as reassessment of psychological tests), and so on. Unless the police force systematically evaluates the contribution of each of these strategies, it is not possible to assess the relative success of each type of recruitment strategy.

As noted earlier, several police forces have developed tracking procedures that can be of great assistance in determining the success or failure of recruitment and selection methods in hiring VM candidates. Under the EE regulation in Ontario, each police force in the province is now mandated to do so.

INFORMATION AND COMMUNICATION GAPS IN RECRUITMENT STRATEGIES

A recent report (*Evaluation* 1990) indicated that Blacks in the Halifax area interviewed for that study felt that the tendency to restrict the recruitment of VMs to university graduates was a problem. More highly educated Blacks felt that the opportunities for advancement were not good with the police, that many Blacks who could be effective on the job were not seriously considered, that the verbal-skills test used by police departments was culturally biased against Blacks, and that spoken communication skills should be weighted more heavily in the selection process.

In Montreal, minority communities targeted for recruitment were also less than enthusiastic, according to the study (*Evaluation* 1990). The VM respondents suggested that the French-language barrier, together with the potential difficulty of cultural integration, contributed to the general feeling of being unwelcome in the ranks of the police force, despite the force's proactive efforts to recruit VMs. In Toronto, researchers found that many minority group members distrusted police at the operational and street levels, and stated that this could be a most significant barrier in obtaining recruits from the high schools and community colleges. Other adverse factors cited in the report (*Evaluation* 1990) were the inability of the Metropolitan Toronto Police (MTP) to retain VM recruits owing to lack of promotions and career opportunities; the inadequacy of the intercultural training program; and a perception of a lack of meaningful participation by the VM community in the MTP's decision-making processes for the selection of VM candidates. As the report noted, the MTP has disputed some of these assertions.

The same report did not find any major communication problems between police and VMs in Calgary and Vancouver. If anything, the VMs interviewed for the study gave high marks to the police departments for their proactive recruitment efforts (*Evaluation* 1990).

RECOMMENDATIONS

1. Tracking

It is important to build a data base in order to find out which recruitment strategies work and the ones that do not. Tracking of sources of recruitment that are used by each police department to attract and hire VM officers, by keeping statistical records, can provide information to form the base for informed judgments on which of the recruitment sources to concentrate on and which should be discarded. Each police force needs to collect such data in order to increase the efficiency and the effectiveness, in terms of costs and benefits, of their outreach efforts.

In large police departments, the tracking of recruitment sources can present problems, as noted earlier in the case of the Metropolitan Toronto Police (MTP). However, the mentoring process, as practised by the MTP, can help keep track of at least some VM applicants; the MTP have been keeping limited data from the stage when an initial contact is made with a VM recruit, to the actual application by the recruit, to the final stage of being hired.[6]

Similarly, tracking at each stage of the selection process will help to uncover the differential effect, if any, of interviews, tests, and so on, on minorities, as opposed to non-minorities. For example, in a recent quarterly 'Recruitment Progress Report,' the Edmonton police found that, of the 195 candidates who were administered written examinations (from January to March 1991), only 10 per cent of the VM candidates passed the tests, as compared to 36.4 per cent of the non-minorities, and 27 per cent of females. If this trend were to continue over a period of time, the Edmonton police department might wish to adopt an appropriate strategy to correct the situation.

In Ontario, the EE regulation requires each police force to track all applicants through the recruitment and selection process, as noted earlier in this paper.

2. *Validation and Adverse Impact*

Human-rights statutes in all jurisdictions across Canada prohibit discrimination on the basis of race, religion, colour, national or ethnic origin, marital status, and age. The age groups protected vary among jurisdictions; most commonly they span the ages 18 to 65. In addition to these grounds, the other grounds prohibited vary according to jurisdiction.

These statutes put the burden on the employer to prove that, in case of a valid complaint, the hiring standards employed – such as cut-off scores on tests, interview results, and age criteria – are reliable and valid or are job-related. Human-rights tribunals and courts have ruled that any requirement that has a disproportionate effect on minority-group applicants is illegal unless it is related to job success or business necessity.

It is in the police departments' self-interest to ensure that selection standards, such as psychological tests and job interviews, are job-related. It might be helpful to collect validity data, if it is not already being collected. However, validity alone may not be sufficient. It may also be necessary to keep data on the adverse impact, if any, of the selection standards on minorities. As noted earlier, several police departments are already doing so.

Several boards of inquiry under human-rights statutes have found that the board of police commissioners, the chief of police, and police officers are all covered by human-rights legislation. In the case of *Prue* v. *City of Edmonton* (1985),[7] the court of Queen's bench confirmed that the Alberta *Individual's Rights Protection Act* does apply to the hiring of police officers. The case dealt with a provision in the collective agreement between the City of Edmonton and the Edmonton Police Association which provided that applicants must be younger than thirty-five years old. Mr Prue, aged forty-eight, had applied to become a police officer. In view of the collective agreement provision, his application was never considered because of his age. In the case of *Kickham* v. *Charlottetown (City of)* (1986), a board of inquiry found that the city had discriminated against Ms. Kickham for the position of police officer because of her sex, based on the results of biased job interviews.[8]

In a landmark decision, the Supreme Court of Canada affirmed (*C.N.R.* v. *Canada* [1987]) the decision of a human-rights tribunal requiring the Canadian National Railways (CN) to abandon certain mechanical aptitude tests and other selection standards, since the CN had no evidence of the validity of these tests and the tribunal had found widespread systemic discrimination against women in the employer's hiring practices.[9]

The purpose of adverse-impact analysis is to ensure not only that selection standards are applied uniformly to all groups of applicants, both minorities and non-minorities, but also that the net result of these standards is not to produce differences in the selection of various groups. A classic example of adverse impact is the requirement for minimum height and weight, which had been used extensively for police, fire-fighters, and some manual-labour positions. As the human-rights board of inquiry noted in *Colfer* v. *Ottawa Board of Commissioners of Police*,[10] the Ottawa police's height and weight requirements had the effect of disqualifying from employment as police officers a much larger per centage of women than men, and therefore had adverse and discriminatory effect. These requirements were declared as illegal.

One way to calculate adverse impact of selection procedures on minorities is to use a rule-of-thumb developed in the United States, called the four-fifths rule. The rule suggests that the hiring rate of any group must be at least 80 per cent of the hiring rate of the most favourably treated group. For example, if 60 per cent of non-minority applicants for police-officer jobs are selected, then the selection proportion of any minority group should be at least 48 per cent. Thus, suppose that 120 white, male applicants are processed through recruitment and 72 (60 per cent) are selected. If 50 VMs apply for the same position through a similar recruitment drive, and if VMs were hired at the same rate as whites, 30 VM applicants ideally would be selected (50 × .60). However, exact parity is not expected. The minimum number of VM hirings would be expected to be 24 (30 × .80), which is 80 per cent or four-fifths of the 60 per cent hiring rate for non-minorities. If the rate is smaller, one might initially conclude that discrimination in selection has probably occurred owing to disproportionate selection rates (Gatewood and Feild 1990).

3. Employment Equity

A majority of police agencies, as noted earlier, have voluntarily adopted EE plans. It is incumbent on other police departments to do the same. Outreach recruitment strategies are not very effective if systemic discrimination in selection, training, and promotion is not removed. EE involves undertaking positive measures and providing special accommodation, where necessary, to encourage VMs and others to apply for police jobs. Some of the positive measures for VMs and others include pre-employment counselling and training, internship programs, career-development and accelerated-promotion programs, short-term or bridging positions, providing for lateral entry into police departments, and special accommodation programs. An example of the latter is the Quebec Human Rights Commission's recommendation that the candidates who meet all the job requirements of the Montreal police department, but are unable to function in French, be given a conditional job offer, with the French course given at the expense of the Quebec government.

Research indicates that EE plans that do not include numerical goals and timetables to achieve eventual parity with the external-labour-force representation of VMs and others are not very effective (Jain and Hackett 1989). Therefore, EE plans must include the removal of job barriers; proactive measures and special accommodation to attract, recruit, train, and promote qualified VMs as police officers; and numerical goals and timetables with responsibility and accountability to achieve these goals (Jain and Hackett 1989, 1992).

4. New and Innovative Recruitment Strategies

It might be worthwhile for police departments to evaluate, on an experimental basis, the impact of the following on recruiting VMs:

- prompt testing and processing, or 'fast tracking,' of VM applicants and

others responding to outreach initiatives as in the case of Metropolitan Toronto, Calgary and other police departments
- building family support for the choice of policing as a career as in the case of (Vancouver, Metropolitan Toronto and others)
- police-selection process changes to eliminate systemic discrimination or obstacles in recruiting VMs, such as changes to the written examinations, interviews, and obstacles course (Metropolitan Toronto, Calgary, and others)
- scholarship programs (Ottawa)
- recruitment of minority youths during summer months (several forces in the study)
- hiring VM youths by proactive recruiting at shopping malls, high schools, and so on (Calgary)
- special recruiting teams, including VMs, to help recruit VMs (RCMP and several other police services).

5. *Organizational Culture*

A recent study (Ungerleider 1989), which examined the attitudinal dispositions of 251 municipal police officers in two major Canadian municipal police forces, found that nearly three-quarters of the officers in the sample made irrational judgments about the members of ethnocultural groups, and therefore lacked awareness and sensitivity to cultural and social diversity in their communities. If this finding holds for other police departments, institutional change, in order to affect the organizational culture, needs to be implemented forthwith so that VMs will feel welcomed and be encouraged to join police forces. Police departments, therefore, may wish to adopt organization development strategies in order to effect attitudinal and behavioural changes that are supportive of diversity.

NOTES

This article has been adapted from a report commissioned by the Solicitor General Canada.

1 In this paper, the term racial minorities is used to include visible minorities and Aboriginals. The term visible minorities refers to non-whites as defined by the *Federal Employment Equity Act*, R.S.C. 1985, c.E-5.4. and excludes Aboriginal people.

2 In some cases, owing to the multiple-hurdles approach, each selection standard could be eliminatory. Hence, the interview could count for 100 per cent in the selection process.

3 The 'community' is defined as (a) those between 15 and 64 years of age; (b) in

the area served by the police force; and (c) any Ontario reserve within 60 kilometres of that area. These data were to be made available by the Ministry of the Ontario Solicitor General (*Overview of Regulation*, undated).

4 The ministry is responsible for monitoring EE plans, and for advising the Ontario Civilian Commission on Police Services when a police service fails to comply with the act or meet its numerical goals and timetables. The Commission can apply sanctions (*Overview*, undated).

5 The Metropolitan Toronto Police was perhaps the first department to develop an EE program with numerical goals and timetables beginning 1986. The OPP has had an EE plan for some time, before the 1990 Ontario legislation.

6 As Superintendent Kerr of the MTP has pointed out (September 1990), 'of all applications given out, 24% are not returned. Of candidates who have submitted application forms, 21% either withdraw or fail to show up for initial testing at C.O. Bick College.' He went on to note that 'this type of analysis will help zero-in on where problems may exist ... [and] where follow-up outreach efforts need to be made.'

7 *Prue* v. *City of Edmonton and the Board of Police Commissions and the Chief of Police of the City of Edmonton and Edmonton Police Association* (1985), 6 C.H.R.R. D/2544.

8 *Kickham* v. *Charlottetown (City of)* (1986), 7 C.H.R.R. Decision 3481 (PEI Board of Inquiry). Ms. Kickham, one of eight final candidates for the position of police officer, was given the highest rating score by the committee appointed by the Charlottetown City Council to recommend a candidate for the position. However, when Ms. Kickham received the highest rating, the committee decided to change the rating method, dropping the highest and lowest scores of the top three candidates. This resulted in Ms. Kickham receiving the lowest score. When the committee subsequently voted on which candidate to recommend, the vote was tied between Ms. Kickham and a male candidate. The chairman of the committee then broke the tie by voting in favour of the male candidate, and the committee recommended hiring him.

The board of inquiry found that the decision to change the scoring method was made because Ms. Kickham had received the highest score. The board also found that the chairman of the committee, Alderman Squarebriggs, was influenced in his voting by discriminatory objections to hiring a woman as a police officer that were raised by the police officials who were members of the committee. The board of inquiry ruled that the City of Charlottetown was liable for the discrimination since it had authorized the committee to make the recommendation, was informed of concerns regarding discrimination, and took no action on them.

9 *Canadian National Railway* v. *Canada (Canadian Human Rights Commission)*, [1987] 1 S.C.R. 1114.

10 *Colfer* v. *Ottawa Board of Commissioners of Police* (1979), unreported (Ontario Board of Inquiry).

REFERENCES

Abbate, G. 1992. 'Police prejudiced, report concludes: Bigotry not deliberate, but Auditor calls for sweeping changes in race relations.' Toronto *Globe and Mail*, 11 September, A18.

Action Travail des femmes v. *CNR* (1987), 8 C.H.R.R. Decision 664 (S.C.C.).

Amalfitano, J.G., and N.C. Kalt. 1977. 'Effects of Eye Contact on the Evaluation of Job Applicants.' *Journal of Employment Counselling* 14.

Appleby, T. 1991. 'Policing the ranks to find right balance.' Toronto *Globe and Mail*, 13 April, A8.

Bellemare, J. (Chair). 1988. *Investigation into Relations Between Police Forces, Visible and Other Ethnic Minorities*. Montreal: Quebec Human Rights Commission.

British Columbia Police Academy. 1989/90. *Annual Report*.

Cascio, W. 1991. 'Reconciling Economic and Social Objectives in Personnel Selection: Impact of Alternative Decision Rules.' In D. Saunders, ed., *Proceedings of the 1991 Conference on Human Rights and Employment*. Montreal: McGill University.

Cawsey, R.A. (Chair). 1991. *Justice on Trial: Report of the Task Force on the Criminal Justice System and Its Impact on the Indian and Métis People of Alberta* (Edmonton).

Cote, M. 1991. 'Visible Minorities in the Canadian Labour Force.' *Perspectives*

Discussion Paper. A Vision of the Future of Policing in Canada: Police Challenge 2000. 1990. Ottawa: Solicitor General Canada, October.

Evaluation of the Police-Minority Initiative in the Multiculturalism Sector. 1990. Ottawa: Carenage Consultants.

Fleras, A., F. Desroches, C. O'Toole, and G. Davies. 1989. 'Bridging the Gap: Towards a Multicultural Policing in Canada.' *Canadian Police College Journal* 13.

Gatewood, R., and H. Feild. 1990. *Human Resource Selection*, 2nd ed. (Fort Worth: Dryden Press).

Glen, I. 1991. 'Police and Visible Minorities.' In H.C. Jain, B. Pitts, and G. DeSantis, eds, *National Conference on Racial Equality in the Workplace: Retrospect and Prospect*. Hamilton: McMaster University and IRRA.

Hamilton, A.C., and C.M. Sinclair (Commissioners). 1991. *Report of the Aboriginal Inquiry of Manitoba: The Justice System and Aboriginal People*. Winnipeg: Queen's Printer.

Hickman, T.A. (Chair). 1989. *Royal Commission on the Donald Marshall Jr. Prosecution.* Nova Scotia: Queen's Printer.

Inkster, N. 1991. 'Luncheon Address.' In H.C. Jain, B. Pitts, and G. DeSantis, eds, *National Conference on Racial Equity in the Workplace: Retrospect and Prospect.* Hamilton: McMaster University and IRRA.

Jain, H.C. 1987. 'Recruitment of Racial Minorities in Canadian Police Forces.' *Relations Industrielles/Industrial Relations* 42.

– 1988. 'The Recruitment and Selection of Visible Minorities in Canadian Police Organizations, 1985 to 1987.' *Canadian Public Administration* 13.

– 1988. *Recruitment and Selection of Visible Minorities in the Montreal and Other Selected Police Organizations.* Montreal: Testimony to the Quebec Human Rights Commission.

Jain, H.C., and R. Hackett. 1989. 'Measuring Effectiveness of Employment Equity Programs in Canada: Public Policy and a Survey.' *Canadian Public Policy* 15, 189.

– 1992. 'A Comparison of Employment-Equity and Non-Employment Equity Organizations on Designated Group Representation and Views Towards Staffing.' *Canadian Public Administration* 35, 103.

Jayewardene, C.H.S., and C.K. Talbot. 1990. *Police Recruitment of Ethnic Minorities.* Ottawa: Canadian Police College.

Kickham v. *Charlottetown (City of)* (1986), 7 C.H.R.R. Decision 3481 (Board of Inquiry).

Laypersons' Guide to Regulation: Employment Equity. Toronto: Ontario Ministry of the Solicitor General. Undated.

Lewis, C. 1990. 'The Report of the Race Relations and Policing Task Force.' *Canadian Police College Journal* 14.

Lewis, C. (Chair). 1989. *The Report of the Race Relations and Policing Task Force.* Toronto: Solicitor General.

– 1992. *The Report of the Race Relations and Policing Task Force.* Toronto.

Lunney, R.F. 1985. 'Police-Minority Relations.' *Currents* 3.

McFarlane, J. *A Career in Policing: Speaker's Kit.* Charlottetown: Atlantic Police Academy.

Marron, K. 1990. 'Accept multiracial society or face unrest, Inkster says.' Toronto *Globe and Mail*, 5 March, D12.

News Release. 1991. Ontario Ministry of the Solicitor General, 10 April.

Normandeau, A. 1990. 'The Police and Ethnic Minorities.' *Canadian Police College Journal* 14.

Normandeau, A., and B. Leighton. 1990. *A Vision of the Future of Policing in Canada: Police Challenge 2000.* Ottawa: Solicitor General Canada.

Overview of Regulation: Employment Equity, Ontario Police Services. Toronto: Ontario Ministry of the Solicitor General. Undated.

Oziewicz, E. 1993. 'Better training on racism urged for Montreal police: Prejudiced attitudes must change, Ryan says.' Toronto *Globe and Mail*, 19 January, A4.

Picton, J. 1992. 'Visible minority population soaring, study finds' *Toronto Star*, 30 May, A1.

Regulation Made Under the Police Services Act. 1990. Toronto: Ontario Ministry of the Solicitor General.

Rolf, C.H. (Chair). 1991. *Policing in Relation to the Blood Tribe, Report of a Public Inquiry*, vol. 1: Findings and Recommendations (February).

Small, P. 1992. 'Report accuses Metro Police of "race bias."' *Toronto Star*, 11 September, A1.

Together, vol. 2 (Winter 1990).

Tugwell, M., and J. Thompson. 1991. *The Legacy of Oka*. MacKenzie Paper 21. Toronto: MacKenzie Institute.

Ungerleider, C.S. 1989. 'Intercultural Awareness and Sensitivity of Canadian Police Officers' *Canadian Public Administration*.

Wiesner, W., and S. Cronshaw. 1988. 'A Meta-Analytic Investigation of the Impact of Interview Format and Degree of Structure on the Validity of the Employment Interview.' *Journal of Occidental Psychology* 61

Young, D.M., and E.G. Beier. 1977. 'The Role of Applicant Non-Verbal Communication in the Employment Interview.' *Journal of Employment Counselling* 14.

PART FOUR: POLICE AND POLITICS

9

The Police and Politics: The Politics of Independence

JAMES C. ROBB

> Most police officers stoutly maintain that policing and politics don't mix. Chief Constables regularly declaim on the political neutrality of the police service and on the dangers embodied in the current campaigns for enhanced accountability to democratically-elected local authorities, denouncing this as an insidious bid for 'political' control. Sir Robert Mark claimed the support of a 'long tradition of constitutional freedom from political interference in our operational role ... the police are not servants of government at any level. We do not act at the behest of a minister or any political party, not even the party in government. We act on behalf of the people as a whole.'[1]

> We are now witnessing the domination of the police service as a necessary pre-requisite of the creation in this country of a society based on Marxist Communist principles. The current concern over policing being expressed by certain political factions has got precious little to do with better community participation in police affairs, or the improvement of democracy – rather it is the first conscious step manifesting itself towards the political control of the police, without which the dream of a totalitarian, one-party state in this country cannot be realised.'[2]

In the above quotations we see a dichotomy of views central to the issue of police and politics. On the one hand, we have the view to which most police would, if asked, ascribe: the police officer is a servant of the people, assigned the task of enforcement of the laws of the state. On the other, we have an overtly political statement emphasizing the potential for political activity by the police.

Yet, each statement is political, having a common genesis in the desire to ward off measures designed to increase police accountability to other public bodies. Equally, however, there are some differences. The first quotation posits the police as enforcing the law of the land as established by others; the second posits the police as the institution that seeks to preserve democratic values as defined by the police. The two statements embody the central dilemma in addressing the question of police and politics. We desire police forces that will apply the law even-handedly and without political considerations entering into police decision-making. At the same time, history and current events press upon us the reality that policing is an inherently political activity.[3]

This paper will attempt to explore our hesitant approach to the central issue of defining the role of the police in its political context and some of the reasons for that hesitation.

CURRENT TENSIONS

If any one period warranted a public review of the issue of police and politics, it should have been the years 1990–1. Consider the following events, which could have triggered far wider public debate on the role of the police in our society:

1 The budget leak: three persons are charged in connection with a leaked budget, resulting in a trial that dissolves amidst allegations of politically influenced prosecutions.[4]
2 The Oka barricade: Mohawk people at the barricade welcome the replacement of the Quebec provincial police by the Canadian military. While one could argue that this demonstrated a consciousness of police paramilitarism,[5] the more likely explanation is a perception of the Quebec police as the coercive instrument of the Quebec state. Either explanation would have warranted greater scrutiny in the aftermath of Oka.
3 Several reports of inquiries into the criminal-justice system and Aboriginal peoples are issued. The vast overrepresentation of Aboriginal peoples in our jails[6] is not something recently discovered. However, the scathing indictment of the treatment of Aboriginal peoples in our justice system by judicial inquiries is concentrated in this period. The Marshall Report,[7] reports from public inquiries in Manitoba and Saskatchewan,[8] and an Alberta inquiry[9] are scathing in tone and content. Issues of selective enforcement, variations in enforcement, and overt racism are raised. The Manitoba inquiry was sparked by the police shooting of a native leader that, the report concluded, had been motivated by racism, with a subsequent inquiry aimed solely at clearing the police of wrongdoing.
4 The activities of CSIS: New Democrat MPs, attending a northern meeting, complain of CSIS surveillance.[10] The Civil Liberties Association had pre-

viously commenced an action to have the mandate of the Canadian intelligence forces ruled unconstitutional as being too vague, too broad, and too zealously enforced.[11]

5 Picket-line violence: once again, striking workers employed by the federal government and Canada Post confront police on the picket lines. Historically, labour strife has contributed greatly to theories of the police as the coercive arm of the capitalist class.[12]

6 Bill C-79: a bill potentially fettering certain police investigations involving MPs and senators is passed with barely a ripple of public comment, save for some muted New Democrat criticism. A few short years ago, administrative memos from the Alberta Attorney General's department to police forces detailing procedures for investigations involving MLAs and other prominent persons, in part, spawned an inquiry.[13]

7 A Manitoba police chief resigns amidst allegations that a prosecution of a prominent lawyer was improperly motivated. An independently conducted report concludes that a charge of sexual assault had been motivated by an intense dislike of the lawyer, who was a harsh critic of the Winnipeg police, particularly during the Aboriginal Justice Inquiry. The report concluded that 'payback' was at work in a not very subtle fashion.[14]

Each of the above, taken alone, would justify much greater public examination of the issue of police and politics than has occurred; in combination, the paucity of comment is truly deafening. Two events particularly stand out.

1. The Budget Leak

The case of *R.* v. *Appleby, Belisle and Small*[15] involved three persons charged with the theft and possession of stolen goods, namely, a copy of a pamphlet disclosing details of a pending federal budget. A motion was brought by the defence to stay the informations on the ground of abuse of process: (1) that the charges were politically motivated; and (2) that the prosecution of journalist Doug Small was an attempt to restrict his freedom of expression.

There were two leaks of the budget document in question. One involved the removal of a copy of the 'Budget in Brief' by a government employee, and its exchange through several hands to the offices of Mutual Life. The second was the apparently innocent removal of a discarded misprint of the budget pamphlet by an employee of a waste-recycling company, and its exchange, through several hands, to the journalist Small, who promptly disclosed the document and contents on television.

The case was investigated by the RCMP, and in particular by Staff Sergeant

Jordan, an experienced officer. As officer in charge of the investigation, Jordan concluded that charges could not properly be brought against the three accused for a number of reasons: (1) confessions of two of the accused were likely inadmissible; (2) the recycling-company employee had successfully passed a polygraph test in which he asserted an absence of dishonest intent in the original taking; (3) the prosecution could be perceived as being unduly selective, since numerous other individuals had at least as much involvement as the three accused; (4) charging only the three would ignore the first leak involving Mutual Life, which was not yet public knowledge and which, the officer concluded, raised the only valid charge; and (5) based on his understanding of the law, the officer also concluded that the trashed document would be construed as having virtually nil value.[16] In short, his opinion that charges should not proceed against the three were predicated upon both ethical and legal considerations.

A series of meetings then ensued involving Jordan, other senior officers, and Crown counsel from both federal and provincial governments. Characterized as unremarkable strategy sessions by the trial judge,[17] the meetings none the less left Jordan with the view that charges were inappropriate. Significantly, Crown counsel at the meetings neither gave appropriate directions to the RCMP on the law, nor took control of the decisions to be made: '"Resolute in their irresolution," the only solace they would offer to the R.C.M.P. was to say that the charges, if laid, would not be withdrawn.'[18] It also appears that a senior RCMP officer expressed the view that it was time to teach journalists a lesson.[19]

Following his continued refusal to lay charges, Jordan was removed from the handling of the case. His immediate superior similarly refused to swear the informations. Ultimately, a corporal was selected, and he swore the informations before a justice of the peace after normal working hours.

The legal result in the case is not remarkable. While it was Jordan's impression that the prosecutions were politically motivated, the court was satisfied that no political pressure had emanated from either the Prime Minister's Office or the Privy Council Office. Absent evidence of 'top down' influence, the motion to stay the informations would have to be dismissed. But, given the paltry value of the document, it would be an abuse of process to permit the prosecution.[20]

The questions raised by the case, however, are remarkable. Jordan was described as an honest witness.[21] Consider the ramifications of the following questions and answers of Jordan:

Q. And, in addition, you are not suggesting, sir, that, for example, any public remarks of elected officials would sway your own decision-making process, that is, yours, Staff Sergeant Jordan?

A. No, they would be taken into account. I would know that they were there. They were part of the reality of the situation, but they would not induce me to act more aggressively, I hope.

Q. And for that matter, I take it, your view is that any such remarks could not possibly sway any other member of the R.C.M.P., right up on to the Commissioner?

A. No, that's not my view. I think it possible.[22]

This statement strikes at the heart of the theory of political independence of the police in Canada.

A further consideration is the individual and combined effect of three factors in the case. First, there is the ruling that only 'top down' political influence can render a prosecution an abuse process. Apparently, the fact that a charge might be laid in anticipation of what politicians may want, or premised on a political viewpoint independently held by the police (for example, that it was time to teach journalists a lesson), is irrelevant.

Second, the position of the Crown counsel in the case was that the matter of the laying of charges is a matter of police discretion: 'He ... said it was the nature of their advice, when it would be given, that if the charges were laid they would not be withdrawn; however, there was no recommendation that the charge be laid. The discretion was in the hands of the police.'[23] This stated position emphasizes that the police have discretionary powers in the matter of the laying of charges and that, notwithstanding the *Nelles* case,[24] some prosecutors would commit to not withdrawing charges.[25] Yet, the role of Crown prosecutor is viewed as an important instrument in restraining the discretionary power of the police and in providing an immediate level of accountability. Weaknesses to the theory that an office equivalent to the Director of Public Prosecution in the United Kingdom could provide a means of restraining police discretion are apparent.[26]

The third factor was the ruling that discriminatory enforcement is not necessarily prohibited in Canada. There is no onus on the Crown to negate the existence of discriminatory enforcement; rather, the accused must show a violation of equality rights under s. 15 of the *Charter of Rights and Freedoms*. In turn, this requires proof that the discrimination was based on the prohibited or analogous grounds in s. 15.[27] It would be gross overstatement to say that this has the effect of legitimating selective enforcement; but it does raise a major issue of the degree to which selective enforcement is part of the pattern and policy of police enforcement in Canada.

While selective enforcement has been the subject of recent close scrutiny in reports dealing with Aboriginal peoples and the criminal-justice system,[28] it has been the subject of relatively mute comment by the courts. In *R.* v. *Ladouceur*[29] the dissenting judgment of Sopinka, J. notes that the powers afforded to police officers to stop vehicles randomly may permit a situation where 'racial considerations may be a factor too.'[30] The majority reviews the powers of the police in accordance with legal doctrine developed under the Charter in the context of powers needed for the police to address drunk driving. The latter approach serves to reinforce the idealization of the police as simply applying the law of the land in a neutral way – as independent, non-political servants of the people.

2. *Bill C-79*

The period from 1990–1 saw the prosecution of several MPs for offences involving allegations of dishonesty. At the same time, it was apparent that other police investigations were underway and, in at least one case, there was a parallel Senate investigation.[31] However, the extent of criminal investigation was not known until December 1989, when the Commissioner of the RCMP, Norman Inkster, appeared before the House of Commons Justice Committee. He confirmed that there were fifteen such investigations underway (thirty since 1985), involving members of all three national parties, and involving offences under the Criminal Code and *Canada Elections Act*.[32] It is important to note that of the several prosecutions underway, some involved allegations of misuse of public, meaning parliamentary, funds.[33]

Movement from Parliament Hill was remarkably swift. Bill C-79 was given first reading on 26 June 1990 and referred to the Special Committee on the Review of the Parliament of Canada. Second reading, following brief comment in the House, was given on 27 June 1990. The all-party committee, under the chairmanship of Minister of State Marcel Danis, reported back to the House on 20 November 1990 with an amended bill that had all-party support. Again, following brief debate, the bill was passed on 30 November 1990.[34]

The bill, as initially passed by the House of Commons, gave Parliament extraordinary authority. Sections 20.3 and 52.6 provide that the Standing Senate Committee on Internal Economy, Budgets and Administration and a newly established Board of Internal Economy of the House of Commons have exclusive authority to determine whether previous, current, or proposed use by a senator or MP of any funds, goods, services, or premises made available is or was proper. Senators or MPs may apply to the board for, or the board may, on its own initiative, provide the peace officer with, an opinion concerning the propriety of the use of funds, goods, services, or premises by a parliamentarian.

Once an opinion is provided to a peace officer, or once an officer is informed that an application for an opinion has been made, that officer is obliged to provide the opinion to a judge in an application for process. The judge must consider the opinion in determining whether to issue process or not. Applications for process include authorizations for wire-taps, special warrants, search warrants, restraint orders, the laying of an information, a summons, or an arrest warrant, or the confirmation of an appearance notice, promise to appear, or recognizance. Furthermore, the issuance of process for search warrants, the laying of an information, issuance of summons or arrest warrants, or confirmation of appearance would hereafter have to be made to a provincial court judge rather than before a justice of the peace. The board, operating under an oath of secrecy, may release their opinions to senators and MPs, and may include in the opinions any comments that the board considered relevant.

Bill C-79 was sent to the Senate for its approval. There, debate centred around the issue of whether the terms of the bill could force delays in police investigations. Under the provisions of the bill, once a police officer was made aware that an application for an opinion had been sought, the officer would be obliged to await the opinion in order to provide it to the judge. No time frames for rendering opinions were provided by the bill. Concluding that delays were possible, amendments were passed by the Senate to the effect that where an opinion is provided to a peace officer, and where an application for process is made, the opinion must be provided to the judge.[35]

The Senate amendments were debated 21, 26, and 27 March 1991 and concurred in by the House on 27 March 1991. Bill C-79 was given royal assent on 11 April 1991. It was only during the debate on the Senate amendments that all-party support for the bill broke down. Declaring themselves to be supportive of the bill in principle, New Democrats argued that the Senate amendments, in plugging one loophole, had created another. Specifically, it was argued that the Senate amendment had removed the obligation upon the board in fact to provide the opinion to a peace officer. Therefore, it was argued, in the event of a failure or refusal to provide the opinion to a police officer, a member could remain under public suspicion.[36] The amendments to the bill were passed without accepting further New Democrat amendments.

The New Democrat objection contained muted suggestions that the public might perceive that parliamentarians were protecting themselves once again; but given their early support for the bill that argument could not be pressed. There were further questions raised by the New Democrats as to the speed of obtaining royal assent and whether this matter had been rushed through at the request of a Conservative MP facing Criminal Code charges, which was hotly denied by the government.[37]

There are important details with respect to the bill that remain uncertain. For example, the discretion to withhold an opinion from an investigating officer raises questions regarding under what circumstances, and for what reason, it can be withheld. Furthermore, the bill simply indicates that the judge before whom an application for process is made must consider the opinion before deciding. Yet, the provisions of the bill also state that the boards have exclusive authority to determine whether there has been impropriety or unauthorized usage of funds, goods, or premises. An uncertain point, bound to be argued, is whether the judge is actually bound by the decision of the board.

There is a related further question as to how detailed the opinions will be: will they be factually based rather than statements of opinion and conclusions of law? These are important details. Ordinarily, a peace officer must, in order to obtain process, establish the existence of reasonable and probable grounds for believing that an offence has been committed. In making that determination, a peace officer cannot simply rely upon suspicion; nor can the officer ignore cogent information indicative of innocence.[38] To the extent that an opinion might assist the officer in determining whether an application for such things as search warrants is required, Parliament has created a special category of 'investigated Person' by permitting potential counterargument, if not binding opinion, to be placed before the judge.

The importance of the bill does not rest on its details and resulting legal arguments. Rather, it resides in the stunning display of a lack of confidence by Parliament in the impartial and independent exercise of police discretionary powers. The bill was a product of panic, seeking to shield parliamentarians from a zealous police force that had trained its attention upon politicians and expenditures of public funds – a sensitive public issue. While the debates in the House of Commons tended to concentrate on justifying the bill by using the example of a member seeking prior authorization for an expenditure (evidencing the unfairness of subsequent investigation and prosecution),[39] the terms of the bill permit the boards to provide retroactive rulings.

A seeming minor detail in the bill requires applications to be made before a judge rather than a justice of the peace, indicative of a belief that judges will provide more careful scrutiny of police applications. Yet, the norm for ordinary citizens under investigation will be applications to justices. Given the lack of confidence exhibited by Parliament, do others have any greater reason for confidence?

Both the budget-leak case and the circumstances surrounding Bill C-79 highlighted the essential characteristic of police powers as being discretionary. Certainly, in the first instance, both the independence and impartiality of the police were brought into question. Each case, albeit in an anomalous fashion, raises the issue of the source and breadth of police discretion and questions whether police truly are politically neutral.

THE CENTRAL QUESTION

The foremost question concerning police and politics, both historically and currently, is: what is the constitutional role that we want police forces to play in our society? There are drawbacks to even asking the question. It is evident that some police forces feel uncomfortable in the light of public scrutiny:

> No occupation in modern North American society has been as picked at, pried apart, put upon and misrepresented as police work, and unfortunately for the truth, the extreme ends of the spectrum of police activity have received the preponderance of attention. A great deal of learned sociological study has been devoted to the role of the police and the impact of their activity. While useful in the academic sense and potentially applicable in the future when sufficient findings are accumulated to permit validation, the great majority of these writings remain sterile, and have made a minimal contribution to the betterment of policing standards or methods. At the opposing end of the scale is that discordant mass of film and television drama on policing themes, replete with exaggerated violence and having little in common with reality. In the middle there are a few well-researched and thoughtful study papers and serious published works, which may be recognized as a contribution to police science or the documentation of the real nature and performance of policing. *The Law Enforcement Handbook* is in this latter category.[40]

The 'real nature and performance of policing' is law enforcement according to the orthodox view. *The Law Enforcement Handbook*, cited in the above quotation as one of the few books on police work worth reading, speaks to that singular view. In essence, and without meaning to disparage it, the book is a practical guide to police investigatory techniques.

Within this context, raising the question of the constitutional role of police can be perceived as yet a further attack upon a profession that generally holds the perception of being 'attacked' from different quarters, and which feels a frustration with the courts, parole system, and the justice system in general, all of which tends to make it more difficult to do its job.[41]

The danger is that raising this question then serves only to marginalize (if not alienate) police from the discussion. This would result in placing the discussion on a wrong footing at its outset. By and large we accept the need for police in a way that defies left-right analysis. During the same period as the debate on Bill C-79, Hansard records numerous reference to members of both opposition parties presenting petitions on behalf of various communities urging the government to conclude contracts ensuring the continuing presence of the RCMP in their communities. It would be fatuous to suggest that any country, socialist or capitalist, has found a means of dispensing with the police.

While there may be consensus as to the necessity of having police, it is not at all clear that there is agreement as to their proper constitutional role. If Reiner is correct, acceptance of the role of police as orthodoxy defines it was achieved by consensus. In his words: 'By the 1950s "policing by consent" was achieved in Britain to the maximal degree it is ever attainable – the wholehearted approval of the majority of the population who do not experience the coercive exercise of political powers to any significant extent, and *de facto* acceptance of the legitimacy of the institution by those who do. Police power, i.e., the capacity to inflict legal sanctions including force, had been transmuted into authority, power which is accepted as at least minimally legitimate.'[42]

Consensus is a fragile creature that can be fractured by events that shake public confidence. Such events can include corruption scandals such as those in the United States and the United Kingdom;[43] incidents of police wrongdoing;[44] indications of improperly obtained convictions;[45] racial tensions[46]; and massive displays of force.[47] Still, while aspects of some of these events were present during the 1990–1 period, we have not declared a crisis of confidence. While there are signs of fractures in the Canadian consensus concerning police (particularly with the ever-increasing demand for a separate justice system for Aboriginal peoples), the topic of the role of the police does not appear anywhere on the political horizon. Why not?

Perhaps it is part of the Canadian culture to be deferential to authority;[48] or perhaps we are preoccupied with economic and seemingly larger constitutional concerns. An equally plausible explanation is simply that we have never debated the constitutional role of the police. Rather, through the unquestioning adoption of the independence theory of the police,[49] we have so depoliticized our conception of the police that the discussion of their constitutional role is unlikely to occur.

Granted, the discussion of constitutional role is notoriously difficult. There has been little enough consensus on the origins of the police and policing. Theories concentrate on the need to respond to rising crime rates and to restore social order in the face of chaos,[50] or the need to respond to gangsterism,[51] through the creation of independent, non-partisan civil police forces. These theories, in turn, have been described as being too ethnocentric in their approach by ignoring the variety of policing models that diverge from the British model and by disregarding the prior development of colonial police forces as a means to establish and maintain social order in the colonies on behalf of the Imperial power.

Given the complexity of argument surrounding the origins of police forces and their reason for existence, it is not surprising that debate on the role of the police is equally varied. It ranges from the theory of the independent, impartial, non-partisan police force that investigates and enforces the law to the revisionist theory that police forces are simply the coercive instruments of an oppressive capitalist class.[52]

In Canada, while it has been recognized that the RCMP had its origins in previous British experience in the development of a civil police force in Ireland, the effects of that recognition have only been considered in the context of the development of paramilitary forces and consequent paramilitary-type structures and discipline processes.[53] What has not been recognized sufficiently as part of the colonialization process is the adoption of the independence theory of the police.

The independence theory has it that police officers exercise an original, not a delegated, authority.[54] That is, it is a police officer's duty to enforce the law of the land. In doing so, the responsibility for law enforcement is upon the officer: the officer 'is answerable to the law and to the law alone.'[55] Thus, the independence theory has three parts to it: (1) that the function of a police officer is to enforce the law of the state; (2) that this duty is owed to the public, not to the executive of government; and, therefore, (3) that in order to be able to comply freely with that function and that duty, independence from political masters is necessary. As noted by the Law Reform Commission of Canada, this theory was adopted in Canada over a hundred years ago.[56] While it has been recognized that police may be subject to *some* statutory regulation,[57] conferral of independence by statute is not necessary. It would simply be declaratory of a long-established constitutional position.

We must not, however, stop with the theory of independence as it relates solely to the police, for its full impact can be felt only if one understands that the theory permeates the whole of the criminal-justice system in Canada. The attorney general is to be, and is considered to be, independent of partisan political motives,[58] notwithstanding the accountability of the attorney general to the legislature. Similarly, the Crown prosecutors, having day-to-day control of the administration of justice, are to be viewed as enjoying a broad and generous area of unfettered discretion.[59] One such area of discretion is the power to stay charges brought by either the police or private prosecutors that, in the opinion of the government prosecutor, ought not to be proceeded with.[60] The *Nelles*[61] case may have had the effect of elevating that discretion to the status of duty, in which case neither the attorney general nor the legislature could restrict it.

In addition, the courts are to be independent of government; indeed, this is a constitutional requirement.[62] Therefore, at each critical stage of the criminal process there is an independent servant of the public, not of the government. The independent police officer determines who will be charged and with what offences; the independent Crown counsel vets the charges and conducts the case in court; the independent judge sits as a neutral arbiter of the dispute between the state and the accused. To admit a political role exercised by the police is likewise to admit a potential political role exercised by the other independent levels of the criminal-justice system.

The one place in the system where we are prepared to assume the possibility of some political contamination is at the level of the attorney general. This recognition leads to advocating (and adopting) the establishment an office of Director of Public Prosecutor (who would presumably be independent)[63] to increase the distance between the attorney general and Crown counsel. Largely ignored, even in light of cases such as *Nelles*, *Appleby et al.*, and *R.* v. *Donaldson*,[64] is the question of whether there is a need to distance the prosecutors and the police from political influence.

The theory of independence is at its heart a political doctrine that assumes a particular role for the police, usually defined as the enforcement of the law through the detection of criminals and the preservation of the peace. As political theory, the independence doctrine, insofar as it defines the role of the police, is clearly subject to political debate and critique.[65] But, as legal, constitutional doctrine, such debate is more problematic, for the role of the police is assumed to have been defined.

In terms of political theory, the political ramifications of discretionary power are open to scrutiny. As Lustgarten has pointed out: 'The fundamental fact about policing is the inevitability and breadth of *discretion*. Concretely this means that the criminal law is never fully enforced: and underenforcement all too easily leads to *selective* enforcement, which has demonstrable class, race and moralistic biases.'[66] Strategies of community-based policing[67] and targeting (of either particular geographic areas or ethnic groups) are proposed to counteract some of the problems of discretion. Such strategies are rarely imposed upon police by government but, rather, are more likely to be joint ventures of police and government.[68] But, as part of the legal doctrine of independence, methods of controlling police discretion are more difficult to implement. Imagine for a moment a government attempting to proscribe or limit police strategies. The issue would not be whether the government was correct in its decision that such strategies should be restricted, but whether the government had the authority to implement such a restriction.

As part of political theory, the overt political activities of police would be viewed as just that – political activity. Clearly, police do engage in such activities. The funding of the Canadian Resource Centre for Victims of Crime by the Canadian Police Association,[69] annual demands by police for the return of capital punishment,[70] and criticisms of the Charter of Rights and Freedoms as impinging on their ability to do their job are surely political in nature, unless one takes a remarkably narrow view of the scope of politics. While not as overt as the efforts of American police associations that engage in partisan politics, the role of Canadian associations as spokespersons for a particular police viewpoint, or as lobbyists, deserves far more attention than it has received.[71] But, in terms of legal doctrine, such activity can be viewed as legitimate activity necessary for the maintenance of a historic function. The issue appears to be whether there is any evidence of overtly partisan behaviour that would be inconsistent with the theory of independence.[72]

CONCLUSION

The unquestioning adoption by Canadian courts of the theory of independence means that, in a very real sense, we have never debated the role of the police in our society and certainly not the constitutional role of the police in society. Such debate is not impossible, but carries with it the baggage of political interference with the police.

One result of the absence of debate is that the political debate concerning police activities tends to be carefully circumscribed, dealing more with issues of police accountability for misconduct or the extent to which extra police powers are required to equip the police with the ability to properly fulfil their role as law enforcers. A proper debate on the role of the police requires us to re-examine the assumptions underlying the theory of independence. That, at a minimum, would require us to recognize police activity for what it is – police activity – and to examine several factors (including the racial and gender make-up of police forces, the values held by police officers, and the values instilled by training) that could help lead to a new consensus on the role of the police.

The Aboriginal inquiries may give us a window of opportunity to begin such a debate, since they represent one of the few occasions in Canadian history in which underlying assumptions in this area have been examined. But we must not make the mistake of assuming that such issues are confined to the lives of Aboriginal peoples. The issues presented here have wider ramifications that deserve examination and debate – a debate that has not occurred, and is not likely to occur, in the Canadian courts.

NOTES

1 R. Reiner, *The Politics of the Police* (London: Harvester Wheatsheaf 1985), 1 [hereinafter *Politics*].

2 Ibid., 2; quote attributed to James Anderton, Chief Constable of Manchester.

3 Reiner, *Politics*, 2–3.
4 *R.* v. *Appleby, Belisle and Small* (1990), 78 C.R. (3d) 282 (Ont. P.C.).
5 An issue being addressed in other jurisdictions: see P. Waddington, 'Towards Paramilitarism? Dilemmas in Policing Civil Disorder.' *British Journal of Criminology* 27 (1987): 37.
6 See J. Bonta, 'Native Inmates: Institutional Response, Risk, and Needs.' *Canada Journal of Criminology* 31 (1989): 49; Indian Justice Review Committee (Canada), *Report of the Saskatchewan Indian Justice Review Committee* (Chair: Judge P. Linn) (Saskatchewan: The Committee 1992), 10–12; Public Inquiry into the Administration of Justice and Aboriginal Peoples, *Report of the Aboriginal Justice Inquiry of Manitoba*, vol. 1 (Winnipeg: The Inquiry 1991), 85–6 [hereinafter *Manitoba Inquiry*].
7 The Commission, *Report of the Royal Commission on the Donald Marshall, Jr. Prosecution* (Halifax: The Commission 1989) [hereinafter *Marshall Inquiry*].
8 See n. 6, above.
9 The Task Force, *Justice on Trial: Report of the Task Force on the Criminal Justice System and Its Impact on the Indian and Métis People of Alberta* (Edmonton: The Task Force 1991).
10 *Canadian Press*, 5 Feb. 1990; *Canadian Press*, 10 Oct. 1990.
11 *Canadian Civil Liberties Association* v. *Canada (Attorney-General)* (1992), 91 D.L.R. (4th) 38 (Ont. Gen. Ct.).
12 See A.L. Morton and G. Tate, *The British Labour Movement* (Westport, Ct.: Greenwood Press 1975); R. de Friend and S. Uglow, 'Policing Industrial Disputes,' in J. Baxter and L. Koffman, eds, *Police: The Constitution and the Community: A Collection of Original Essays on the Issues Raised by the Police and Criminal Evidence Act 1984* (Abingdon: Professional Books 1985), 62.
13 Canadian Bar Association Inquiry into the Administration of Justice in Alberta (1986) [unpublished].
14 'Winnipeg Police Chief resigns,' *Canadian Press*, 18 Sept. 1991.
15 See n. 4, above.
16 His understanding was stated to be correct by the trial judge; ibid., at 302–5.
17 Ibid., at 294.
18 In fact a charge against a fourth individual involving the leak to Mutual Life was withdrawn.
19 *Appleby*, at 300.
20 Ibid., at 306–7.
21 Ibid., at 292.
22 Ibid., at 299.
23 Ibid., at 295.
24 *Nelles* v. *R.* (1989), 71 C.R. (3d) 358 (S.C.C.), in which it was held that the

Crown did not have immunity from actions for malicious prosecution in circumstances where a prosecution is a result of improper motives.

25 In the earlier, corollary case of *R.* v. *Catago* (1977), 38 C.C.C. (2d) 296 (Man. C.A.) it was held that a blanket commitment to withdraw charges would be illegal.

26 The adoption of a Director of Public Prosecutions was a key recommendation of the *Marshall Inquiry* (see n. 7, above).

27 *Appleby*, at 300–1. See also *R.* v. *Paul Magder Furs Ltd.* (1989), 49 C.C.C. (3d) 267 (Ont. C.A.).

28 Selective enforcement was a major issue in each of the Marshall, Alberta, Saskatchewan, and Manitoba inquiries into Aboriginal peoples and the criminal-justice system.

29 (1990), 56 C.C.C. (3d) 22 (S.C.C.).

30 Ibid., at 29.

31 See Canada, *Proceedings of the Special Committee of the Senate on the Propriety of the Conduct of the Honourable Senator Cogger*, 5 Dec. 1989, 21 Feb. 1990, 10 Apr. 1990, 10 May 1990, 14 May 1990.

32 *Ottawa Letter*, 18 Dec. 1989, 51.

33 Ibid., 20 Nov. 1989, 372.

34 *An Act to Amend the Parliament of Canada Act*, S.C. 1991, c.20.

35 Senate, *Debates*, 6 March 1991, 5448–50.

36 House of Commons, *Debates*, 26 March 1991, 18997ff.

37 House of Commons, *Debates*, 15 May 1991, 89; 17 May 1991, 254.

38 *Chartier* v. *Quebec* (1979), 9 C.R. (3d) 97 (S.C.C.).

39 See Senate, *Debates*, 6 March 1991, 5448, in which the example of a member seeking and obtaining approval for the purchase of a Mercedes-Benz with public funds was actually disapproved of.

40 R. Lunney, 'Preface,' in D. Rowland and J. Bailey, *The Law Enforcement Handbook* (Toronto: Methuen 1983). R. Lunney was at the time the Edmonton chief of police.

41 R.L. Jackson, *Canadian Police Labour Relations in the '80's: New Environmental Concerns* (Kingston: Industrial Relations Centre, Queen's University 1986), 11.

42 Reiner, *Politics*, 51.

43 Ibid., 65.

44 In Manitoba, part of the inquiry into the Winnipeg police force centred around allegations that some police officers were engaged in a theft ring; see n. 14, above.

45 See *R.* v. *Marshall* (1983), 57 N.S.R. (2d) 286 (N.S.C.A.); *Reference Re Milgaard* (1992), 71 C.C.C. (3d) 260 (S.C.C.); *R.* v. *Nepoose* (1992), 71 C.C.C. (3d) 419 (Alta. C.A.).

46 Which created virtual 'no go' areas for police in the UK.
47 None more so than during the Oka crisis, but repeated to some degree at picket lines.
48 E.Z. Friedenberg, *Deference to Authority: The Case of Canada* (New York: Random House 1980).
49 Reiner *Politics*, 1–2.
50 Ibid., 32–9.
51 M. Brogden, 'The Emergence of the Police – The Colonial Dimension,' *British Journal of Criminology* 27 (1987): 6–7.
52 Reiner *Politics*.
53 The Commission of Inquiry, *The Report of the Commission of Inquiry Relating to Public Complaints, Internal Discipline and Grievance Procedure Within the Royal Canadian Mounted Police* (Ottawa: Information Canada 1976), 16–19.
54 I.T. Oliver, *Police, Government and Accountability* (Great Britain: MacMillan Basingstroke 1987), 16–17.
55 *R.* v. *Commissioner of Police of the Metropolis, Ex parte Blackburn*, [1968] 2 Q.B. 118 at 136, per Lord Denning.
56 Law Reform Commission of Canada, *Controlling Criminal Prosecutions: The Attorney General and the Crown Prosecutor* (Working Paper 62) (Ottawa: Law Reform Commission of Canada 1990), 29.
57 Reiner, *Politics*, 17.
58 J. Edwards, *The Law Officers of the Crown* (London: Sweet & Maxwell 1964), 223.
59 Law Reform Commission, *Controlling Criminal Prosecutions*, 16.
60 *R.* v. *Bradley* (1975), 34 C.C.C. (2d) 482 (Ont. C.A.). In *Kostuch* v. *Kowalski* (1990), 75 Alta. L.R. (2d) 110 (Prov. Ct.) it was found that it was the policy of the Alberta Attorney General's Department to stay all private prosecutions in the environmental area, a number of which had been directed at the government.
61 See n. 24, above.
62 *Charter of Rights and Freedoms*, Part I of the *Constitution Act, 1982*, being Schedule B of the *Canada Act 1982* (U.K.), 1982, c. 11, s. 11(d); *Valente* v. *R.* (1985), 49 C.R. (3d) 97 (S.C.C.).
63 See *Marshall Inquiry*, n. 7, above), 52.
64 (1991), 58 C.C.C. (3d) 294 (B.C.C.A.), in which it was found that a police officer had deceived a justice of the peace on the advice of Crown counsel.
65 Reinter, *Politics*, 2–3.
66 L. Lustgarten, 'The Police and the Substantive Criminal Law,' *British Journal of Criminology* 27 (1987): 25.
67 Community-based policing is often advocated as a necessary step to reducing racial tensions between police and Aboriginal peoples: see Law Reform Commis-

sion of Canada, *Aboriginal Peoples and Criminal Justice* (Ottawa: Law Reform Commission of Canada 1991), 45; *Manitoba Inquiry*, 597–600.

68 See, for example, C. Murphy, *Community Based Policing: A Review of the Critical Issues* (Ottawa: Programs Branch, Ministry of the Solicitor General 1985), a joint project of the RCMP and the Solicitor General of Canada. In the *Manitoba Inquiry* (p. 600), the RCMP indicated that community-based policing should become the standard approach for all detachments.

69 With plans to create a television series highlighting controversial crimes: see 'High-profile prosecutor writes TV crime series,' *Edmonton Journal*, 26 Nov. 1992, B3.

70 In 1984 police demonstrated on Parliament Hill calling for its reinstatement.

71 It has been alleged that John Sewell lost a re-election bid as mayor of Toronto partly as a result of political action by the Toronto police association. See Jackson, *Canadian Police Labour Relations* (n. 41, above), 8–11, for a discussion of trends in police-association political activity and Philip Stenning, 'Police and Politics: There and Back and There Again?' in this volume.

72 Clearly, proposals that conform to a crime-control model would appeal more to one ideological persuasion than another, and in that sense are political.

10

The Police and Political Science in Canada

DAVID E. SMITH

When I was invited to present a paper at this symposium, I welcomed the opportunity to explore a subject new to me. I did not realize that it was new to Canadian political science as well. Why I should have been surprised I am not sure, since in the quarter-century I have taught Canadian politics the subject of policing has never arisen in any substantive way. I assumed, I suppose, that political scientists elsewhere must be studying the topic. That supposition now appears invalid, as a bibliographic search quickly makes evident. In the *Directory of Political Scientists in Canada*, compiled in 1989, only one of the 699 respondents listed police or policing as subjects of specialization: Professor Allan R. McDougall is unique among Canadian political scientists in having written a monograph on the topic, *Policing: The Evolution of a Mandate*, an essay as much historical and comparative in design (looking at British and U.S. practices as well as Canadian) as it is politically analytic.[1] Again, there is no article on policing in the *Canadian Journal of Political Science* (published since 1968) and only one, a historical treatment of 'The Ontario "Gestapo" Affair,' in its predecessor, the *Canadian Journal of Economics and Political Science* (published between 1935 and 1967).[2]

It is possible that a study of policing might appear under the guise of public-policy analysis, and one such article, by a non-Canadian, has appeared in *Canadian Public Administration*, the journal of the Institute of Public Administration of Canada, founded in 1958. That article, entitled 'The Police and the Implementation of Public Law,' is unusual not only for its subject-matter but also for the link it makes between police and the implementation of law.[3] Part of its argument concerns the discretionary power of the police to invoke the criminal law and the variability in law enforcement that may result from the exercise of this discretion. In a federal country as large and diverse as Canada, it is not hard to see the political implications of this argument. Canadian political scientists, however, have been slow to explore its implications. Indeed, none of the principal texts used to teach Canadian politics – *The Government of Canada* by R. MacGregor Dawson (now *Dawson's The Government of Canada* by Norman Ward), Richard J. Van Loon and Michael S. Whittington, *The Canadian Political System*, and Robert J. and Doreen Jackson, *Politics in Canada* – cite either the subject of policing or specific police forces in their indexes.[4]

On several counts the omission is instructive about the discipline of political science in Canada and about its priorities. First, Canadian political scientists have been preoccupied with nationalism questions for more than half a century, beginning with the quest for constitutional autonomy from Great Britain and, then, concern for national unity (that is, the federalism question). In Quebec, the nationalism issue is, if anything, more dominant than elsewhere in Canada, but the perspective of its scholars is fundamentally different from that of colleagues in the rest of the country.

Second, because scholarly research follows academic preoccupations, political scientists devote extraordinary attention to constitutional questions, such as the division of powers and amending formulae, or to institutions and processes presumed to promote national integration. This explains the long but selective fascination political scientists have shown for studying political parties and elections. The research agenda of the Macdonald Commission (The Royal Commission on the Economic Union and Development Prospects for Canada), as far as political topics were concerned, accurately reflected the discipline's priorities.[5] An apparent exception to this generalization only proves its accuracy: concerns about regionalism or province-building, as it is sometimes called in the political-science literature, are from another perspective concerns about national unity. How else to explain the perennial interest in Senate reform? Senate reform is never proposed as a way of improving the legislative process or even the policies that process gives rise to, except to make them more acceptable to the regions or provinces.

Where Canadian political science has broken with past preoccupations and where it might be expected to approach the topic of this symposium is in its examination of the Canadian Charter of Rights and Freedoms and the implications of the Charter for traditional politics. Even here, however, old categories of interpretation persist: the Charter is viewed more as a political than as a legal agent. Its significance lies, it is said, in its potential to nationalize politics by empowering the previously powerless to challenge established élites and to check the fissiparous tendencies of modern Canadian federalism.[6] Interest in the Charter has stimulated interest in the courts, particularly the Supreme Court of Canada, and has directed attention to the long neglected role of law in politics.

But, again, the familiar concerns of political scientists – in the aggregation of interests and in the formation, structure, and performance of institutions – have been translated into the judicial realm. The same questions are asked of judicial activity as are asked of legislative and executive activity: how is policy made?, who influences it?, what shape does it take?

To the implementation of judicial decisions, as to the implementation of legislation, political scientists pay meager attention. Part of the reason is that outputs of institutions are more difficult to study than inputs. Inputs are both more public and less precise than outputs, although even here it is a question of degree; the activity of interest groups (an area of Canadian political science that still remains underdeveloped) is harder to investigate than that of political parties. Also, outputs are detailed (delegated legislation is a good example) and, if not actually secret, considerably less easy to scrutinize than inputs.[7] (For these same reasons, Canadian political scientists, as opposed to the media, have been slow to take advantage of data on government operations that freedom-of-information legislation offers). A further explanation for this lack of inquiry has to do with what Roger Tasse, a former Canadian deputy solicitor general, has labelled 'problem definition.'[8] Applied to the subject at hand, what Tasse says is that unless questions with a political dimension are asked, there will be no reason for political scientists to investigate policing.

Political scientists have failed in this regard because, as students of political pathology, they have been blind to the political problems associated with policing. In their defence, it might be said, they reflect the society they serve. Over time the majority of Canadian citizens have demonstrated consistent support for the police. Professional acceptance, however, reflects something more: an assumption among students of politics that the police are instrumental enforcers of the law or, phrased more colloquially, that the police and the law are one and the same.[9] Society's view of this matter may be changing as a result of a series of incidents touching on the administration of justice as it affects Native peoples and other visible minorities. Yet, in the academy, it is the disciplines of sociology and criminology, not political science, that are responding to this change. In the absence of either a civil-rights movement, as in the United States, or organized and militant labour protests, as in Great Britain, there is no politicized debate in Canada about the organization, actions, accountability, or constitutional position of the police.

The high status of the police in Canada – elevated in the case of the Royal Canadian Mounted Police (RCMP) to that of a national symbol, with a 'prestige and experience' superior to that of the governmental agency that is supposed to control it, and with a reputation for non-partisanship as well – explains why the police are undervalued and overlooked as a subject for political researchers.[10] It might also be noted that two-thirds of these same researchers live in the two provinces that do not contract with the RCMP to provide provincial policing. Outside of Quebec the study of provincial politics trails in academic prestige behind the study of national politics, with knowledge of the Ontario Provincial Police only one of a number of provincial subjects to suffer as a result of this research pecking order. In Quebec, the study of its politics is treated not as the politics of a province but as a coequal of national politics. As a consequence, while it is not surprising to learn that 'the Quebec provincial police force has progressively evolved into an organization much more befitting an independent state than a province,'[11] it is remarkable that this development has not directed more academic attention to the Sûreté du Québec.

Excluding for the moment the distinct question of police and national security, of which more will be said later in this paper, the significance for the Canadian political system of what is apparently a disinterestedly loyal police force eludes political scientists. This paper will argue that there are good reasons for making the effort to see the significance, because some of the traditional concerns of the discipline and some new questions confronting it find common ground in the subject of police and policing.

FEDERALISM

There is no subject more central to the study of Canadian politics than that of federalism: the late Donald Smiley, a senior scholar of the topic, once observed that Canada is the only country in the world where airport news-stands sell books on federalism. The subject permeates all elements of our public and a good part of our private lives, although, as Smiley also warned: 'We know a good deal less about how federalism in government shapes and is shaped by other aspects of human organization.' At one level of analysis, policing would seem to confound the pre-eminence of federalism. Along with courts and the legal system, the police as instruments of the state appear to violate the division of powers that is the hallmark of Canadian federalism. A single system of appellate jurisdiction and centrally appointed judges, when combined with the dominance of the RCMP, who provide one-third of all public police in Canada (including eight of the ten provinces who contract for their services), are countervailing, and unexpected, forces in a federal system of government.

On the other hand, the *Constitution Act, 1867* provides for provincial administration of the courts and of the law, while judges are appointed from the bar of the province in which they sit. In a rare comment on the relationship of the courts to federalism, a political scientist, Edwin R. Black, has stated that 'far more significant for the federal situation than the judge's enjoyment of the traditional type of independence from the executive is his almost complete reliance on provincially-directed officers both for prosecution of cases in his court and execution of his judgements.'[12] The consequences of this distribution of functions has been to provincialize (or to federalize, since Canadian political scientists use the terms interchangeably) the legal system.

Thus, while on the constitutional surface there is not the duplication of institutions in the legal realm that is found among executives and legislatures, there is in the administration of law the practice of de facto federalism. Practitioners here are every bit as sensitive to provincial distinctiveness as are the authorities who formulate and execute provincial policy. There is, of course, the exception of a single criminal law. For while Parliament may possess the residual power to legislate for peace, order, and good government, judicial interpretation of SS-91 and SS-92 has limited use of the general power to extraordinary situations. In contrast, the criminal law is less constrained in its nationalizing effect, an influence that the Saskatchewan government in its brief to the Fraser Committee noted is growing in response to 'recent developments under the *Charter*, S.15 and the judicial trend towards requiring uniformity in the application of criminal legislation across the country.'[13] As a result of this trend, provincial power to complement the criminal law by regulation – in this instance as regards the display and sale of sexually explicit materials – may, said Saskatchewan, be 'futile.'

Yet in the exercise of the discretionary power that the police have to lay charges in criminal matters lies the potential for the practices of law enforcement to sustain societal and, in turn, political federalism: 'By responding to deviance, intervening and pressing charges on behalf of the public or by ignoring offences, the police participate in the definition of social norms or moral standards, as exemplified by their selective enforcement of pornography violations.'[14] The implications of this discretionary power and, more particularly, the variability in its use, are apparent although unstudied by political scientists. The degree of oversight exercised by provincial ministers of justice in the laying of charges, an aspect of the question of accountability to be discussed in the next section of this paper, varies so much among Canadian jurisdictions that a former deputy minister of justice in New Brunswick has described 'the very basic differences from province to province [as] amazing.'[15]

The variation may arise from different interpretations of prevailing moral standards or, equally, from different interpretations of the role of policing. Of this latter debate, for example, commentators have distinguished between the role of the police in repressing crime as opposed to containing it. The desire to contain, according to Jean-Paul Brodeur, explained the persistence of Montreal's 'red-light district' from 1880 to 1944, when public officials recognized prostitution as inevitable but when Roman Catholic opposition to the practice made its legalization politically impossible.[16] If the sources of this variation are multiple, so too are the consequences, for law enforcement is more than instrumental – it is also symbolic. According to Allan McDougall, 'the style of policing will have a direct impact on the citizen's view of the character of the rulers, and thus general acceptance of the state.'[17]

Because of the different arrangements for policing in Canada (federal, provincial, and municipal), variations in law enforcement may produce different perceptions of politics and government. To that extent, policing replicates other federal institutions; like them, it has the potential to reinforce territorially based differences among the units of the federal system. But, more than most public services, policing also exerts a differential impact on the citizens it touches. According to a British writer on the subject: 'The practical experience of different segments of the population with the police is very uneven.'[18] It is, he says, those 'at the base of the social hierarchy' on whom police activity 'bears most heavily,' a truth borne out by the proliferation of inquiries into the administration of Native justice and into charges of racism in police forces at the municipal level and above. Whether these serious indictments of systematic discrimination are sustained will be determined elsewhere, but the outcome of the investigations should not disguise the political significance of the events themselves.

At issue is the influence of these events on the conduct of policing in the Canadian federation. The relationship is not simple, since the context in which such conflicts take place will be changed by them. For example, whatever the jurisdiction of the police – provincial or municipal – implicated in the Donald Marshall case, the inquiry itself is neither: it is a national matter. Similarly, while controversy surrounding the actions of the police that led to protests of racism in Montreal in the summer of 1991 may be viewed by authorities as a local matter, the issues that flow from the controversy cannot be confined within local (or even provincial) boundaries. Thus, in some instances, the territorial specificity of politics, which federalism in Canada elevates and which the discretionary power of the police may on occasion reinforce, is reversed, and what in other circumstances might be conceived as being of local significance becomes national.

The tension arises when there is a conflict between maintaining local values and preserving social harmony across the nation. Canadian federalism has more usually accepted the diversity attendant upon the first of these options than sought to enforce national values from the centre. In the matter of rights and equality of treatment, this pattern of response may no longer be generally tolerated in the era of the Charter and instantaneous communication. That at least is one conclusion to be drawn from the failure of the Meech Lake Accord at the hands of some of its most vigorous critics: those who opposed the distinct-society clause and its putative override of the equality provisions of the Charter.[19]

The experience of the United States in the matter of policing is apposite. There the imposition of national, due-process norms has transformed policing down to the precinct level. Despite the overwhelming state and municipal base to police organization in that country, policing has ceased to be a federalism issue and has become, instead, a separation-of-powers issue. Beginning with the *Miranda* case, the United States Supreme Court imposed one 'code of behaviour' on the previous mosaic of local values in policing; in consequence, legal-process values have replaced community-public-order values.[20]

Though topically apposite, perhaps, United States experience is not socially or politically comparable to that of Canada. Seymour Martin Lipset is one commentator who has long cited the contrast in legal values and respect for the law between the two societies. In his most recent work on this theme, *Continental Divide: The Values and Institutions of the United States and Canada*, he has posited the 'due process model' in the former and the 'crime-control model' in the latter.[21] Canada, he says, is a country of 'generalized deference' and 'diffuse elitism' and, as a consequence, is less aggressive and more law-abiding than its neighbour. But that assertion, which repeated demonstrations of empirical evidence support, gives inadequate attention to the rapid emergence of an equality consciousness in Canadian society; this consciousness runs counter to and is even stronger than traditional beliefs (at least outside of wartime) in the virtues of a decentralized Canada. Part of the explanation for this change in attitude lies in the fact that élitism is no longer so 'diffuse' as it once was. The extent to which the change in attitude is nation-wide, and in particular its potency in Quebec when confronted by strong local values embedded in Québécois nationalism, is a crucial question to determine. Notwithstanding that unknown, outside of Quebec Charter-inspired beliefs in equality are certain to be invoked in controversies involving the police and disputable uses of their discretionary power, while inside Quebec the same response can be expected when minority rights are perceived to be adversely affected. In this manner, Charter beliefs will seek to temper the autonomy that the politics of federalism have in practice conferred on policing.

It is not the intent of this discussion to attribute a monocausal explanation for these complex events, still less to identify the police or policing as their genesis; it is, instead, to emphasize that in the politics of federalism the police have a role to play, one that grows in importance as the politics of federalism themselves change. If McDougall is right in his claim that the quality of policing determines the legitimacy of the state for its citizens, then political scientists need to look more closely than they have at the institutions and processes of policing. In particular, they need to study the effect of these factors on the politicization of visible minorities. Historically, immigrants have been accommodated within Canada's traditional political structures and, it may be assumed, that process is continuing. Arguably, the concentration of today's immigrants in a few large metropolitan centres, as opposed to the waves of rural settlers in the past, has localized the politics of immigrants to an extent not seen before. The extent is unknown, because the national perspective favoured by political scientists is responsible for the political experience of recent immigrants being vastly understudied. But it is exactly in this demographic configuration where policing practices can exert their greatest impact to reinforce or alienate support for the political system. American experience has shown how police behaviour, among other factors, can discredit traditional institutions and direct the disadvantaged (in this case urban blacks) to form political organizations outside the local political structures.[22]

The effect of policing on the politics of Native people would seem to be the reverse of that on immigrants. Rather than fracture and localize their politics, controversies surrounding police and Natives today are helping to nationalize Native politics. There are structural reasons as well for this difference, beginning with the constitutional responsibility of Parliament for 'Indians and lands reserved for the Indians.' But the 'rights dialogue' has aggregated Native politics in an unprecedented manner and, in contrast to a condition Alan Cairns once described as 'a classic case of state-sponsored fragmentation of the Canadian community' that hindered Aboriginal political unity, now promotes those politics.[23]

If the reciprocal effect of federalism and policing has been ignored in the past, to the disadvantage of understanding one part of the political system, there is a danger now in attributing too much influence to the relationship. The police are only one of many actors in the political system, and most of what they do has minimal direct bearing on politics. But there is a dimension to their work that has repercussions for federalism, both on structures and attitudes, and to that extent police make a contribution to one of the central concerns of Canadian politics.

ACCOUNTABILITY

In the exercise of their discretionary power the police, like Caesar's wife, must be above reproach. Yet while independence from the influence of government and private interests is essential, it should not be equated with an absence of responsibility. There are at least three external mechanisms of accountability that constrain the police in their duties: established political structures, instruments of public accountability, and jurisdictional limitations. Each is enveloped in politics, not all of it partisan in nature, and for this reason, notwithstanding its neglect by political science, police accountability has implications for the political system.

Established Political Structures

The concept of political accountability is central to the study of Canadian politics; the Whig interpretation of Canadian history in fact begins with the struggle for colonial self-government. But because Canadian politics is party-driven, Canadian political science gives pre-eminence to party matters and interprets accountability in peculiarly restrictive partisan terms. Its analytical focus is set more resolutely on parliamentary debate and procedures than on policy formulation and implementation. Therefore, because policing is about administration and details, and because politicians are reluctant to submit it to the kind of scrutiny that would open the matter to potential politicization, policing does not receive sustained legislative attention. In the normal course of events, the police appear exempt as a subject of investigation in the grand forum of the nation or the province, as the case may be.

The divide between police and politicians appears to have widened as a result of federal legislation proclaimed in May 1991. An amendment to the *Parliament of Canada Act* (Bill C-79) goes some way to placing Members of Parliament beyond the reach of the police. In future, the Board of Internal Economy of the House of Commons (an all-party management committee) has 'exclusive authority' to determine whether an MP has spent his office budget properly, while the RCMP are allowed to ask for a report from the board on an MP or senator under police investigation. The board's opinion is to be considered by a judge in any application by police for a search warrant, wire-tap, or interception of mail. Media and public attention momentarily focused on the genesis of this amendment – in response to reports late in 1989 that fifteen MPs and senators were under police investigation; on its formulation – at in-camera meetings of an all-party committee; and on its unorthodox proclamation – by order-in-council under the signature of four unidentified cabinet ministers on the day before a Conservative MP was charged on fourteen counts of fraud and breach of fraud. But outside of limited criticism from the New Democratic Party, the principle of the legislation – greater protection of elected politicians who are under police investigation – went unchallenged.[24]

Thus, the focus of political accountability lies not in Parliament but elsewhere, in the ministries concerned with police administration. At the national level this involves the solicitor general, who is responsible for the RCMP,[25] but also the attorney general, who in his or her prosecutorial function completes the act begun by the police when they lay charges. As a former deputy minister of justice of New Brunswick has observed: 'The general supervisory influence of the Minister of Justice plays a large role in influencing police activity and the manner and occasion for the exercise of police power.'[26] It is in this latter office that the interaction of politics and policing occurs in government.

Legal scholars have written extensively on this interaction, and for this reason it is unnecessary (and, probably, rash for a political scientist) to do more than quote these authorities in this discussion. For instance, John Ll.J. Edwards summarizes one aspect of the nature of the problems this arrangement of function poses: '[T]he Attorney General's authority ... derives from the Crown and is inherently an exercise of the prerogative powers of the Crown. Any attempt to invest the Crown's prosecutorial powers in the Government of Canada (or for that matter in the Government of a province) is to open the gates to the kind of partisan political abuses ... against which the independent nature of the office of the Attorney General is the constitutional shield.'[27]

To potential influence on the police of the attorney general, or more specifically his or her officials including Crown prosecutors, must be added the potential influence of government on the attorney general. British governmental structures offer a shield to this threat by excluding the attorney general from cabinet. By contrast, in Canada he or she is a high-ranking member of cabinet. Edwards asserts that until the late 1960s 'most Ministers of the Crown would have viewed their involvement in the disposition of such prosecutorial questions in Cabinet as a natural application of the principle of collective responsibility for unpalatable political decisions.'[28]

The implication of Canadian practice (in the provinces as well as at the federal level) is obvious for external accountability mechanisms. What Alan Grant describes as 'political discretion in the organization of law enforcement capability' has the potential to undermine confidence in both the legal and political systems. Which is not to say that the political discretion may not be used beneficially or that it is regularly abused, but to stress that the potential for conflict of interest opens the system to criticism and suspicion. In 1991, the claim was made that 'political manipulation delayed the laying of [fraud] charges' against a Progressive Conservative leadership candidate in Nova Scotia, so that he might stay in the race and divide delegate support to the benefit of the eventual winner;[29] that senior officials of the RCMP conspired 'to obstruct the course of justice by causing investigations of a political nature to be limited or cease' (at issue were charges against thirteen prominent Tories of conspiracy to defraud the federal government 'by bribery, bid-rigging, kickbacks, falsehood or other fraudulent means');[30] and that the RCMP laid criminal charges against a television reporter and two others in the matter of a federal budget leak for reasons a judge later attributed to 'unfairness and vexatiousness.'[31] How much direct political interference, if any, there was in these cases or whether, as was said by one RCMP officer in the budget-leak case, the 'charges were intended to please the RCMP's political masters' is tangential in this discussion to the damage each has caused the principle of ministerial accountability for police actions. More damning still, is the finding of the Marshall inquiry that in Nova Scotia there is a 'two tier system of justice,' one where the conduct of officials in both the RCMP and the Department of the Attorney General exemplified the attitude that 'status is important, and that one is not blind to influence in enforcing the law.'[32]

Traditional structures of political accountability are flawed if police independence is compromised on behalf of those who direct the police or who are associates of those who direct the police. Proposed remedies for the problem include enhancing the independence of the police by keeping government ignorant of police activities, a remedy that would ensure the end of political accountability altogether. In any case, recent Canadian experience casts doubt on the wisdom of proposals to augment police powers. Police forces as distinct as the Sûreté du Québec and the Winnipeg City Police have been described as having either a 'political agenda' or attitudes tantamount to one. In the first instance, the Oka crisis of 1990 resulted in a change in responsibile ministers and a move to check the autonomy of a force one observer said 'was never accountable to any of its masters.' In the second instance, the shooting death of Native leader J.J. Harper while undergoing arrest (itself a determinative event leading to that province's Native justice inquiry) prompted an investigation into the laying of criminal charges against Harper's lawyer and the claim by Manitoba's assistant deputy justice minister that a police officer admitted this was done so the lawyer would 'know how [the accused in the Harper case] feels.'[33]

Another possible remedy to the dilemma created by the conflicting demands for police independence and ministerial accountability for police action is found in proposals to create an office of public prosecutions 'to ensure the independence of the prosecution service from partisan influences, and reduce potential conflicts of interest within the Office of the Attorney General.'[34] The proposal has the virtue of removing discretion in the laying of charges from both partisan and police hands, and thus reduces the potential for conflict of interest as well as the suspicion of its presence. Yet the responsibility for laying charges does not disappear; it is only less visible and answerable in a public forum. The relationship that must necessarily (and often beneficially) exist between prosecutors and police remains. And as political-science students learn early in their careers, whenever there is a relationship there is politics. The absence of a linkage to partisan politics is not in itself a commendable feature; for while partisan considerations may distort aspects of police work, in the general matter of legislative oversight, partisanship promotes the acuity and perseverance of opposition.

Instruments of Public Accountability

If the Canadian governmental system is strong on political accountability, it is deficient in mechanisms to promote public accountability. Party discipline in Parliament and the patronage of the Crown exercised on advice of a partisan executive concentrate power and limit choice. Periodic revolts in the form of third parties and proposals from the regions for institutional reform have failed to democratize structures that pre-date Confederation. Arrangements for policing in Canada reflect this larger institutional structure. Crown appointment and centralized policy-making characterize both the RCMP and the provincial police forces of Ontario and Quebec.

Only at the margins of the political system has reform calculated to promote participation and accountability begun to appear in the last quarter-century. Competitive leadership selection and regularized policy conventions in political parties, election finance legislation to subsidize campaigns, and a series of procedural reforms to promote backbench activity in the House of Commons are innovations that originated in the 1960s, the decade of participatory democracy. In the same decade 'there was a marked shift in social attitudes in the area of civil rights. This new era of social awareness also brought an increasing demand for accountability on the part of the police and other public bodies. The rapid growth of ombudsman offices across Canada is one example of this.'[35] That quotation from the Marin Commission initiated the idea of a federal police ombudsman, a proposal that was repeated (using different nomenclature) by the McDonald Commission. In 1986 an amendment to the RCMP Act established the RCMP Public Complaints Commission, and a public-complaints process came into effect in 1988.

In its first *Annual Report, 1988–1989*, the Public Complaints Commission stated that 'external review and investigation of police conduct is emerging as an essential safeguard for free and democratic societies.'[36] Subsequent annual reports indicate the limitations of a complaints-focused procedure, beginning, in the words of its chairman, with the '"perception that a conflict of interest exists" because [the] watchdog committee is financed by the same minister who is responsible for the RCMP.'[37] That impression is reinforced when, as happened in 1991, the federal Department of Justice disputed the commission's jurisdiction to investigate senior RCMP officials implicated in the budget-leak case. Whether or not the commission possesses the necessary powers to conduct this particular investigation will be clarified if the commission seeks a ruling from the Federal Court of Canada. From the perspective of this paper, the controversy demonstrates the gap that may appear between intent and realization in institutional reform.

A fundamental question that needs to be asked of structural reform is, Whom does it serve? According to its *Annual Report, 1989–90*, approximately one-third of all complaints about RCMP activity in the previous year were made via the commission. As a mechanism to enforce public accountability, more needs to be known about the complainants who avail themselves of this route, as opposed to approaching the force directly: wherever there is a choice, there is politics. Since the adequacy of a remedial instrument depends upon its being known and available, there is a more basic question still: Who files complaints against the police? In the absence of more information to the contrary, it is reasonable to doubt that the persons who have most contact with the police in situations that give rise to controversy are those best prepared and ready to file complaints. Studies of political participation, including the act of voting, illustrate that the active citizens are the efficacious, those who feel able to effect change.

In his study of the municipal police boards that originated in the mid-nineteenth century, Professor Stenning has identified multiple causes and contradictory results in institutional reform.[38] On the one hand, the boards may be interpreted as a structural innovation to remove local politics from policing but, on the other hand, as Stenning convincingly argues, they can be viewed as part of a centralizing thrust by provincial governments to take control out of the hands of local authorities. The boards were most prominent in Ontario, and their introduction to limit municipal control of police is one aspect of the larger story of Oliver Mowat's policy of province-building.[39] Thus, the evolution of the police boards had as much to do with intergovernmental politics as it did with improving policing techniques. Furthermore, Stenning demonstrates the boards' modern-day limitations as instruments to enforce accountability. Among these are the part-time and short-term appointments of board members charged with the oversight of a permanent police force, the representative basis of board membership versus the increasing professionalism of the police, and the restraints on board jurisdiction that flow from such developments as collective bargaining. In other words, the factors that account for bureaucracy's advantage over the legislature and the consequent decline in legislative control of the executive are echoed in the particular world of police accountability.[40] Here, as in the matter of ministerial responsibility, policing constitutes a microcosm of the larger political concern about accountability.

Jurisdictional Limitations

Multiple jurisdictions impose, or should impose, the preconditions for accountability, since they limit the scope and focus of public policy. That is one of the customary reasons given for federalism: to allow the unit governments to act as social laboratories. The same argument applies to municipal government where, in the case of policing, the local community sets boundaries to municipal police activity. Jurisdictional determination is less simple than this, of course; under the *Constitution Act* municipalities are creatures of the province and municipal police forces may be subject on occasion to provincial dictation or supervision or, again, regional police structures may combine several municipal services. The principal Canadian exception to jurisdictional simplicity in the matter of policing is the performance by the RCMP of contract policing in eight of the provinces. In 1988 half of the RCMP's 18,000 members were designated as performing federal policing functions, the other half (in a ratio of approximately 2:1) provincial and municipal functions.[41] Provisions for contract policing are found in provincial police legislation whose details are discussed in Stenning's study paper, *Legal Status of the Police*.[42]

The history of contract policing goes beyond the bounds of this paper, although it is germane to note that Saskatchewan disbanded its provincial police force in the late 1920s – it had been introduced during the First World War – after relations between the general public and the force were found, in the words of the premier, J.G. Gardiner, 'too ... intim[ate].'[43] More revealing of the interpenetration of police and politics was a later royal-commission report that described the provincial-police policy 'a mistaken one ... because it brought the administration of the police in such proximity to the political side of the Government as to be too likely to encourage designing persons to try and affect it on political grounds, while it laid Government too easily open to the implication that the police were subject to political control.'[44]

By way of contrast, the politics of contract policing lie in the area of traditional federal-provincial relations. Since the agreement that provides for the contract is scheduled for renewal every ten years, the discussion of its terms becomes an occasion for federal-provincial bickering. The most recent example of this occurred early in 1991, when Ottawa pressed the provinces to increase their share of costs by 5 per cent. The provinces resisted, in Saskatchewan's case beyond the 31 March expiration of the agreement, thus necessitating a provincial order-in-council designating all members of the RCMP as special constables with authority to enforce all provincial and municipal laws.[45] Ultimately, the old agreement was extended for a year while discussions between the two levels of government continued.

In the realm of Canadian federalism the negotiations of the policing agreement are standard fare and touch not at all the matter of accountability. Since 1981 and the decision of the Supreme Court of Canada in *Attorney General of Alberta and Law Enforcement Appeal Board* v. *Putnam and Cramer* (1981), the relationship between contract policing and accountability, however, has entered a new era. In that case both the Alberta Court of Appeal and the Supreme Court found *ultra vires* provincial legislation empowering a provincial board to inquire into the conduct of RCMP members and, where appropriate, to impose discipline. That decision would appear to jeopardize the harmonization of federal and provincial interests in the matter of the policing made possible by the contract. That at least was the concern expressed in the same year by then RCMP Commissioner R.H. Simmonds. The commissioner noted that Canada's 'political arrangement allows for a high degree of local autonomy and local control,' that the RCMP had provided policing in the area that was Alberta for eighty-six years between 1874 and 1981 (for a time Alberta, too, had a provincial police force), and that the *Cramer* decision could promote an unravelling of Canada's legal and policing systems. He went so far as to propose a review of the criminal law and its procedures 'to determine which crimes should be regarded as local offences and thus the responsibility of local [i.e., provincial] governments for investigation and prosecution, by institutions that are created by and fully accountable to those governments, and which crimes by either their very nature – or the way in which they are conducted – should be the responsibility of the senior government.'[46] Contracting would cease when 'the cataloging [sic] is complete.' Disclaiming any suggestion that the provinces should have the power to enact criminal law, the Commissioner pressed his case on the grounds that 'the accountability issues' needed clarification. The alternative, he suggested, was the 'dismantling [of] a system that had promoted coordination and expertise.'[47]

This plea underlines the tension that exists between concern for maintaining local control and accountability, on the one hand, and promotion of national standards of law enforcement, on the other. Since it is in essence a political question, involving a choice between competing policy priorities, it is also a classic illustration of the tension endemic to federalism. Yet, the dilemma the choice presents, and which Commissioner Simmonds clearly articulates, is exceptional in the context of Canadian federalism because it is devoid of any partisan content. This is an instance where the goal of accountability penetrates federal structures and, in so doing, would, I believe, intrigue that Albertan, Donald Smiley, who perceived more acutely than most of his contemporaries the dynamic relationship of society and federal government.

REPRESENTATION

Although representation is a venerable concept in the literature of political science and although it is a prominent concern in the national-unity debate today, attention to the topic is recent in Canada. The mechanisms of the electoral system are only now the subject of investigation (through the Royal Commission on Electoral Reform and Party Financing), and while Senate reform is a familiar enough topic, current proposals are innovative in their singular goal to improve the capacity of the upper house to represent the units of the federal system.

Nor is the current focus limited to territorial matters. In the last twenty-five years representation has been recognized as having to do with more than geography. Royal commissions in the 1960s – on bilingualism and biculturalism and on the status of women – encouraged Canadians to think of representation in both linguistic and gender terms, as well as in the context of non-elected office. Sensitivity to the composition of institutions now extends beyond the world of government to, among other spheres, business, the media, and universities. Part of the explanation for the wider perception is the growing understanding among political scientists at least that politics cannot be confined only to the activity that occurs within the traditional governmental institutions of Western countries.

In turn, that change signifies what is not always made explicit: that representation is now conceived in symbolic as well as relational terms. If electoral representation is about a disposition to discover public opinion and to promote it, non-electoral representation (appointed boards and commissions, for example) is about mirroring society. This is not to say the reflection is necessarily accurate; usually it is distorted in favour of white, middle-aged, middle-class males.[48] Both symbolic and relational representational help to legitimate the existing arrangements of political and societal power. It is with the (comparatively) new perspective on symbolic representation that policing assumes political importance. This explains the critical attention that police recruitment and training policies receive.[49]

Changes in analytical concepts are not alone responsible for the interest expressed in police as representative bodies. The imperative is demographic as well. Canada is a much more heterogeneous society today than half a century ago, and 'the police are frequently the only front-line officials with whom many citizens are likely to interact. This is especially so in the case of non-whites, including recent third-world immigrants.'[50] Although Canada is a country of immigrants, in the first decade of this century immigrants settled in rural communities in western Canada. Although there has always been a large Native population, these persons used to be isolated on reserves or in provincial hinterlands. Now, immigrants and Natives congregate in large cities, with the former particularly concentrated in such metropolitan centres as Toronto, Montreal, and Vancouver. The result brings visible minorities (including Native persons) into close contact with white society, in part because rather than being self-sufficient like earlier immigrants, they are now dependent in such matters as employment, education, and housing.

Equally important, the change in living conditions occurs in the context of radically different public policies. At the opening of the century, immigration was expected to reinforce the values of a predominantly Anglo-Saxon society (thus the preference given British and northern European settlers); today immigrants arrive in a society that is officially bilingual and multicultural. Instead of reinforcing a common set of norms, immigrants contribute their own values, which are constitutionally protected (s. 27, *Constitution Act, 1982*). It is in this context that the police, as part of the state structure, assume a new and 'very special role' in community relations,[51] one that cannot escape being perceived as political, either by themselves or by the members of the communities they serve.

This is not the place to analyse the extent or effectiveness of police policies on minority recruitment; that has been done by others. Nor is it the place to evaluate the contributions these policies make to community stability or harmony. It is the place to underline, first, that in either activity the police play a symbolic representational role and, second, that the police are instruments of policy even though in the case of the large metropolitan centres they may be one or more jurisdictions removed from the federal or provincial formulators of that policy. It is not a matter of whether the police personally agree with multicultural policies or whether they have good personal relations with visible minorities. As Harish Jain has observed, the police participate more directly than that:

> The first major initiative was launched by the federal Multiculturalism Directorate in October 1984 in the form of a national symposium on policing in multicultural multiracial urban communities in Vancouver. The symposium was attended by police chiefs, visible minority representatives and government officials. Following the symposium, a National Police Multiculturalism Liaison Standing Committee consisting of visible minority community leaders and selected police chiefs was established under the

auspices of the Canadian Association of Chiefs of Police (CACP), funded by the government. The committee's role was to work with the CACP membership to implement major recommendations from the symposium aimed at increasing the number of visible minorities in police forces, improving cross-cultural training for police, and promoting liaison between ethnic and visible minority communities and the police. The committee was established in 1986. Following the symposium, CACP commissioned a survey of recruitment and selection of visible minorities in selected Canadian police organizations in 1985. The study was funded by Multiculturalism Canada.[52]

Because of their tradition of independence, the role of the police in helping to deliver multiculturalism policy is analogous, in some respects at least, to that of private organizations who deliver other social policies (for example, the John Howard Society). These bodies and the police share the problems associated with the direction and coordination of multiculturalism policy, a subject little explored by political science.[53] It is the immediacy and frequency of police contact with visible minorities (their 'clients,' so to speak) that explains the controversy that periodically arises.

Because the demographic pattern with regard to immigrants and Native people is not uniform across the country, the representational role the police are now expected to play is not consistent. In areas like Alberta, with large concentrations of Native persons, 'even-handedness' in dealing with 'other cultures' can lead to 'an inequity of results.' That is the finding of the Report of the Task Force on the Criminal Justice System and Its Impact on the Indian and Métis People of Alberta: 'Although it is clearly recognized that police services must be multiculturally sensitive, it is equally clear that, given the disproportionately large number of Aboriginal people involved with the Criminal Justice system, a specific Aboriginal-only awareness program is more appropriate than a broader multicultural program of which Aboriginal culture is only a part.'[54]

There are other dimensions than demography to the representational role of the police: To what degree do they represent (and enforce) the economic or social values of the ruling class? To what extent do the police set the terms of debate on law and order and on social policy? These are legitimate questions, though evidence through which to provide answers is difficult to gather. The use of the police by Canadian politicians in conflicts with organized labour is documented (Maurice Duplessis and the Asbestos strike, 1949, and Mitch Hepburn and the Oshawa GM strike, 1937, are two prominent examples); but the incidents are dispersed and sporadic and reflect the decentralized structure of labour relations in Canada's federation. While Canadian police do express views on social-policy issues that touch the performance of their duties (for example, soliciting by prostitutes), this is commonly done through traditional means such as testimony before legislative committees.[55] 'There is,' said a former RCMP commissioner, 'something vaguely disquieting "about 'large bodies of uniformed officers parading in support of their views,"' a sentiment his successor, the current commissioner, has echoed.[56] Disquieting or not, in 1992 Canadians witnessed uniformed police parading in the streets of Montreal and Toronto in protest against public criticism of police methods and attitudes and at governments who respond to that criticism by tightening their control of the police.[57]

SECURITY

If overt examples of the police acting as a pressure group in the furtherance of a policy objective are rare, this does not mean that it is unknown for them to act covertly to influence or alter policy. That at least would seem to be the conclusion to be drawn from the RCMP's activities in regard to security matters in the 1970s, when members of the service were 'willing ... to systematically deceive senior officials of the government outside the Force as well as responsible Ministers.'[58] It would be misleading to draw any general inference about police and politics from instances of police behaviour in the realm of national security, since that is an area distinct from the day-to-day politics of a democracy. Yet it would be equally blind to ignore the effect, however aberrant it may have been, of RCMP security activities on Canadian politics.

To begin with, these events led to the most extensive academic discussion and investigation of policing practices to date in Canada. The Commission of Inquiry Concerning Certain Activities of the Royal Canadian Mounted Police (the McDonald Commission) undertook original research into previously neglected areas. Studies for the commission by J.Ll.J. Edwards (*Ministerial Responsibility for National Security*, 1980)[59] and C.E.S. Franks (*Parliament and Security Matters*, 1980)[60] are prime examples of this contribution; so, too, is the monograph by Richard French and André Beliveau, for the Institute for Research on Public Policy (*The RCMP and the Management of National Security*, 1979). Together they reveal more precisely than most of the other literature on the topic the capacity of the police to affect politics. For instance, they illustrate how subjects discussed earlier in this paper, federalism and mechanisms of accountability, have operated to reinforce the separation of police from political supervision in matters of security. And they pose important questions for students of policing and politics, not least how to reconcile the enforcement of security, which is implicitly and invariably perceived as having a national dimension, with policing practices that are conventionally viewed in Canada as operating within a federal framework. Or, again, if security is a national matter, where then does accountability lie for its enforcement? The answer to that question would seem to be obvious: the locus of control must rest with Parliament and the responsible minister of the central government. Yet these studies demonstrate that, during the 1970s, management of security was far from certain, with the police and not the politicians making what amounted to policy decisions.

The intricacies of the relationships and the reason why 'institutionalized accountability' failed to operate are discussed extensively in this literature.[61] There is not space here to explore these matters, only to emphasize the direct influence that police had on politics during the period – an influence, it might be argued, that continues today in the form of the Canadian Security Intelligence Service (CSIS), itself a political response to the earlier controversy. CSIS marks the first time in Canada that a security agency has 'a statutory mandate' and the first time that its activities are subject to external review.[62] In light of the McDonald Commission's findings and recommendations, the structure of CSIS and its relations with the more visible world of democratic politics go some way to regularizing security operations, especially as regards the question of ministerial responsibility for these operations. The federalism issue, that is, the extent to which provincial attorneys general are involved or kept informed about 'the operational activities' of CSIS, is more problematic.[63]

CONCLUSION

This paper began with the observation that most political scientists in Canada have ignored police and policing as components of the political system. It offered reasons why this is so – principally, the preoccupation of political scientists with the question of national unity – and it suggested that both the old and new concerns of the profession would be rewarded if its members cast aside their apparent indifference to the topic.

Policing in Canada embraces some of the great issues of politics: federalism, accountability, and representation; at the same time, it is relevant to analyses of political culture, political socialization, and political stability, topics to which Canadian political scientists must increasingly pay attention. Because of the discretion and independence they possess and because of their proximity to the communities they serve, the police constitute a determinative factor in establishing or confirming society's values.

It has been said that 'to the extent that police activism means that government cannot always count on the police to carry out its policy ... the police may make a significant though unconscious contribution to radical change.'[64] Policing experience in Canada does not appear to confirm so extreme an evaluation, although it must be admitted that Canadian society to date has not confronted strains serious enough to elicit sustained police activism. Yet the implication of the statement – that those who enforce the law are not automatons, that they have the autonomy, the resources, and the need to make choices among competing priorities – underlines the essentially political character of the police. Unlike the excesses of the RCMP in the 1970s, which had as their specific political objective the discovery of subversion, the political influence of the police in their daily tasks at all levels of government is both more subtle and more pervasive. As such, it warrants the recognition that political scientists have long withheld.

NOTES

1 A.R. McDougall, *Policing: The Evolution of a Mandate* (Ottawa: Canadian Police College, Minister of Supply and Services 1988).
2 G.L. Caplan, 'The Ontario "Gestapo" Affair, 1943–1945,' *Canadian Journal of Economics and Political Science* 30 (1964): 343.
3 G.C. Sharman, 'The Police and the Implementation of Public Law,' *Canadian Public Administration* 20 (1977): 291. Two other articles in the same journal deal with 'police culture': H.C. Jain, 'The Recruitment and Selection of Visible Minorities in Canadian Police Organizations, 1985 to 1987,' 31 (1988): 463, and C.S. Ungerleider, 'Intercultural Awareness and Sensitivity of Canadian Police Officers,' 32 (1989): 612.
4 R. MacGregor Dawson, *The Government of Canada* (Toronto: University of Toronto Press 1947) and N. Ward, *Dawson's The Government of Canada*, 6th ed. (Toronto: University of Toronto Press 1987); R.J. Van Loon and M.S. Whittington, *The Canadian Political System: Environment, Structure and Process*, 4th ed. (Toronto: McGraw-Hill Ryerson 1987); R.J. Jackson and D. Jackson, *Politics in Canada: Culture, Institutions, Behaviour and Public Policy*, 2d ed. (Scarborough, Ont.: Prentice-Hall Canada 1990).
5 J.R. Mallory, 'The Macdonald Commission,' *Canadian Journal of Political Science* 19 (1986): 597.
6 A.C. Cairns, 'Political Science, Ethnicity and the Canadian Constitution,' in D.P. Shugarman and R. Whitaker, eds, *Federalism and Political Community: Essays in Honour of Donald Smiley* (Peterborough: Broadview Press 1989), 113.
7 In his study, *Parliament and Security Matters* (Ottawa: Minister of Supply and Services 1980), for the Commission of Inquiry Concerning Certain Activities of the Royal Canadian Mounted Police, C.E.S. Franks noted that during the early 1970s, at the time proposals to create a new civilian security group were being debated in Parliament, 'no academics, and no journalists, had however twigged to

the problems. The secrecy surrounding security matters, and attendant ignorance, handicapped perception of the problems' (p. 60).

8 R. Tasse, 'The Role of Social Science in Crime and Delinquency Policy,' *Canadian Public Administration* 19 (1976): 273.

9 F.K. Zemans, 'Legal Mobilization: The Neglected Role of the Law in the Political System,' *American Political Science Review* 77 (1983): 697.

10 A. Grant, *The Police – A Policy Paper* (Study Paper, Law Reform Commission of Canada) (Ottawa: Minister of Supply and Services 1981), 35. A further reason for neglect, explored by G. Marquis elsewhere in this volume, is the municipal provenance of policing for most of Canada's history. Only recently have academics begun to probe the autonomous world of municipal government.

11 J.P. Brodeur, 'Legitimizing Police Deviance,' in C.D. Shearing, ed., *Organizational Police Deviance: Its Structure and Control* (Toronto: Butterworths 1981), 139.

12 E.R. Black, *Divided Loyalties: Canadian Concepts of Federalism* (Montreal: McGill-Queen's University Press 1975), 121.

13 Conference of the Council of Provincial and Territorial Attorneys General and Ministers of Justice, *Pornography and Prostitution: Provincial Response to Badgley and Fraser Reports: Saskatchewan* (Discussion Paper) (Regina, Sask.: 19, 20 Sept. 1985), 10.

14 D. Forcese, 'Policing' in *The Canadian Encyclopedia*, 2d ed. (Edmonton: Hurtig Publishers 1988), 3:1706.

15 G.F. Gregory, 'Police Power and the Role of the Provincial Minister of Justice,' *Chitty's Law Journal* 27 (1979): 14.

16 Brodeur, 'Legitimizing Police Deviance,' 148–9.

17 A. McDougall, 'The Police Mandate: An Historical Perspective,' *Canadian Police College Journal* 12 (1988): 17.

18 R. Reiner, *The Politics of the Police* (London: Harvester Wheatsheaf 1985), 137.

19 See, for instance, D. Coyne, 'Commentary,' in D.E. Smith, P. MacKinnon, and J.C. Courtney, eds, *After Meech Lake: Lessons for the Future* (Saskatoon: Fifth House Publishers 1991), 139.

20 D. Fellman, 'The Nationalization of American Civil Liberties,' in M.J. Harmon, ed., *Essays on the Constitution of the United States* (Port Washington, NY: Kennikat Press 1978), 56.

21 Lipset, 'Law and Deviance,' in S.M. Lipset, *Continental Divide: The Values and Institutions of the United States and Canada* (New York: Routledge 1990), 93.

22 See T.B. Edsall, book review of *The Promised Land: The Great Black Migration and How It Changed America* by N. Lemann in *The New Republic*, 27 May 1991, 35.

23 A.C. Cairns, 'Introduction,' in D.E. Williams, ed., *Constitution, Government and*

Society in Canada: Selected Essays by Alan C. Cairns (Toronto: McClelland and Stewart 1988), 14.

24 Toronto *Globe and Mail*, 10 May 1991, A1–2; *Ottawa Citizen*, 9 May 1991, 1; and Saskatoon *Star-Phoenix*, 9 May 1991, D6. Bill C-79 is discussed in more detail in the paper by J. Robb, 'The Police and Politics: The Politics of Independence,' in this volume, and in J.R. Robertson and M. Young, 'Parliament and the Police: The Saga of Bill C-79,' *Canadian Parliamentary Affairs* 14 (1991–92): 18.

25 According to a recent report of the Law Reform Commission of Canada, *Controlling Criminal Prosecutions: The Attorney General and the Crown Prosecutor* (Working Paper 62) (Ottawa: Law Reform Commission of Canada 1990), 7 [hereinafter *Working Paper 62*], 'In Nova Scotia, New Brunswick, Ontario, Alberta, and British Columbia, the Solicitor General is responsible for the Police, and in Quebec, the police are under the Minister for Public Security.'

26 Gregory, 'Police Power,' 14.

27 Commission of Inquiry Concerning Certain Activities of the Royal Canadian Mounted Police, *Ministerial Responsibility for National Security as It Relates to the Office of Prime Minister, Attorney General and Solicitor General of Canada* (Ottawa: Minister of Supply and Services 1980), 68.

28 J. Edwards, *The Attorney General, Politics, and the Public Interest* (London: Sweet and Maxwell 1984), 362; quoted in *Working Paper 62*, at 9 (see n. 25, above).

29 Toronto *Globe and Mail*, 23 Feb. 1991, A8.

30 Ibid., 18 July 1991, A1, A4.

31 *Ottawa Citizen*, 4 May 1991, B2.

32 Royal Commission on the Donald Marshall, Jr., Prosecution, *Findings and Recommendations*, vol. 1 (Halifax: Province of Nova Scotia 1989), 220–1.

33 Toronto *Globe and Mail*, 18 July 1991, A5 and Saskatoon *Star-Phoenix*, 6 Jūly 1991, C19.

34 *Working Paper 62*, 53.

35 The Commission of Inquiry, *The Report of the Commission of Inquiry Relating to Public Complaints, Internal Discipline and Grievance Procedure Within the Royal Canadian Mounted Police* (Ottawa: Information Canada 1976), 67.

36 RCMP Public Complaints Commission, *Annual Report, 1988–1989* (Ottawa: Minister of Supply and Services 1989), 11 [hereinafter *RCMP Report*].

37 Toronto *Globe and Mail*, 24 July 1991, A6.

38 P.C. Stenning, 'The Role of Police Boards and Commissions as Institutions of Municipal Police Governance,' in C.D. Shearing, ed., *Organizational Police Deviance* (Toronto: Butterworths 1981), 161.

39 S.J.R. Noel, *Patrons, Clients and Brokers: Society and Politics, 1791–1896* (Toronto: University of Toronto Press 1990).

40 A.P. Pross, 'Space, Function and Interest: The Problem of Legitimacy in the Canadian State,' in O.P. Dwivedi, ed., *The Administrative State in Canada: Essays for J.E. Hodgetts* (Toronto: University of Toronto Press 1982), 107.

41 *RCMP Report*, 9 (see n. 36, above).

42 Law Reform Commission of Canada, *Legal Status of the Police* (Study Paper) by P.C. Stenning (Ottawa: Minister of Supply and Services 1982).

43 National Archives of Canada, W.L. Mackenzie King Papers, Gardiner to King, 3 Jan. 1927, 121655-60; quoted in D.E. Smith, *Prairie Liberalism: The Liberal Party in Saskatchewan, 1905–1971* (Toronto: University of Toronto Press 1975), 186–7.

44 Saskatchewan, *Report of the Royal Commission to Inquire Into Statements Made in Statutory Declarations and Other Matters* (Regina: King's Printer 1930), 81.

45 Saskatoon *Star-Phoenix*, 3 Apr. 1991, C10.

46 R.H. Simmonds, 'An Address to the International Conference on Police and Accountability,' *Canadian Police College Journal* 6 (1982): 183.

47 Ibid., 185.

48 See Stenning, 'The Role of Police Boards,' 179.

49 Standing Committee on Justice and Solicitor General, *Minutes of Proceedings and Evidence* (No. 18, 26 May 1987) [hereinafter *Minutes of Proceedings*]. On this occasion the majority of the questions addressed to Norman Inkster, slated to become commissioner of the RCMP on the following 1 September, dealt with the hiring of women, visible minorities, and homosexuals, and with the force's bilingualism policy.

50 Jain, 'Recruitment and Selection of Visible Minorities,' 468 (see n. 3, above).

51 Ibid., 469.

52 Ibid., 468–9; see also 'Summary Report of Symposium,' *Canadian Police Chief Newsletter* 3, no. 9 (1984).

53 An exception is J.L. Langford, 'The Question of Quangos: Quasi-Public Service Agencies in British Columbia,' *Canadian Public Administration* 26 (1983): 563.

54 Task Force, *Report of the Task Force on the Criminal Justice System and Its Impact on the Indian and Métis People of Alberta*, vol. 1 (Edmonton: The Task Force 1991), 2.36.

55 Submission to the Special Committee on Bill C-49, Canadian Association of Chiefs of Police, 'Soliciting,' *Canadian Police Chief Newsletter* 4, no. 9 (1985).

56 R.H. Simmonds, in news release, *RCMP*, 26 Oct. 1984, quoted in R.L. Jackson, *Canadian Police Labour Relations in the '80's: New Environmental Concerns* (Reprint series no. 66) (Kingston: Industrial Relations Centre, Queen's University 1986), 43; see remarks by N. Inkster in *Minutes of Proceedings*, 24 (see n. 49, above).

57 Toronto *Globe and Mail*, 15 May 1992, A9, and 29 Oct. 1992, A7.

58 Department of Justice, *The Position of the Attorney General of Canada on Certain Recommendations of the McDonald Commission* (Ottawa: Department of Justice, August 1983), 6.

59 See n. 27, above.

60 See n. 7, above.

61 Department of Justice, *Position of the Attorney General*, 16.

62 P. Rosen, *The Canadian Security Intelligence Service* (Ottawa: Research Branch, Library of Parliament 1990), 7–8.

63 Peter H. Russell, 'The Proposed Charter for a Civilian Intelligence Agency: An Appraisal,' *Canadian Public Policy* 9 (1983): 326. The subject of this paper is Bill C-157, introduced in 1983 but after strong criticism allowed to die; a revised bill (C-9), introduced in 1984, provided the statutory basis for CSIS. None the less, the discussion of the proposed agency's powers and the role of provincial attorneys general is relevant to the topic of this paper. So, too, Department of Solicitor General, *Report of the Federal-Provincial Committee of Criminal Justice Officials with Respect to the McDonald Commission Report* (Ottawa: Department of Solicitor General, June 1983), 105.

64 C.D. Robinson, 'The Deradicalization of the Policeman: A Historical Analysis,' *Crime and Delinquency* 24 (1978): 151.

11

Police and Politics: There and Back and There Again?

PHILIP C. STENNING

The dilemma for a liberal democratic society is to acknowledge the political nature of policing and yet to ensure that it is carried out in a non-partisan way.

(Cranshaw 1987: 72)

Ever since the modern public police force was first created in the early nineteenth century, questions and controversy have arisen over the relationship between police and politics. Indeed, as many writers have pointed out, opposition to the very concept of the 'new police' at the time it was being advocated by reformers hinged around expressed fears that this institution would become a political instrument of government or of the monarchy, as it was said to have become in France (Radzinowicz 1956: 570–4; Reiner 1985: chap. 1).

The response of reformers to these fears involved a two-pronged argument. The first part of this argument was to the effect that the new police force would in effect amount to no more than a bureaucratic rationalization of the old constabulary that for centuries had been such a familiar part of the English local-government scene. By retaining the familiar title of constable, the reformers hoped to dispel fears of some radical and dangerous innovation. This strategy was further pursued by placing the first such new police force in mainland Britain (the London Metropolitan Police) under the leadership of two commissioners who were justices of the peace, thus reinforcing the traditional relationship between justices of the peace and constables. A similar strategy was adopted when many of the early police forces in Canada were established. Indeed, until 1985 the commissioner and every deputy commissioner, assistant commissioner, and chief superintendent of the RCMP was 'ex officio a justice of the peace having all the powers of two justices of the peace' (*R.C.M.P. Act*, s. 17(1), repealed in 1985).

The second part of the strategy to counter fears of a political police force was encapsulated in the oft-repeated 'seventh principle' of modern British policing, as formulated more recently by Reith (1952: 163): 'To maintain at all times a relationship with the public that gives reality to the historic tradition that the police are the public and that the public are the police; the police being only members of the public who are paid to give full-time attention to duties which are incumbent on every citizen, in the interests of community welfare and existence.'

These two arguments – that the modern public police officer is merely a refurbished version of the ancient office of constable, and that he or she is to all intents and purposes indistinguishable from the citizens he or she is appointed to serve – provided the starting-point for a succession of attempts to promote public police as 'non-political' in virtually all jurisdictions in which the British model has been emulated.

Attractive as they may have appeared to those who sincerely desired a more efficient system of public policing, the two arguments were quickly belied by the realities of the new institution. Indeed, the history of public police forces in Canada and other Commonwealth countries, as well as the United Kingdom itself, is replete with examples of public police forces being deployed for sometimes overtly political purposes (see, for instance, Morgan 1987 with reference to the U.K.; Brown and Brown 1973 with reference to Canada). Brogden (1987) and Cain (1979) have both argued that the principal role of the police in British colonial jurisdictions was the obviously political one of 'pacification' and suppressing adherence to pre-existing local customs and laws in favour of compliance with the laws and values of the colonial power. Cain, in fact, has gone further, cogently arguing that 'the real police task,' in all instances, is 'the maintenance of an internal order satisfactory to the state and the ruling class' (1975: 157).

A recent incident in Moscow provided a dramatic illustration of this claim. One of the first acts of the newly elected reformist president of the Russian Federation, Boris Yeltsin, was to appoint a new police chief for the city of Moscow, the republic's capital, who was to be answerable to Russian authorities. Moscow was also the capital of the Soviet Union at that time, however, and the national Soviet government immediately revoked the new chief's appointment and named a Soviet interior-ministry general to the job. Soviet newspapers characterized the situation as a 'battle of laws' and a 'paralysis of power' (*Globe and Mail* 1991a). Such an incident provides an exceptional insight into the inherently political nature of the police role, and it is perhaps not inconceivable that similar struggles over control of the police could occur in Canada, should Quebec ever decide unilaterally to separate from the rest of the country.

The idea that public policing can be regarded as 'non-political' is, historically speaking, a relatively new one, and its credibility has always been difficult to sustain. The fact that the two words, 'police' and 'politics,' both spring from the same etymological root (the Greek word *polis*) is indicative of the problem. Dr Johnson included the word 'police' in his famous dictionary, 'but only as a French word used in England,' and as meaning 'the regulation and government of a city or country so far as regards the inhabitants' (Maitland 1885: 105). Only in the late eighteenth and early nineteenth centuries did an important shift in the meaning of the word begin to occur, whereby it came to connote the new institution given responsibility for 'police' (in the old sense), rather than the function itself. A footnote in Harrison's *The New Municipal Manual for Upper Canada* (1859), in which the editor sought to explain to his readers the new power of municipalities to 'establish, regulate and maintain a police,' provides a telling illustration of this shift in meaning: 'The word "police" is generally applied to the internal regulations of Cities and Towns, whereby the individuals of any City or Town, like members of a well governed family, are bound to conform their general behaviour to the rules of propriety, good neighbourhood, and good manners, and to be decent, industrious and inoffensive in their respective situations ... but the word, as here used, has a still more restricted meaning, for it is intended to apply to those men who in every City and Town are appointed to execute police laws, and who in many respects correspond with Constables of Rural Municipalities' (1859: 158).

It was the need to insulate this new institution from partisan political influence that provided impetus to characterize the police, and the function of policing that they performed, as 'non-political.' The attempt to do so occurred within the context of attempts to differentiate the law and its administration more generally from 'politics.' By characterizing the police as 'officers of the law,' whose principal role is 'law enforcement,' it became relatively easy to construct arguments and strategies for 'depoliticizing' them.

In Canada, the two principal strategies for presenting the police as 'non-political' have involved the reform of police governance arrangements and restrictions on political involvement by police officers. In this paper, we shall examine both aspects of the relationship between police and politics, within the Canadian context and from both historical and contemporary perspectives.

KEEPING POLITICS OUT OF THE POLICE: THE EVOLUTION OF POLICE GOVERNANCE

The earliest constables in Canada were under the authority of justices of the peace, following the system that had grown up in England during the fourteenth to seventeenth centuries (Stenning 1982, chaps. 1, 2; Talbot et al. 1986: chap. 2). Although justices of the peace were judicial officers during this period, they were politically appointed and performed numerous administrative and executive, as well as judicial, duties. The distinction between politics and law, which is so familiar to us today, would have been much less easily recognizable with justices of the peace at this time (Landau 1984; Lewthwaite 1987).

With the reform of local government during the first half of the nineteenth century (Aitchison 1949), the authority for establishing and governing municipal police forces fell to the new elected municipal councils. An illustration of the extent to which judicial and political functions remained intermingled even at this time is provided by the charter that incorporated the City of Toronto in 1834 (S.U.C. 1834, 4 Wm. IV, c. 23). The charter provided for the government of the city by a common council of elected aldermen, presided over by an elected mayor. The council had legislative, executive, and judicial functions, including the authority to establish and govern a police force for the city. The charter provided that 'the City Constables shall be bound to obey the orders of the Mayor and Aldermen, or any or either of them, in enforcing the laws of this Province, and the ordinances of the said City' (s. 65). In addition to being the governing authority for the police, the mayor and aldermen together constituted a court of record, called the Mayor's Court, which had, within the city limits, the same criminal jurisdiction as the courts of general quarter sessions of the peace elsewhere (ss. 77, 78).

These kinds of arrangements, in which municipal police forces were under the direction and control of elected municipal politicians, were the norm in the Canadian colonies during the first half of the nineteenth century (Stenning 1983: 49–55). Although precious little research has been undertaken into policing during this era, we do know that in some cases the results of these arrangements were quite unsatisfactory.

A good deal more light has been shed on the reforms of municipal police governance that occurred in Ontario in 1858 since this author first wrote about them a decade ago (Stenning 1983). In a very detailed account of the early years of the Toronto police force, Rogers (1984) has provided graphic descriptions of its partisan activities under a city council dominated by Orangemen. His account makes clear that the provisions of the *Municipal Institutions of Upper Canada Act, 1858*, which required the appointment of boards of commissioners of police to govern the police forces in the province's five cities, in place of the city councils, had indeed been designed to distance the governance of the police from local partisan influences. The fact that these provisions were originally proposed by the Toronto city council, with support from both of its political factions (Rogers 1984: 121), provides the clearest evidence for this conclusion. This reform, however, was strenuously resisted, albeit unsuccessfully, by other cities and towns to which it came to be applied (Stokes 1991: 37).

The fact that this reform was designed to insulate these city police forces from local partisan influences does not detract from this author's earlier assessment (Stenning 1983: 218–30) that the 1858 provisions cannot convincingly be viewed as an adequate measure to remove politics from the governance of the police altogether. Not only did they, and subsequent reforms of municipal police governance in the province, leave plenty of room for provincial political influence over the governance of the city police forces to which they applied, but they did not apply to the majority of municipal police forces in the province, which continued to be governed by elected municipal councils. Indeed it was only with the passage of the *Police Services Act* of 1990 that all municipal police forces in Ontario were required to be governed by 'police services boards' consisting of a majority of provincial appointees and a minority of locally elected municipal politicians.

That the creation of boards of commissioners of police as municipal-police governing authorities is more realistically viewed as a measure to redistribute political control and influence over municipal policing than as a measure to eliminate it has been borne out by more recent experiences with them in Ontario. Provincial appointments to such boards have long been regarded as political appointments, a conclusion that is reinforced by the appointment process itself (described in Stenning and Landau, 1988: 16–18).

There is evidence, too, that provincial governments have been quite willing to exert political pressure on municipal police boards, directly or through the provincial appointees, when it suited them. In the 'Syd Brown Affair' in Waterloo Region in 1978, the provincial attorney general of the day publicly announced that if the regional police commission did not follow the 'recommendations' of an inquiry by the provincial police commission, he did not 'intend to let the matter lie there,' adding that if necessary he would amend provincial legislation to 'clarify' his powers in such cases (*Globe and Mail* 1978). Allegations of a similar, but more covert, exercise of provincial pressure on a regional police commission came to light in a more recent study that the author undertook of the Niagara Regional Board of Police Commissioners (Stenning and Landau 1988: 19).

In an assessment of the arrangements for police governance in the Waterloo Region, the Waterloo Regional Review Commission observed: 'the arguments for "keeping politics out of the police" are largely fraudulent. No matter how the system is structured, the police governing authority must ultimately be responsible to the public – that is accountability and that is politics. The present system where the Provincial Government, elected through a party system, appoints a majority of the police commission is every bit as "political" and more potentially dangerous than a situation in which a government composed of twenty-four separately elected individuals with at least three different political stripes and seven different factions appoints the police governing body' (Ontario, Waterloo Region Review Commission 1979: 156). Three other regional review commissions in Ontario have reached similar conclusions (Ontario, Ottawa-Carleton Review Commission 1976: 114–16; Ontario, Royal Commission on Metropolitan Toronto 1977: Vol. 2, 276–7; and Ontario, Niagara Region Review Commission, 1989: 157–62), each arguing either, as did the Waterloo Region Review Commission, that governance of regional police forces should be returned to committees of the regional councils, or that regions should at least have majority representation on regional-police governing authorities.

Looking more generally at the situation across Canada, it is noteworthy that British Columbia and Ontario are the only provinces that have insisted that municipal-police governing authorities be composed of a majority of non-elected, provincial appointees. Whatever may have been the intent of the reforms in these two provinces, therefore, it is clear that keeping local politics out of municipal police governance has not been the dominant trend in this country, at least in terms of the legislated arrangements for municipal-police governing authorities. Nor, until quite recently, was there any attempt to legislate restrictions on the authority of municipal-police governing authorities to govern, and exercise oversight over, their police forces. When it comes to the provincial and federal police forces, no form of governance other than direction by elected ministers of cabinet rank ever seems to have been contemplated (see Stenning 1983: 40–9, 65–81 for a review).

Where legislatures have hesitated, however, senior police officers and courts have stepped in. Beginning in the very late nineteenth century, and culminating in the now oft-quoted words of an English Court of Appeal judge written in 1968, there has evolved the crucially important legal doctrine of 'police independence,' which has had more influence over the realities of police governance in this country than any legislated mandate ever did.

It is not necessary to trace the tortuous legal history of this critical doctrine here (see Stenning 1983 for a review of its history in Canada). The essence of the doctrine, however, is that in matters of law-enforcement (or with respect to law enforcement decisions in particular cases, depending on which version of the doctrine you read), the police are constitutionally immune to any supervision or control other than by the courts. In its most extreme version, epitomized by the following famous dictum of Lord Denning in *R.* v. *Metropolitan Police Commissioner, ex parte Blackburn,* the doctrine appears to rule out not only political control or direction in matters pertaining to law enforcement, but also political accountability:

I hold it to be the duty of the Commissioner of Police, as it is of every chief constable, to enforce the law of the land. He must take steps so to post his men that crimes may be detected; and that honest citizens may go about their affairs in peace. He must decide whether or not suspected persons are to be prosecuted; and, if need be, bring the prosecution or see that it is brought; but in all these things he is not the servant of anyone, save of the law itself. No Minister of the Crown can tell him that he must, or must not, keep observation on this place or that he must, or must not, prosecute this man or that one. Nor can any police authority tell him so. The responsibility for law enforcement lies on him. He is answerable to the law and to the law alone. ([1968] 1 All E.R. 763, at 769)

Lord Denning went on to indicate that only in most exceptional circumstances would the courts even interfere with this discretionary authority of the police.

The doctrine represents the zenith of the attempts to equate the police with the judiciary in terms of their constitutional status and their immunity from political control and accountability. Despite the fact that it has been discredited by every legal analyst who has seriously examined it, in terms of both its historical and its legal authenticity (Marshall 1965; Brogden 1982; Stenning 1983; Lustgarten 1986), the doctrine persists as conventional wisdom among police officers, policy-makers, and judges alike.

Even if one were to assume that the doctrine has some legitimate basis in English legal history as applicable to English chief constables, it flies in the face of some of the clearest language to the contrary in Canadian statutes concerning police governance. In its inquiry report concerning the RCMP in 1981, the McDonald Commission considered how the doctrine might be reconciled with the apparently clear wording of section 5 of the *R.C.M.P. Act*, to the effect that the commissioner of the force 'has the control and management of the force and all matters connected therewith,' 'under the direction of the Minister.' The commission concluded that the terms of this section left it uncertain whether, and if so to what extent, the *Blackburn* doctrine has any application to the RCMP, noted that this matter has not been resolved, and recommended that the *R.C.M.P. Act* be amended to clarify it with respect to the issues of political accountability and control of the force.

The commission's recommendations in this regard are worth quoting in full, if only because they constitute an unusually clear discussion of the issues at stake.

We believe that those functions of the R.C.M.P. which we have described as 'quasi-judicial' should not be subject to the direction of the Minister. To be more explicit, in any particular case, the Minister should have no right of direction with respect to the exercise by the R.C.M.P. of the powers of investigation, arrest and prosecution. To that extent, and to that extent only, should the English doctrine expounded in *Ex parte Blackburn* be made applicable to the R.C.M.P. Even though the Minister should have no power of direction in particular cases in relation to the exercise by the R.C.M.P. of these 'quasi-judicial functions,' the Minister should have the right to be, and should insist on being, informed of any operational matter, even one involving an individual case, if it raises an important question of public policy. In such cases he may give guidance to the Commissioner and express to the Commissioner the government's view of the matter, but he should have no power to give direction to the Commissioner. (Canada, Commission of Inquiry 1981: vol. 2, p. 1013, para. 19)

The commission added an important rider to these general propositions. Writing of the minister's general authority to direct the commissioner on matters other than those just described, the commission insisted: 'On no account should the Minister or his deputy give direction based on partisan or personal considerations. If the Deputy Solicitor General does so, the Commissioner should take the matter up with the Minister and if necessary the Prime Minister. If the Minister gives such an improper direction the Commissioner should speak to the Prime Minister directly' (Ibid.: 1014). The commission did not discuss what it thought to be comprehended by 'partisan' considerations. Its consultant, Professor John Edwards, however, did try to elaborate a distinction between partisan and non-partisan political considerations:

It is my contention that there exists a fundamental demarcation that needs to be constantly borne in mind when analysing the application of the doctrine of ministerial accountability in the area of policing and prosecutions. We begin with the proposition ... that anything savouring of personal advancement or sympathy felt by an Attorney General or Solicitor General towards a political colleague or supporter (or opponent) or which relates to the political fortune of his party and the government in power should not be countenanced if adherence to the principles of impartiality and integrity are to be publicly manifested. This does not mean that the Attorney General in the realm of prosecutions, or the Solicitor General in the area of policing, should not have regard to political considerations in the non-partisan interpretation of the term 'politics.' Thus, it might be thought that there are legitimate political grounds for taking into account such matters as the maintenance of harmonious international relations between states, the reduction of strife between ethnic groups, the maintenance of industrial peace and generally the interests of the public at large in deciding whether (or when) to initiate criminal proceedings or whether (or when) to terminate a prosecution that is in progress.

All these broad political considerations, whether domestic or international in character, must be seen to involve the wider public interest that benefits the population at large rather than any single political group or factional interest. In my perception of the term, 'partisan politics' has a much narrower focus and is designed to protect or advance the retention of constitutional power by the incumbent government and its political supporters. It is the intervention of political considerations in this latter sense that should have no place in the making of prosecutorial decisions by the Attorney General of Canada or in the making of policing or security decisions by the Solicitor General of Canada. Adherence to the same doctrine should be universally evident on the part of the Commissioner of the Royal Canadian Mounted Police and the officers of the force when executing any general mandates issued by the Government. (Edwards 1980: 70)

This author has argued elsewhere (Stenning 1983: 438–9) that, attractive as this distinction appears to be in theory, in practice it is virtually unworkable as a guide to action within our democratic system. Others (such as Turk, 1982: chap. 1) would go further and assert that the distinction is not even sustainable in theory. When the *R.C.M.P. Act* was amended in 1985, however, the commission's advice in this regard was not followed, with the result that the applicability of the doctrine of police independence to the RCMP remains as unclear now as it has always been.

The doctrine, however, has found a firm place in the ideological armoury of both senior police officers and judges, as well as many politicians. For the RCMP it has acquired near-biblical status, intoned at virtually every available opportunity. In 1959 it was the principal pretext – quite inappropriately under the circumstances – for the resignation of the commissioner of the force. The police view that even broad (let alone partisan) political considerations are to be given no weight in individual law-enforcement decisions was reflected in the terms of the commissioner's letter of resignation to the minister of justice, in which he wrote: 'I realise that other issues are before you which arise from this strike but I feel most strongly that the matter of law enforcement should be isolated and dealt with on its own merits. This is the attitude the force has taken throughout. It has not concerned itself with the issues back of the strike, but has merely tried to maintain law and order in the area' (Canada, House of Commons, *Debates*, 16 March 1959: 2005–6). The fact that the particular agreement under which the relevant decision had to be made expressly gave the minister the final authority to make the decision does not appear to have counted for anything in the commissioner's eagerness to uphold the 'independence' of the force. (For a fuller account of this incident, see Stenning 1983: 440–6).

A quarter of a century later, in 1985, the commissioner of the RCMP again found occasion to publicly proclaim the independence of the force in his report on its investigation of the premier of New Brunswick. In an addendum to the report he wrote: 'I accept that the Minister has broad powers of direction over the Commissioner with respect to *control* and *management* of the Force, and all matters connected with that *control* and *management*. However, I do not accept that the Minister's powers of direction over-ride the inherent responsibilities, authorities and powers that are given to every member upon appointment to the office of "Peace Officer"' (Simmonds 1985: addendum, p. 6) (emphasis in original). The *Blackburn* case was cited in support of this position.

In the interim, the concept of the independence of the police from political accountability as well as political control in matters of law enforcement had been expressly endorsed by none other than the prime minister of Canada as a general principle of democratic government. In a press conference in 1977, Prime Minister Trudeau, in response to a journalist who had asked him 'just how ignorant does a minister have to be before, at the very least, some responsibility is applied to the advisers who seem to have kept him ignorant?' was reported as having replied:

> I have attempted to make it quite clear that the policy of the Government and, I believe, the previous governments in this country, has been that they, indeed, – the politicians who happen to form the Government – should be kept in ignorance of the day-to-day operations of the police force and even of the security force. I repeat that it is not a view that is held by all democracies, but it is our view, and it is one we stand by. Therefore, in this particular case, it is not a matter of pleading ignorance as an excuse. It is a matter of stating, as a principle, that the particular minister of the day should not have a right to know what the police are doing constantly in their investigative practices, in what they are looking at and what they are looking for, and in the way in which they are doing it ...
>
> ... That is our position. It is not one of pleading ignorance to defend the Government. It is one of keeping the Government's nose out of the operations of the police force, at whatever level of government.
>
> On the criminal law side, the protections we have against abuse are not with the Government, they are with the courts. (*Globe and Mail* 1977)

Trudeau's version of the police-independence doctrine, like Lord Denning's version that it closely emulates, declared the police to be independent from both political control and political accountability with respect to individual law-enforcement decisions. Other versions of the doctrine, however, emphasize a distinction between 'policy' and 'operational' decisions, indicating that the former are within the purview of police governing authorities, while the latter are not. The advice given by the *Handbook* for municipal-police governing authorities published by the British Columbia Police Commission in 1980 illustrates this approach:

> The Chief Constable is accountable to the Board for the overall policy of the force and the level and quality of service provided to the community. It is important to stress, however, that day-to-day professional policing decisions are matters that are reserved to the force itself. The authority of the individual constable to investigate crime, to arrest suspects and to lay informations before a justice of the peace comes from the common law and the *Criminal Code* and must not be interfered with by any political or administrative person or body. Overall policies, objectives and goals, however, are matters that properly belong to civilian authority and police boards have the duty to see that the force operates within established policy and has the right to hold the Chief Constable accountable for these matters. (British Columbia Police Commission 1980: 13)

A study of municipal-police governance in Canada, undertaken under the sponsorship of the Canadian Police College in Ottawa in the early 1980s, found that this policy/operations distinction, attractive as it is, was not well understood by members of municipal-police governing authorities or their police chiefs, and did not appear to explain when municipal-police governing authorities became involved in decisions with respect to their police forces, and when they did not (Hann et al. 1985).

There can be no question, however, that the doctrine of police independence, vague and contentious as it is, has had a profound effect on attitudes towards police governance in this country. In the 1970s a major overhaul of legislation concerning the police began to take place across the country. Many provinces imitated each other's initiatives in this regard, with the result that standard formulations began to appear in the new provincial Police Acts that were enacted during this decade. One of these involved the provisions concerning the respective roles of police governing authorities and chiefs of police. In 1971, Alberta passed a major revision to its *Police Act*, which contained the following sections:

> 18(3) Every member of the police force of a municipality, however appointed, is from and after the passing of a by-law establishing a board, subject to the jurisdiction of the board to the same extent as if appointed by the board and shall obey its lawful directions.

23(1) Notwithstanding the right of a municipality to direct its own police operations, the functions of any board or police committee shall primarily relate to the administrative direction, organization and policy required to maintain an efficient and adequate police force.

(2) Except when inconsistent with the provisions of the Act, the actual day to day direction of the police force with respect to the enforcement of law and the maintenance of discipline within the force shall rest with the chief of police or person acting for him. (Alberta *Police Act, 1971*, c. 85)

Unclear as these provisions were, they seemed to reflect a legislative intent to adopt, to some degree, the principle of police independence. The provisions were virtually copied in revisions to police legislation in Saskatchewan and Nova Scotia in 1974, and in Prince Edward Island in 1977. The version in the Prince Edward Island *Police Act,* however, did not have the qualifying words 'Except when inconsistent with the provisions of the Act' at the beginning of its clause specifying the chief as having the day-to-day direction of the force (1977, c. 28, s. 18).

New Brunswick also revised its *Police Act* in 1977, but did not opt for this formulation. Instead, its legislation stated quite specifically that a chief of police 'shall be responsible directly' to the board or municipal council, as the case may be (1977, c. P-9.2, ss. 10(1)(a) and 11(1)(a)). The act did, however, also stipulate: 'The chief of police is the chief executive officer of the police force and shall have all necessary powers to direct the police force in carrying out its duties and responsibilities' (ss. 10(3) and 11(3)).

Ironically, in Ontario – the province in which the move to insulate municipal police from local political influence had begun over a century before – the *Police Act* still provided simply: 'the board is responsible for the policing and maintenance of law and order in the municipality and the members of the police force are subject to the government of the board and shall obey its lawful directions' (R.S.O. 1970, c. 351, s. 17(1)). In a controversial court case involving the attempted firing of a chief of police in the province in 1957, however, the Ontario Court of Appeal had held that: 'while members of a police force must obey "the lawful direction" of the board, neither the board nor any municipality not having a board can lawfully give directions to any member of a police force prescribing the duties of his office' (*Re a Reference under the Constitutional Questions Act* [1957] O.R. 28, at p. 30). While the precise implications of this ruling were far from clear – especially as, in the case before the court, the municipality had not sought to 'prescribe the duties' of the chief's office, but rather to fire him – the case was widely interpreted as proclaiming the independence of the police from political control or accountability with respect to their law-enforcement duties (see, for instance, McDougall 1971).

It was not, in fact, until 1990, when Ontario replaced its *Police Act*, that the principle of police independence found legislative expression in that province. The new *Police Services Act* defined in much greater detail the authority of the new 'police services boards' that it established as municipal-police governing authorities. Two of the key provisions in this regard required boards to:

(b) generally determine, after consultation with the chief of police, objectives and priorities with respect to police services in the municipality.

and

(e) direct the chief of police and monitor his or her performance.
(1990, c. 10, s. 31)

The bill also included the following clause: 'The board may give orders and directions to the chief of police, but not to other members of the police force, and no individual member of the board shall give orders or directions to any member of the police force' (s. 31(3)).

When these provisions were discussed in legislative committee, they were the subject of considerable disagreement, some arguing that the board's powers should be strengthened, others (including the Ontario Association of Chiefs of Police) that chiefs should be given more operational autonomy. The government's response was to introduce an amendment to the bill, adding the following clause, which was eventually enacted: 'The board shall not direct the chief of police with respect to specific operational decisions or with respect to the day-to-day operation of the police force' (31(4)).

It remains to be seen, of course, how this provision is interpreted in practice by boards, police chiefs, and the courts. The provision is of considerable importance, however, representing as it does the first unequivocal inclusion of the doctrine of police independence in a statute governing the police in Canada.

KEEPING THE POLICE OUT OF POLITICS: CURTAILING THE POLITICAL RIGHTS OF POLICE OFFICERS

While much has been written on the attempts to keep politics out of the police, surprisingly few scholars have given attention to the history of the political rights of police officers. Indeed, in the most recently published history of public police forces in Canada (Talbot et al., 1986) the subject is barely mentioned.

As noted earlier, the political loyalties of members of the Toronto police force were seen as a problem almost from its inception in 1835. Rogers (1984: 119) reports: 'In 1844 six of Toronto's ten aldermen were known to be Orangemen, and from 1845 the order enjoyed near monopoly of mayoral office. Moreover, roughly half of the police force, including at least two high bailiffs, were recruited from Orange ranks. Given these links, it was hardly surprising that the police role in curbing sectarian demonstrations was severely compromised.' Because the British government was not prepared to tolerate limits on the membership of political organizations, however, it appears that the political rights of police officers in the city initially remained unaffected, and reforms of the governing structure (discussed above) solely were relied upon as a means to disengage the Toronto force from political partisanship.

It appears to have been the experience of the British in Ireland that first led to explicit attempts to curtail the political rights of police officers in the common-law world. Thus, the 'Standing Rules and Regulations for the Government and Guidance of the Royal Irish Constabulary' included the following provisions: '6. Partisanship prohibited – It cannot be too strongly or frequently impressed upon both the officers and the men of the establishment, that as its character and efficiency would be seriously injured by even a suspicion of its partisanship, the expression or any other manifestation of political or sectarian opinions on the part of the Constabulary is most strictly forbidden.' This paragraph was followed by another that urged members of the force 'to avoid altercations or squabbles of every kind.'

In his book *The Constable's Guide*, published in 1859, A. Wilson indicates that one of the first acts of the newly created board of commissioners of police in Toronto was to introduce a rule requiring that 'each [police] man, upon his appointment, should declare upon oath, that, with the exception of the order of Freemasonry, he was not connected with any secret society' (1859: 83). In justification of this rule, he wrote: 'The exclusion of all secret society men is found to prevail in every part of the old country, in the United States, and in Australia; and from the repeated complaints against the partizan character of the force in this city, it had become necessary, even in justice to the force itself, to introduce the rule here which had been found to be so necessary and beneficial elsewhere' (Ibid.). Wilson went to some lengths to deny that the rule had been adopted for the purpose of excluding anyone 'who is or ever has been an Orangeman' from the police force. He noted that immediately prior to the introduction of the rule there were still many Orangemen on the force, and argued that the rule 'does not exclude the secret society; he may be and is in fact yet taken as readily as anyone else; all he is asked to do is not connect himself with the society or to attend its meetings while he is a policeman' (Ibid.: 84).

Arguing that 'the police is not established for the purpose of representing any particular party, sect or country,' and that the introduction of the rule about secret-society membership had had a beneficial effect on the police force, Wilson concluded: 'The newly organized body has now the perfect confidence of the public, and for that, among many other reasons, they are, if not so useful as partisans, at any rate a far more valuable body of peace officers' (Ibid.).

It is not known how many police forces in Canada introduced such rules restricting the political affiliations and activities of their members. It is noteworthy, however, that the original 1829 instructions issued to the London Metropolitan Police in England – the force on which most of the new municipal police forces in Canada were modelled – apparently included no provisions restricting the rights of force members.

Although the North-West Mounted Police, formed in 1873, were modelled on the Royal Irish Constabulary, the paragraph of the latter's regulations that banned partisanship was not included in the original 'Regulations and Orders' promulgated for the Canadian force. When the British Columbia Provincial Police Force was formed in 1895, however, the 'Provincial Police Regulations' contained the following rule: '48. Members of the force shall abstain from the expression of political or religious opinions which may in the slightest degree be calculated to give offence, and shall not, after appointment (except as a matter of police duty), attend any political meeting' (British Columbia, Superintendent of Police 1896: 885).

During the twentieth century, many other police forces have sought to curtail the political rights of their members in one way or another. Since no one has charted these kinds of provisions in any systematic manner, it cannot be said for sure how widespread the practice has been.

Regulations under the *Police Act* of Ontario included the following provisions concerning members of the Ontario Provincial Police Force:

62. No member of the Force shall

(a) join or associate himself with any union connected with any labour organization or any body not belonging to or affiliated with the Force or the civil service except where a membership in the organization or body is authorized by the Minister of Justice and Attorney General;

(b) take any part in politics or occupy an official position in a party organization, but this does not affect the right of the member to private political views or to vote;

(c) sign any petition on any subject to the government;
(R.R.O. 1970, Reg. 680)

Members of the OPP, however, were also 'Crown employees' subject to the Ontario *Public Service Act*, which gave much more extensive political rights, including the right to run for elective office in municipal, provincial, or federal elections while on a leave of absence, to all but a small group of designated senior civil servants.

In 1980, an OPP officer applied for, and was granted, a leave of absence to run as a Conservative candidate in the federal election of that year. He was not elected and, when he returned to his duties, he was charged with 'discreditable conduct' for his political activities. He filed a grievance, forcing a resolution of the apparent conflict between the provisions of the regulations under the *Police Act* and the express provisions of the *Public Service Act*. In 1983, the Ontario Divisional Court ruled that the provisions of the *Public Service Act* should prevail (*Re Mahlberg and Ferguson et al.* (1983), 44 O.R. (2d) 239), thus precluding further disciplinary action against the constable. The response of the government, however, was to include all OPP officers within the category of designated public servants who did not enjoy the political rights guaranteed in the *Public Service Act*.

There was no general prohibition of political activities for municipal police officers in the Ontario *Police Act*. Section 38 of the *Municipal Act*, however, provided that a municipal employee was entitled to a leave of absence to run for a municipal elected office, but if elected must resign. In 1985, a Durham Regional Police officer took a leave of absence, was elected to municipal office, and resigned from the force. He took legal action, however, to challenge the requirement that he resign. The action was settled by way of Minutes of Settlement under which the officer's resignation was withdrawn, and he was granted an unpaid leave of absence while he continued to hold elected office (RCMP, External Review Committee 1991: 36).

The extent to which police officers in Ontario were permitted to engage in political activities was, until very recently, determined by the internal regulations of individual police forces. A recent survey of thirty-five police forces in the province, ranging in size from nine to five thousand uniformed officers, revealed that sixteen had policies that in some way restricted the political rights of their officers. Policies ranged from outright prohibition of political activity in two forces to quite permissive policies in others, which required officers to obtain the permission of the police chief and a leave of absence before running for political office. Seven of the thirty-five forces reported that officers had held, or were still holding, political office. Ten of the forces reported that none of their officers had ever run for elected office (Ontario, Ministry of the Solicitor General 1991: 15–16).

In 1990, Ontario passed its new *Police Services Act*, section 46 of which stipulates: 'No municipal police officer shall engage in political activity, except as the regulations permit.' Relevant regulations were promulgated in 1992, after the Ontario Ministry of the Solicitor General had put out a discussion paper inviting public comment as to what the regulations should say (Ontario, Ministry of the Solicitor General 1991).

Compared with those that have been (and in many cases still are) in force in other jurisdictions, the new Ontario regulations on this issue are quite permissive. They allow wide latitude to police officers, while off duty and not in uniform, to engage in such political activities as attending and participating in political meetings, canvassing during an election, and 'expressing views on any issue not directly related to the police officer's responsibilities as a police officer.' The general intent of these regulations is summed up in the 'Rationale' for them that appears in the *Policing Standards Manual*: 'Municipal police officers are permitted to engage in most political activities while off duty and not in uniform, and to express views as long as they do not associate their position as a police officer with the issue or represent their views as those of the police service' (Ontario, Ministry of the Solicitor General 1992: Tab 0104, p. 1). The regulations also allow a police officer, with the permission of his or her police services board or chief of police, to express views on any issue 'on behalf of the police force,' and to attend and participate in a public meeting for this purpose, 'as long as the police officer does not, during an election campaign, express views supporting or opposing, (i) a candidate in the election or a political party that has nominated a candidate in the election, or (ii) a position taken by a candidate in the election or by a political party that has nominated a candidate in the election.'

It will be apparent that these regulations go much further than any of the others previously cited in permitting police officers to engage in overtly partisan political public speech and other activities (other than during the course of an election campaign) while they are on duty, and at virtually any time while they are off duty and not in uniform or on a leave of absence. They reflect the commitments of the present NDP government in Ontario to 're-enfranchise' public servants more generally. It is, of course, too soon to be able to determine how these regulations will be interpreted and applied in practice within police forces in Ontario. They reflect, however, what can only be described as a radical rethinking of the acceptable political role of police officers in Canada.

In Quebec, which has the largest number of municipal police forces of any province, somewhat different rules apply to the provincial police force (the Sûreté du Québec) than to municipal police forces. Section 6 of the *Police Act* currently states:

On pain of dismissal, no member of the [provincial] Police Force shall be a candidate in any federal, provincial, municipal or school election, or engage in partisan activity in favour of any candidate or political party.

The provisions of the preceding paragraph shall apply to every special constable within the limits of the territory for which he is appointed; they shall also apply to every municipal policeman but the latter may be a candidate or engage in partisan activity at the time of a municipal or school election outside the limits of any judicial district of which the municipality that employs him forms part.

The regulation respecting the code of ethics and discipline of members of the Sûreté du Québec imposes further restrictions in addition to those in the *Police Act*:

21. A member must be politically neutral in the performance of his duties.

The following in particular constitute breaches of discipline:

(a) being present in uniform at a political meeting, unless he is on duty at that place;
(b) failing to show moderation in publicly expressing his political opinions;
(c) during an electoral period, publicly expressing his political opinions, soliciting funds for a candidate for election, a party authority or a political party, or publicly expressing his support for a candidate for election or for a political party.

The regulations of the Winnipeg Police Department are similarly explicit with respect to permitted and forbidden political activities by force members:

124(16) POLITICAL PARTISANSHIP, that is:

(a) wearing any political party badge, button, pin or emblem at any time while on duty,
(b) unless on duty, attending any political meeting in uniform,
(c) membership in any subversive organization,
(d) membership in any union, party, group or organization which by its nature or objectives might influence or constrain the impartial discharge of police duty, except the Winnipeg City Police Senior Officers' Association or the Winnipeg Police Association, as certified under the Labour Relations Act,
(e) officiating in any matter in connection with the Dominion, Provincial or Municipal elections, other than in the normal course of police duty.
(f) Nothing in this sub-section shall affect the right of a member to hold private political views or his right to vote, or to be nominated as a Candidate for the

> Provincial Legislature or the House of Commons, but if elected to either office, he must forthwith sever his connection with the Department.

(Regulations of the Winnipeg Police Department, 1974 – Schedule 'A' of By-Law no. 1 of the Winnipeg Police Commission)

In a brief review of this issue undertaken in late 1990 as part of a wider study of the control and regulation of the off-duty conduct of police officers in Canada, this author learned that in many jurisdictions in Canada police officers have been permitted to hold elected political offices in neighbouring municipalities (for instance, as municipal councillors or school-board trustees) while retaining their police employment. In one case, a police officer sat as a member of the local police commission in a neighbouring community (RCMP, External Review Committee 1991: 37).

Practice on this issue in Canada makes it clear that in many jurisdictions in Canada a distinction is made between local municipal politics and provincial and federal politics, the assumption apparently being that the former is less 'partisan' than the latter. In 1980, it was reported that a Niagara Regional Police officer had been given permission by his chief to run for a seat on a county board of education within the force's geographical area of jurisdiction. The police chief was reported in the press at the time to have said that he gave his permission because 'it is not a political thing. Police have a sense of duty the same as any fellow citizen, but they must remember that they are policemen 24 hours a day. I would not sanction anyone running for councillor of regional council where, for example, he may be required to vote on the police budget' (*Globe and Mail* 1980a).

While the extent to which the political rights of individual police officers have been curtailed thus varies significantly across the country, there is also the question of collective political action by police officers. As Jackson (1980: 12–13) has noted, in four of the ten provinces police associations are legislatively denied the right to affiliate with other labour unions, and in five they are denied the right to strike.

With respect to collective political action that is not so directly related to police working conditions, the situation is quite unclear. Both police associations and associations of chiefs of police, however, have regularly conducted lobbies with respect to particular causes, the restoration of capital punishment being the most well known (see, for example, McDougall 1971; Forcese 1980; and Marquis 1993).

In 1979 the Metropolitan Toronto Police Association made a very public display of withdrawing its 'collective and individual support' from the incumbent mayor of Toronto, apparently in response to criticisms of the police force that he had voiced in preceding months. The move was interpreted by many as a first step in the association's active involvement in the municipal elections scheduled to take place the following year, and the propriety of police officers becoming individually or collectively involved in electoral politics, by either openly supporting or opposing individual candidates, was the subject of much debate in the city. The views expressed by political leaders in this debate illustrated the lack of public agreement on this topic, ranging as they did from outright opposition to virtually unqualified support for police involvement in electoral politics. Between these extremes were positions such as that, while individual involvement of officers was considered acceptable, involvement by the association as a collectivity was not, and that it was acceptable for police to be involved in this way, but that 'it would be wise for them not to be too visible about it' (*Globe and Mail* 1979).

Early in the following year, the president of the Metropolitan Toronto Police Association announced that the association would 'in all probability' endorse candidates in the upcoming municipal elections who would 'work in the best interests of good policing.' He indicated that the association would push for a 'bill of rights to protect' the police, and would lobby to oppose domination of the local police commission by politicians. He added that the association 'would probably support a suitable candidate who would be opposing' the incumbent mayor of the city (*Globe and Mail* 1980b). When the elections finally came later in the year, however, the association publicly announced that it would not become involved in partisan politics 'unless unusual circumstances dictate otherwise' (*Globe and Mail* 1980c). It did not elaborate on what such 'unusual circumstances' might be.

In late 1992, the Metropolitan Toronto Police Association mounted an aggressive political campaign against the NDP government in Ontario. The immediate trigger for this action was a new regulation, introduced by the government, that required stricter controls over, and accountability for, police use of firearms. It quickly became clear, however, that the concerns of the Association were broader than this, as they accused the NDP government of always placing the complaints of 'minority special interest groups' over the legitimate interests and concerns of police officers. With explicit support of other police associations in the province, the Toronto association staged a work slowdown, refusing to issue traffic tickets and trading their regulation caps for baseball caps while on duty. The campaign was relatively short-lived, as the association members were the subject of a court order requiring them to give up their 'job action,' and the provincial government agreed to negotiate with them further over their concerns.

PUTTING POLITICS BACK INTO POLICING? – 'COMMUNITY-BASED POLICING'

Triggered largely by a controversial book by the chief constable of Devon and Cornwall in England (Alderson 1979), and in the context of a more general movement towards greater accountability of public services (Day and Klein 1987), there has been a growing interest in Canada during the last decade in what is said to be a new style of public policing, variously called 'community-policing' or 'problem-oriented policing' (Greene and Mastrofski 1988).

While the community-based policing philosophy involves some sweeping changes to the conception of the public police role, the organization and management of public police forces, and the ways in which policing services are delivered, the principal interest that it has for a discussion of police and politics derives from its vision of a new relationship between the public police force and the community it serves. While descriptions of the 'new strategic partnerships' that would be required between elected officials, police managers, and police associations/unions and officers in order to successfully implement community-based policing are typically quite imprecise (see, for instance, Normandeau and Leighton 1990: 77–82, 90–1), the gist of virtually all community-based policing proposals involves a greater involvement of the community, both directly and indirectly (through elected politicians) in the determination of the objectives, priorities, and policies that will guide the police force in performing its role. In England (Taylor 1981: 146–64) and in Canada (Normandeau and Leighton 1990) this philosophy has translated into demands for an enhanced role for municipal-police governing authorities, and greater locally elected representation within these bodies. As the following quote indicates, however, the vision of community policing would not limit the political accountability of the police to the area of police governing authorities:

> Accountability to the community is of the foremost concern with the increasing popularity of community policing and the vision of the public as consumers of police services. With the idea that members of the community should have an agenda-setting role as well as a say in operational matters (e.g., problem-solving), it becomes obvious that ongoing consultations need to take place between the police and the public. The 'public' can mean various things. Individuals may bring relatively limited matters or concerns to the attention of the police. Neighbourhood groups and associations may make representations to the police or even constitute a form of town council that has a continuing role in setting police policies. The business community, too, will want input into the activities of the police. Finally, the media, with the ability it has to shape public opinion about crime and the efficacy of police efforts, needs to be dealt with in a

serious and competent way so as to provide a favourable image of the police and an accurate picture of the crime problem. (Normandeau and Leighton 1990: 73)

While the concept of community-based policing is clearly intended to allow 'political' factors, in the broadest sense of the term, to play a greater role in the determination of police policy and practice, its proponents rarely make clear what mechanisms will prevent the police from coming under the control of partisan interests. Bayley, writing as the 'devil's advocate' on this subject, has drawn attention to these concerns:

Community policing makes a virtue of command discretion with respect to priorities and operations and hopes to make it responsible. The problem is that enforcement of law is rarely altogether popular. Community policing can easily be read as bending the law so as not to offend. Local commanders may begin to think it is more important not to alienate loud voices than to protect quiet ones. Moreover, communities are complex. Whose interests, priorities, and values are the police to consider? And have they the capacity, indeed the wisdom, to manufacture a consensus? Perhaps it is better in the long run to say that the law should be equally enforced – even though that is often unrealistic – than to say that the law should be used by the police to maintain order acceptable to local communities?

... Decentralization under police control may seem less political than decentralization by community demand, but the possibility of decay in the rule of law is only slightly reduced. (Bayley 1988: 232)

Since 'community-based policing' has so far remained largely a creature of rhetoric rather than being to any substantial degree fully implemented in Canadian jurisdictions, one can only speculate at this point as to what implications it may have in practice for the relationship of police and politics.

In Ontario, however, the beginnings of implementation have occurred with the enactment of the new *Police Services Act* in 1990, which was expressly intended to provide a legislative framework for the introduction of community-based policing. The act begins with a 'Declaration of Principles,' stating that police services throughout the province are to be provided in accordance with six basic principles, the third of which refers to 'the need for co-operation between the providers of police services and the communities they serve.' As noted earlier, however, the act preserves the earlier provisions concerning the composition of municipal-police governing authorities (now called 'police service boards'), with a majority of provincially appointed members and a minority of locally elected members. In addition, the act sets out in detail the responsibilities of police services boards, which include the following:

31(1)(b) generally determine, after consultation with the chief of police, objectives and priorities with respect to police services in the municipality;

(c) establish policies for the effective management of the police force; ...

(e) direct the chief of police and monitor his or her performance;

It is doubtful whether these provisions provide police-services boards with any greater legal authority over their police forces than their predecessors, the boards of commissioners of police, had (Stenning 1981: part 3, chap. 3). Since the political composition of police-services boards is essentially not different from that of their predecessors and, as noted earlier, the principle of 'police independence' has now been enshrined in the legislation in fairly broad terms, it is arguable that the new act actually places more restrictions on political control of the police by police governing authorities than did the *Police Act* that it replaced.

Of critical importance, however, will be how the new act is perceived by police-services boards (and police chiefs) to have affected their role, their relationships with their police forces, and with the communities they serve, and how the provisions of the act are interpreted and implemented in practice. It is thus possible that even though the act itself may not provide any clear additional authority for the political control or accountability of police forces, its general spirit (and the climate of opinion on these matters in which it was introduced) may nevertheless lead to significant changes in practice, with police-services boards being more ready to exercise an authority that their predecessors were notoriously reluctant to exercise (Hann et al. 1985).

PUTTING THE POLICE BACK INTO POLITICS? – 'COMMUNITY-BASED POLICING' AND THE *CHARTER OF RIGHTS AND FREEDOMS*

Two aspects of the philosophy of 'community-based policing' that are potentially relevant to the political nature of police work are the expectations first, that the police be more proactive in their policing efforts and, second, that they address themselves to identifying and rectifying 'underlying causes' of crime and disorder, rather than simply reacting, after the fact, to actual manifestations of them.

Taken together, these two elements require the individual police officer to become much more deeply involved with the community that he or she is assigned to police. As Bayley has pointed out, there is a distinct possibility that this involvement may lead to a greater politicisation of the individual police officer as well as of the police force as a whole: 'The diversity of today's police work comes from the nature of the calls that individuals make to the police, not from governmental design. Community policing may reverse this trend as police consciously develop their capacity to assist neighbourhoods as minicenters of government service, all in the name of convenience, crime prevention, and community development. Community policing, then embeds police not only in communities, but at the heart of government' (Bayley 1988: 230).

At a seminar on community policing held at the Canadian Police College in 1986, one of the foremost U.S. exponents of community-based policing was recounting early experiences with this style of policing in Flint, Michigan. He described how particular officers had been given great autonomy and flexibility to develop links with their local communities and to develop 'problem-oriented' rather than 'incident-oriented' solutions to policing problems, in conjunction with community members. Police officers were encouraged to become 'social activists' within their communities. All was thought to be going well with this program, until one day an officer of the force, during his off-duty hours and not in uniform, was seen to be leading a march of community residents on the city hall, demanding more efficient garbage collection in their neighbourhoods. The speaker noted that it was at this point that police officials began to realize that there might be more to community-based policing than they had bargained for.

Quite apart from the political activism among individual police officers that community-based policing might encourage, however, concerns have also been expressed that the greater penetration of communities that this style of policing involves may also be exploited for political ends, providing new grounds for the kinds of fears that led English sceptics in the early nineteenth century to be wary of the proposals for the introduction of the 'new police.' As Bayley has commented: 'Western political theory as well as practice has tried, increasingly vainly, to separate public from private domains. Community policing seeks to make that division indistinguishable. It tries to enlist the public in the state's maintenance of order just as it tries to insinuate police officers into private spheres of activity. Overcoming distrust of the police may improve public safety, but at what cost? Perhaps suspicion of the police is essential to our freedom?' (Bayley 1988: 231). For some, the prospect of community policing conveys uncomfortable reminders of the 'high policing' that characterized the French police of the seventeenth and eighteenth centuries, described by one commentator as 'a form of political activity through the medium of the police' (quoted in Radzinowicz 1956: 572; see also Brodeur 1983).

Whether or not 'community-based' policing becomes a reality, or has these effects, in Canada, a second recent trend has the potential for affecting significantly the extent to which police officers may be permitted to engage in political activity. With the enactment of the *Charter of Rights and Freedoms* and its constitutional guarantees of 'freedom of expression' and 'freedom of association' (section 2) have come a number of legal challenges to statutory provisions that seek to restrict the political rights of public servants. Until recently, these challenges were unsuccessful, but in June 1991 the Supreme Court of Canada ruled key provisions of the federal *Public Service Employment Act* unconstitutional on the ground that they were in violation of the Charter's guarantee of freedom of expression (*Osborne, Millar and Barnhart et al.* v. *Canada* (1991) 125 N.R. 241).

Sections 32 and 33 of the *Public Service Employment Act* stated:

> 32. For the purposes of sections 33 and 34, 'candidate' means a candidate for election as a member of the House of Commons, a member of the legislature of a province or a member of the Council of the Yukon Territory or the Northwest Territories.
>
> 33(1) No deputy head and, except as authorized under this section, no employee, shall
>
> (a) engage in work for or against a candidate;
> (b) engage in work for or against a political party; or
> (c) be a candidate.
>
> (2) A person does not contravene subsection (1) by reason only of attending a political meeting or contributing money for the funds of a candidate or of a political party.

Subsection 33(3) provides that the Public Service Commission, 'if it is of the opinion that the usefulness to the Public Service of the employee in the position the employee then occupies would not be impaired by reason of that employee having been a candidate,' may grant leave of absence without pay to allow the employee to run for elected office.

The Supreme Court ruled that these provisions violated the guarantee of freedom of expression in section 2 of the Charter (there was no ruling on whether they also violated the guarantee of freedom of association), and that they could not be saved by recourse to section 1 of the Charter, which provides: 'The *Canadian Charter of Rights and Freedoms* guarantees the rights and freedoms set out in it subject only to such reasonable limits prescribed by law as can be demonstrably justified in a free and democratic society.' The majority of the Court held that the provisions of section 33 of the *Public Service Employment Act* could not be regarded as such a 'reasonable limit' on freedom of expression guaranteed by the Charter. They acknowledged that political neutrality of the public service is an undisputed constitutional convention in Canada, adopted in section 33 of the act, and was a valid governmental objective, the achievement of which could justify overriding the Charter's guarantee of freedom of expression. They held, however, that the terms of section 33 were unnecessarily broad to achieve this purpose, and therefore could not be upheld by virtue of section 1 of the Charter. Specifically, they held that the Section covered too wide a range of activities (they held that it covered all partisan political activities), and applied indiscriminately to too wide a range of public servants. Accordingly, they held that paragraph (a) of subsection 33(1) (which was the only provision directly challenged in the case) was of no force and effect except as it applied to a 'deputy head.'

Since the political rights of police officers were not in issue in the *Osborne* case, its implications for police officers remain a matter of speculation. Two aspects of the case, however, may provide clues to how the Supreme Court might view the kinds of restrictions on the political rights of police officers that were outlined earlier in this paper.

In the first place, it can be noted that some of the existing restrictions on the political rights of police officers in Canada are much more expansive than those that were at issue in the *Osborne* case. Thus, although the Court acknowledged that the term 'engage in work for or against' in section 33 of the *Public Service Employment Act* was difficult to interpret and apply in practice, it seems at least possible that the Court would not have thought that it covered the mere expression of (even partisan) political views. Yet, as has been noted earlier, the mere public expression of political (and in some cases religious) views by police officers has been prohibited in some jurisdictions in Canada. Also, restrictions of political activities by the police frequently cover municipal, as well as federal, provincial, and territorial politics. Arguably, then, if the Court found the restrictions in section 33 of the *Public Service Employment Act* constitutionally unacceptable, it might react even more negatively to the more embracing restrictions that are applied to some officers.

On the other hand, the Court's second objection to the legislation – that it applied to too wide a range of public servants – perhaps provides a more important clue as to the attitude the Court might take to restrictions on police officers' political rights. In explaining the Court's objections on this ground, Mr Justice Sopinka, writing for the majority of the Court, wrote: 'The result of this broad general language is that the restrictions apply to a great number of public servants who in modern government are employed in carrying out *clerical, technical or industrial duties that are completely divorced from the exercise of any discretion that could be in any manner affected by political considerations*' (emphasis added). The clear implication of these words would seem to be that the restrictions that the Court was considering would not be regarded as unconstitutional in the case of public servants whose jobs involved 'the exercise of any discretion that could be in any manner affected by political considerations.' This suggests that the Court may be very unreceptive to any claim by police officers to have such restrictions struck down as unreasonable violations of the guaranteed freedom of expression, since the impartial exercise of discretion is arguably at the very heart of the police's law-enforcement function.

As was noted earlier, in the case of the OPP in Ontario, the courts have favoured the less restrictive provisions of the Ontario *Public Service Act* over the more restrictive provisions of the regulations under the former *Police Act*. The political rights under the *Public Service Act* that the OPP won in the *Mahlberg* case, however, have since been taken away by a change in the regulations under the *Public Service Act*, whereby OPP officers were placed in the category of designated public servants who do not enjoy these rights. Although this change in designation has not been legally challenged, the constitutionality of the relevant provisions of the Ontario *Public Service Act* was upheld by the Supreme Court of Canada in 1987 (*O.P.S.E.U.* v. *Ontario (Attorney General)*, [1987] 2 S.C.R. 2).

Thus, at the present time, it remains an open, and somewhat confusing, question, as to whether – and if so, to what extent – police officers in Canada can look to the *Charter of Rights and Freedoms* to guarantee their political rights. In view of the large number of jurisdictions in which the political engagement of police officers appears in practice to be regarded with considerable permissiveness, however, it may not be in their interests to put this question to a legal test.

CONCLUSIONS

Even a cursory review of the relationship between police and politics in Canada, both historically and at the present time, reveals that the dilemma of recognizing the political nature of policing while ensuring that it is carried out in a non-partisan way remains unsolved in Canada. Each of the two main strategies for ensuring non-partisan public policing has had a very chequered history among the multiple public police jurisdictions here, and to this day neither seems to be generally accepted or agreed upon.

With respect to the structure and role of municipal-police governance, the issue has been consistently confounded by ongoing provincial-municipal struggles for control. In two provinces, provincial governments have succeeded in wresting considerable control over municipal policing from local municipal authorities. As has recently been pointed out, this has been largely achieved through financial incentives rather than any very convincing arguments of principle, and is intimately linked to more general relationships between provincial and municipal governments (Apostle and Stenning 1989: part 10). There is little evidence to suggest, however, that reforms in this area have rendered the public police significantly more or less susceptible to political influence or control (Hann et al. 1985).

With respect to the political rights of police officers, the situation has been and remains remarkably uneven, despite the growing organization and sophistication of police associations and unions. While it may be true, as some have claimed (such as, Wilson 1981), that police officers, as a group, tend to be disinclined towards political involvement, there appear to be enough examples to the contrary to conclude that this is not a universal characteristic of the police. In fact, the police job provides police officers with plenty of opportunities to become aware of the details of political conflicts.

Opinions about the desirability of political involvement by police officers seem to be as divided in Canada now as they ever were. Influences from south of the border, where there has historically been quite a different tradition in the relationship of police and politics, are not insignificant in this regard and, as exchanges become more common (for example, through Canadian participation in the International Association of Chiefs of Police and American participation in the Canadian Association of Chiefs of Police), may be expected to grow rather than diminish. Both scholars and police leaders in the United States have been aggressive in urging greater involvement of the police in political affairs. Thus, for example, Professor William Ker Muir, Jr (1983) has argued that police officers' involvement in politics strengthens public debate about police issues and leads to more open police institutions whose leaders are more focused on the larger community rather than just on the police. In addition, he argues that such involvement develops police officers' communications and negotiation skills and dissipates police cynicism about the world being divided into good and bad people. More recently, the executive director of the International Association of Chiefs of Police has argued that it is time to abandon the idea that police involvement in the political process is unprofessional, as it appears 'almost unprofessional to sit silently on the sidelines while legislative issues [are] hammered out by politicians and special interest groups, often to the long-term detriment of public safety' (Vaughn 1988).

Such sentiments have found sympathetic listeners among Canadian police officers. Recently, the Police Association of Ontario, probably sensing that the new NDP provincial government might be more receptive to such demands, urged that police officers should not be required to resign if elected to political office (*Globe and Mail* 1991b). The new regulations in Ontario allow police officers to take a leave of absence in such circumstances, rather than requiring them to resign.

There can be little doubt, however, that the British tradition of police neutrality and 'independence' has also exercised a significant influence over the attitudes of police, politicians, and the courts in Canada, and has contributed to what is still probably the majority view here that police should maintain an arms-length relationship to politics. The view that policing, and law generally, should be regarded as non-political arenas, however, is coming under pressure from a number of different quarters. On the one hand, critical legal scholars, criminologists, and 'revisionist' historians (Reiner 1985: chap. 1) have been increasingly arguing that the distinction is an untenable one that has itself been exploited for political advantage. The view that 'law is simply politics by other means' (Kairys 1982: 17), while certainly not subscribed to by the majority of scholars, is one that has a growing number of adherents.

As has been noted, the advent of the *Charter of Rights*, with its guarantees of equality and individual freedom, has also led to questioning of the conventional wisdom that engagement in public service necessarily involves forgoing one's rights as a citizen, although how this will eventually affect the political rights of police officers remains unclear at present. Perhaps most significant in this regard, however, is the current popularity of the concept of community-based policing, with its significantly different vision both of the role of the public police and of the relationship that should exist between the police and the communities they are appointed to serve. Up to this point, the questions that community-based policing will inevitably raise about the relationship between police and politics have remained largely unaddressed. If the concept ever extends beyond rhetoric, and serious attempts are made to implement it in a systematic way, it will almost certainly require some fundamental reassessments of the role of politics in policing, and of the police in politics.

REFERENCES

Aitchison, J. 1949. 'The Municipal Corporations Act of 1849.' *Canadian Historical Review* 30: 107.

Alderson, J. 1979. *Policing Freedom*. Plymouth: Macdonald & Evans.

Apostle, R., and P. Stenning. 1989. *Public Policing in Nova Scotia*, vol. 2. Report of the Royal Commission on the Donald Marshall, Jr., Prosecution. Halifax: Government Printer.

Bayley, D. 1988. 'Community Policing: A Report from the Devil's Advocate.' In J. Greene and S. Mastrofski, eds, *Community Policing-Rhetoric or Reality*, 225. New York: Praeger Books.

British Columbia, Superintendent of Police. 1896. *Annual Report of the Superintendent of Police Respecting the Police and Prisons of British Columbia for the Year Ending 31st October, 1895*. Victoria: Queen's Printer.

British Columbia Police Commission. 1980. *B.C. Police Boards Handbook*, Vancouver: BC Police Commission.

Brodeur, J-P. 1983. 'High Policing and Low Policing: Remarks about the Policing of Political Activities.' *Social Problems* 30(5): 507.

Brogden, M. 1982. *The Police: Autonomy and Consent*. London: Academic Press.

– 1987. 'The Emergence of the Police: The Colonial Dimension.' *British Journal Criminology* 27: 4.

Brown, L., and C. Brown. 1973. *An Unauthorized History of the R.C.M.P.* Toronto: James Lorimer.

Bunyan, T. 1976. *The Political Police in Britain*. London: Quartet Books.

Cain, M. 1979. 'Trends in the Sociology of Police Work.' *International Journal of Sociology and the Law* 7: 143.

Canada, Commission of Inquiry into Certain Activities of the Royal Canadian Mounted Police Second Report. 1981. *Freedom and Security under the Law*. Ottawa: Minister of Supply & Services Canada.

Cranshaw, R. 1987. 'Police and the Political System – A Systems Analysis Approach.' *The Police Journal* 60(1): 72.

Day, P., and R. Klein. 1987. *Accountabilities – Five Public Services*. London: Tavistock Publications.

Edwards, J. 1980. *Ministerial Responsibility for National Security*. Ottawa: Minister of Supply & Services Canada.

Forcese, D. 1980. 'Police Unionism: Employee-Management Relations in Canadian Police Forces.' *Canadian Police College Journal* 4(2): 79.

Globe and Mail 1977. 'Trudeau: Keep politicians ignorant of police actions.' 12 December, 7.

– 1978. 'Fire Brown and 2 Police Officers – Waterloo Police Probe.' 30 November, 1.

– 1979. 'Jab at Sewell called first step in police election involvement.' 2 October, 5.

– 1980a. 'Policeman allowed to run for county board of education.' 23 October.

– 1980b. 'Police urged to lobby for political change.' 21 February, 1 and 2.

– 1980c. 'Won't take political action, police association promises.' 21 October.

– 1991a. 'Appointment of police chiefs splits soviets.' 8 April, A10.

– 1991b. 'Police should be allowed to enter politics, association says.' 14 August, A4.

Greene, J., and S. Mastrofski, eds. 1988. *Community Policing – Rhetoric or Reality*. New York: Praeger Books.

Hann, R., J. McGinnis, P. Stenning, and A. Farson. 1985. 'Municipal Police Governance and Accountability in Canada: An Empirical Study.' *Canadian Police College Journal* 9(1): 1.

Harrison, R., ed. 1859. *The New Municipal Manual for Upper Canada*. Toronto: Maclear & Co.

Jackson, R. 1980. 'Police Labour Relations in Canada: A Current Perspective.' In B. Downie and R. Jackson, eds, *Conflict and Cooperation in Police Labour Relations*, 7. Ottawa: Minister of Supply & Services Canada.

Kairys, D., ed. 1982. *The Politics of Law*. New York: Pantheon.

Landau, N. 1984. *The Justices of the Peace*. Berkeley: University of California Press.

Lewthwaite, S. 1987. 'Keepers of the Peace: The Magistrates of Georgia Township, 1830–1850.' M.A. thesis, History Department, University of Toronto.

Lustgarten, L. 1986. *The Governance of the Police*. London: Sweet & Maxwell.

McDougall, A. 1971. 'Policing in Ontario: The Occupational Dimension to Provincial-Municipal Relations.' Ph.D. thesis, University of Toronto.

Maitland, F. 1885. *Justice and Police*. Reprint. New York: AMS Press 1974.

Marquis, G. 1993. *Policing Canada's First Century: A History of the Canadian Association of Chiefs of Police*. Toronto: The Osgoode Society.

Marshall, G. 1965. *Police and Government*. London: Methuen & Co.

Morgan, J. 1987. *Conflict and Order: The Police and Labour Disputes in England and Wales, 1900–1939*. Oxford: Clarendon Press.

Muir, Jr, W.K. 1983. 'Police and Politics.' *Criminal Justice Ethics* 2(2): 3.

Normandeau, André, and B. Leighton. 1990. *A Vision of the Future of Policing in Canada: Police Challenge 2000*. Ottawa: Supply and Services.

Ontario, Ministry of the Solicitor General. 1990. 'Political Activity Rights for Police Officers in Ontario: A Discussion Paper.' Toronto: Ministry of the Solicitor General of Ontario.

– Policing Services Division. 1992. *Policing Standards Manual*. Toronto: Ministry of the Solicitor General of Ontario.

Ontario, Niagara Region Review Commission. 1989. *Report and Recommendations*. Toronto: Queen's Printer.

– Ottawa-Carleton Review Commission. 1976. *Report*. Toronto: Queens's Printer.

– Royal Commission on Metropolitan Toronto. 1977. *Detailed Findings and Recommendations*, vol. 2. Report. Toronto: Queen's Printer.

– Waterloo Region Review Commission. 1979. *Report*. Toronto: Queen's Printer.

Radzinowicz, L. 1956. *A History of English Criminal Law and Its Administration from 1750*. Vol. 3: *Cross-currents in the Movement for the Reform of the Police*. London: Stevens & Sons Ltd.

RCMP, External Review Committee. 1991. *Off-Duty Conduct*. Discussion Paper 7, by P. Stenning. Ottawa: RCMP External Review Committee.

Reiner, R. 1985. *The Politics of the Police*. Brighton: Wheatsheaf Books.
Reith, Charles. 1952. *The Blind Eye of History*. London: Faber and Faber.
Rogers, N. 1984. 'Serving Toronto the Good.' In V. Russell, ed., *Forging A Consensus*, 116. Toronto: University of Toronto Press.
Simmonds, R. 1985. *Internal Review of the Royal Canadian Mounted Police Investigation of the Hatfield Case*. Ottawa: Royal Canadian Mounted Police.
Stenning, P. 1983. 'Trusting the Chief: Legal Aspects of the Status and Political Accountability of the Police in Canada.' Unpublished S.J.D. thesis, Faculty of Law, University of Toronto.
Stenning, P., and T. Landau. 1988. *The Niagara Regional Board of Commissioners of Police: Its Role and Accountability*. Niagara Falls: Niagara Region Review Commission.
Stokes, M. 1991. 'Law Reform from Below: Petitions to the Legislative Assembly of Ontario from Local Government, 1867–1877.' Unpublished paper.
Talbot, C.K., C.H.S. Jaywardene, and T.J. Juliani. 1986. *Canada's Constables: The Historical Development of Policing in Canada*. Ottawa: Crimcare.
Taylor, I. 1981. *Law and Order: Arguments for Socialism*. London: Macmillan.
Turk, A. 1982. *Political Criminality*. Beverly Hills: Sage Publications.
Vaughn, J. 1988. 'Police and Politics,' *The Police Chief* 55 (10): 8.
Wilson, A. 1859. *The Constable's Guide: A Sketch of the Office of Constable*. Toronto: Maclear and Co.
Wilson, I. 1981. 'Political Awareness in Policing.' In D. Pope and N. Weiner, eds, *Modern Policing*. London: Croom Helm.

PART FIVE: TWO CASE STUDIES – MONTREAL AND EDMONTON

12

Police Accountability in Crisis Situations

JEAN-PAUL BRODEUR AND
LOUISE VIAU

INTRODUCTION

As its title indicates, this paper raises the issue of police accountability in crisis situations. The concepts of crisis and of accountability are both difficult to define. Without attempting to provide a formal definition of them, we will explain how they will be used in the context of this study.

Crises

First of all, the type of crises that we want to discuss are triggered by criminal behaviour and not by natural events. Second, the word 'crisis' is used here to refer to collective events, that is, events that implicate whole communities for an extended period of time. Finally, these crises are formally acknowledged by the authorities that have to deal with them. Their existence is officially recognized by the invocation of emergency legislation, such as the former *War Measures Act*[1] or the present *Emergencies Act*,[2] or by the application of a set of police procedures that are actually labelled 'emergency measures.' Emergency legislation usually implies that a state of emergency or its equivalent (for example, an apprehended insurrection) is formally proclaimed.

As is obvious from our description, the kind of crisis that we have in mind is exemplified by the October Crisis of 1970 and the Oka Crisis of 1990. These two crises have been associated in Québec and, to a significant extent, in Canadian public opinion. There are substantial similarities between the two crises:

- Although both crises occurred in Québec, they had national implications and were perceived to be national crises.

- Both crises were extended in time, the October Crisis lasting approximately six weeks and the Oka Crisis twelve weeks.
- Both crises were fuelled by claims to political autonomy and self-government.
- Both crises involved the intervention of several police forces and of the Canadian Armed Forces.
- Both crises were characterized by widespread police abuse of power.

This list is not exhaustive, and an even longer list of differences between these two crises could conceivably be drawn. Although we believe that the two crises are comparable in several aspects, such a comparison is too complex to be undertaken systematically within the limited scope of this paper. We focus mainly on the Oka Crisis and raise the issues of police accountability in crisis situations within the context of this crisis. The Oka Crisis is more recent than the October one and has not yet been the object of much research. The October Crisis can be used as a point of reference for stressing an issue and for broadening the scope of our discussion of police accountability.

With regard to one crucial aspect of police accountability, there is an obvious difference between the October and the Oka crises. No police were disciplined for having violated a citizen's rights after the October Crisis. In contrast, thirty-nine members of the Sûreté du Québec (SQ) are now facing disciplinary charges, including high-ranking officers (one chief inspector and one captain), for misconduct during the Oka Crisis.

As regards the October Crisis it must be said that, following the recommendations of the Keable inquiry,[3] members of the Royal Canadian Mounted Police (RCMP) were charged with criminal offences.[4] However, all the offences they were charged with were committed at least one year after the October Crisis. In contrast with the Oka Crisis, no disciplinary action of any kind was taken against members of the police forces – or members of the armed forces – for wrongful behaviour displayed during the October Crisis itself. We should stress that in the mid-1970s, no formal independent structure to process citizens' complaints existed in Canadian police forces. Thereafter, civilian review of police misconduct was progressively instituted in relation to Canada's main police forces.

There is, however, another factor that played a decisive part in moving authorities to bring disciplinary charges against members of the SQ. The medium of the October crisis was the word, either in its spoken or written form. The written press and radio did most of the reporting on this crisis. The Oka crisis was a war of images, television being the main source of reports on what was happening. The result of TV coverage was that, with the exception of the initial assault on the Mohawks' barricade on 11 July, the most violent confrontations between police, Mohawks, and residents of Oka and Châteauguay were watched by millions of viewers. The shocking display of police brutality was witnessed by so many persons through television that the authorities were compelled to react officially. Furthermore, television tapes could be used in certain instances to identify police who had engaged in brutality.

Accountability

There is now a great deal of discussion revolving around the issue of accountability. Although the general meaning of the word appears to be clear, there are no legal definitions of it in relation to the police. According to the *Oxford English Dictionary*, 'accountability' means 'liability to give account of and answer for, discharge of duties or conduct.' The same dictionary defines 'liable' as 'bound or obliged by law or equity.'

This significant relationship between the concepts of accountability and obligation is also reflected in *Webster's Third New International Dictionary,* which defines being accountable as 'being subject to giving an account.' The idea of being *subjected* to accountability is clearly expressed in the French translation of accountability. 'Accountability' is translated in French as '*l'obligation de rendre compte*' (being obligated to account for). Such emphasis upon the compulsory character of accountabilty would lead us to make the following distinction:

- *Accountability as an internal obligation.* The prototype of this kind of accountability is budgetary or financial accountability. Almost all public and private organizations are compelled to account on a regular basis for their spending. The crucial point here is that this obligation does not stem from external allegations of overspending or of any kind of financial wrongdoing. Within the course of ordinary business, the organization is compelled by law or by regulation to provide a statement on what it is spending. Likewise, in the field of political policing, the Canadian Security Intelligence Service (CSIS) is under legal obligation to account for its operations before the Solicitor General and the Security Intelligence Review Committee (SIRC), whether or not there are rumors of scandal.[5]
- *Accountability as created by external pressure.* The paradigm case for this kind of *forced* accountability is the external complaint, which implies that an organization (or an individual) does not have to account for the behaviour of its members unless it is compelled to do so by external allegations of wrongdoing. In the case of external pressure, we have to make a distinction

between two kinds of instances. First, there may be a formal mechanism that automatically processes complaints made against an organization or its members. A civilian police review board is such a mechanism. However, there are cases where such a process has not been developed. In this second instance, allegations made by an individual complainant or by a group may often not be sufficient in themselves to compel accountability. They have to be supplemented by a public campaign orchestrated by the media. Such 'accountability' really betrays the sense of the word. An organization or an individual may be profoundly deviant. Yet, as long as nobody complains, neither the individual nor the organization have to account for their decisions or their behaviour.

There is yet another fundamental distinction that needs to be made with regard to accountability:

- *Organizational vs. individual accountability.* Although it is to a certain extent problematic, this distinction is referred to more frequently than the previous one in the research literature. Either it is the behaviour of an organization, taken as a whole, that is questioned or it is the behaviour of one or several of its members. The crucial difference between these two types of accountability is the following. As a whole, an organization is accountable, usually through its chief, to a higher-level authority. In contrast, its individual members are accountable to the organization itself and to its internal hierarchy. This opens up the possibility that an organization might want to subject some of its members to internal discipline in order to shield itself from external scrutiny. The members who are thus subject to internal sanctions may feel that they are being used as scapegoats. Two problems related to this distinction deserve to be mentioned. A complainant that cannot identify the person against whom he or she wants to complain will tend to make a complaint against the whole organization, despite the fact that it is not as such involved in wrongdoing. Furthermore, the distinction between organizational and individual accountability may be variously drawn because there is no clear threshold beyond which it cannot be claimed that we are only dealing with individuals (in other words, we do not know what proportion of an organization needs to be involved in wrongdoing to justify the assertion that the issue has become one of organizational accountability). Both problems are emphasized in the context of a crisis.

We shall use both pairs of distinctions in our study. The paper is divided in two parts. First, focusing on the Oka Crisis, we discuss the issues of police accountability in situations of emergency from the perspective of a political sociology of organizations. Second, we consider these issues from a legal standpoint. Our claim is that in the aftermath of the Oka Crisis, police accountability was entirely the result of external pressure and that it only extended to individual members of the SQ. We argue that the issue was not individual but organizational, accountability and that the SQ leadership entirely failed to take a critical look at its organization and to draw the lessons of the crisis. In our conclusion, we discuss the meaning of police accountability in the context of police emergencies, and also offer suggestions to increase police accountability in the context of crises.

POLICE ACCOUNTABILITY: AN ORGANIZATIONAL PERSPECTIVE

The Oka Crisis happened in the summer of 1990 and was extensively covered by the media. We can assume that most of our Canadian readers are still familiar with the general aspects of this crisis. However, since it will provide the main background for our discussion of police accountability in situations of crisis, it may be useful for our Canadian and a fortiori for our foreign readers to briefly recall these events.[6]

The Oka Crisis

The Mohawk Nation reserve of Kanesatake is adjacent to the town of Oka, which is near Montreal in the province of Quebec. In the fall of 1989, the authorities of Oka announced their intention to expand its municipal golf course. This expansion threatened to uproot a Mohawk burial ground. As expected, the Band Council of Kanesatake officially stated that it was opposed to it. However, the land that was to be used for expanding the golf course – including the Mohawk burial ground – was not 'owned' by the Mohawks. Hence, they did not have legal recourse for stopping the expansion of the golf course on what they considered sacred land.

On 11 March 1990 residents of Kanesatake mounted a barricade on a dirt path leading to the burial ground. In the following weeks, they were joined by a contingent of heavily armed Mohawks who belonged to a society of Warriors. Many of the Warriors are believed to have come from the reserve of Akwasasne, which is located on territory spreading across the boundaries of Quebec, Ontario, and the state of New York. On 29 June the municipality of Oka was granted an injunction to evict the Mohawks who had protested the expansion of the golf course by mounting a barricade. In the early morning of 11 July, a contingent of approximately one hundred SQ police mounted an assault against the barricade in an attempt to dislodge the Mohawks by force. They were repelled by gunfire and retreated in disarray. One SQ officer, Corporal Marcel Lemay, was hit by a bullet during the assault and died shortly thereafter. The SQ then erected its own barricade a hundred metres from the Mohawks'.

On the same day, in a gesture of support, the Mohawks of the neighbouring reserve of Kahnawake blocked all the roads leading to the Mercier Bridge to Montreal and occupied the bridge itself, thus denying access to residents of the region of Châteauguay. This occupation of the Mercier Bridge was a major source of inconvenience for the many Châteauguay residents who worked in Montreal. They had to use an alternative route to get to the city which, it must be remembered, is situated on an island. Having to use another bridge to get into Montreal, they needed at least two extra hours of driving time to get to work and back. It was calculated that some 60,000 motorists had to be rerouted every day of the crisis. As the crisis dragged on throughout the summer of 1990, the residents of Châteauguay experienced intense frustration and became very hostile to the SQ, because of its perceived inaction.

From then on, until the end of the occupation of the Mercier Bridge on 6 September and until the final surrender of the Warriors of Kanesatake on 26 September, the tension mounted steadily and erupted in several violent confrontations involving the SQ, the Mohawk communities of Kanesatake and Kahnawake, and the residents of Châteauguay. A particularly violent incident occurred on 12 August, when the SQ charged into a crowd of Châteauguay residents who were occupying a bridge at St-Louis-de-Gonzague in an attempt to block maritime traffic on the St Lawrence Seaway. On 29 August, in what was probably the most disgraceful event of the crisis, a convoy of cars that was evacuating Mohawk women, children, and elderly people from Kahnawake across the Mercier Bridge was stoned by rioters in LaSalle, a Montreal suburb. Although numerous police witnessed the stoning, they apparently were caught unprepared and did nothing to prevent or stop the incident.

A contingent of approximately 240 RCMP police was sent to support the SQ. Finally, on 27 August, the Canadian Armed Forces were called in and progressively succeeded in dismantling the barricades, thus putting an end to the crisis. We are now suffering from the sequels of this crisis and will still be in the coming years.

Major Impediments to Accountability

Before reviewing the various types of police accountability, we will describe briefly five major obstacles to making the police accountable for their behaviour in the context of this crisis. Apart from the last one discussed, all these obstacles are generally found in all crises.

The Suspension of Individual Rights

The Oka Crisis was precipitated by a conflict between two communities. It involved large numbers of people, some of them heavily armed, who engaged in mass demonstrations that often erupted into violence and threatened to bring chaos to this whole part of the province. Such a crisis is essentially a collective phenomenon wherein the individual person is engulfed and individuality loses at least part of the significance it normally has. It does not necessarily follow from such a characterization that *individual rights* become irrelevant during a crisis. However, they do become more vulnerable, not because they are rights but mostly because they are *individual* rights. In other words, when individuals are swamped by a mass phenomenon, individual rights also tend to dissolve.

In order to support our point, we shall quote parts of two decisions rendered by the Quebec commissioner for police deontology on 18 March 1991. These decisions followed complaints made M. Bernard Petit, a resident of Oka, to the effect that he was submitted to police harassment and unjustified searches, and that the protection afforded by the Charter of Rights and Freedoms was suspended. These complaints were made against the SQ during the summer of 1990, through a series of five telegrams sent to the chairman of the Quebec Police Commission; on 3 September of the same year, this citizen also sent a formal complaint by letter to the commissioner for police deontology. All six complaints were processed by the commissioner and were rejected by him, for the following reasons:

> [Translation] It also came out during the inquiry and is judicial knowledge that the total population living in this part of the province's territory had experienced for several long months, a state of siege where force was used. As Commissioner for police deontology, we have no mandate to judge whether this use of force was necessary or futile. However, two observations can be made. First, during these periods of confrontation and violence, individual rights are the first to suffer, in order to safeguard collective interests. The *Charter of Rights and Freedoms* is then put under the bushel. Second, peace officers only execute tasks demanded by those who judge confrontation to be necessary and extraordinary measures also to be necessary.
>
> Is this a question of reprehensible obedience to which the police should not have suscribed? This is not the time for philosophy, but it seems to the Commissioner that the constraints and harassing of the citizens by police acting under orders, were not violations so serious that the police should have refused to inflict them upon citizens.

Another point should be brought up. In all the documents that fill our files, it seems that M. Petit says it is impossible for him to identify the policemen he accuses of harassment. Even more, he admits that, in the case where he might recognize some faces, he would not be able under oath to point to one or another officer as the author of a derogatory act.

This essential proof being inaccessible, any inquiry would be doomed to failure.[7]

[Translation] In brief, a state of emergency can require that individual rights be violated in the command of general interest.[8]

These quotes clearly support our point about the precariousness of individuality in the context of mass crises. In such instances, personal identity is subverted in more than one way. Individual persons are impossible to identify, either physically or even morally, as they can claim not to be acting on their own but following orders from their superiors. It is this general predicament that is conducive to a suspension of individuals rights. It also neutralizes the application of such mechanisms for making police accountable that can only be triggered by external complaints against individual officers.

Failures of Identification

We previously distinguished between accountability as an internal obligation and accountability as the result of external pressure, such as complaints from the public. Both kinds of accountability depend on the possibility of identifying who is responsible for what.

This issue is quite obvious in the case of external complaints: no official body that receives complaints from the public can process a complaint directed against one or several unidentified police. The quotes given above provide a striking illustration of this kind of obstacle.

In the context of a crisis, the identification of individual police that may be guilty of misconduct in the midst of action is extremely problematic. First, riot squads usually wear helmets and protective garments such as bullet-proof jackets, which bear no marks of identification and protect the identity of the individuals wearing them. Second, the police may remove their identity badges before going into action. The alleged pretext is that the steel pin fastening the identity badge to the uniform might be used as a weapon against the police by a rioter tearing off the badge. Actually, police need no pretext to remove their identification marks when going against demonstrators and do so as a matter of course. Third, skirmishes between demonstrators and police unfold so fast that nobody has the time to identify any of the parties involved. All these factors played a part during the October[9] and Oka crises.

Even when accountability is conceived as an internal obligation, a police force that is reporting on itself – say, to the minister responsible for policing – must be able to identify who charted a particular course or who gave the order to undertake an operation. When no clear chain of command can be delineated, such identification becomes impossible. This was the situation during the Oka Crisis, as it was during the 1970 October Crisis,[10] and, generally speaking, in other crises of such nature.

Faulty Reports

Experience acquired by one of the writers of this paper when he was director of research for the Keable inquiry into RCMP wrongdoing taught him that it is relatively futile to interrogate police officers on the part they played in certain events, unless it is possible to check what they say against their own and other written reports. The possession of these reports is also vital for an inquiry, because their content reveals what are the most relevant questions to raise.

Unfortunately, police reports written during a crisis are very difficult to use. First, they are generally incomplete, being written in great haste at the end of eventful days. For example, Crown prosecutors whom we interviewed had to drop a great number of charges against demonstrators during the Oka Crisis because the investigators' reports were only partially filled and full of mistakes. Second, they are occasionallly deliberately misleading, if not downright false. Finally, when compared with each other, these reports contain inconsistent information. Taken together, these shortcomings become a major obstacle to police accountability.

Suspicion Against the Structures of Accountability

With very few exceptions, the Mohawks did not make any official complaint against SQ police before the SQ's Committee for Studying Complaints, the majority of which is staffed by civilians.[11] There are two possible reasons for this reluctance to use the available structures for ensuring police accountability. The first is that, for the Mohawks, any body emanating from the SQ totally lacks credibility. The second reason is that the Mohawks consider themselves to be a nation. Hence, they will more readily appeal to international bodies such as the International Federation for Human Rights (or even the United Nations) than they will to a provincial body.

However, this strategy tends to undermine police accountability. International bodies are very remote from the reality of Canadian policing and can only perform the role of a distant moral authority devoid of any power to remedy police abuse in Canada. In contrast, the SQ complaint committee actually charged thirty-nine members of the force with violations of their code of ethics, as we previously said. However, this committee cannot take any action on behalf of the Mohawks if it does not receive any complaint from them. The same is true for the Quebec commissioner for police deontology.

There may also be a more general explanation for this apparent reluctance to complain against individual members of a police force. To our knowledge, no complaints against individual police were made during or after the October Crisis. Being collective confrontations, such crises pitch entire communities against each other and against institutions such as the police or the army, which are perceived as a whole to favour one side against the other. In the context of such group polarization, individualized processes such as making a complaint against a particular person seem to lose their point.

Amnesty as Anti-accountability

One officer from the SQ, Corporal Lemay, was killed by gunfire on the first day of the crisis. The killing of a police officer is regarded by the police as the ultimate crime. The police were extremely frustrated to find that sympathy for the Mohawks did not abate after their failed assault on the Kanesatake barricade. On the contrary, after 11 July, public support for the Mohawk cause actually increased both in Quebec and in the rest of Canada. Furthermore, there was so much confusion during that first assault on the Kanesatake barricade that the police had no clue as to who killed Corporal Lemay (the case is still unsolved today and is now the focus of a public inquiry conducted by a Quebec coroner). It was by no means proved that the SQ officer had been killed by a bullet fired by the Mohawks; the Mohawk Warriors claimed for a time that Lemay may have been hit by a stray bullet fired by the police – this was later disproved by a ballistic examination – and demanded to have a Mohawk representative on the team investigating the death of Corporal Lemay.

What had the most debilitating effect on police morale, however, was the Mohawks' demand for amnesty. Although both the federal and the Quebec ministers of justice repeatedly denied that amnesty for the killing of Corporal Lemay would ever be granted the Mohawks, the police were never certain that the government negotiators would not give in to all the demands of the Warriors. The SQ suspicions were justified to a significant extent.

First, numerous intelligence officers – from the SQ, the RCMP, and also the CSIS – claimed that they had regularly informed the government since 1989 of the illegal activities of the Warriors, such as cigarette smuggling across the U.S./Canada border and firearms contraband, including prohibited weapons such as fully automatic rifles. High-ranking Quebec civil servants also warned the government of an impending crisis. Yet, the Warriors seemed to enjoy some form of immunity because the government never took any action against them, for reasons that are still unclear. During the night of 31 August, when the end of the crisis was in sight, several small planes, presumably meant to fly out men and weapons from Kahnawake, were heard coming into the reserve and then leaving it. Even today, it is public knowledge that the Mohawks continue to be heavily involved in cigarette smuggling with the apparent blessing of the authorities.

We are not claiming that the frustration experienced by the police was a factor that led to their brutal treatment of the Mohawks and of Châteauguay demonstrators, although it may have played such a role. However, the bitter contrast between the blame that was heaped on the SQ and the manifest reluctance of public opinion and of government authorities to condemn the Warriors' behaviour can explain, at least in part, the adamant refusal of the police to account for their behaviour and to admit that anything had gone wrong during the crisis. Even faced with crushing evidence of brutality, such as the filming of unjustifiably violent action against demonstrators, very few SQ police were willing to accept any blame. This unwillingness to admit guilt is largely to be expected from individual policemen, who can be said to be exercising their basic right to remain silent when faced with accusations of wrongdoing. Indeed, following brutal events that took place on 12 and 13 August, the director general of the SQ announced that disciplinary investigations were to be conducted against SQ members who had abused their power.

What is more unexpected, however, is the organization's stern denial that its performance was below standard. After the violent confrontation between the SQ and Châteauguay citizens who occupied a bridge at St-Louis-de-Gonzague on 12 August 1990, the SQ's director general publicly apologized to the population of Châteauguay – the only time that the SQ leadership was critical of the performance of the organization. Since the end of the crisis, neither the SQ nor the minister responsible for public security have announced any measures to reform the SQ. On 15 January 1991, the Montreal daily *Le Devoir* reported that the SQ was trying to buy three powerful armoured amphibious vehicles – Leopard tanks – at a cost of US $800,000 in the United States. The president of the SQ's police union confirmed this information. Fortunately, Mr Claude Ryan, the present minister for public security, decided later against the acquisition of such weapons by the SQ.

Having discussed major impediments to police accountability, we shall now review the main types of accountability and assess whether police are subjected to them in times of crisis.

Financial Accountability

As the word 'accountability' itself indicates, financial or budgetary accountability is probably the oldest form of accountability. With regard to our previous distinctions, it can be described as an internal obligation that an organization itself has to meet.

Representatives of the Quebec government and of the SQ released figures on the cost of the Oka Crisis in mid-July 1991. Approximately one-third of the SQ's manpower (1500 police) had been working seven days a week, on shifts of 12–15 hours. The costs in extra personnel were close to $1 million per day during most of the crisis ($840,000 in overtime pay and $130,000 for food and shelter). Numerous SQ police made, in overtime pay, as much as their whole year's salary.

However, the fact that the Quebec government and the SQ could assess how much it was spending is no evidence that it was controlling its financial situation. Actually, an examination of the allocation of police manpower during the crisis could reveal that very little control was exercised. In crisis situations, police are hurriedly allocated on the basis of perceived needs, which are not carefully assessed.

Such a situation was observed during the 1970 October Crisis. Lawyer Jean-François Duchaîne, who was appointed by the Quebec government as a special investigator into the crisis, reported that the police felt compelled to follow up any lead that might reveal where the hostages were being held captive, thus stretching their resources in personnel to the breaking-point.[12] After the October Crisis, Pierre Vallières, who was believed to be an FLQ leader, went into hiding, thus triggering one of the biggest manhunts in Quebec history. When he decided to come out of hiding and give himself up to the SQ, the policeman who was on duty at the SQ headquarters where Vallières surrendered himself, accompanied by his lawyer, exclaimed, 'Pierre, what about my overtime!'[13]

To sum up, police financial accountability may take the form of recording what monies are spent during a crisis. How these monies are spent is only justified by the very general rule that in times of crisis every police officer is tacitly allowed to work himself or herself to the point of exhaustion.

There is a further point to be made with regard to financial accountability. No study has yet been made on whether there is any double-checking of the amount of overtime that is claimed by individual policemen. Our own hypothesis, based on the fact that the paperwork is extremely sloppy in a time of crisis, would be that there may be a significant amount of overbilling.

Political Accountability

Political accountability has a double meaning. It may refer to the need for elected officials to be accountable to the community. It may also mean that the police are accountable to elected officials as an organization; it is so accountable most especially to the minister responsible for public security. At the federal level, this minister is the solicitor general; during the Oka Crisis this was Mr Pierre Cadieux. In Quebec, this minister is called the minister for public security; this office was held at the time by Mr Sam Elkas.

We shall restrict our discussion to an examination of political accountability in the second sense, that is, the relationship between the police and political authorities. We must, however, stress that we do not consider this relationship to be one-sided. The police must account for their behaviour before the relevant political authorities, but it is also incumbent upon these authorities to exercise the proper form of control over the police.

Before discussing political accountability within the context of the Oka Crisis, a word should be said about the relationship between the SQ and the government. Up until the early sixties, the SQ – then known as the Provincial Police – was the strong arm of the provincial government and was directly under the control of the premier, who used it as a private army to implement his conservative labour policies. This was especially true under the government headed by Mr Maurice Duplessis.[14] After a long period of subservience to the political power, the SQ progressively grew more autonomous. It is now a powerful agency within the government and its power has to be reckoned with. When the government froze the salaries of all its employees in 1981–2, it conceded an 18 per cent pay increase to the members of the SQ. A minister responsible for public security who wanted to reform the SQ in 1986, Mr Gérard Latulippe, suddenly found himself in the midst of a minor political scandal and had to resign from the provincial cabinet (he subsequently became the Quebec delegate in Mexico). During the Oka Crisis, the deputy minister for public security was Mr Jacques Beaudoin. Before becoming deputy minister, Mr Beaudoin was director general of the SQ. He was succeeded by Mr Robert Lavigne, who is still its chief.

Several times during the Oka Crisis, Mr Sam Elkas, the minister of public security, admitted that he did not know who had given the order to mount an assault against the Kanesatake barricade on 11 July 1990, thus triggering the crisis (Mr Elkas was on holidays on 10 and 11 July). Not only did he not know who gave the order, but at the end of the crisis, on 27 September, he confessed to not being able to find any such order. However, in an article published on

12 September by the Montreal daily *La Presse*, the vice-president of the SQ police union, Mr André Malouf, quoted Mr Elkas as saying on 6 July, during an interview broadcast by radio station CJMS, that the police would have to act if the Mohawks did not respect a court injunction ordering them to dismantle their barricade at Oka. In his article, Mr Malouf gives several indications that the Quebec government was aware that an assault against the Mohawk barricade was imminent.

The premier, Mr Robert Bourassa, promised to call a public inquiry into the crisis and subsequently appointed Mr Claude Ryan, one of the strongest ministers of his cabinet, as minister of public security. Apparently, Mr Ryan conducted his own inquiry and, in a declaration to the Quebec National Assembly made on 16 October 1990, the new minister presented his version of how the decision to mount an assault against the Mohawks' barricade on 11 July was taken. According to the minister, this decision was taken by a special committee appointed by the SQ and was approved by the head of the force, Mr Lavigne. The minister did not reveal who were the members of this committee. On the 10th of July, Mr Lavigne informed Counsel Ménard, a 34-year-old lawyer who was a political attaché in Mr Elkas's cabinet, that the assault would take place the following day. This information was given to Ms. Ménard in the context of a briefing on another subject and no details were specified. She waited until 11 July, when the assault was well under way, to inform Mr Elkas. Ms. Ménard confirmed this account in an interview with *Le Devoir* on 8 November 1990. She has resigned, as have two other political attachés of Mr Elkas, from the cabinet of the minister for public security. It was said by the PQ opposition in the National Assembly that junior political personnel had to take the blame for the incompetence of the ministers involved (Mr Elkas and Mr Sciaccia, minister for indian affairs, who was said to have urged that no police action be taken against the Mohawks at the beginning of July).

No public inquiry has yet been called by the provincial government and it is now completely unlikely that one will ever be called. Furthermore, no public announcement has been made of any steps taken to remedy the SQ operational failures that were revealed during the crisis. A series of new promotions at the highest levels of the SQ was anmounced on 6 February 1991. According to an SQ spokesperson, these promotions were unrelated to the Oka Crisis. The most significant appointment was the replacement of Mr André Dugas, who was in charge of press relations during the crisis, by SQ agent Poéti. Mr Poéti was formerly the personal driver of SQ chief Lavigne and now heads the force's office of public communications. Captain J. Trudel, who was chief of the emergency unit during the Oka Crisis was promoted to inspector.

At first glance, then, it would appear that the SQ largely succeeded in avoiding political accountability. This conclusion is too simple, however, and assumes that two important questions have been resolved:

1 Were the Quebec political authorities willing to assume their responsibilities in relation to the SQ?
2 Granting that they were, were they not, in fact, prevented from assuming their responsibilities by the way the SQ operated during the crisis?

With regard to the first question, it is of paramount importance to consider that negotiations with the federal government to have the army intervene in Oka began very early in the crisis. Hence, the Quebec government distanced itself from the SQ early on. Actually, on the day following the failed SQ attempt to dismantle the Mohawk barricade at Kanesatake, Mr Sam Elkas began negotiations with the federal minister of defence, Mr Bill McKnight, in order to have the Canadian Armed Forces sent to Oka. The federal government was at first extremely reluctant to intervene, claiming that the administration of justice was a matter of provincial jurisdiction. At all levels of government, the main political strategy seemed from the outset to have been one of conflict avoidance, aimed primarily at gaining time for the crisis to wear itself down. The Quebec government faced a crushing dilemma. On the one hand, it could not call for another SQ assault on the Mohawk barricades without facing the very real possibility that it would fail again and cause a great deal of bloodshed. On the other hand, it could not officially call on the federal government to send the army in without admitting its failure to solve the crisis and without appearing at the same time to disavow the SQ. More important, it must be stressed that the Oka Crisis occurred after the failure of the Meech Lake accord, at a time when the Quebec government was asserting the distinct character of the province and was even threatening to break its links with the rest of Canada. In this context, any recognition by Quebec that it relied on the federal government to solve the Mohawk crisis would have been a major political embarrassment.

The Bourassa government tried to have it both ways: the Canadian Armed Forces were called in, not to lead operations, but, in theory, to provide a supporting role vis-à-vis the SQ. In calling for the assistance of the army, the government was, in fact, responding to a request expressed on 13 August by the director general of the SQ. After the storming of the bridge at St-Louis-de-Gonzague had triggered widespread rioting in Châteauguay, Chief Lavigne admitted that the SQ was no longer able to control the situation. His admission met with a great deal of hostility from the SQ rank and file and, particularly, from the powerful SQ police union (L'Association professionnelle des policiers du Québec).

The passive attitude of the Quebec and federal political authorities during the Oka Crisis was in marked contrast with the proactive approach taken by the Trudeau government at the time of the October Crisis. It must be emphasized, however, that the federal government had no more control over police abuse of their powers during the October Crisis than did the Quebec government during the Oka Crisis. In fact, the federal government disclaimed any responsibility for the gross violations of civil liberties that occurred during the October Crisis.

To conclude, it appears that there was a lack of political will to police the crisis. This indecisiveness in dealing with the crisis completely undermined the legitimacy of politicians to bring the police under account. In a remarkable inversion of responsibility, it is the police who passed judgment on their political masters. In the aftermath of the Oka Crisis, the SQ conducted an opinion survey of its 5650 members (police and civilian). The Montreal daily *La Presse* got hold of a copy of the questionnaire used in this opinion survey, which was dated 20 November 1990 and had to be completed by 4 December. It contained questions such as :

> According to you, to what extent did the Goverment of Quebec hinder or help the Sûreté in its operations, in the exercise of its powers, in the fulfilling of its mandate during the crisis?
>
> Did the Quebec government adequately control the SQ during the Aboriginal crisis?[15]

This questionnaire consisted of forty-four questions that addressed most significant aspects of the crisis from a police perspective (for example, were the police paid enough overtime, what effect had the media's coverage on their self-image, and what degree of confidence do they have in politicians, in their leadership, and so on). Its results were never made public. Nor do we know if it was used to introduce reforms into the SQ's decision-making, as was its stated purpose.

Control and Supervision by the SQ Hierarchy

We shall now try to answer our second question: Was the operational structure of the SQ open enough to satisfy legitimate demands with regard to police accountability? When Mr Sam Elkas was the minister for public scurity, could he have found out who gave the order to charge the Kanesatake Mohawk barricade, if he had tried hard enough? The answer is at best doubtful.

One of the biggest failures of the SQ during the crisis was a failure in command, which can be shown in several ways.

The Chain of Command

According to SQ regulations, a special chain of command is to be applied in a state of emergency. Several local *command posts* conduct the operations in the field. They are under the supervision of an *operation centre*, which coordinates all operations for one district. Above the district operation centre is the *control centre*, which is vested with ultimate authority. Both operation and control centres are situated at the SQ headquarters in Montreal.

This fairly straighforward structure was undermined in three basic ways during the Oka Crisis. First, the control centre was superseded by yet another body called the *strategic committee*. Its composition was somewhat mysterious. In theory, it consisted of three Quebec ministers – those for public security, indian affairs, and municipal affairs – and the SQ high command. Very little has publicly filtered through on the part played by the ministers in this committee, if they played any part.[16] After the middle of August, when the situation was threatening to get out of hand, the strategic committee became a *decision centre* that interfered more actively in the daily operations of the SQ.

Second, not only had the structure of command become complex, but some of its crucial links were systematically bypassed. Hence, if a field officer in a command post enjoyed the confidence of the high command, he could be in direct contact with the decision centre. Not only did such bypassing have a demoralizing effect on the officers who were passed over, but it may have resulted in crippling failures of intelligence. In situations where centres of decisions are needlessly multiplied, crucial intelligence is not disseminated throughout the whole structure of command.

Finally, there were divisions within the high command. The SQ has long been reputed to have two chiefs: the director general, its official chief, and the director of investigations. This traditional antagonism between uniformed officers and plain-clothes investigators became a source of enduring conflict during the crisis. For instance, it later surfaced that the high command was deeply divided over the conduct of the first assault on the Kanesatake barricade on the morning of 11 July. The men who conducted the assault in the field were also divided.

There is one feature of this structure that must be emphasized. It is fairly opaque, since it vests authority in committees, without specifying who (what individual officer) precisely answers for these committees' decisions. For example, this kind of structure allowed the head of the SQ to apologize for the brutality of his men without having his own responsibility questioned. Nevertheless, when Mr Lavigne asserted that his men acted outside their orders, he was referring to an operation – the clearing of the bridge at Saint-Louis-de-Gonzague – that was, according to the SQ structure of command, under the direct supervision of the decision committee, of which he was himself a part.

Ambiguous Commands

The SQ displayed so much violence in having demonstrators evacuate a bridge crossing the St Lawrence Seaway at St-Louis-de-Gonzague, on 12 August 1990, that, as we have mentioned, the director general of the SQ felt obliged to apologize to the Quebec population. He was quoted as saying during his press conference: '[Translation] If SQ members used their truncheons against citizens *after* the bridge was cleared, they acted outside their orders' (our emphasis).[17]

This declaration implies that it was wrong to club citizens with truncheons only after the bridge had been cleared with utmost brutality (as anyone could see on the television news). Furthermore, it does not reveal the actual content of these orders. Actually, a close reading of the DG's statements in a press conference leads us to believe that the high command of the SQ did not so much give explicit orders to the officers in the field as show tacit approval of their decisions by not openly disagreeing with them.

Split Command

The structure of decision-making applied by the SQ in a state of emergency resulted in splitting the chain of command between line officers who were operating from command posts in the field and high-ranking officers who staffed no less than three committees – the operational centre, the control centre, and the strategic committee, which was to become the decision centre. In theory, this last committee also included members of the Quebec cabinet. These bodies were remote from operations and only met at headquarters. This structure was unbalanced, since the number of committee staff officers far outnumbered the number of high-ranking line officers deployed on the terrain.

Among the thirty-nine members of the SQ facing disciplinary charges, there are, with the exception of Inspector Michel Scott, no officers from the committees that were operating at headquarters. Following the standard set by the SQ director general, it would appear that their way of authorizing the field officers to follow a specific course of action seemed to have been entirely by omission: they merely had to show that they did not oppose it. For instance, it was asserted by the press that Inspector Scott, who was sent by helicopter from headquarters to assume command of the situation in Saint-Louis-de-Gonzague, acted on his own initiative when he ordered the riot squad to clear the bridge. He was, nevertheless, in constant radio contact with the decision centre at headquarters.

The complete lack of a clear line of police authority during the Oka Crisis would explain the impossibility of identifying who actually gave the final order to mount an assault on the Mohawk barricade at Kanesatake on the first day of the crisis. This reluctance to exercise command also permeated the theatre of operations, where the commanders (captains) delegated to lower-ranking officers the conduct of the action. It is significant to note in this regard that the highest-ranking field officers facing disciplinary charges are facing accusations of carelessness and neglect of duty.

This split in command afforded the police involved the possibility of invoking the so-called 'Nuremberg defense,' according to which those who ambiguously authorized misconduct did not actually engage in it, and those who did engage in it can claim that they were following orders. This defence is a very efficient way to neutralize accountability. Its efficiency is clearly illustrated by the March 1991 decisions of the Quebec commissioner for police deontology. We quoted his words to the effect that the police who violated the rights of citizens during the crisis were acting legitimately under orders from their superiors. The problem with the Oka Crisis is that there is not one police officer who cannot claim to have been following orders. It was repeatedly argued by representatives of the police that the assault on the Mohawk barricade, which initially triggered the crisis, was conducted in reaction to a court order.

Lack of Supervision

The NCOs – corporals and sergeants – completely failed to control their men, who were left free to rampage, after a crowd of demonstrators had been successfully dispersed. The rank and file – sometimes encouraged by their officers – engaged in the wanton destruction of private property (motor vehicles), in the wild chase of isolated demonstrators or innocent bypassers who were returning home after the incident, and in serious misconduct with the press. Again, all this was thoroughly documented by camera crews and broadcast on television.

When he apologized to the Quebec population, after the violent events of 12 and 13 August, the director general of the SQ announced that disciplinary procedures would be initiated against the police who had acted 'outside their orders,' instead of taking the situation into his own hands. This was a rather poor show of leadership and one that also was ill-timed. The crisis would last for six weeks more, during which the SQ police could have felt that it was operating under the threat of being disciplined by a civilian review board rather than under the control and supervision of their own officers. This was bound to undermine morale even more.

To sum up, it can be said that the internal mechanisms to ensure accountability largely failed in this crisis situation. We shall now describe how external pressure increased and how a public outcry finally led the SQ to resort to its civilian review board to produce a show of accountability.

External Pressure

The October Crisis of 1970 was the object of extensive coverage by the press – both national and international. Part of this coverage was critical of Canada's handling of the crisis. However, Canada's position in reacting to FLQ terrorism was secure with respect to world public opinion: terrorists did not generate a lot of sympathy. The situation was entirely different during the Oka Crisis: the Mohawks appeared fully justified in resisting the expansion of a golf course over sacred burial ground, thus making police action against them suffer from a huge legitimacy gap at the outset. This lack of legitimacy and the consequent critical attitude were to increase because of three factors.

The SQ's Inept Handling of the Press

The SQ's public-relations office had a long-standing reputation of arrogance in its dealings with the press. However, when the SQ started to seize films shot by cameramen from the various TV networks, at first in an attempt to identify who might have shot Corporal Lemay and, later, in attempts to gather evidence against alleged rioters, its action drew strong protest from the Professional Federation of Quebec Journalists, the Canadian Press Council, and the Canadian Association of Journalists. At the end of the crisis, several journalists openly sided with the Warriors and waited with them for the final siege against the treatment centre, where they had barricaded themselves.

There is no doubt that this antagonistic relationship with the media accounted in part for the very bad press that was received by the SQ and, more generally, by the police forces involved in the crisis (the Canadian Armed Forces, which had a carefully planned media strategy, fared much better).

International Bodies

Canada is sensitive to its international reputation of respect for human rights. Yet, on 11 September, the European Parliament blamed Canada for having confiscated Mohawk lands in order to expand a golf course. Agreeing to Mohawk demands, the International Federation of Human Rights sent representatives to Oka in order to supervise the negotiations between the government and the Mohawks and to ensure that human rights were not violated. This internationalization of the conflict was reflected in the press coverage given to the crisis, which threatened to damage Canada's cherished reputation as a defender of human rights.

The Canadian Political Context

A book was published in Quebec shortly after the crisis. Its title (in translation) is *Oka: English Canada's Last Alibi.*[18] Its argument was that the Oka Crisis was used by English Canada to show that the distinct Quebec society, rejected in the failure of the Meech Lake Accord, was in fact only a 'distinctly repressive society.' The holier than thou attitude manifested by Toronto civil-rights pundits in a petition to Prime Minister Mulroney was particularly upsetting to the people of Quebec ('We will never forget Oka'). This petition explicitly mentioned the SQ: 'We plead for an end to all further military action and any acts of intimidation or reprisal by the Sûreté du Québec.'[19]

The SQ was extremely sensitive to the beating that its image took. In what can only be termed as an overreaction, it issued on 7 September 1990 a garbled press release accusing the Mohawks and the anglophone media of trying to take revenge upon Quebec after the failure of the Meech Lake negotiations by discrediting the SQ. This press release directly violated section 21 of the SQ's code of ethics and discipline, which stated that a member of the SQ must be politically neutral in performing his or her duties.

The SQ was severely blamed by the francophone and, needless to say, the anglophone press for politicizing the crisis. Added to its inept handling of the press and its being criticized by international bodies, this politicization of the crisis resulted in a great deal of external pressure on the SQ and on the government of Quebec to remake the image of the provincial police force. However, the SQ had no inclination towards self-criticism. The measures that it took, or attempted to take, in the aftermath of the crisis show clearly that its leaders believed that external factors were at the root of its failure to solve the Oka Crisis and that there was nothing wrong with the organization itself. These external factors were identified as the lack of heavy equipment such as armoured vehicles, the mistreatment of the SQ by the media, and political interference. Unwilling to take a critical look at its organization, the SQ would attempt to rebuild its image by using its civilian review committee to discipline some of its men, who had blatantly abused their power.

We shall now discuss the action taken by this committee. We must stress that it might never have been given the mandate to review the behaviour of the SQ in the absence of strong external pressure.[20] Hence, the kind of accountability that we shall now discuss is not the result of an internal obligation, but stems from a response to criticism from the outside.

The SQ Civilian Review Board

The whole structure for processing complaints from the public was recently changed in Quebec with the appointment of a commissioner for police deontology, pursuing the coming into force of the *Code of Ethics of Québec Police Officers*.[21] This commissioner is the recipient of all public complaints made against any member of a Quebec police force. However, this new legislation only began to be applied after the Oka Crisis. Although the new commissioner ruled, as we saw above, on a few complaints, it was the earlier complaint structure that was used to make individual members of the SQ account for their behaviour during the Oka Crisis.

We shall briefly review this structure. First, it was a decentralized one, with each police force having its own mechanism for processing complaints from the public. This feature of the structure for processing complaints from the public raises the important question of the independence of the bodies reviewing the behaviour of the members of a particular police force. Whether or not the bodies that we describe were part of the SQ and under its authority was an issue that was never solved and that generated constant conflict.[22]

Second, there are two basic models of complaint committees. They either act as a lower court, through which all complaints are processed, or as a body to which a citizen can appeal, if he or she is not satisfied with how the police first handled his or her complaint. Generally speaking, Quebec applies a lower-court model, whereas Ontario uses civilian review boards as a forum for appeal. With regard to the SQ, then, all complaints made against members of this force had to go through its civilian review committee.

Third, the SQ process for handling complaints is two-tiered. One body – the Commitee for Studying Complaints – is responsible for screening complaints.[23] It determines whether there are sufficient grounds for a complaint to be sent before a second body – called the 'disciplinary authority'[24] – which will determine guilt and recommend a sanction. Furthermore, the screening committee also chooses the kind of disciplining authority the accused member will appear before (one high-ranking SQ officer, a committee comprising two SQ officers and one civilian, or a committee of two civilians and an SQ officer). The most serious charges are prosecuted before a committee with a majority of civilians. The screening committee sits in camera, does not hear witnesses and, in consequence, deliberates on the basis of an examination of a dossier put together by investigators of the SQ internal-affairs unit. The disciplinary authority holds its hearing in public; it can hear witnesses and the accused is entitled to legal counsel. The director general of the SQ has the power to review the sanctions imposed by the disciplinary authority. Hence, he may confirm or alter such recommendation or disregard it.[25] If the final sanction is either demotion or discharge of an SQ member, it must be approved by the minister of public security.[26] In all cases, a convicted member of the SQ can appeal his or her case before a labor arbitrator.[27] The DG is not under the authority of any of these committees, since this would imply that he might be in the situation of reviewing a sanction imposed upon him. According to section 25 of the SQ Code, any complaint against the DG must be made directly to the minister for public security.

There is one last feature of this structure that is of paramount importance. A distinction is made in Quebec between police discipline and police deontology, or police professional ethics. In theory, a code of police discipline regulates the behaviour of individual members of a police force towards the organization to which they belong. A code of deontology regulates the behaviour of the police towards the public. In practice, many violations of deontology are also seen by the SQ as violations of police discipline, since they tarnish the image of the force.[28] Hence, whether or not there is a complaint from the public, the policy of the SQ is to have its screening committee investigate any public allegation of misconduct by one of its members *as if it were an internal complaint originating from the organization* (criticism by the press was considered to be an instance of a public allegation of misconduct). It was pursuant to this policy that the complaint committee was asked in the past to review events such as the death of a demonstrator in La Malbaie, after he had been arrested by the SQ during a labour conflict. In this case, no official complaint had been made to the SQ review board by a private citizen, although the head of a labor union had accused the SQ in the press of having murdered this demonstrator.

It was also pursuant to this policy that the Committee for Studying Complaints was asked to review the behaviour of all SQ members who may have been guilty of misconduct during the Oka Crisis. The committee had received a number of complaints from the public. However, the mandate that it was given by the SQ was much broader than the investigation of a few civilian complaints. As we mentioned, it was to review all major violent incidents that had occurred during the crisis, except for the 11 July assault that triggered the crisis.

There is a crucial point to be made with regard to the mandate given to the screening committee. As we previously said, the SQ considered public allegations of misconduct against its members as matters of internal discipline, even if no individual citizen had made an official complaint to the committee. Since there had been numerous allegations of misconduct made by the press, the committee was asked to cover all aspects of the crisis that generated bad press for its members, regardless of whether there was or was not a specific complaint made by a member of the public. Consequently, the committee's authority for investigating the whole Oka Crisis was basically grounded in *the need to uphold internal discipline.*

Not surprisingly, the SQ essentially views internal discipline as an administrative instrument for managing the organization. Since the complaint committee's authority rested much more on internal discipline than in police deontology, the SQ may have felt that it was in a position to dictate to the committee how it should fulfil its mandate. That this, indeed, was the case can be shown by indicating which part of the work of the Committee for Studying Complaints was eventually made public.

Previously, when it examined incidents that were the object of extensive media coverage, the complaint committee usually wrote a report on the event rather than limiting itself to sending disciplinary indictments to individual police, who were then compelled to appear subsequently before the disciplinary authority. Being authorized by the *Regulation Respecting the Code of Ethics and Discipline of the Sûreté du Québec*[29] to make recommendations promoting respect for discipline and deontology, the Committee for Studying Complaints formulated such recommendations in the report that it sent to the SQ director general. The content of the committee's report was at times released to the press. In one instance, the press even reported that there was a dissenting opinion appended to one of the committee's reports.

After its examination of the Oka Crisis, the screening committee decided, as we said previously, to charge thirty-nine members of the SQ with breaches of both discipline and deontology. The press also revealed that the Committee had produced a report that formulated general recommendations to the director general. However, contrary to past practice, the content of the report was never disclosed to the public by the SQ. Whether the recommendations were followed is also not known. In marked contrast to this reluctance to reveal the content of the report of the committee, the SQ leaked to the press the number and rank of the police who were directed to appear before the disciplinary authority even before the committee had completed its investigations.

Clearly, the SQ's policy was to favour individual accountability over organizational accountability. Also clear was the fact that the SQ chose to placate public opinion by eventually disciplining a number of its members in highly visible proceedings rather than by reforming the organization itself.

POLICE ACCOUNTABILITY: A LEGAL PERSPECTIVE

We now turn to a discussion of the issue of accountability from the perspective of the remedies available to a citizen who considers himself or herself a victim of police illegality. This requires analysing of the legality of police action and, more precisely, addressing the question of the scope of police power during a crisis. We have already quoted the Quebec commissioner for police deontology, who considers that these powers are very broad – so broad, indeed, that no disciplinary charges could be sustained. This is a blatant illustration of the inadequacies of the legal system to provide a satisfactory answer to this issue of police accountability. As this question is extremely general, we shall exclude from our study conduct that is obviously unlawful, such as the action of the SQ when it cleared the bridge at St-Louis-de-Gonzague, to concentrate our analysis on borderline conduct that was complained of by citizens and by the press. As a matter of comparison, we will analyse the legal situation that prevails now in the Province of Quebec, along with the one that prevailed during the October Crisis, to determine the impact of the legislative changes that have occurred since the October Crisis. From a purely theoretical standpoint, the current trend is towards more accountability but, in practice, citizens still have a lot to complain about.

The police behaviour most frequently under attack during the October Crisis was the number of so-called preventive arrests[30] and the searches and seizures conducted on mere suspicion. During the Oka Crisis, there were fewer complaints of allegedly unlawful arrests, but citizens challenged the legality of roadblocks and of the search and seizure of motor vehicles conducted at the entry to the security perimeter established by the SQ. However, all legal actions taken by citizens in ordinary court – as well as those taken before the Quebec commissioner for police deontology – led nowhere.

Furthermore, pursuing our comparison between the two crises, we can say that, during the Oka Crisis, we witnessed unprecedented recriminations by members of the media. Indeed, the press suffered almost the same inconveniences as ordinary citizens, being forced to stop at police barricades, to identify themselves, and to submit to summary search before being allowed to go inside the security perimeter. Although the press severely criticized these measures, they did not go to court to challenge them until they experienced more difficulties in performing their jobs, towards the end of the crisis. They then took legal action on the basis of subsection 2(b) of the Canadian Charter of Rights and Freedoms, which guarantees the freedom of the press, but they were unsuccessful. It must be said in all fairness, however, that the press was almost an active participant in the crisis and that some members of the media (for example, TV cameramen) came very close to siding with the Mohawks. Hence, it was to be expected that they would experience inconveniences in performing their tasks.

Despite the major legislative changes that have occurred during the last twenty years, the constitutionalization of citizens' rights in the Canadian Charter of Rights and Freedoms being the most important of them, the Oka Crisis dramatically illustrates that no legal action can successfully be taken to curb the exercise of extraordinary police powers, when the need for these powers can apparently be justified by the existence of a crisis situation. This observation is quite disturbing considering the fact that, during the Oka Crisis, no law of exception was adopted to grant the police extraordinary powers.

The Legal Environment

It must be remembered that in October 1970 the political authorities considered themselves unable to cope with the terrorist actions of the *Front de libération du Québec* without resorting to extraordinary powers that involved a suspension of certain civil rights enjoyed by Canadians.[31] The *War Measures Act*[32] provided the legal framework for such a suspension. It authorized the Governor in Council to issue a proclamation that an apprehended insurrection existed[33] and to adopt regulations: 'to ensure that lawful and effective measures can be taken against those who thus seek to destroy the basis of our democratic governmental system on which the enjoyment of our human rights and fundamental freedoms is founded and to ensure the continued protection of those rights and freedoms in Canada.'[34] Among those measures were the power of arrest without warrant on mere suspicion,[35] the suspension of the bail provisions of the *Criminal Code*,[36] and the possibility to detain an arrested person for seven days before charging that person with an offence under the regulations and bringing that person before a justice. Furthermore, the attorney general of a province had the authority to order that this delay be extended to twenty-one days.[37] The regulations also provided for search and seizure without warrant on mere suspicion.[38] All this was possible despite the *Canadian Bill of Rights*[39] because Parliament had included in the *War Measures Act* a 'notwithstanding clause,' which enabled the act to operate notwithstanding the bill of rights.[40] Thus, it was almost impossible for any citizen to challenge the legality of the state's action taken against him or her.

Despite the repeal of the *War Measures Act*,[41] the federal government still has the power to adopt special temporary measures, although these measures can hardly be as disrespectful of citizen's legal rights as were the measures adopted in 1970, which allowed police officers to act with total impunity. Furthermore, at the time of the October Crisis, civilian control over the internal disciplinary process of the Service de police de Montréal and the SQ was nonexistent. Also, as mentioned in our introductory remarks, no disciplinary measures were taken against any member of these police forces.

During the Oka Crisis, it would theoretically have been possible for the federal government to resort to the *Emergencies Act*.[42] It must be remembered that the Quebec government asked for the assistance of the Canadian Armed Forces[43] to cope with the situation after the violent incident on the bridge at St-

Louis-de-Gonzague. Allegedly, that request showed the incapacity of the police forces, and more specifically of the SQ, under whose jurisdiction the troubled areas fell and where their duty lay, as described in laconic terms in the *Police Act*: 'The Police Force, under the authority of the Minister of Public Security, shall be charged with maintaining peace, order and public safety in the entire territory of Québec, preventing crime and infringements of the laws of Québec and seeking out the offenders.'[44]

The Oka situation could have been called a 'national emergency' within the meaning of the *Emergencies Act*.[45] It was also within the purview of section 2 of the *Canadian Security Intelligence Service Act*,[46] which sets out the requisite conditions for the proclamation of a public-order emergency.[47]

The reasons why the federal government did not resort to the *Emergencies Act* were political, rather than legal.[48] The advantages of resorting to such a proclamation in the context of a crisis such as Oka might be questioned. Indeed, it would not have been possible, under the authority of the *Emergencies Act*, to adopt a regulation similar to the one adopted in 1970 because that act does not contain a disposition to the effect that its regulations shall operate despite the legal rights guaranteed by the Canadian Charter of Rights and Freedoms.[49] It should also be noted that the *Emergencies Act* stipulates: 'Nothing in a declaration of a public order emergency or in an order or regulation made pursuant thereto shall be construed or applied so as to derogate from, or to authorize the derogation from, the control or direction of the government of a province or a municipality over any police force over which it normally has control or direction.'[50]

However, all of this is purely theoretical since no such declaration was issued. From the perspective of police accountability, this was a major change over the situation that prevailed at the time of the October Crisis, since police are still submitted – with or without a declaration of a public-order emergency – to internal directives and are therefore still subject to disciplinary measures in case of a breach thereof.

As a matter of fact, during the Oka Crisis, the legal rights guaranteed by the Canadian Charter of Rights and Freedoms were not in any way affected by the crisis situation that existed. Despite recourse to the army, no extraordinary powers were enacted to cope with the situation. Still, citizens felt that their rights were being trampled upon. This perception can be explained by the vagueness of the legislative framework concerning police powers. When such legal imprecision is coupled with deficiencies of control and supervision by the police hierarchy, the end result is, arguably, massive abuse of power. Hence, many questionable actions were taken against law-abiding citizens and these persons were left with almost no remedy at all.

The Vagueness of the Definition of Certain Police Powers

We shall illustrate this vagueness with three examples:

- the setting-up of a security perimeter guarded by heavily armed members of the SQ and, later, of the Canadian Armed Forces
- the road blockade and the consequent obligation of citizens living inside the security perimeter to pass through police barricades and to submit to formalities to get to their homes located inside the security perimeter
- the search of motor vehicles at both the entrance and the exit of the security perimeter

These three examples concern routine activities that happened at Oka and in the vicinity of the Mercier Bridge.[51]

Security Perimeters

The major complaints were about the establishment of a security perimeter, which had the effect of limiting the comings and goings of the citizens who resided within that perimeter. Let us try to determine the legal authority under which police can establish such a perimeter.

There is no direct authority that prescribes the establishment of a security perimeter. In fact, section 39 of the *Police Act* reproduced above is the only section of that act describing the scope of the powers attributed to the SQ.[52] This section is a codification of the duties and powers of a constable at common law.[53] It is, thus, on a case-by-case basis that the scope of police powers is defined, usually in the context of criminal charges of obstructing a peace officer[54] or of assaulting a peace officer.[55]

The key case in that respect is the English Court of Appeal decision in *R.* v. *Waterfield*,[56] which proposes a two-stage analysis to determine the legality of any police action: 'In the judgment of this court it would be difficult, and in the present case it is unnecessary, to reduce within specific limits the general terms in which the duties of police constables have been expressed. In most cases it is probably more convenient to consider what the police constable was actually doing and in particular whether such conduct was prima facie an unlawful interference with a person's liberty or property. If so, it is then relevant to consider whether (a) such conduct falls within the general scope of any duty imposed by statute or recognised at common law and (b) whether such conduct, albeit within the general scope of such a duty, involved an unjustifiable use of powers associated with the duty.'[57] The Court of Appeal further says: 'Thus, while it is no doubt right to say in general terms that police constables have a duty to prevent crime and a duty, when crime is committed, to bring the offender to justice, it is also clear from the decided cases that when the execution of these general duties involves interference with the person or property of a private person, the powers of constables are not unlimited.'[58]

The Supreme Court of Canada referred to that case to substantiate its decision in the cases of *R.* v. *Stenning*[59] and *Knowlton* v. *R.*[60] The *Knowlton* case gives us the most relevant guidelines with which to address the question of the legality of a security perimeter in a context akin to the one that prevailed during the Oka crisis.

In that case, the Edmonton City Police Force had put in place a safety cordon to assure the security of Premier Alexei Kosygin, who was visiting the city. A man tried to push his way past a police officer on duty as part of the security arrangements and was charged with having unlawfully and wilfully obstructed a peace officer in the execution of his duty. It should be noted that the *Alberta Police Act* contained a general provision very similar to section 39 of the Quebec *Police Act*. Police duty and the use of powers associated with such duty were the sole questions at issue before the Supreme Court of Canada. *Waterfield*'s two-fold analysis was adopted by the Court.

After noting that Premier Kosygin had been attacked a few days before his visit to Edmonton, Chief Justice Fauteux, speaking for the Court, said with respect to the first question – the scope of police duty by virtue of the *Criminal Code* and the *Alberta Police Act* or under common law:

> According to the principles which, for the preservation of peace and prevention of crime, underlie the provisions of subs. 30, amongst others, of the *Criminal Code*, these official authorities were not only entitled but in duty bound, as peace officers, to prevent a renewal of a like criminal assault on the Premier Kosygin during his official visit in Canada. In this respect, they had a specific and binding obligation to take proper and reasonable steps. The restriction of the right of free access of the public to public streets, at the strategic point mentioned above, was one of the steps – not an unusual one – which police authorities considered and adopted as necessary for the attainment of the purpose aforesaid. In my opinion, such conduct of the police was clearly falling within the general scope of the duties imposed upon them.[61]

Chief Justice Fauteux also ruled that the police conduct did not involve an unjustifiable use of powers associated with that duty since the accused had not acted with due diligence: 'He might possibly have obtained the privilege extended to members of the press and others to access to the restricted area had he applied for a pass at the proper time, at the proper place and from the proper authorities.'[62]

The British author L.H. Leigh, after reviewing the Canadian cases, says that our Supreme Court has developed an 'ancillary powers doctrine' that justifies the incidental measures necessary to achieve police duty.[63] However, the *Knowlton* decision was issued prior to the coming into force of the Canadian Charter of Rights and Freedoms. Therefore, one may challenge its actual authority, particularly on the basis of section 7 of the Charter,[64] which reads as follows: 'Everyone has the right to life, liberty and security of the person and the right not to be deprived thereof except in accordance with the principles of fundamental justice.'

Of course, the establishment of a security perimeter infringes the citizen's liberty and significantly so in the case of a citizen who is prevented from travelling on a public road or gaining access to his or her home. It is true that such a right is not an absolute one because of the qualifier of the right resulting from the portion of the section that states: 'and the right not to be deprived thereof except in accordance with the principles of fundamental justice.'[65] To determine the scope of these principles, the Supreme Court of Canada said, in *Beare* v. *R.*: 'While the common law is, of course, not determinative in assessing whether a particular practice violates a principle of fundamental justice, it is certainly one of the major repositories of the basic tenets of our legal system referred to in *Re B.C. Motor Vehicle Act, supra.*'[66] Accordingly, it is doubtful that a court would conclude that the establishment of a security perimeter that meets the *Waterfield* criteria is incompatible with the principles of fundamental justice and therefore in contravention of section 7 of the Charter.

Road Blocks

However distasteful they are, roadblocks do not seem to contravene the common law or the Canadian Charter of Rights and Freedoms. The cases decided by the Supreme Court of Canada[67] in that respect resulted from the random stopping of motor vehicles in the course of checkpoint programs whose purpose was the detection of impaired drivers. None the less, the rulings are applicable to a situation such as the one in Oka and near the Mercier Bridge.

The *Dedman* case was decided before the Charter came into force. Once again, the English case of *Waterfield* was resorted to in order to determine the scope of police powers concerning the random stopping of motor vehicles. Applying *Waterfield*'s test, Mr Justice Le Dain, speaking for the majority of the Supreme Court, concluded that random stops were lawful under common law as an ancillary power to the duty of controlling traffic for the protection of life and property. In the application of the second part of that test, he said: 'Turning to the second branch of the *Waterfield* test, it must be said respectfully that neither *Waterfield* itself nor most of the cases which have applied it throw much light on the criteria for determining whether a particular interference with liberty is an unjustifiable use of a power associated with a police duty. There is a suggestion of the correct test, I think, in the use of the words "reasonably necessary" in *Johnson* v. *Phillips, supra.*[68] The interference with liberty must be necessary for the carrying out of the particular police duty and it must be reasonable, having regard to the nature of the liberty interfered with and the importance of the public purpose served by the interference.'[69]

In *Hufsky* v. *R.*[70] and in *R.* v. *Ladouceur*,[71] a roadblock and a random stop were respectively attacked on the basis that they infringe sections 8 and 9 of the Charter. Concerning section 9, it was the arbitrary character of the stopping that was the key issue. Since all motor vehicles were stopped at the entrance of the security perimeter laid out during the Oka Crisis, it cannot be said that the measure was an arbitrary one. Therefore, we will address only the question of the roadblock's conformity with section 8 of the Charter which guarantees the right to be secure against unreasonable search or seizure.

Assuming that the police had authority to lay down a security perimeter for the reasons mentioned above, entrance into the restricted area became a matter of privilege rather than right. Consequently, it can be argued that the stopping of drivers who sought to enter and the demand that they identify themselves was not an unreasonable search. As Le Dain J., speaking for the Supreme Court in the *Hufsky* case, said: 'the demand by the police officer (...) that the [citizen] surrender his driver's licence and insurance card for inspection did not constitute a search within the meaning of subs. 8 because it did not constitute an intrusion on a reasonable expectation of privacy: *cf. Hunter v. Southam Inc.*, [1984] 2 S.C.R. 145. There is no such intrusion where a person is required to produce a licence or permit or other documentary evidence of a status or compliance with some legal requirement that is a lawful condition of the exercise of a right or privilege.'[72] Although that ruling was made in a case pertaining to the stopping of vehicles for a purpose in direct relation to driving, which is no more than a privilege, it is submitted that it applies also in a situation like the one that happened in Oka. Even though the Supreme Court has said recently that 'the rights granted to police to conduct check stop programs or random stops of motorists should not be extended,'[73] it can still be argued that there was no infringement of the right to be secure against unreasonable search or seizure, when the police officers located at the entrance of the security perimeter asked the citizens to identify themselves. Indeed, this pronouncement occurred in a case involving ordinary police action and does not preclude an opposite ruling in a crisis situation. Although the Quebec commissioner for police deontology has ruled otherwise, thorough searches of motor vehicles are more questionable.[74]

Search of Motor Vehicles

It should be remembered that neither the common law nor the Criminal Code generally authorize search and seizure without warrant.[75] In England, the Royal Commission on Criminal Procedure concluded that, under the common law: 'The police have no general authority to search members of the public. They may only do so where the person concerned agrees or in certain limited circumstances prescribed by law. A search in the absence of authority or consent will constitute an assault, and an action in the civil or criminal courts may follow. There are two situations in which a person may lawfully be searched against his will: where there is specific statutory authority to stop and search short of arrest, and in certain circumstances where he has been arrested.'[76]

The same conclusion has been arrived at by the Supreme Court of Canada in many recent decisions based on the Canadian Charter of Rights and Freedoms.[77] In *Wong* v. *R.*, Mr Justice La Forest explained why, apart from arrest situations, search powers should be confined to those prescribed by written laws: 'it does not sit well for the courts, as the protectors of our fundamental rights, to widen the possibility of encroachments on these personal liberties. It falls to Parliament to make incursions on fundamental rights if it is of the view that they are needed for the protection of the public in a properly balanced system of criminal justice.'[78] In *Mellenthin* v. *R.*, Mr Justice Cory reinforced this statement by saying: 'Random stop programs must not be turned into a means of conducting either an unfounded general inquisition or an unreasonable search.'[79]

Since no written law authorized most of the warrantless searches that occurred at the entrance of the security perimeter, most were probably unreasonable.[80] Actually, all searches were more intrusive than 'the visual inspection of the car by police officer'[81] that was considered permissible in the *Mellenthin* case. Indeed, considering the La Forest J. dictum cited above, it may be difficult to convince a court that, although unlawful, they were none the less reasonable. Though, arguably, a situation of crisis might render reasonable a search without warrant that would normally have been qualified as an unreasonable search, the fact that a state of emergency had not been proclaimed must be taken into account, even more so since such a proclamation would not have authorized a departure from compliance with Charter requirements.

In discussing these decisions of the Supreme Court of Canada, our purpose is not to settle these matters conclusively but to show how difficult it is to determine the legality of the police conduct and also the limits of the protection offered by the Canadian Charter of Rights and Freedoms to those citizens who felt that their rights had been infringed. In that respect we must add that the vagueness of the guarantee offered by section 8 is not the only obstacle to overcome. For example, it would be necessary to determine if the warrantless search authorized by section 101 of the Criminal Code is justified in a free and democratic society under section 1 of the Charter.[82] If that were so, the section would accordingly be held constitutional despite the infringement of subsection 8.

As Lamer J. (as he then was) said in *Reference re Motor Vehicle Act*: 'Section 1 may, for reasons of administrative expediency, successfully come to the rescue of an otherwise violation of subs. 7, but only in cases arising out of exceptional conditions, such as natural disasters, the outbreak of war, epidemics and the like.'[83] It is difficult to determine if Lamer J. had in mind any exceptional situation that might be determined by a judge's personal appraisal or only those that would have called for the application of the *Emergencies Act* by the Governor in Council.

If a search is based on a law that is ruled reasonable within the purview of section 8, it cannot per se be unreasonable. However, the question of reasonableness must always be addressed because a search otherwise lawful may be conducted in a manner that renders it unreasonable. For example, mere suspicion is an insufficient ground for conducting a search under any circumstances. Would a crisis situation lessen that usual standard of reasonableness? The purpose of our paper is not to answer that question either, but simply to address the question of the limits of the Charter's response to allegedly unlawful police conduct occurring during a crisis.

Recriminations of the Press

When the Canadian Armed Forces gained control of the last barricade erected by the Warriors at Oka (Kanesatake) on 3 September 1990, many natives and a few journalists retreated into a detoxification centre that was located on that same reserve. From that date on and until the final surrender of the natives within the compound, there was a tense stand-off between them and the besieging army. After a week, the Canadian Armed Forces adopted measures to break the impasse. Two of these measures were challenged by the press agencies before the Quebec Superior Court as well as before the Federal Court of Canada.

The first measure was intended to cut off all communication between the barricaded people and the outside world. In order to achieve this goal, a search warrant was issued to break all the cellular telephone lines, including those that belonged to the press agencies and that enabled reporters to communicate with their editors. *Southam Inc.* and *Canadian Newspapers Inc.* presented a petition for *certiorari* and for a remedy under subsection 24(1) of the Canadian Charter of Rights and Freedoms alleging, inter alia, that the seizure infringed the fundamental rights of freedom of speech and freedom of the press as guaranteed by section 2(b) of the Charter and asking that the search warrant be quashed.[84] The Warriors surrendered to the army before a Quebec Superior Court judge had time to decide the issues.[85]

The second measure concerned the delivery of food and other essential supplies to the persons besieged. Because there were women and children among them, the army adopted a policy authorizing essential supplies to pass through the perimeter, and until 11 September it allowed the delivery of food and supplies directly to the journalists and separately from that delivered to the natives. On 12 September, a new directive was issued by which no separate deliveries were to be made to journalists. Two of the latter challenged the directive in applications for an interlocutory injunction filed in the Federal Court of Canada.[86] As summarized by Joyal J., the journalists referred to subsections 2(b) and 7 of the Charter:

> The plaintiffs argue that the defendants' refusal to permit separate delivery of food and supplies to the journalists inside the center infringes upon the latter's right to freedom of the press, as is guaranteed by subs. 2(b) of the *Canadian Charter of Rights and Freedoms*, Part I of the *Constitution Act, 1982*, being Schedule B of the *Canada Act 1982* (U.K.), 1982, c. 11. Subsidiarily, the plaintiff Southam Inc. claims that the defendants' actions infringe the plaintiffs' right to life, liberty and security of the person, as is guaranteed by subs. 7 of the *Canadian Charter*. More specifically, the plaintiffs argue that the journalists are being forced to rely upon the good will of the Warriors inside the compound with respect to the proper distribution of food. This reliance threatens their objectivity and independence in reporting on matters as they arise at Oka.[87]

These applications were heard on 26 September 1990. The surrender of the Warriors on the same evening made the issues moot. Nevertheless Joyal J. was asked to rule on them and agreed to do so. Relying on American decisions, he dismissed the applications because the strict requirements for an interlocutory injunction were not met. As summarized in the headnote of the case, he concluded: 'Freedom of the press does not confer any special status upon the media. Journalists have no constitutional right of access to scenes of crime or disaster when the general public is excluded. Should a journalist put himself in a dangerous situation, he has no greater right to protection than the ordinary citizen. Under condition of siege, and in a compound defended by armed Warriors who effectively controlled the journalists' conduct, their status did not impose on the defendants a special affirmative duty of care in the manner the plaintiffs had claimed. The defendants had not forced the plaintiffs to enter, or to remain in the compound. The plaintiffs were remaining on the scene voluntarily and their liberty to leave the compound at any time was no more restricted than that of anyone else.'[88]

This ruling is one more illustration of our general thesis on the difficulty of being successful before the courts in an action attacking the exercise of police powers in a situation of emergency.

The Remedies Available under the Charter

We shall address in our conclusion the question of remedies to the legal difficulties already discussed. However, we shall first briefly review the jurisprudence concerning the remedies available under the Canadian Charter of Rights and Freedoms to show their limits.

Section 24 of the Canadian Charter of Rights and Freedoms provides that:

(1) Anyone whose rights or freedoms, as guaranteed by this *Charter*, have been infringed or denied may apply to a court of competent jurisdiction to obtain such remedy as the court considers appropriate and just in the circumstances.

(2) Where, in proceedings under subsection (1), a court concludes that evidence was obtained in a manner that infringed or denied any rights or freedoms guaranteed by this *Charter*, the evidence shall be excluded if it is established that, having regard to all the circumstances, the admission of it in the proceedings would bring the administration of justice into disrepute.

The question of remedies must be addressed from two different perspectives. First, what are the remedies immediately available to a citizen or to a press agency when an alleged infringement of rights occurs? Second, what remedies can be sought after the crisis has ended?

During the Oka Crisis both ordinary citizens[89] and the press[90] petitioned the Superior Court of Quebec to obtain interlocutory injunctions seeking immediate relief for the alleged unlawful conduct they endured. For many reasons, mainly procedural in nature, these remedies that could clearly be asked for under section 24(1) of the Charter were not granted.

Under section 24(1), some remedies can also be asked for afterwards, that is, when the infringement no longer exists. Among these, damages is probably the most usual remedy granted to a person aggrieved and, in a situation like that arising from the Oka Crisis, it is almost the only available remedy.[91] Although some other remedies, such as a stay of proceedings, an acquittal, or a lesser penalty, can also be considered, in all circumstances, as was recently decided by the Quebec Court of Appeal in *R.* v. *Latulippe*, 'it is the compensatory purpose that prevails, the punitive effect being only incidental.'[92] In that case, it was said that a citation for contempt of court in regard to those who had infringed citizens' rights was not a remedy available under subsection 24(1). In that respect, Tyndale J.C.A. cited with approval what Ewaschuk E.G., Q.C. (as he then was) wrote in an article entitled 'The *Charter*: An Overview and Remedies': 'Finally, it should be noted that the word "remedy" does not mean "sanction." Thus a remedy is to be provided to the applicant, not a sanction imposed on the contravener. For example, a peace officer who contravenes the applicant's constitutional right against unreasonable search or seizure may be ordered in a civil proceeding to pay damages as a remedy to the applicant. But the judge would not be empowered to imprison the police officer or order that he be suspended from his force. The remedy must result in personal benefit to the applicant as opposed to merely punishing another party or person.'[93] Mr Justice Tyndale also agreed with the following ruling of McDonald J. in *R.* v. *Hay*:

> To the extent that the conduct of the police is relevant, that is not because the purpose of subs. 24(1) is to discipline the police or to enhance the possibility of compliance with the *Charter* by the police in the future. The purpose of subs. 24(1) is to afford a 'remedy' ('réparation') to the person applying for it. The notion of the court granting a remedy to a person who has been the victim of an infringement or denial of a *Charter*-guaranteed right is not necessarily co-extensive with the notion of imposing a sanction on the person whose conduct has infringed or denied that right. While the remedy chosen may have the consequence of a sanction (e.g. an order for compensation in a separate proceeding seeking compensation using normal court process), the remedy chosen may altogether lack an element of sanction (e.g. an acquittal or the reduction of the fine or other sentence). Pursuing a line of inquiry as to the conduct of the police does not imply that the objective in applying subs. 24(1) is to impose some sanction on the police: rather, such questions are designed to advance the objective of providing a remedy, or redress (that being an adequate connotation of the French word 'réparation') to the person seeking a remedy.[94]

Accordingly, internal discipline to which police officers are subjected is not a remedy that can be asked for under subsection 24(1) of the Charter. Moreover, citizens have no constitutional right or interest in the disciplinary proceedings and these might be abolished without any possibility of constitutional challenge.

The application of subsection 24(2) in the context of the Oka Crisis is more limited. In fact, with respect to the alleged infringements of the Charter examined above, it is only if a seizure had occurred as a consequence of a motor-vehicle search, and then a person had been charged with an offence, that the exclusion of evidence under section 24 of the Charter could have been considered as a remedy. In that case, the kind of evidence obtained and the circumstances of the *Charter* violation would have been relevant factors. It has been said authoritatively in *R.* v. *Collins*, that: 'Real evidence that was obtained in a manner that violated the *Charter* will rarely operate unfairly for that reason alone. The real evidence existed irrespective of the violation of the *Charter* and its use does not render the trial unfair.'[95] And in *R.* v. *Therens*: 'The relative seriousness of the constitutional violation has been assessed in the light of whether it was committed in good faith, or was inadvertent or of a merely technical nature, or whether it was deliberate, wilful or flagrant. Another relevant consideration is whether the action which constituted the constitutional violation was motivated by urgency or necessity to prevent the loss or destruction of evidence.'[96] These rulings offer sufficient flexibility to allow the court to take a state of emergency into account. However, each case would have had to be considered on its own merits.

It does not seem that self-incriminating evidence within the purview of the *Collins* case was obtained through unlawful search conducted during the Oka Crisis. Nor are we aware of any application for an authorization to intercept private communications.[97] It was, rather, the interruption of communication services that was sought by the application for a search warrant that has been challenged by the media. Therefore, no evidence could have been obtained as a consequence of it. Accordingly, subsection 24(2) of the Charter could not have been a remedy for that alleged infringement of guaranteed rights.

CONCLUSIONS

We began this paper by noting that a significant difference between the October and the Oka crises was that the latter was followed up with the prosecution before a disciplinary authority of thirty-nine members from a police force. Are we justified in saying that this result marks progress with regard to accountability? The answer to this question is complex. It is both yes and no and probably more no than yes. Let us first discuss why it does not represent progress.

Fragmentation

The SQ civilian complaint review committee's action resulted in a complete diffusion of the responsibility for the SQ's utter failure to prevent and, later, to resolve the Oka Crisis. In deciding that the complaint committee would be the only official body that would review the SQ's behaviour during the Oka

Crisis, the SQ and the Quebec government prevented any questioning of the behaviour of the organization itself – its leaders, its structure of command, its training, its recruitment practices, its use of intelligence, and its public-relations strategy. Although neither the federal government nor the RCMP should be credited for appointing the public inquiries that examined the action of the police during the October Crisis and its aftermath, the fact remains that the organizational behaviour of the RCMP and of the Quebec police forces were scrutinized in later inquiries.[98] In a way, the SQ's complaint committee performed a pre-emptive strike against any further examination of the organization's behaviour by focusing on the misconduct of its individual members.

It was, from the start, highly doubtful that the investigation conducted by the complaint committee would succeed in shedding real light on what really happened during the crisis. As the investigation was conducted by the internal-affairs unit, all police interrogated knew that they were potentially facing disciplinary charges. Hence, they exercised their right to remain silent. Because of the adversarial relationship between internal affairs and its 'witnesses,' and the implication with regard to the right to remain silent, relying on a complaint committee to unearth the causes of apparent police misconduct is a self-defeating endeavour.

Finally, it must be said that the recent reform of police deontology in Quebec will only make matters worse. A centralized mechanism for processing complaints against the police will be more independent of any one police force. Having, however, severed its ties with all police forces, an independent commissioner for police deontology will not be privy to inside information from any police force, and will be limited to its role as an arbitrator in individual complaints from private citizens. Hence, its capacity to see the broader picture will be significantly diminished.

Making the Mid-rank Officers Accountable

The two most significant failures of accountability in the Oka Crisis that we described in the first part of this paper related to political accountability and the lack of supervision by the police hierarchy. By the latter, we mean most of all the complete absence of control over their men by officers of low and middle rank, such as corporals, sergeants, and lieutenants.

We tried to show how unclear the law was in relation to the exercise of police powers in situations of emergency. It could be inferred that we should fill the legal gaps and formulate rules that are more precise. This is perhaps necessary. However, we would like to point out that legal control is time-consuming, because it mainly consists of compelling the police to get an official (that is, judicial) authorization for undertaking certain operations. It was rumoured that the police made an extensive use of electronic surveillance and systematically intercepted private communications during the Oka Crisis. It would be interesting to know whether the police were granted judicial authorization to intercept private communications as required by the Criminal Code or if they felt that such authorization was not needed because the Mohawks and the citizens who were organizing the demonstrations in Châteauguay had no reasonable ground to expect that their private communications would be kept private, since they were engaged in massive civil disobedience and violation of the law.[99]

Legal control could be compared to a film that is projected in slow motion, whereas a crisis usually happens suddenly and consists of a chain of events that occur in 'fast forward,' so to speak. Hence, we believe that the most adequate control that can be exercised in this kind of situation is by field officers over their men. In this regard, one of the unexpected outcomes of the investigations of the SQ Committee for Studying Complaints was that several mid-rank officers were charged with violations of SQ regulations on deontology and discipline. This outcome is relatively surprising, because it seldom happens that ranking officers are charged with breaches of discipline (or of deontology). Since civilian complaint committees usually react to external complaints directed against the rank and file, they have few opportunities to question the behaviour of the officers. Although it is premature to speculate on the outcome of the eventual proceedings before the disciplinary authorities, it is to be hoped that having made mid-rank and higher-level officers accountable for their behaviour will result in a better performance of their duties. Seen in this way, the work of the SQ screening committee resulted in a fragmentation of responsibility, but will also be beneficial if the persons that it has charged are prosecuted.

Whether these police officers will be prosecuted is, at the present time (March 1993), uncertain. The lawyers for the police officers argued successfully in court that, in order to assure full defence and answer for their clients, the disciplinary proceedings had to be postponed until the end of the inquiry of Coroner Guy Gilbert, who is investigating the circumstances of the death of Corporal Marcel Lemay on 11 July 1990. This inquiry has only recently begun. Furthermore, the legality of the charges brought against thirty-nine members of the SQ by the complaint review board is now being challenged in court.[100] It is alleged, inter alia, that the term of two members of the committee was illegally renewed when they started to examine the Oka file, and that this illegality invalidates all the decisions of the committee regarding police misconduct during the Oka Crisis. It is impossible to predict what the government and the SQ will do if the court rules that all the proceedings of the complaint committee in relation to the Oka Crisis were illegal.

Political Accountability

At the end of the Oka Crisis, Mr Sam Elkas, then minister for public security, admitted that he still did not know who had given the order to storm the Mohawk barricade at Kanesatake on 11 July 1990. His successor, Mr Claude Ryan, stated before the Quebec National Assembly that the order was given by a special committee, the members of which are not known.

We believe that these declarations are as embarrassing for the Quebec government as they are for the SQ, perhaps even more so. The government of Quebec had known since at least 1989, from police intelligence reports, that a crisis of major proportions was building in the reserves of Kanesatake, Kahnawake, and Akwesasne. It can be argued that the decision to mount an assault on the Mohawk barricade on 11 July 1990, because of its possible implications for the Oka communities, should have been considered as a political decision and should not have been made by the police alone. The fact that, during the crisis, the minister for public security could not account in the National Assembly, and ultimately before the Quebec people, for the behaviour of the organization for which he was legally and politically responsible is liable to undermine seriously the credibility of the minister himself. A minister who cannot account for the organizations that are accountable to him compromises his own political accountability.

To a large extent, the relationships between the police and political authorities are still governed by the doctrine of 'plausible deniability.' A minister should, apparently, always be in a position to dissociate himself or herself from a police action. We believe that the police should be protected against political interference in their operations and must at all costs remain politically unbiased. However, this is not to say that political authorities should abdicate their responsibilities for overseeing the general behaviour of policing organizations. In certain areas – for instance, regarding police willingness to abide by the rulings of the Supreme Court on police powers – the minister should play a much more active role. There are many other areas that could be identified where the minister responsible for policing could provide police agencies with directives and guidelines.

We are convinced that police forces would not oppose an initiative to develop a framework that would delineate ministerial accountability in Parliament with respect to policing. The development of such a framework would make it more difficult for a minister to evade his responsibilities with regard to policing and would be an incentive to fully exercise legitimate political authority. Another advantage of developing such a framework is that it would clarify the policing areas where ministerial activism is undesirable. Spelling out in clear language what the minister is accountable for and what he or she is *not* accountable for would, it is hoped, deprive police agencies of their blanket alibi of having been under pressure from their 'political masters,' which they have a tendency to invoke when they have taken questionable action.

Legal Remedies

We raised the issue of legal remedies in an earlier section of this conclusion. We hypothesized that legal/judicial control may not fit the nature of an emergency situation because of its procedural and time-consuming character. However, our previous remarks far from exhaust the issue of legal remedies, and we would like to make two additional points.

The first point is obvious. Without being unduly pessimistic, we can assume that there may be an increase in civil disorders in the future (most Western countries are now experiencing such an increase). Hence, issues such as security perimeters, roadblocks, and routine search and seizures will arise again. Without demanding that elaborate legislation be enacted in respect to these issues, it seems to us beyond doubt that legal clarification of the powers of the police in maintaining public order is desirable. Despite an abundant jurisprudence that specialists can resort to, one of the most acute problems is that citizens are completely in the dark with respect to the legality of police action in securing perimeters, mounting roadblocks, requesting identification, and conducting routine search and seizures. Modest amendments to the present law would not only provide better safeguards for citizens' rights, they would also educate the public on what the police legally can and cannot do.

It could be argued against our proposal that it is self-defeating to regulate through the general (non-emergency) law police powers that are to be exercised only in exceptional circumstances. It is not, the reasoning would go, legislation such as the *Criminal Code* that should be made more precise but the *Emergencies Act*. At first appearance, this objection seems well founded. However, we must point out that amending such legislation as the *Emergencies Act* may only provide theoretical protection to Canadians. The crux of the matter is that a state of emergency has to be proclaimed in order for the *Emergencies Act* to apply. We saw that such a state of emergency was never officially proclaimed during the Oka Crisis, although *in practice* the police applied their own emergency procedures and acted accordingly. To a certain extent, the reasons for this reluctance were and will always be political. A provincial premier may find it highly embarrassing to use this kind of legislation, which shows his province's dependence on the federal government. Even the federal government may have great reservations about using such legislation, as the proclamation of a national state of emergency might damage Canada's international image as a peaceful and law-abiding country.

It would seem then that we are facing an unhappy dilemma with regard to legal remedies. On the one hand, the legal instruments, such as emergency laws, that would be the most adequate to afford citizens protection may be neutralized by a lack of political will to use them. On the other hand, incorporating safeguards into the criminal law may prove to be cumbersome and stand needlessly in the way of police efficiency in their daily operations.

Furthermore, it could be argued that emergency laws are not primarily instruments to protect civil liberties; they are tools to increase the powers of the police. Even if we grant the objection, it must be noted that safeguards against abuse can actually be introduced in such legislation. As we have seen, some guarantees are now present in the *Emergencies Act*. However, the real answer to the objection is that in crises such as that at Oka, the police grant themselves all the powers that are provided by emergency legislation and even go beyond what would have to be specified according to such legislation. We regard these situations where police powers are extended de facto, without any state of emergency having been legally proclaimed, as the most objectionable of all.

There is no easy solution to the dilemma facing us in seeking legal remedies to police abuse of power. We would suggest that the present dichotomy between a state of emergency, which is proclaimed only under the most extraordinary of circumstances, and everyday law enforcement is much too rigid. Numerous situations requiring police intervention, such as public demonstrations, civil disobedience, racial confrontations, and youth riots, fall in the uncharted area between a state of emergency and routine law enforcement. Since there is a very real possibility that the frequency of these incidents will increase in the future, there may be no better time to consider a more flexible and searching approach to these problems than the present.

NOTES

The authors wish to thank the Canadian Donner Foundation for the support that they provided for this research on police accountability.

1 R.S.C. 1970, c. W-2.

2 S.C. 1988, c. 29.

3 Gouvernement du Québec, *Rapport de la Commission d'enquête sur les opéra-*

tions policières en territoire québécois (Rapport Keable) (Québec: Gouvernement du Québec, Ministère de la Justice 1981) [hereinafter *Keable Report*].

4 The results of the court proceedings against these 24 members are as follows. One policeman pleaded guilty to a reduced charge and was released unconditionally. Another was found guilty by the court and received a suspended sentence along with six months' probation. Four policemen were acquitted and the complaints were rejected in four other cases. As late as the end of 1991, seven RCMP members were still on trial for offences allegedly committed 20 years ago and for which charges were laid in 1981. In one of these cases, the accused was released by the court for reasons of undue delays in the court proceedings (*Canadian Charter of Rights and Freedoms*, Part I of the *Constitution Act, 1982*, being Schedule B of the *Canada Act 1982* (U.K.), 1982, c. 11, s. 11(b)). This decision was applied to all pending cases against RCMP members. All court proceedings initiated after the release of the Keable report are now terminated. For a detailed discussion of the court proceedings that followed the Keable inquiry, see R. Doyon and J.P. Brodeur, 'Legal Action Taken Following the Recommendations of the Commission of Inquiry on Police Operations in the Province of Quebec,' C.A.S.I.S. *Newsletter* 15 (1990): 28.

5 See *Canadian Security Intelligence Service Act*, R.S.C. 1985, c. C-23, s. 20(2), s. 30(2)c), s. 33 and ss. 38–41.

6 See the appendix to this article for a chronological study of the events. Generally speaking, our sources for the Oka Crisis consist of the articles that were published in Canada's main newspapers in French and English. Few books have been published so far on the Oka Crisis. We have consulted R. Philpot, *Oka: Dernier alibi du Canada anglais* (Montréal: VLB Editeur 1991); R. Hornung, *One Nation Under the Gun* (Toronto: Stoddart Publishing Co. 1991). None of these books qualifies as an unbiased study of the crisis. Philpot argues that the crisis was used by English Canada to undermine Quebec's constitutional position. Hornung is an New York journalist who reviews these events through a U.S. perspective.

7 Commissaire à la déontologie policière du Québec, dossiers P-90-4330 and P-90-4345, p. 3:

Il est aussi ressorti de l'enquête et il est de connaissance judiciaire que toute la population vivant dans cette partie du territoire de la province a vécu, au cours de quelques longs mois, un état de siège où a primé le coup de force, qu'il n'appartient pas au Commissaire à la déontologie de juger qu'il fut nécessaire ou futile. Deux constatations peuvent être faites cependant. La première est que durant ces périodes d'affrontement et de violence, ce sont les droits individuels qui, les premiers, sont brimés pour que soient sauvegardés les intérêts collectifs.

Alors, la Charte des droits et libertés se met en veilleuse. La seconde est que les agents de la paix ne font qu'exécuter les tâches de ceux pour qui l'affrontement est nécessaire et, par conséquent, nécessaires les mesures extraordinaires.

S'agit-il d'une désobéissance condamnable à laquelle ne devraient pas souscrire les policiers? L'heure n'est pas à la philosophie, mais il semble au Commissaire que les contraintes et les brimades imposées par les policiers aux citoyens, par obéissance, ne sont pas des fautes lourdes au point qu'ils auraient dû refuser de les faire subir.

Un autre point doit être soulevé. Dans tous les documents que renferment nos dossiers, il apparaît que monsieur Petit se déclare impuissant à identifier les policiers qu'il accuse de harcèlement. Bien plus, il admet que, dans l'hypothèse où il reconnaîtrait quelques visages, il ne pourrait désigner sous serment tel ou tel agent comme l'auteur de tel acte dérogatoire.

Cette preuve essentielle étant inaccessible, toute enquête serait vouée à l'échec.

8 Commissaire à la déontologie policière du Québec, dossier 90-0001, p. 3: 'Bref, l'état d'urgence peut exiger que des droits individuels soient brimés lorsque l'intérêt général le commande.'

9 The main source of information on the October Crisis is J.F. Duchaîne, *Rapport sur les événements d'octobre 1970*, 2e édition comprenant les passages retenus dans la première édition et les annexe A, B, C et D (Québec: Gouvernement du Québec, Ministère de la Justice) [hereinafter *The Duchaîne Report*]. Other useful sources are the *Keable Report*, (see n. 2, above) and the second and third reports of the McDonald Commission: McDonald Commission, *Second Report of the Commission of Inquiry Concerning Certain Activities of the Royal Canadian Mounted Police: Freedom and Security Under the Law* (Ottawa: Minister of Supplies and Services); *Third Report of the Commission of Inquiry Concerning Certain Activities of the Royal Canadian Mounted Police: Certain RCMP Activities and the Question of Governmental Knowledge* (Ottawa: Minister of Supplies and Services).

10 *Duchaîne Report*, 74ff. The *Duchaîne Report* shows convincingly that the chain of command during the October Crisis was broken into so many components that one cannot even identify with certainty who first decided that the *War Measures Act* was to be invoked. The report identifies, with reservations, the legal counsel of the Montreal Municipal Police, Mr Michel Côté, as the initiator of this move.

11 This committee has been appointed in compliance with the *Regulation Respecting the Code of Ethics and Discipline of Members of the Sûreté du Québec*, adopted under the authority of the *Police Act*, R.S.Q., c. P-13, s. 57.1. Jean-Paul Brodeur has served as a member of that committee since its appointment in 1987. Al-

though he was an acting member of the committee during the Oka Crisis, all the information mentioned in this paper is derived from public sources. Louise Viau was appointed president of that same committee, commencing 1 September 1991.

12 The *Duchaîne Report* describes the climate that prevailed in the police forces after the kidnapping of Pierre Laporte as complete panic. It is reported that 1200 police were engaged in the massive arrests conducted during the night of 16 October 1970 (p. 118). It is also reported that, during the period from 18 October to 6 November, information was being given to the police forces at a daily rate of 1200 items. The RCMP and all other police forces confessed their incapacity to process such an amount of data (p. 165). They initially attempted to follow every lead; this practice resulted into chaos.

13 Personal communication of Jacques Bellemare, QC (Mr Vallières's counsel) to J.P. Brodeur.

14 J.P. Brodeur, *La délinquance de l'ordre* (Montreal: Hurtubise HMH 1984).

15 *La Presse*, 30 Nov. 1990.

16 It might be interesting to note that the actual minister of public security, Mr Claude Ryan, served on that committee. He was then and still is the minister of municipal affairs. After the crisis, Mr Ryan was also appointed as minister of public security in replacement of Mr Sam Elkas. During the October Crisis, he was the publisher of *Le Devoir* and its most prominent editorialist. It is reported in The *Duchaîne Report*, (p. 146), that, on 17 October 1970, he had severely criticized the adoption of the *War Measures Act* and questioned the motives behind the radical position adopted by the different levels of government, which had first appeared to take a conciliatory approach.

17 The original French text is: 'Si des agents de la Sûreté du Québec ont matraqué des citoyens après l'ouverture du pont, ils ont agi en dehors des ordres donnés par la direction de la Sûreté du Québec (*Le Devoir*, 14 août 1990).

18 Philpot; see n. 6, above.

19 Quoted in Philpot, ibid., 159.

20 One of the authors of this paper – J.P. Brodeur – was frequently asked by the English speaking media to give interviews on the behaviour of the SQ at different points during the Oka Crisis. The first question that was unavoidably asked at the beginning of these interviews was, 'Why is the SQ the most violent police force in Canada?'

21 See Title II of *An Act Respecting Police Organization*, R.S.Q. 1990, c. O-8.1 (as amended by S.Q. 1990, c. 27), that came into force on 1 September 1990.

22 The complaint procedure is prescribed by the *Regulation Respecting the Code of Ethics and Discipline of Members of the Sûreté du Québec*; see n. 11, above.

23 Ibid., chapter V.

24 Ibid., chapter VI.

25 Ibid., s. 78.
26 Ibid., s. 81.
27 Ibid., s. 85. That section stipulates: 'This Regulation may not be interpreted as affecting a labour contract within the meaning of the Act respecting the Syndical Plan of the Sûreté du Québec' (R.S.Q., c. R-14). We shall mention that the new *Code of Ethics of Québec Police Officers* prescribes that the decision of the ethics committee cannot be submitted to an arbitrator; See *An Act Respecting Police Organization*, s. 134 (n. 21, above).
28 See chapter II, *Breaches of Discipline*, and chapter III, *Duties of a Member*, of the *Regulation Respecting the Code of Ethics.*
29 S. 48.
30 According to the *Duchaîne Report*, 119 (see n. 9, above), nearly 450 persons were arrested during the arrest operation of 16 October 1970.
31 Ibid., 113–17, 119–31.
32 See n. 1, above.
33 The original proclamation occurred on 16 October 1970: SOR/70-443. It stayed in force until the coming into effect of the *Public Order (Temporary Measures) Act, 1970*, S.C. 1970-71-72, c. 2, which received royal assent on 4 December 1970. That last-mentioned legislation expired on 30 April 1971. For a general overview of the legal impact of the proclamation, see J.-L. Baudouin, J. Fortin, and D. Szabo, *Terrorisme et justice* (Montréal: Les Editions du Jour 1970), 133–49.
34 See the preamble to the *Public Order Regulations, 1970*, SOR/70-444.
35 Ibid., s. 9(1).
36 Ibid., s. 7. According to the *Duchaîne Report*, 118, an order from Inspector Jodoin required the police to arrest all persons found on premises where searches were conducted who would refused to identify themselves: 'Il donna alors instruction d'arrêter toute personne qui refuserait de s'identifier, puis de l'interroger et, s'il était clair qu'elle n'avait rien à voir avec cette affaire, de la relâcher.' The requirement that the attorney general himself authorize the release of arrested persons from custody explains the high number of citizens detained after the arrest operation of 16 October 1970.
37 Ibid., s. 9(2).
38 Ibid., ss. 10–11.
39 S.C. 1960, c. 44.
40 See s. 6(5) of the *War Measures Act* and s. 6 of the *Canadian Bill of Rights.*
41 That repeal is provided by s. 80 of the *Emergencies Act*, S.C. 1988, c. 29.
42 Ibid.
43 As authorized by *National Defence Act*, R.S.C., 1985, c. N-5, part XI.
44 S. 39 (see n. 11, above).

45 S. 3(a): 'an urgent and critical situation of a temporary nature that [...] seriously endangers the lives, health or safety of Canadians and is of such proportions or nature as to exceed the capacity or authority of a province to deal with it.'

46 See n. 5, above.

47 *Emergencies Act*, s. 16. According to s. 2(c) of the *Canadian Security Intelligence Service Act*, a public-order emergency arises when there is a threat to the security of Canada, which means inter alia: 'activities within or relating to Canada directed toward or in support of the threat or use of acts of serious violence against persons or property for the purpose of achieving a political objective within Canada or a foreign state.'

48 Indeed, it should be mentioned that s. 25(3) of the *Emergencies Act* prescribes that a declaration of a public-order emergency whose effects would have been confined to only one province cannot be issued unless 'the lieutenant governor in council of the province has indicated to the Governor in Council that the emergency exceeds the capacity or authority of the province to deal with it.' For the premier of Quebec to admit such incapacity might have been politically suicidal.

49 Arguably, such a clause cannot be adopted by the Governor in Council without the previous authorization of Parliament: see the wording of s. 33 of the Charter. However, the constitutional validity of regulations of that nature would have had to be considered not only with respect to the legal rights guaranteed by s. 7 and following sections of the Charter but also in the context of s. 1. It is conceivable that the judicial approach adopted in ordinary circumstances would be distinguished in a crisis situation so as to validate extraordinary police powers.

50 S. 20(1).

51 Their legality was challenged in a petition for the granting of a interlocutory injunction, a proceeding that illustrates the recriminations of those residing inside the security perimeter; see *Ronald Bonspille and Nicholas Livingston* v. *Procureur général du Québec et Sûreté du Québec*, C.S.Mtl. no 500-06-000006-904. The interlocutory injunction asked for was refused by Gomery J.C.S. on 30 July 1991. In the court's file, no written reasons are given for its dismissal. That proceeding was joined to a motion for authorization to institute a class action on behalf of all the citizens living within the limits of the security perimeter. The petitioners abandoned the whole proceedings on 9 October 1990.

52 *Criminal Code*, R.S.C. 1985, c. C-46 [hereinafter *Criminal Code*], is no less general: see ss. 25, 30, and 495(1).

53 These duties and powers are described in Lord Hailsham, ed., *Halsbury's Laws of England*, 4th ed. (London: Butterworths 1981), 200–10:

320. General functions of constables. The primary function of the constable remains, as in the seventeeth century, the preservation of the Queen's peace. From

this general function stems a number of particular duties additional to those conferred by statute and including those mentioned hereafter.

The first duty of a constable is always to prevent the commission of a crime. If a constable reasonably apprehends that the action of any person may result in a breach of the peace it is his duty to prevent that action. It is his general duty to protect life and property. The general function of controlling traffic on the roads is derived from this duty.

However, a constable is himself subject to the law, and he cannot claim immunity from it by reason only that he is acting in pursuance of his duty; indeed a constable who flouted the law (whether civil or criminal) could scarcely be said to be acting in the execution of his duty as such. Whether or not the conduct of a constable is inconsistent with his acting in the execution of his duty is very much a matter of degree; for example, touching a person on the shoulder for the purpose of attracting his attention may be an assault in law, but such a trivial interference with a citizen's liberty would not be sufficient to take a constable out of the course of his duties.

54 *Criminal Code*, s. 129 (see n. 52).

55 Ibid., s. 270.

56 [1964] 1 Q.B. 164.

57 Ibid., 170–1.

58 Ibid., 171.

59 [1970] S.C.R. 631.

60 [1974] S.C.R. 443.

61 Ibid., 447–8.

62 Ibid., 448.

63 L.H. Leigh, *Police Powers in England and Wales* (London: Butterworths 1975), 33: 'Other cases appear to move tentatively towards an ancillary powers doctrine which would enable the police to perform such reasonable acts as are necessary for the due execution of their duties.' This quotation has been cited with approval by the Supreme Court of Canada in *Dedman* v. *R.*, [1985] 2 S.C.R. 2 at 34.

64 It is unlikely that s. 6 of the Charter could be invoked to challenge the legality of a security perimeter, having been interpreted as forbidding the free interprovincial mobility of citizens: see *Malartic Hygrade Gold Mines Ltd.* v. *R.* (1982), 142 D.L.R. (3d) 512; *McDermott* v. *Nackawic (Town)* (1988), 53 D.L.R. (4th) 150 (C.A.N.B.).

65 See *Reference Re Section 94(2) of the Motor Vehicle Act*, [1985] 2 S.C.R. 486, which ruled that this section encompasses substantive principles of criminal law as well as procedural safeguards.

66 [1988] 2 S.C.R. 387 at 406.

67 *Dedman* (see n. 63); *R.* v. *Hufsky*, [1988] 1 S.C.R. 621; *R.* v. *Ladouceur*, [1990] 1 S.C.R. 1257; *R.* v. *Mellenthin* (1993), 76 C.C.C. (3d) 481 (S.C.C.).

68 [1975] 3 All E.R. 682.

69 *Dedman*, at 35.

70 [1988] 1 S.C.R. 621.

71 [1990] 1 S.C.R. 1257.

72 At 638 (see n. 67).

73 *Mellenthin*, at 490 (see n. 67).

74 See n. 7 and 8, above.

75 Under the Criminal Code, a search warrant is required by ss. 487–487.1. However s. 101 authorizes a search without warrant of a person or vehicule, or place or premises, when a peace officer believes on reasonable ground that an offence in relation to firearms is being committed or has been committed.

76 Royal Commission on Criminal Procedures, *The Investigation and Prosecution of Criminal Offences in England and Wales: The Law and Procedure* (London: Her Majesty's Stationery Offices 1981), cmnd 8092-1 at 8, no. 20.

77 See *R.* v. *Landry*, [1986] 1 S.C.R. 145; *Wong* v. *R.* (1991), 1 C.R. (4th) 1 (S.C.C.); *Mellenthin*. In the *Wong* case, Mr Justice La Forest, citing with approval Martin J.A.'s observation in *R.* v. *Rao* (1984), 40 C.R. (3d) 1 (Ont. C.A.), leave to appeal refused: [1984] 2 S.C.R. ix (note), reiterated that 'at common law there is no power to search premises without a warrant, except as an incident of a lawful arrest' and added, 'I do not think judicial development of new search powers should be encouraged' (15). La Forest J.'s opinion was shared by Dickson C.J.C. and L'Heureux-Dubé and Sopinka JJ. Though dissenting on the issue of the admissibility of evidence under s. 24(2) of the Charter, Wilson J. also agreed with him on the question of law under discussion in our paper.

78 At 17.

79 At 487. In fact, the burden of proving that a search is unreasonable is not a heavy one since the Supreme Court of Canada held, in *R.* v. *Collins*, [1987] 1 S.C.R. 265 at 278, that a warrantless search is prima facie unreasonable. See also *R.* v. *Dyment*, [1988] 2 R.C.S. 417 at 436, La Forest J.; *R.* v. *Kokesch* (1991), 1 C.R. (4th) 62 at 81 (S.C.C.), Dickson C.J.

80 It cannot be argued that the searches of motor vehicles conducted at the entrance of the security perimeter established at Oka occurred as an incident to a lawful arrest and, as a matter of fact, no search warrant authorized them: see *Langlois* v. *Cloutier*, [1990] 1 S.C.R. 158. Some of them might have been supported by s. 101 of the Criminal Code, which authorizes a search without warrant of a motor vehicle conducted in connection with a firearms offence, but certainly not all searches. Furthermore, these warrantless searches are also questionable because the constitutionality of s. 101 was unclear. Actually, Parliament has modified this

section by Bill C-17 to prescribe that such a search be conducted only *where the conditions for obtaining a warrant exist but, by reason of exigent circumstances, it would not be practicable to obtain a warrant.* A search warrant cannot be obtained on mere suspicion: see *Criminal Code*, s. 487.

81 *Mellenthin*, at 487.

82 Section 1 of the Charter provides that '[t]he Canadian Charter of Rights and Freedoms guarantees the rights and freedoms set out in it subject only to such reasonable limits prescribed by law as can be demonstrably justified in a free and democratic society.'

83 At 518 (see note 65). This ruling is also applicable to a violation of s. 8 of the Charter because *Reference Re Section 94(2)* further established that '[s]ections 8 to 14 address specific deprivations of the "right" to life, liberty and security of the person in breach of the principles of fundamental justice, and as such, violations of section 7' (512).

84 See *Southam Inc.* v. *Judge E.R. Iuticone and Cpl. Gilles Charette and A.G. Quebec*, S.C. Mtl. No 500-36-000605-900; *Canadian Newspapers Inc.* v. *Judge E.R. Iuticone & Cpl. Gilles Charette and A.G. Quebec*, S.C. Mtl. No 500-36-000610-900.

85 Counsel acting on behalf of Southam Inc. discontinued the suit on 27 September 1990. The proceedings taken on behalf of Canadian Newspapers Inc. were abandoned on 4 October 1990.

86 *MacLeod* v. *Canada (Chief of Defence Staff, Canadian Armed Forces)* (1991), 2 C.R. (4th) 213 (Fed. T.D.).

87 Ibid., at 216.

88 Ibid., at 213–14.

89 See n. 51, above.

90 See n. 84.

91 However, there are uncertainties about the possibility of awarding punitive damages as a remedy under s. 24(1) of the Charter; see R. Provost, 'Emergency Judicial Relief for Human Rights Violations in Canada and Argentina,' *University of Miami Inter-American Law Review* 23 (1992): 758.

92 *R.* v. *Latulippe* (1991), 69 C.C.C. (3d) 365 at 377 (Que. C.A.). Tyndale J. cited the following doctrinal authorities on this point: M.L. Pilkington, 'Damages as a Remedy for Infringement of Canadian Charter of Rights and Freedoms,' *Canadian Bar Review* 62 (1984): 517; A. Morel, 'Le droit d'obtenir réparation en cas de violation de droits constitutionnels,' *Revue juridique Thémis*, 1984: 253; E.G. Ewaschuk, 'The Charter: An Overview and Remedies,' *Criminal Reports* 26, 3d ser. (1982): 54.

93 Ewaschuk, ibid., 73–74, cited at 377 of *Latulippe*, ibid., Tyndale, J.

94 (1986), 30 C.R.R. 96 at 105, reproduced at 377 of *Latulippe*, ibid., Tyndale J.

95 At 284 (see n. 79).

96 [1985] 1 S.C.R. 613 at 652, Le Dain J., cited with approval by Lamer J. in *Collins*, at 285 (see n. 79).

97 To that effect, a written authorization might have been asked for under the conditions specified in Part VI of the *Criminal Code* or in s. 21 of the *Canadian Security Intelligence Service Act.*

98 See *Duchaîne Report*, *Keable Report*, and the three reports of the McDonald Commission (nn. 3, 9, above).

99 *Criminal Code*, s. 183 defines a 'private communication' in a manner that puts some emphasis on the reasonableness of the expectation of privacy: '"private communications" means any oral or any telecommunication made under circumstances in which it is reasonable for the originator thereof to expect that it will not be intercepted by any person other than the person intended by the originator thereof to receive it.' Nevertheless, if the rumours that we acknowledged earlier in our paper are true, we are inclined to consider such an interpretation as being abusive.

100 *Louis Côté et al.* v. *Gilles St-Antoine et al.*, C.S.Mtl. 500-05-017965-920; *Lieutenant Jean-Luc Lemieux et al.* v. *Le Comité de discipline de la Sûreté du Québec*, C.S.Mtl. 500-05-017951-920. Since the writing of this paper, the Court found that three members of the civilian review board were illegally renewed by the minister in order to investigate the Oka crisis. The Court also found other breaches of procedure, such as the absence of complaints against individual SQ officers. Consequently, all disciplinary charges against 39 SQ police were dropped. The SQ has now definitely closed this file.

Appendix: Chronology of Events in the 'Amerindian Crisis,' March–September 1990

11 March 1990: The Mohawks of Kanesatake erect a barricade in order to stop the city of Oka from enlarging a golf course on land that had been given to the municipality but is claimed by the Mohawks.

26 April: The town of Oka obtains an injunction enjoining the Mohawks of Kanesatake to take down the barricades, but the mayor, Jean Ouellette, chooses not to apply it in order not to provoke the Mohawks.

1 May: The town of Oka opens negotiations with representatives of the Band Council (the elected government) and the Longhouse (the traditional government).

2 May: A representative of the Quebec government is sent as negotiator to try to find a solution to the dispute.

9 May: The minister of public safety, Sam Elkas, states that he does not intend to ask the Sûreté du Québec (the Quebec police force) to intervene.

16 May: The Quebec minister of indian affairs, John Ciaccia, announces that he hopes the town of Oka will suspend its project of enlarging the golf course.

4 June: The town of Oka proposes that it will declare a moratorium of three months on the project if the Mohawks will agree to end their occupation.

7 June: The town of Oka is denied two new provisional injunctions against the Mohawks in Quebec Superior Court.

29 June: A judge of the Superior Court grants the town of Oka an interlocutory injunction enjoining the Mohawks of Kanesatake to take down their barricades. The municipal administration decides to wait and try to get the Band Council to agree to take down the barricades without a confrontation.

4 July: The Mohawks of Kanesatake state that they will not obey the injunction against them and intend to resist in the case of intervention by the Sûreté du Québec. The chief of the Band Council, George Martin, says that a majority of Mohawks are in favour of occupying the Oka lands, but have reservations about the methods to be used, fearing a violent confrontation with the Quebec police.

6 July: The town of Oka grants the Mohawks of Kanesatake a new deadline of three days. The mayor, Jean Ouellette, states he will ask for the intervention of the Sûreté if the barricades have not been taken down by the deadline.

The lawyer for the Band Council of Kanesatake speaks to the minister of public safety, Sam Elkas, to warn him that if the Warriors (the armed faction of the traditionalist Mohawk movement) are sent to Oka, confrontation with the Sûreté du Québec is probable. The minister's office responds, saying that Mr Elkas will not order the police themselves to dismantle the barricades: the police will only intervene if there are any criminal acts, but they could also escort the battering rams for dismantling the barricades if the town so demands.

The Quebec Human Rights Commission asks the Canadian and Quebec ministers responsible for Indian affairs to create a special committee to 'restore social peace and suggest a satisfactory solution to the demands of the Mohawks of Kanesatake.'

8 July: The mayor of Oka grants the Mohawks occupying the barricades one more day. The members of the Longhouse of Kanesatake, sure of the support of the friendly nations of Quebec, Ontario, and the United States, reaffirm their intention to maintain the blockade in spite of the injunction against them.

9 July: The federal minister of indian affairs, Tom Siddon, commissions the negotiator Yves Désilets to find a peaceful solution to the demands of the Mohawks. At the same time, Mr Siddon obtains the mayor of Oka's promise to postpone temporarily any taking down of the barricades by the police.

In a letter addressed to the mayor of Oka, the provincial minister of indian affairs, John Ciaccia, asks that the project for the enlargement of the golf course be abandoned. While recognizing the legality of the injunction obtained by the town, the minister states that 'the conflict goes far beyond the strictly legal aspect of the case.'

The mayor of Oka declares that he opposes any negotiations with the Mohawks as long as the barricades remain.

10 July: Refusing to abandon his project for the development of a golf course on the disputed land, the mayor of Oka, enforcing a Superior Court injunction, asks the Sûreté du Québec to proceed with the removal of the barricades.

Ciaccia states he has warned his public safety colleague, Sam Elkas, responsible for the Quebec police, of the danger of armed intervention.

11 July: At 5:30 a.m., a contingent of about one hundred men of the Sûreté du Québec is sent to level the barricades. One policeman (Corporal Marcel Lemay) dies during the fusillade provoked by the confrontation between the police and Mohawks. The police are forced to retreat, leaving behind several vehicles and a battering ram, which the Mohawks use to block route 344 at the entrance to Oka. The Sûreté police erect their own barrier a hundred metres further away.

On the same day, in a gesture of support, the Mohawks of the neighbouring reserve of Kahnawake block all the roads leading to the Mercier Bridge to Montréal and occupy the bridge itself, thus denying access to residents of the region of Châteauguay.

12 July: The Sûreté du Québec justifies the raid on Oka by the need to obey the injunction issued by the Superior Court and because of suspicions concerning the activities going on in the territory occupied by the Mohawks.

Minister John Ciaccia undertakes to negotiate with the Mohawks of Kanesatake. A representative of the Kanesatake Longhouse, Ellen Gabriel, lets it be understood that the Mohawks would end their occupation on condition that the Sûreté du Québec withdraw all its men, and that judicial immunity be granted for misdeeds committed before and during the raid.

Minister Sam Elkas undertakes negotiations with the national defence minister, Bill McKnight, with a view to getting the support of the Canadian Armed Forces at Oka. The department lets it be defence understood that the decision to call up the army depends on the success of Mr Ciaccia's negotiations.

13 July: Indian Affairs Minister Ciaccia, after leaving the negotiation table, says he now knows the position of the Mohawks and asks the federal government to assume its responsibilities in the case. The minister declares that he will not intervene in the Oka crisis as long as there is still armed confrontation.

More than 500 citizens of Châteauguay charge the barricades of the Sûreté du Québec near the Mercier Bridge in protest against the 'intrusion' of the Mohawks of Kahnawake who go to Châteauguay for their provisions.

The Sûreté searches the vehicle of journalists from Télé-Métropole and confiscates a cassette. It accuses them of having crossed one of the police barricades without authorization.

The Mohawks of Kahnawake threaten to blow up Mercier Bridge if one of their members is a victim of the Sûreté du Québec. This declaration is taken all the more seriously because of the theft of a large amount of dynamite that had taken place in the Désourdy warehouse a short time before.

14 July: The Mohawks demand the presence of observers during the negotiations. Their demand is granted and a group of about a dozen persons, mainly from religious communities, is formed.

An agreement is reached between Minister Ciaccia and traditionalist Mohawks of Oka on opening the Mercier Bridge, but a leader of the Kahnawake Warriors declares that his group is in no way bound by Mr Ciaccia's promises.

15 July: The mayor of Châteauguay asks Prime Minister Mulroney to intervene personally in the conflict. The residents of Châteauguay, for their part, demand the immediate intervention of the army.

Negotiations between Indian Affairs Minister, Ciaccia, and the Mohawks cease. The points now under negotiation are

- a large decrease in the number of police from the Quebec force, estimated to be between 1000 and 1500 men;
- the creation of a group of observers;
- recognition of Minister Ciaccia's office as mediator between the federal government and the Mohawk nation;

- an inquiry into the attitude of the federal government in the crisis, in which the Mohawks should participate;
- the participation of Mohawks in the inquiry into the shooting during which Corporal Lemay lost his life; and
- retreat from the barricades at Oka and the Mercier Bridge, conditional on the withdrawal from the barricades of the Quebec police.

16 July: Regarding the negotiations, the Mohawk's spokesperson Ellen Gabriel states that any commitments of the Mohawk negotiators should be the subject of a consensus of the entire population of the Kanesatake community.

In a letter Ms. Gabriel sent to the chief of the Kanesatake Band Council, she states that the Quebec police maintain that they have substantially reduced their manpower in the Oka region. They also confirm that no contingent of the RCMP is now stationed at Oka.

17 July: Some one hundred demonstrators, mostly citizens of Châteauguay, force the roadblocks of the Quebec police near the Mercier Bridge. The police retaliate with force, but no one is hurt.

18 July: The Mohawks of Kanesatake make new conditions public:

- that the whole project of developing the golf course at Oka be stopped;
- that of the territorial claims of the Amerindians in the region be recognized;
- that the entire Mohawk population be allowed to leave the barricades in the 48 hours following the signing of an agreement without being searched or arrested; and
- that all civil and potentially criminal matters, as well as litigation over territorial rights and sovereignty, be submitted to the International Court of Justice at the Hague.

The federal minister of indian affairs officially offers to buy back the golf course and certain neighbouring lands from the town of Oka.

It is estimated, unofficially, that the police operations of the Sûreté du Québec cost at least a million dollars every day in additional expenditures. There are about 1000 police at Oka and 500 at Châteauguay – in all, almost a third of the Quebec force's manpower; 800 officers come from outside the district of Montreal. All the officers of the Sûreté are now working from 12 to 15 hours a day, 7 days a week. Additional costs of the operation include:

- overtime: $840,000 per day;
- lodging: $80,000 per day; and
- per diem ($33.50) given the policemen: $50,000 per day.

23 July: Minister Ciaccia fails in his attempt to get the discussions with the Mohawks of Kanesatake and Kahnawake resumed.

The Quebec government creates a strategy committee comprising the head of the Sûreté du Québec and Ministers Sam Elkas (Public Safety), John Ciaccia (Indian Affairs), Claude Ryan (Education), and Yvon Picotte (Municipal Affairs). These ministers, moreover, are representatives of the constituencies where the Kanesatake and Kahnawake reserves are situated. All the decisions regarding the crisis now go through this committee.

The United Nations Organization says that it holds no jurisdiction concerning the request of the Iroquois Confederation of Six Nations to send forces to keep the peace in Quebec.

24 July: The Quebec Human Rights Commission and the Red Cross complain that the Quebec police are rationing the provision of food and medicine to the Mohawks inside the barricades.

25 July: The town of Oka takes advantage of its option to buy the land for the golf course. The owner of the land gives up his rights to the property for a sum estimated at $90,000, based on a conditional offer to buy in 1989.

27 July: The federal minister of indian affairs, Tom Siddon, announces that the government is buying a large portion (12 hectares) of the territory claimed by the Mohawks of Oka, at a cost of $1.4 million.

Indian Affairs Minister Ciaccia makes the Mohawks a global offer to settle the matter, in which the government promises to:

- withdraw its police from Oka and Kahnawake, except for eight men from the Sûreté du Québec at each of the control points and those necessary to patrol and maintain order; and
- name a member of the Mohawk nation to assist the coroner in the inquiry into the death of Corporal Marcel Lemay.

Amnesty concerning this homicide, however, is out of the question. In return, the Mohawk nation promises:

- to leave the barricades erected in Kanesatake and Kahnawake;
- that an inventory will be made of the arms and explosives until such time as they can be disposed of legally at the conclusions of negotiations; and
- to allow the inhabitants who had to be evacuated to return home.

This agreement would be conducted under observation of a surveillance commission of seven persons named by the government and the Mohawk nation.

30 July: A spokesperson for the Warriors of Kahnawake says that Mr Ciaccia's proposal does not contain the guarantees demanded by the Mohawks, particularly the one concerning the presence of outside observers. However, the secretary of the International Federation of Human Rights, on a mission in Quebec, would agree to participate in the surveillance commission proposed by the government of Quebec.

An injunction requested by two Mohawks of Oka demanding the removal of the Sûreté du Québec barriers on the highway is refused by the Superior Court.

31 July: The town council of Oka refuses to ratify the sale of the disputed lands to the federal government so long as the Mohawks' barricades are not removed. The preliminary agreement provided for the expenditure of $1.34 million for the lands and $2.5 million as compensation for the loss of revenues following the abandonment of the project to extend the golf course and develop a housing project.

3 August: Claude Ryan, minister of education, announces that the Quebec government will compensate the families that were forced to leave their homes for the cost of food and lodging.

A group, Solidarité Châteauguay, blocks off autoroute 15 at Delson. With the aid of a search warrant, Sûreté du Québec officers seize 34 video cassettes from 11 July, the day of the police raid at Oka, from five television stations. The force alleges that this seizure will enable the police to pursue their investigations of the events that took place on 11 July at Oka, and of a series of infractions committed by the Mohawks before that date.

4 August: Solidarité Châteauguay blocks a harbour bridge in St Laurent for five hours.

5 August: Premier Bourassa gives the Mohawks a 48-hour ultimatum to dismantle the barricades.

6 August: Solidarité Châteauguay blocks route 20 near Dorval for an hour.

8 August: Prime Minister Mulroney appoints a mediator for the crisis, Chief Justice of the Québec Superior Court Allen B. Gold.

Premier Bourassa calls up the Canadian Armed Forces, specifying that their intervention is primarily to support the Sûreté du Québec.

12 August: Judge Gold manages to get an agreement between the representatives of the two levels of government and the Mohawks. Three conditions are attached:

- the unrestricted furnishing of food, clothing, medical supplies, health care, and other necessities of life, to be delivered to Kanesatake and Kahnawake;
- the free movement of spiritual leaders, clan mothers, chiefs, advisers, and lawyers named by the Mohawk nation; and
- the presence of an international group of observers to oversee the implementation of the agreement and to observe the proceedings between the parties during the negotiations.

Two violent confrontations take place between the police and demonstrators near the Mercier Bridge. In the second, a crowd of demonstrators estimated at 3000 or 4000 come to blows with about 80 policemen, armed with truncheons, on the St-Louis-de-Gonzague Bridge. Several persons are injured. During the mêlée, a cameraman has his cassette seized and a photographer his film.

The citizens of Châteauguay go to the Quebec police station in the region to free the demonstrators who were arrested following the confrontation.

13 August: The Quebec Federation of Professional Journalists and the Press Council complain about the brutality of certain policemen of the Sûreté du Québec. According to these two organizations, the seizures of material are violations of the freedom of the press. The Sûreté gives back the cassette seized the previous day at Radio-Canada.

Following these recent events, the director general of the Sûreté du Québec apologizes for the brutality of his men and admits he is incapable of restoring peace and order in the present conflict. The director asks Premier Bourassa to call in the army. Twenty or so representatives of the International Federation of Human Rights arrive at Oka.

14 August: Another confrontation takes place between demonstrators and the Quebec police at Châteauguay.

15 August: Negotiations between the representatives of the government and the Mohawk nation are started again. Priority is given the dismantling of the barricades at Kanesatake and Kahnawake.

The army takes up its position in the Oka and Châteauguay regions and waits to learn what its mission will be.

According to an international inquiry held by the Quebec Association of Provincial Police (QAPP), the administrative staff of the Sûreté du Québec was divided over the decision on 11 July to resort to armed intervention. The officers called upon to intervene would have opposed the assault in any case, because they felt they did not have the means to bring the operation to a successful conclusion. The intelligence services and security branch of the force would also have advised against trying to dislodge the Warriors.

16 August: The international observers are officially installed near the barricades.

The Canadian and American intelligence services had warned the Quebec and Canadian governments three years ago that the Mohawk reservation contained an arsenal and that a military infrastructure was in place.

17 August: Premier Bourassa asks the Canadian Armed Forces to relieve the police of the Sûreté du Québec of the surveillance of the barricades. The police remain, but confine their policing to areas outside the barricades.

20 August: About 900 soldiers of the Canadian Armed Forces take up their positions at the Kahnawake and Kanesatake barricades to replace the police of the Sûreté.

Mohawk negotiators stay away from the negotiating table to protest against the army's plan to move the Sûreté's barricades closer to the position held by the Mohawks.

21 August: The Sûreté du Québec had never reduced its manpower; there are between 1400 and 1800 police of the Quebec Force installed close to Oka and Châteauguay. There is also a contingent of about 240 men of the RCMP.

In Ottawa, senior officials of the Department of Indian Affairs let it be understood that an addition of $2 billion over a period of 10 years could solve most of the territorial claims of the country's native peoples.

For ten days the group Solidarité Châteauguay has been blocking an exit of the Mercier Bridge used by the Mohawks of Kahnawake.

22 August: Negotiations are begun once more between the Mohawks and the two levels of government. The Mohawk negotiators submit the following proposal:

- Give the Mohawks the land in question. The federal government has just spent $5.12 million to buy these 39 hectares of land.
- Stop legal proceedings connected with the operation of bingo games on the Kahnawake reserve.
- Promise to create Kanienkahaka (a unified Mohawk nation) within a period of three years, as a means of resolving the question of territorial claims and sovereignty. This Mohawk nation would include the reserves of Kanesatake, Kahnawake, Akwasasne, Ohsweken, Tyendinaga, and Ganienkeh.

Dorval. The police are called to Dorval, where about 100 persons are trying to stop the residents of Kahnawake from transporting provisions and oil by boat. The demonstrators object particularly to the fact that the wharf used by the Mohawks is situated on a property belonging to John Ciaccia. Later, the Peacekeepers of Kahnawake destroy the fateful wharf with the consent of officers of the Montreal Urban Police.

Châteauguay. A group of residents in the region erect a barricade at the northern end of the Mercier Bridge to protest against the use of the bridge by the Mohawks; other users now have to make long detours to get to Montreal.

23 August: A spokesperson for the Mohawks states that the declarations made the evening before, to the effect that the Mohawks were demanding the creation of a new nation, had been wrongly interpreted by journalists. He says that it was not a new demand and not a demand that had to be accepted before the barricades were taken down. He also states that the bingo games were not part of the negotiations.

The army advances to within 1.5 km of the perimeter occupied by the Mohawks of Kanesatake.

The Mohawk negotiators do not come to the negotiation table, protesting the army's 'intimidation manoeuvres.'

Quebec. The minister of 'Sécurité du revenu' declares that $300,000 have been paid to residents and businesses in the regions of Châteauguay and Oka that had sustained losses during the six weeks of conflict. (More than 5000 persons had been evacuated from the vicinity of Kahnawake and Kanesatake.)

Representatives of the International Federation of Human Rights question the willingness of the governments to arrive at a solution within a reasonable time and also the role of their observers in the field. They particularly accuse the police of hindering the free movement of the observers and of doing nothing to prevent white demonstrators from hampering the flow of vehicles bringing food and medicines to the Mohawks.

24 August: Mohawk negotiators return, not wanting to be blamed for being an obstacle in the way of the negotiations. They present two sets of proposals: the first concerns short-term demands that would result in the removal of the barricades; the second is a list of basic items such as territorial demands and self-government.

25 August: A meeting of the 'condoled,' the chiefs of the Confederation of Six Iroquois Nations, takes place in the Onandaga reserve near Syracuse, NY. Condolence is an ancient Iroquois ceremony that officially recognizes the wisdom of and respect for the hereditary chiefs. One of the chiefs declares that the Mohawk negotiators are hypocrites who are hiding behind tradition in order to protect their interests in the lucrative and immoral activities of gaming and the illegal sale of cigarettes. The chiefs say they are the legitimate government of the Mohawk people and, as such, would ask the government representatives to negotiate with them rather than with the present team.

The negotiations are suspended in the afternoon to allow the two parties to discuss their positions.

There are now two groups of demonstrators that block the exit of the Mercier Bridge – the greens, members of Solidarité Châteauguay, and the reds, who say they support the Solidarité, but believe in 'using the force necessary to convince the Mohawks that they are not welcome on the Island of Montreal.'

26 August: The federal negotiator meets with Prime Minister Mulroney and representatives of Quebec's Indian and Northern Affairs ministries to discuss the situation.

The provincial negotiator meets with the emergency committee of the provincal cabinet to decide whether or not negotiations should be opened again.

27 August: Premier Bourassa declares that negotiations with the Mohawks are no longer possible; he accuses them of making all sorts of unacceptable demands since the negotiations began.

The commanding officer of the armed forces receives the order from the Quebec government to proceed with the dismantling of the barricades in Kanesatake and Kahnawake. The dismantling is to begin in the two Mohawk reservations as soon as the plans for the intervention are finalized.

George Erasmus, National Chief of the Assembly of First Nations, for his part, hopes negotiations will be resumed, saying he does not see the use in stopping them.

28 August: The army starts removing the secondary barricades. Prime Minister Mulroney asks the Warriors to stop the confrontation and remove the barricades themselves.

A meeting is held in Ottawa by the minister responsible for indian affairs, Tom Siddon, and the leaders of the native peoples. Unofficial secret negotiations take place between the ministers of the provincial cabinet and Mohawk leaders in an effort to prevent a violent confrontation between the Warriors and the army. Chief Billy Two River of Kahnawake negotiates directly with the army concerning removal of the barricades blocking access to the Mercier Bridge and the roads leading to it.

The army publishes a videotape presenting its point of view of the situation: it presents the information gathered so far and shows the arsenal used by the two parties.

A group of 500 demonstrators on the Mercier Bridge attack a convoy of about 60 cars transporting Mohawk families preparing to leave Kahnawake, throwing rocks at them: several Mohawks are injured.

29 August: The army goes ahead with the dismantling of the barricades: on the Mercier Bridge, the army gets assistance from the Mohawks, first on route 132 and next on route 138; at Oka, the barricades of Kanesatake are still intact, and nothing has been moved.

Last-minute negotiations take place between the representatives of both levels of government and the Mohawk negotiators.

30 August: Mohawk leaders threaten to stop dismantling the barricades on the Mercier Bridge, accusing the police and government representatives of acting in bad faith concerning the delivery of food and medicines.

The last-minute negotiations break down, the representatives of the Iroquois Confederation saying they are unable to be present at the meeting as expected. Premier Bourassa, for his part, says there will be no negotiations with the government because the Iroquois Confederation had withdrawn, which could mean, in his opinion, that the negotiations had been taken over by radicals. But a representative of the Confederation says they had withdrawn because their work was finished: their mandate was limited to such time as the parties actively negotiated.

The principal points in the conflict that, by this time, should have been the subject of an agreement in principle are:

- a promise of the federal government to create economic programs for Kahnawake and Kanesatake;
- a promise of the provincial government to offer the same compensation to the Indians evacuated as that received by the residents of the neighbourhood; and
- the creation of a committee for the establishment of procedures concerning territorial claims and sovereignty.

Montreal. The Quebec police ask journalists to help them identify the demonstrators who had thrown rocks at the natives who were trying to leave Kahnawake by the Mercier Bridge on 28 August. The Sûreté states, furthermore, that it had obtained a number of visual documents from certain media, but the main media say they never supplied the police with any material whatsoever. For their part, the Mohawk representatives accuse the Sûreté of not having given the members of the convoy sufficient protection.

The National Assembly is called into session in order to adopt a law providing for the lengthening of autoroute 30; this route would offer a way of avoiding the Kahnawake reserve.

31 August: The dismantling of the barricades near Kahnawake is making good progress, but the discussions continue as to the dismantling of those at Kanesatake (Oka).

Chief Joe Norton says that the negotiators are in agreement on 15 different points of contention, but there is still disagreement concerning the administration of justice and especially the matter of the jurisdiction of the Sûreté du Québec on Indian territory.

Light airplanes are seen landing and leaving the Kahnawake reservation.

1 September: The army undertakes the dismantling of the barricades at Oka (Kanesatake) after a report that Chief Francis Jacob and his son were beaten by a group of Warriors.

2 September: The army dismantles the last barricade at Kanesatake on route 344, as well as the last barricade at Kahnawake.

3 September: Despite the dismantling of all the barricades at Kanesatake, the Mohawks are still entrenched in the detoxification centre in Oka, which serves as a refuge and general headquarters.

George Erasmus would like to see a police force composed of the RCMP and native constables used to keep the peace at Oka instead of the Sûreté, in order to lessen the fear of reprisals on the part of the Sûreté police.

A committee is formed at the last minute to meet the crisis. It comprises top representatives of the armed forces, the Sûreté du Québec, and the RCMP, its purpose being to decide on a final strategy that would put an end to the siege.

At least three policemen of the Sûreté du Québec pass themselves off as journalists during a visit by the media to territory belonging to the Warriors of Kanesatake. The journalists feel that their safety could have been compromised if the presence of these policemen had been known.

4 September: Premier Bourassa accuses the Mohawks of mounting a propaganda campaign to discredit the Sûreté du Québec.

5 September: The Sûreté tightens its perimeter around Oka in order to prevent any Warriors from escaping.

Indian Affairs Minister Tom Siddon meets a delegation composed of representatives of the Confederation of Six Iroquois Nations and Manitoba MLA Elijah Harper, and is handed three demands:

- free access to the detoxification centre in Kanesatake for the spiritual leaders of the Mohawk community;
- a widening of the military perimeter; and
- the return of the two governments to the negotiation table.

The army withdraws some of its heavy equipment that is close to Kahnawake, in an effort to reduce its visibility.

The leader of the Liberal opposition at Ottawa, Jean Chrétien, in his first intervention in the matter, asks the police authorities to temporarily suspend their activities against the Warriors 'to allow everyone to get out of the conflict with dignity.' By this time, the Quebec government has already spent close to $3.7 million on relocating the people directly affected by the crisis.

7 September: After almost two months, the Mercier Bridge is re-opened. The army warns journalists who are within the Warriors' territory that they stay there at their own risk and that remaining there could place them in danger.

In answer to Mr Chrétien, Solicitor General of Canada Pierre Cadieux declares that the siege can only be terminated by the arrest of the Warriors involved. Chief Joe Norton of Kahnawake announces that the Mohawks have asked for an injunction in federal court ordering the armed forces off the reservation.

Army headquarters submits a proposal for the surrender of the Warriors:

- They must put down their arms and be placed under guard by the military authorities;.
- They will be taken to an area under military guard until such time as a final decision is made concerning them. Their protection and safety will be guaranteed by the army. First, they will be identified, then liberated or charged at the discretion of the Sûreté du Québec. Those who are charged will remain under guard by the army until their release by the competent court.

The Warriors reject the army's proposal, stating that it is absolutely unacceptable and there is simply no question of their surrendering to the Sûreté du Québec. A Quebec government document, obtained by a journalist at Radio-Canada, shows that the council of ministers had known since 21 June 1989 that a crisis was brewing at Oka and that at all costs the Sûreté du Québec should not be called upon to intervene.

According to Canadian and American police intelligence services, most of the Warriors entrenched at Kanesatake come from the State of New York.

8 September: A confrontation between soldiers and Warriors within the Mohawk perimeter of Kanesatake during the night results in the hospitalization of a Mohawk.

9 September: The federal minister of justice, Kim Campbell, states that Ottawa will not negotiate any form of amnesty for the Warriors of Oka.

10 September: Indian Affairs Minister Tom Siddon meets with the chiefs of the Assembly of First Nations at an emergency meeting in Ottawa. The minister urges the leaders to demand that the Warriors give up their arms.

The hospitalized Warrior is now held in detention by the army at the military base in Farnham, which has become the provincial detention centre by decree of the Quebec government.

Two Peacekeepers of Kahnawake have been arrested by army soldiers and accused by the Sûreté of possession of a weapon (their service rifles), thus violating an agreement by the Peacekeepers not to carry a weapon outside the reservation.

11 September: The government of Quebec rejects the nine-point peace plan of the Warriors for their surrender. The Warriors, among other things, demand the setting up of a mixed commission involving representatives of the governments of Ottawa and Quebec, the Iroquois Confederation, and human-rights organizations.

The European Parliament maintains that 'Canada had unjustifiably confiscated Mohawk territory in order to extend a golf course.'

15 September: The army formulates a different proposal for the surrender of the Warriors, but it remains a secret.

All telephone lines of the Warriors' general headquarters, including those of the journalists, with the exception of one, are cut by the army and the Sûreté du Québec. The only line not cut is the direct line between the Warriors' headquarters and the military base at Long-Point. Both the army and the Sûreté had obtained the authorization to cut the telephone lines because of an accusation before the Quebec Superior Court that the Warriors had been using these lines to plot against public order.

The Sûreté du Québec seizes journalistic material (cassettes and film).

Representatives of the Canadian Association of Journalists and the Professional Federation of Journalists of Quebec denounce the shutting down of the cellular telephone lines, which they consider a restriction of civil liberties, and in particular, of freedom of the press.

16 September: The Mohawks of Kahnawake serve the army with an eviction notice from the Confederation of Six Nations.

The army is given 'carte blanche' to bring discussions with the Warriors to a successful conclusion.

Châteauguay. Some 150 white residents of the 'Solidarity' movement march in the streets to demand greater surveillance by the Sûreté in Châteauguay around the Kahnawake reservation.

17 September: The discussions continue between the army and the Warriors, but none of these telephone exchanges has leaked out.

A federal court judge rejects the request of an injunction submitted by the Mohawks of Kahnawake declaring the presence of the army illegal.

18 September: A violent confrontation takes place at Kahnawake between Mohawks and the military during a joint operation by the army and the Sûreté du Québec. Close to 100 persons are injured. This operation, carried out on the basis of a search warrant, makes possible the seizure of 47 weapons.

One of the Mohawk negotiators, Bob Antone, declares that a wave of civil disobedience could take place among the country's native peoples if the siege is not resolved by a promise to negotiate the question of territorial claims and sovereignty. The negotiations come to grief over the concept of a Mohawk nation. The Mohawks assert that they will not abandon their position as long as a process of political negotiation on the future of the Mohawk nation has not been started.

19 September: The brigadier-general of the army gives the Warriors an ultimatum: 'there is nothing to clarify and from now on all discussions will concern the military offer of disengagement.'

22 September: The Sûreté du Québec proposes the creation of a temporary police force to maintain order at Kanesatake. It would be composed of about 20 native and non-native policemen placed under the authority of the Sûreté du Québec.

26 September: The Warriors and persons entrenched in the detoxification centre at Kanesatake give themselves up to the military police.

The Mohawks of Kahnawake block the Mercier Bridge a second time: the army has to intervene.

The journalists who were entrenched with the Mohawks in Kanesatake are told by the army that they could face criminal charges for having participated in a riot.

Two photographers are arrested at Oka during the Mohawk surrender for interfering with the work of the police, but no charge is laid (their equipment also would have been seized).

27 September: Public Safety Minister Sam Elkas still says he does not know who gave the order to the Sûreté du Québec to intervene on 11 July.

Premier Bourassa promises to hold a public inquiry into the crisis and to keep the armed forces in Quebec as long as the safety of every citizen is not guaranteed.

13

Policing: From the Belly of the Whale

CHRISTOPHER BRAIDEN

FIRST WORD

A few words about myself to provide a backdrop for this paper. I am fifty-three years of age. I have been in policing for thirty years. Getting in wasn't easy. I first tried in Ireland where I grew up, but was rejected because I couldn't speak Irish. I moved to England and tried to join the London Metropolitan Police. They rejected me because I have a finger missing. I came to Canada and applied to the Edmonton Police Department. They too rebuffed me because I'm colour-blind. (Today, I get to park in the handicapped zone!) Undaunted I applied in 1962 to the town of Jasper Place, which was a separate community contiguous to Edmonton at the time. The chief, Rodney Stevenson, God rest his soul, interviewed me on Friday afternoon and I started work the following Monday – without uniform or training. In 1964, Edmonton expanded and absorbed Jasper Place and its employees. You might say I got in the back door.

Perhaps my unorthodox entry into policing was a portent of things to come. From the very start I have been at odds with the xenophobia and senselessness of conventional policing. There is a debilitating bitchiness throughout the service. I encountered the same apathy in the provincial and federal civil service whilst on secondments to both. Being forced to perform mindless functions on a daily basis does that to people. When there is a universal predetermined way of doing something, people will park their brains and function robotically. The demise of the communist system proved that.

My first clash with the police culture was when I tangled with a sergeant who tried to convince me that punching a wife was not the same as punching a stranger. His rationale was, 'You don't make a family problem a police problem.' This seemed odd to me. I presumed that human problems were our business. In my defence, I pointed out that there were no categories of puncher and punchee in the criminal code. He angrily countered that it would be pointless to charge the puncher in a family assault because the punchee would probably refuse to testify at trial. When I pointed out that we seemed to be able to convict murderers even though the victim never testifies I was really in trouble. From that point on I was labelled. Early in life I discovered that the pack doesn't like it when one strays. I have never liked packs. I don't think much of the psychology of sheep. I believe what Sean O'Casey said in his autobiography: 'You can't put a rope around the neck of an idea; you cannot put it up against the wall and riddle it with bullets.' I was soon to learn that the police culture prized deference. Free thought was a ticket to nowhere. Sadly, submission to the myth that rank or title confers wisdom and knowledge is still the norm. I believe that people who don't think for themselves don't think at all. That single issue goes to the heart of the malaise that afflicts conventional policing. It must change.

WHAT THE PAPER IS ABOUT

In this paper I will describe the policing problems facing contemporary society as I see them, present what I believe are the solutions to those problems, and then describe how we went about implementing those solutions in Edmonton. I do not want to regurgitate what scholars and researchers have already discovered and presented on the subject. Researchers, by training, are question-focused. My aim is to present answers. I will talk honestly and openly about policing from the inside looking out so as to provide a unique insight that remains hidden to the external scrutineer. At times my comments will seem harsh. Sometimes one must be cruel to be kind, but if we are genuinely interested in doing what is right in the interests of community welfare, we will work through the pain. Policing has been very good to me. I arrived in Canada as an immigrant with eleven dollars in my pocket. Today my family and I enjoy a comfortable lifestyle. I have the Edmonton Police Service and the citizens of our city to thank for that. As well, I have two sons who plan on police careers after university. I want to contribute my bit to prepare the way so that they become peace officers instead of law-enforcement officers and so they serve in a healthier intellectual environment than I did. My singular objective is to help policing move from where it is to where it needs to go to catch up with contemporary society. I want to help policing return to its true mandate. In order to do that I must talk straight.

So let us start.

THE PROBLEM

The beginning of wisdom is to call things by their right name.
– Chinese proverb

Today we speak in clichés. I don't like clichés. They breed mental indolence and can wipe out years of thought. I believe in calling things by their right name. I think policing is screwed up and that it needs to be fixed. Cliché policing won't get it done. Over the past several decades cliché policing has been the in-thing. There has been zone policing and team policing, proactive and reactive policing, hard and soft policing. In recent times there has been great hype around community-based and problem-oriented policing, yet few agencies have progressed past changing the signs on doors. Having travelled the continent and beyond extensively over the past five years I can state confidently that convention has barely budged. Meanwhile, society races exponentially ahead while policing marks time insisting that society hold back to its pace.

As evidence of what I say, witness the closing of ranks by the Winnipeg Police Department following the J.J. Harper killing several years ago. Witness the demonstrations in Montreal by hundreds of police officers who marched against their chief because he had the audacity to admit to the public that police screw-ups had led to the death of an innocent person. Witness the work-to-rule and baseball-cap infantile behaviour of members of the Metropolitan Toronto Police Force in rebellion against the requirement that they fill in a few lines on a form each time they draw their firearm, claiming that police lives would be endangered in the process. Witness the unruly march by thousands of police officers in New York railing against the suggestion that they be answerable to the people who pay their salaries – the citizens of New York. The Rodney King beating in Los Angeles and the subsequent Christopher Commission investigation, the recent beating death of a person by police officers in Detroit while fellow officers stood by, and the even more recent beating of a motorist (who turned out to be an undercover police officer) in Nashville simply drive the point deeper that many in policing presume they live in a world not answerable or accountable to anyone but themselves. Sergeant Stacey Koon, one of the officers involved in the Rodney King incident, revealed much in an interview with *Law Enforcement News* in October 1992. When asked to describe his mandate, he said that he was a law-enforcement officer – the key word being force!

What started out as consent policing, a public institution entrusted with a peacekeeping mandate on behalf of the community, has been bent into a heavy-handed law-enforcement job. The human animal has a compulsion to makes thing over in its own likeness if allowed to. We see this compulsion manifest itself every day in politics, the civil service, the criminal-justice system, education, and medicine. All are monopolies of the public dollar. In such a work environment, drift from cause is assured. Put as simply as I can say it, policing has become what police(men) want it to be. This has happened because few police officers, anywhere at any rank, know from whence they came. They know nothing of the original mandate of consent policing or even what the term means.

After thirty years on the inside I have come to the conclusion that policing is cultist, functioning more upon myth than reality. Within, allegiance is to the cloth. The notion of public service is a foreign thought to most. For many, the trappings of the myth are far more attractive than the reality of the vocation because, done right, policing is a vocation. Unfortunately, for too many it is just a job with a hoped-for pension (Guth, this volume). The trappings of conventional policing connote a particularly acute image, that of a warlike mission (Bittner 1974) with flashy uniforms and brightly painted cars loaded with gadgetry racing about with lights and sirens flashing. The term paramilitary is routinely used to describe the conventional model, but this military model needs an enemy to legitimize its existence. The dominant presumption is that the role of police is to 'ride herd' on the public to keep them in line. For many the uniform connotes power, not service. Witness the wave of new cop shows on television. They present a portrait of policing that appeals to the egocentrist – and appals the altruist. Based upon my thirty years' experience, nineteen of which were spent directly on front-end operational work, it is the wrong portrait. I am convinced that the dominant imagery has attracted – and continues to attract in spite of the hype around how well-educated today's recruits are – personalities that use the office of constable as a vehicle for their ego. Because imagery works both ways, ironically we are attracting the wrong kind of person and turning off the right one. Conventional policing appeals to a personality type drawn to the law-enforcement function and repulses a personality type more suited to the broader peacekeeping vocation.

CULTURE – AROUND HERE, HERE'S HOW WE DO THINGS

All organizations live two lives; there is the structural life – and then there is the culture. The structure is formal and represents the theory of what is *supposed* to happen. Culture is informal and represents the reality of what *actually* does happen. Make no mistake about it, it is the culture that runs things. The Oxford dictionary defines culture as 'a socially accepted set of values and practices.' That is too refined for me. Here is my definition of culture: 'Around here, here's how we do things.' The incidents in the various cities described above were demonstrations of the culture of those police organizations in action. They reveal the pack mentality in action. For me the most significant contributing factor in the Rodney King beating that triggered the cultural response was the helicopter overhead with spotlight shining and an audience of police officers, especially from other agencies. Simply put, it was show time; a time to make a reputation within the culture.

For those who will say I am wrong, listen to the chatter on a police radio or read the pidgin slang of MDTs. Check out the banter when a bunch of cops go for a beer. Read the Rodney King or J.J. Harper reports. For those who think I am referring only to the grunts of policing, wander around the display area at a typical police chiefs' conference and check out the hardware for sale. Check out the advertising in most police periodicals. One could be excused for thinking they were reading *Soldier of Fortune*. The manufacturers of this hardware pay good money to know where police chiefs' heads are at. Too often they are right. The culture is at the root of the worst problems in policing. That culture is at odds with the mandate of consent policing. But it is not alone. There are other contributing factors.

THE IMPENDING CRISIS

> We cannot walk before we toddle,
> but we may toddle much too long
> if we embrace a lovely Model
> that's consistent, clear – and wrong.
> – Kenneth Boulding

David Bayley, a personal friend, in a recent monograph on policing in Canada, wrote: 'Policing in Canada is not in crisis. Crime and drugs are not out of control.' I disagree strongly with David's conclusion. His definition of 'not out of control' means that Toronto and Calgary are not as crime-ridden and murderous as New York and Los Angeles. Some comparison indeed – Canada only has the second-highest reported crime rate in Western society. But surely out-of-control crime and drugs is not the only measure of impending crisis. It wasn't out-of-control crime or drugs that brought down Chiefs of Police Darryl Gates in Los Angeles or Herb Stephen in Winnipeg. It was an absence of leadership. In both cases, it was prolonged neglect of internal danger signals coupled with an obsession with one's personal external image. From beer with grunts to martinis with mandarins, so to speak. In both cases the catastrophe that followed was precipitated by a spontaneous individual incident over which neither executive had any personal control. Invariably it is a single, spontaneous incident that commences the unravelling. The independent inquiry that is sure to follow completes the downfall by exposing the neglect, lassitude, and cultism that drives the day-to-day workings of the organization. The Montreal and Toronto police demonstrations are further evidence that Bayley may have spoken too soon. I am convinced that Canadian policing is indeed on the verge of crisis, but the motive power of that crisis will not be crimes or drugs.

Every time I think about the problems facing policing the old adage 'We have met the enemy, and he is us' comes back to haunt me. I am convinced that the primary factor fuelling the looming crisis in policing is the collective inability of the current senior officer corps (I am one myself), with rare exceptions, to lead policing out of the fog of cultism and myth that is the legacy of the closed-shop 'everyone through the front door' history and xenophobic culture.

To compound the problem, even if some flair and originality survives the acculturation process, by the time we reach the higher ranks, more often than not, we are in the twilight of our careers, so that whatever passion and originality we once possessed are on the wane. Also, when people have been around each other for a quarter-century, collective intellectual boredom sets in. In such a state of ennui people are more apt to be cynics than champions, crotchety than creative. Most senior officers got where they are by being good followers. The dilemma we face is this. While turbulent contemporary society has been screaming out for free-thinking leaders of people, conventional policing has been churning out obedient systems managers. At a time when leaders are needed as never before, conventional police culture has produced a mind-set more suited to follow than lead, while at the same time prohibiting the lateral entry of diverse talents. Put simply, when the times are calling for a 'run-and-shoot' offence, we are overloaded with drop-back passers and lumbering fullbacks.

There are two reasons for the dilemma. I call them the Winejug and Monopoly factors.

THE WINEJUG FACTOR

The un-examined life is not worth living.
– Socrates

Once upon a time there was a farmer who had a pumpkin patch. He went out in the spring of the year and, noticing a little pumpkin growing on a vine, idly kicked it into the neck of a winejug that was lying nearby. He thought no more about it until he returned to the patch in that autumn. Lo and behold, the pumpkin had grown up to the full size of the winejug and of course had taken on its unique shape. He thought that was cute, and so he cut it off, took it home, and set it on the veranda of his house. Sometime later, his son who was a teacher came over to visit and, spotting the pumpkin, asked his dad how it came to be. Dad told him. The son asked if he could take the pumpkin with him and the dad asked for what purpose. The son said, 'Well, I want to show the kids at school what happens to them when they allow their minds – and ultimately their lives – to be moulded and stultified by either people or things around them. I want to show them what happens when they set predestined boundaries on what it is they can become in life.'

Mind-set is what I'm talking about, and we all have one, like it or not. Mind-set influences everything in our lives. It dictates our thoughts, which in turn dictate our actions. Our lives become what our thoughts make them. We are not what we think we are – but what we think, we are. Dwell on this for a bit, for there is much to it. The very essence of this idea was captured by Ortega y Gasset, who put it this way: 'Tell me what you think about and I'll tell you who you are.'

What does the typical police bureaucrat think about? Well, research and experience reveals that this person is ultra-conservative, process-oriented, and preoccupied with *control* rather than *creation* – control of people rather than creation of solutions to community problems. Good work doesn't generate policy; screw-ups do. Therefore, the message is perpetually negative. Because we cannot trust everyone, we trust no one. Centralized command likes one thing of a type, and so policing is buried in blanket rules of behaviour (they are even called general orders) generated by the screw-ups of the most inept and dishonest among us. Everyone is held back to the speed of these few, and form dominates. Policing goes out of its way to hire the brightest people we can find and immediately tells them to follow orders. The upshot of it all is that people chain their brain to the gate on the way in, function through their day, and collect their brain on the way out. The 'winejug' leading policing today is the wrong one. That is why policing has remained relatively unexamined for decades.

THE MONOPOLY FACTOR

If oxen and lions had hands and could paint, then oxen would paint God in the likeness of an ox and lions would paint God in the likeness of a lion.

– Zenophanes

All bureaucracies feeding on the public dollar suffer from a congenital disease; it is called monopoly. William Whyte said, 'Monopoly is business at the end of its journey.' But it is the journey that keeps an enterprise rooted to its fundamental cause by focussing on effectiveness. Policing hadn't had to make the journey. We got a free ride because we are the only ticket in town. Free enterprise gets paid for pleasing customers; monopolies get paid out of a budget. Peter Drucker said that all monopolies concentrate on efficiency at the expense of effectiveness. Efficiency is doing things right; effectiveness is doing the right things. It naturally follows that no amount of efficiency can replace a lack of effectiveness. If we are doing the wrong thing, it matters little how well we do it. As Drucker explains it: 'There is nothing so senseless as doing efficiently that which need not be done at all.' Efficiency locks on function; function locks on the status quo. Dwell on the status quo too long and you have obsolescence.

The Winejug and Monopoly factors are compounded by one another. Today we live in a mass-media world. Mass media breed mass thought, which breeds mass behaviour. Nike cannot afford to pay Michael Jordan $15 million a year if only a few hundred people buy Air Jordans. Today's mass-media world is only a more sophisticated version of Hitler's propaganda machine. The entire advertising industry exists upon a single principle – to get the masses to see what the advertiser sees. As a consequence, modern society's most powerful influence, the mass media, condition us to park our brain and follow. Many within policing do just that.

The conventional model of policing is obsolete for two reasons. It has bastardized the true mandate of consent policing; even then it doesn't achieve what it has structured itself to achieve. Consider these figures. In the ten years 1975–84, the Canadian population increased by 11 per cent. In that same period the number of police officers increased by 30 per cent, the crime rate by 22 per cent, and the incarceration rate by 52 per cent. In their frustration with the failure of convention, the public demand more of the same. In a Gallup poll in 1970, 58 per cent of Canadians interviewed said they felt the criminal-justice system was too lenient. A similar poll in 1983 showed that the dissatisfaction level had risen to 80 per cent (Stuebing; 1991). The truth is that the entire criminal-justice system has fallen prey to the monopoly disease as it was exposed by Chief Justice (as he then was) Warren Burger in 1985. He said: 'The entire criminal justice system – judges, lawyers, law teachers and police officers – have become so mesmerized by the courtroom drama, we have forgotten our fundamental mandate – healers of conflict.'

The structure of conventional policing must be creatively destroyed and rebuilt around a new culture. As things stand, we too often have people in the wrong places doing the wrong things. Conventional policing because of its obsession with law enforcement, has locked onto the criminal-justice system as a baby clings to its mother. Unfortunately, that system too has taken on a life of its own independent from its original mandate. Both were intended to serve the best interests of the community. Today they serve the best interests of those on the inside. In the process, we have locked ourselves into an élitist mind-set and locked out the people we serve. This drift from the original goals of policing is compounded by the driving force of our system of justice, the tradition of common law. With its reverence for precedent it is perpetually looking backwards. The regard for precedent is sacred, therefore, and direction is sought not from a logic dictated by contemporary society, but from history. I too am a lover of history, but for a pragmatic purpose. George Bernard Shaw said, 'Life must be lived forward – but it can only be understood backwards.' History is fact. It happened. By reading and understanding it, we can better prepare and plan for the future. However, reverence for tradition must serve the future, not hold it ransom. 'We do it this way because we have done it this way for four hundred years' rings hollow in the light of what we know now about our system. For that reason, I would abolish jury trials across the board. They have become a contradiction of their original mandate. They are redundant.

THE SOLUTION: TIME FOR A MINDSET TRANSPLANT

Radical change in the way we do business will only follow radical change in the way we organize ourselves.

– Tom Peters

The primary task is to de-cultify and de-mythologize the conventional police model. To achieve this, the heads of the brass must be retooled before we worry about the feet of the grunts. Be forewarned that rhetoric and slogans alone will change nothing. We must get beyond good intentions and slick acronyms to courageous, radical, fundamental change. I don't claim to know the secret of success for anything in life, but I know the secret of failure. Try to please everyone. Any organization intent upon meaningful structural change in order to create a new culture had better expect many noses to be out of joint.

The first order of business is a mind-set transplant throughout the senior officer corps. This requires that we redefine our concept of leadership and accept that real leadership is needed at all levels. Ben Franklin had it right when he told his fellow patriots as they prepared to revolt: 'Gentlemen, we had better all hang together or most assuredly we will hang separately.' Police leaders, commissioners, and politicians must work together and have the same target. Personal agendas must not get in the way. The people who control the moneybags must pay for the right things and refuse to pay for the wrong things. There must be a moratorium on 'stuff' acquisition. Surely by now we have discovered that we cannot buy quality policing. An enlightened system of policing must become a mentality first of all. Nice words, but where to start? First, there must be leadership, vision, and – perhaps most important of all – enthusiasm.

LEADERSHIP: WHAT IS IT?

There is no shortage of leadership among us. Every generation of every race and culture gets its fair share. There is a twofold problem, however. Leadership is rarely found where we expect it to be – attached to high position or title – and so we presume it doesn't exist. Where it does exist, more often than not those who have it don't know it. If the only thing generating respect for a person is their position or title, you have an *official*. If esteem attaches to their name, you have a *leader*. Title conveys authority; esteem bestows power. The two are not the same.

In his book *Journey to the East*, Herman Hesse presents an allegory about leadership. A group of people who have achieved great success in the business world set out on an expedition. Leo, a native, joins the expedition as a servant to the rest. In addition to caring for their every need, Leo tells stories around the campfire at night, listens to the troubles of all, and becomes, with the passage of time, a confidant to them. Although only a servant, Leo becomes the one upon whom the rest depend for everything. He is the glue that holds the group together. The expedition has been very successful; morale is high, and there is great cooperation by all. One morning, they awake to find Leo gone. They try to carry on without him, but in short order the group splits into factions, they begin to fight among themselves, and eventually the expedition grinds to a halt. Without realizing it, they had become so dependent upon Leo they could not function without him. Leo had become their informal leader. One fellow in the group sets out to find Leo. Several years later he does, and discovers Leo in his original role; as chief and guiding spirit of a great race of people who love and respect him. The moral of the story is that leadership is rarely found where we expect it to be. It is a rare find at the top. True leadership often goes about its business – unnoticed – on the edges. All true leaders, whether captaining a hockey team or running a giant corporation, have one common trait – a devotion to the welfare of others. A leader is a servant as a leader.

MANAGING IS NOT LEADING

The leadership drought in policing exists because we have been very good at developing systems managers but not so good at creating leaders. Managing is not leading. I will explain the difference this way. I am colour-blind. No matter how hard I try, I cannot see the difference between certain colours. It is the same with intellectual eyesight. *Some people see. Some people see what they are shown. Some people cannot see at all.* It is just the way of things. Leaders have the innate ability to *see new things*. Managers can only *see what has been shown before*. Managers like things *known*; leaders seek out the *unknown*. Managers *control and contain*; leaders *create and liberate*. Managers like *followers*; leaders champion *free-thinkers*. Managers *administer systems*; leaders *inspire people*. Managers are *process driven*; they like *efficiency* and so jump all over the place. Leaders are *cause driven*; they focus on *effectiveness* because they have constancy of purpose. If we are doing the wrong things, then it matters little how well we do them. Managers *distrust* and so rely on *systems* to control. Leaders *trust* and so rely on *values* to inspire. Perhaps the most fundamental difference between managers and leaders is this: *managers* think *it is their job to run the organization well*. Thus, more often than not they give themselves ulcers trying to know and control everything. *Leaders* know *it is their job to make sure the organization is run well by others*. Leaders concentrate on having the right people in the right places, doing the right things.

LEADERSHIP QUALITIES

Leadership is a human quality. It has nothing to do with position or profile, title or trappings. The qualities found in leaders are many and varied, but one is constant and irreplaceable. Character. Character is society's greatest need – and its greatest safeguard. Too bad we cannot test for it like steroids or manufacture it in the form of an injection. No combination of other talents can replace the absence of character. People of character won't let themselves down because they have a high personal standard of integrity. By definition, they won't let others down. The *definition* of leadership is simple: *Going out ahead to show the way*. The *test* to determine whether one is a leader is just as simple: *Do those who follow become better servants of others?* Mother Teresa is a tremendous example of leadership. Though old, frail, and humble, she has inspired thousands of professional people – many leaders in their own right – to 'down tools' on their own careers and aspirations in order to follow in her footsteps.

LEADERSHIP – FIRST AMONG EQUALS

Leaders don't choose themselves, followers do. The only true power a leader has is that which is willingly given by those who choose to follow. Leadership is the one thing we cannot have unless we are willing to give it away. The Romans, when their empire was at its strongest, had it right with their First Among Equals system of governance – a team of leaders with a common title but singular esteem for one, the principal leader. Principal leaders never forget that the only true power they possess is the freely given esteem of the other leaders. The other leaders may temporarily assume the lead position from time to time, but all the while everyone knows who the principal leader is. There is no need for a sign on the door! In such an environment, everyone thinks *lead.* While all share the leadership role with the principal leader, they do not abdicate their responsibilities. A 'We' mindset develops.

MANAGEMENT – BY STOMPING AROUND

The CEO model of management predominates across North American policing. The chief of police sits enthroned atop a pyramid of ranked senior officers. This model accepts the myth of an omnipotent supreme leader known as 'The Boss.' It creates the delusion that all leadership resides in that one lofty position. The natural consequence is that all other ranks think *follow*. Inevitably these followers abdicate their responsibility to lead at their own level and blame everything on 'the boss' when things go wrong. A we–they mind-set dominates. The CEO model is like a giant tree that blots out the sun and rain, and so no other trees can grow underneath. Few senior officers think of themselves as leaders. They don't see themselves as part of the problem or the solution. Everyone defers to – and everything is left to – the chief. In such a culture chiefs hear only echoes of their own opinion. Everyone looks for – and sees – the same things. There is no intellectual diversity; consensus rules and so when things go wrong, everyone gets blind-sided. And because it is human to choose in our own image, *managerial inbreeding* develops and the process perpetuates itself. You can't get a racehorse by mating two cart-horses. Over time, *bureaucratic sclerosis* develops and whatever leadership existed is soon cleansed.

I call this Management by Stomping Around. Everyone is so busy looking up the derrière of those above they blindly stomp all over the very people they are supposed to be leading. Of course the front end of the organization, in this case the police officer on the street, is looking up too, and in the process walking all over the people we are all supposed to be serving. These heads need to be turned around. The pyramid must be turned on its head so that each level is looking out for the welfare of those below and in the process making new leaders. Eventually, leadership inbreeding will replace managerial inbreeding.

But there is an even more practical reason for turning the pyramid on its head. Layers of managers contribute little to the cause of any organization. Recently, John Reed, CEO of Citibank in the United States, after reluctantly axing five vice-presidents and six hundred managers worldwide, found that in fact their leaving had no ill effect on company revenues. Reed said: 'We discovered that they didn't make any contribution. I don't mean they were bad people. They just didn't add anything.'

CREATING NEW HEROES

Leaders naturally seek out ability in others. When they find it they have the courage to liberate it. Leaders seem to have the peace of mind to champion the cause of others. The great leaders of history were invariably mentors to others. Eugene Debs was such a person. He helped found the American Railway Union towards the end of the last century. Once the union was up and running the workers wanted Debs to become their first president. This is the advice he gave them: 'I am not your leader. I don't want you to follow me, or anyone else. If you are looking for a Moses to lead you out of the wilderness, you will stay right where you are. I wouldn't lead you into the promised land, even if I could, because if I could lead you in, someone else could lead you out.'

Debs knew that these people needed to develop leadership within themselves. He knew the only way they could do that was to become servants of those who would follow, thereby perpetuating the process and entrenching their achievement. Lao Tzu, the great philosopher of antiquity, displayed the same wisdom as Debs when he said, 'When the great leader's work is done the people say, We did it ourselves.'

VISION

> They can – because they think they can.
>
> – Virgil

The first step in the good management of our business or personal life is to ask the question, 'Where do you think you're going?' No matter how long it takes to find the answer to that question, find it we must before we move on. Getting the question right the first time invariably points us in the direction of the answer. If we rush off in search of answers too precipitously, we increase the chances of ending up at the wrong destination.

I think vision is best described in the little story of Michelangelo and the young boy. One day as Michelangelo commenced to sculpt a large block of marble a little boy sat down to watch. The lad came every day thereafter, until the artist had finished his work and a beautiful statue of David had emerged. This prompted the lad to ask, 'How did you know he was in there?' The great lesson of this little story concerns vision. I'm sure Michelangelo didn't know that particular statue of David was in there when he started his work. At the outset he probably used hammers and chisels and heavy strokes to do the rough work, but as the project progressed, I imagine his instruments became more precise and his strokes more deft.

Vision is having better intellectual eyesight than others – being able to see that which is still unseeable by others. By vision, I do not mean a Vision of the Month Club whereby the vision keeps changing after each conference! Intellectual acuity is like all other human talents; some people have more of it than others. Vision, by itself, will get little done. The world is full of unfulfilled visionaries who didn't have the energy to give their vision wheels. Vision must be supported by the daily banging away at a bureaucracy that is sure to resent any efforts to move it, just like an old cat asleep on a chair. A little nudge won't make much happen. You have to pick it up by the scruff of the neck, open the door, and throw it outside in order to bring about significant change in its behaviour. That is exactly what is needed to move conventional policing to where it needs to go. This effort will require courage and confidence; most of all, the courage of one's convictions to do what is right in the face of castigation and ostracism by one's peers. And it will require enthusiasm.

ENTHUSIASM

> Nothing great is ever achieved without enthusiasm.
> – Ralph Waldo Emerson

Enthusiasm is a rare find within police management. The first order of business for leadership is to create enthusiasm for the cause. Leadership and vision are wonderful things. Down through the centuries, tremendous feats have been accomplished by people who possessed them, but alone they are not enough. They need fuel to drive them. Michelangelo's talent would have achieved little without his enthusiasm for the work. It is not technology that puts people in space, it is enthusiasm for the task. For me, enthusiasm is imagination over intellect; it is instinct over second-guessing; it is the kid in us winning out over the adult. I think G.B. Shaw described enthusiasm best this way: 'Some people see things as they are and ask, "why." Others see things as they are not and ask, "why not?"' Most important of all, enthusiasm is contagious.

THE CHIEF'S PRIMARY AUDIENCE

I must dwell here before I move on, because the point I want to make is such an important part of the whole. It is a touchy subject that needs to be discussed because quality leadership is critical to all else. In my view, too many police chiefs spend too much of their time focused on the wrong audience. More than a few become recluses from the people they are supposed to be leading.

How many times have we heard about the workaholic who puts in long hours at the office, is 100 per cent loyal to the company and the life of the party with the guys – but to his wife and children he is a stranger. So it is with some chiefs of police. They're so riveted on the external audience, they become cowed by the media and overawed by their lofty position and the social strata in which they now move. This is a heady change of environment for most; some are in over their heads. As a consequence, their agenda becomes personal. Pandering overshadows doing what is right. Eventually, they turn their backs on the people who can either make – or break – them. Such executives are fundamentally insecure, lack confidence, and so are easily intimidated by politicians and bureaucrats whom they come to regard as their absolute masters. It happened to Darryl Gates in Los Angeles and it happened to Herb Stephen in Winnipeg, and they are gone. It didn't happen to Bob Lunney, the current chief in Ontario's Peel Region, who is still a highly respected police chief after nearly two decades. This shifting of agendas is a fatal error, not only for the police chief whose scam will eventually be exposed, but for the public who will be the ultimate loser. It happens because such executives have no constancy of purpose. Their silent goal is to ingratiate themselves with those they see as their political masters. As a consequence, they are all over the place, focussing on 'look good' issues.

I must be very clear on this point. I realize that what I am saying here at first glance could seem contrary to the idea of community-based policing, a cause to which I have devoted much energy. Some may interpret what I have said to mean that the chief should pander instead to the inner audience by catering to their creature comforts. Nothing could be further from the truth. Many grunts need a boot in the ass. The chief must work closely with his board of police commissioners and, of necessity, rub shoulders often with politicians and bureaucrats, but these people must not be the his *primary* audience. My position is based on the clear lesson of the ages – that the quality of any product is a function of human commitment. That lesson was stated so simply by the manager of an automobile plant, who said, 'I'll tell you all you need to know about quality and I'll tell it to you in one sentence. The person in control of quality in this outfit is the guy on the loading dock who decides not to throw the —— box into the back of the truck.' Such are business's moments of truth.

THE MOMENTS OF TRUTH OF POLICING

During the three years I commanded South Division of the Edmonton Police Service, I received about three hundred letters from citizens about the work of my people, good and bad. I read every letter and talked in person or by telephone to as many of those people who would talk to me. I did so to find out what it was that turned people on and off about the way we did things. Not one of those people or letters complained about us not catching the bad guy or not recovering their stolen property. Every one, however, spoke about one or both of two things: caring and trying hard. These people seemed to understand, perhaps better than we in policing do, that what the police – working alone – can do about crime is debatable. They did, however, expect us to *care* about their problems and to *try hard* to do something about it. As things stand, too often we are doing neither. Too often we are throwing the box into the back of the truck.

The chief's *primary* audience must be the internal one, because only that group can deliver the goods to the ultimate customer, the people we serve. Further, the inner audience must know they are the chief's primary audience. The first rule of police management must be that those who do not serve the customer directly must serve those who do. For that very reason, the chief must have the ability to connect with the front end and to be seen as a servant to others himself. If the perception is that the chief is pursuing a personal agenda, that will set the tone for others to do the same. He must set the example for all other managers. The chief must have the confidence and respect of the grunts, so that when he goes out ahead to show the way, they will follow. This requires constancy of purpose and vision. If this confidence and respect is absent, then the media image of the chief will count for little with the folks on the loading dock.

The office of chief of police is apolitical. The chief should be the most politically unattached person in the community. Institutionalized segregation from the *political* and *judicial* arms of government is fundamental to the

Peelian model upon which North American urban policing is based. There must be no sign of cosiness between the elected and enforcement arms of local government. My experience tells me that many politicians and members of the judiciary overestimate their control of police. I have talked with jurists who presume that the sole function of the police is to be an appendage to the criminal-justice system. They are wrong.

A police constable does not swear allegiance to a political or judicial master. To do so would suggest control by these components of the system. Police officers in Canada swear allegiance to the monarch on behalf of all people. The monarch is apolitical. A civil war was fought over that issue. Swearing allegiance to the monarch is a statement that the police are answerable directly to the people through their law, which is made by their representatives. Thus, no authority can tell a constable beforehand which laws to enforce and which not to. The chief of police must exemplify this autonomy from political control. Control of the police by local politicians and their hacks in the United States was the main contributing factor to the massive corruption of policing in the past in that country.

Quite apart from these legal and policy reasons why the workers should be the chief's primary audience, consider the opinions of several high-profile CEOs and consultants in the business world on the topic. Leonard A. Schlesinger and James L. Heskett contributed an article to the *Harvard Business Review* (*HBR*) in September 1991 entitled 'The Service-Driven Service Company.' In it they emphasize the point that front-line service workers must be the primary audience of executives and that the entire service strategy should be designed around this audience. Their reasoning was simple. The boss must serve the person who serves the public. The last person to touch the product is the most important. Tom Peters makes the same point in his book, *Thriving on Chaos*, with this succinct statement: 'The best way for the CEO to put the customer first is to put the employee first.'

Another *HBR* article (December 1988) presents an interview with James R. Houghton, CEO of Corning Inc. Houghton was asked to describe how he allocates time to the various aspects of his work. He first drew up an ideal scenario in which he broke down his workday by the amount of time devoted to the internal and external audiences. In it he allotted 5 to 10 per cent of his time to his board of directors and shareholders and 70 per cent to the internal audience. Houghton then checked his daily diary for 1989 to determine how he had actually spent his working hours during that year. *Seven per cent was devoted to the board of directors and shareholders – 67 per cent was spent working with the internal audience.*

BUILDING BLOCKS

Our todays and yesterdays are the blocks with which we build.
– Søren Kierkegaard

I will now describe how police work must change by describing the building blocks for the future. It is one thing to throw out convention, but quite another to replace it. This chapter describes reconstruction for the future. With the innovations of the past, more often than not it was only *presumed* that the tactics employed would achieve the results expected; we now know that many did not. Evaluation of strategies in policing was non-existent until recent times. For example, it was presumed that rapid response, random patrol, and follow-up investigations by detectives would achieve great things. We now know such faith was misplaced.

I have come to accept certain things in policing as givens, aspects of police work revealed by research and then corroborated by my own experience. Our experience with conventional police practices has taught us much. It is now time to rebuild around these lessons. What follows are some of the revelations of research and experience that were not known to our predecessors but are known to us. They are the building blocks for a new model of urban policing.

The Village in the City

Consider what Plato said about cities 2400 years ago: 'Any ordinary city is, in fact, two cities; one for the rich and one for the poor, each at war with the other. And in either, there are smaller ones. You would make a great mistake if you treated them all alike.' What has changed?

O.W. Wilson, the guru of police management from the forties to the seventies, borrowing from business-management thinking of the day when corporate headquarters controlled everything, centralized all decision-making and control of policing in Chicago in order to combat the rampant corruption he was hired to stamp out. Central to Wilson's management theory was a generic police product: one thing of a type. Although sensible and effective for the times, Wilson's model still dominates today in a society that bears little resemblance to that of the sixties. Conventional policing treats cities as though they have a single personality and a single need. In fact, we have learned that cities are not globs of people but rather collections of 'villages' stuck together, but as unique as if they were villages in the traditional sense. These villages may be created by various factors: economics, culture, ethnicity, demographics, lifestyle, or geography. As a result, they have unique personalities and unique police needs. Logic dictates that the police product accommodate this reality if it is to be community-based. The policing of cities has to be broken down into smaller pieces – from a department-store to a specialty-shop approach, so to speak.

Some Villages Are Sicker Than Others

Experience and research tell us that many villages don't require much policing. In Edmonton, we proved this point to ourselves with our workload analysis in 1987 (153,000 occurrences) and corroborated those findings with our omnibus workload analysis in 1991 (204,000 occurrences). This second analysis gave us snapshots of each of the 273 neighbourhoods in our city by total workload and by 12 different categories of occurrence: residential break-ins, commercial break-ins, family-related, neighbourhood-related, young offenders, drugs, violence, weapons, criminal driving, stolen autos, theft from autos, and false alarms. City-wide maps were created for each occurrence type. We now have a map room. A glance around the walls quickly illustrates the diverse personality of our city.

Fish Where You Are Likely to Catch Something

Certain locations or addresses are spawning grounds for crime, especially violent crime. Professor Ron Clarke at Rutgers University has done much work in this area. When three ingredients come together there will be a lot of crime: a likely target; a motivated offender; an absence of supervision. While it might be impossible to eliminate all the ingredients, if any one can be eliminated or even diminished, crime is likely to decrease. It is like targeting career criminals, only easier. Criminals move around and so it is difficult and expensive to stay with them. It is easier to target a building or location, neither of which move.

Most Work Comes from Steady Customers

Ten per cent of a doctor's patients generate 90 per cent of the work. So it is with policing. A small proportion of the total population consumes most of the time and energy available. The poor and powerless are odds-on favourites to become criminals or victims of crime and so they need police attention far more than the affluent and powerful. Most calls involve continuing problems that are treated as single events, which leads to the next given.

Most Police Work Is Not Lights-and-Siren Stuff

In Edmonton we find consistently that only about 5 per cent of all incoming telephone calls are true emergencies. Thus, with 95 per cent of the work, response time is not critical. The basic conventional strategy is to have everyone deployed in the rapid-response mode, waiting for the big stuff. With this approach police administrators have helped create their primary problem: a public addicted to immediate, doorstep police response to their slightest needs. As a result, response times have become a key measure of police effectiveness. But this strategy is a contradiction in terms. If we promise to get to all calls quickly, we cannot spend much time at any single call, and so the package becomes more important than its contents. Solving problems must replace response times in the psyche of police managers.

The Family Doctor Approach

Conventional policing is built around specialization by function. It needs to be rebuilt around ownership of turf. The degenerative disease of specialization is tunnel vision. Consider the health-care system for comparison purposes.

Specialization by function is like specialization in medicine. Let's use the example of an orthopaedic surgeon specializing in hip replacements, who is very interested in hips but oblivious to the rest of the patient. He works on hips, not people. Once a hip is fixed, the patient is passed on to someone else. Paths are not likely to cross again, and so there is little interest in the patient as a whole person. A 'one-night-stand' relationship occurs. As a consequence, certain talents are honed at the expense of others. Health-care research reveals that few malpractice suits emanate from careless scalpel work. Most are the product of poor bedside manners – usually demeaning treatment of the patient during the hospitalization process.

Contrast the doctor-patient relationship of the hip specialist with that of the family doctor. The chemistry changes dramatically, because the family doctor is responsible for the general health and well-being of the whole patient on a permanent basis. The family doctor treats a group of perpetual customers who happen to live in a particular neighbourhood. The family doctor needs the patient to come back and so she or he must treat them well, or lose them. If one member of a family is mistreated, they might all be lost. Over time, the family doctor comes to know the patient's body very well because he or she treats everything except that which requires emergency or specialist care.

I believe that the bulk of policing needs of an individual, family, or company are best delivered by one police officer they know and trust. For that reason, policing should build its non-emergency delivery system around the family-doctor idea as much as possible. Most good family doctors recognized long ago that they don't control health; such factors as life-style, heredity, smoking, booze, and sitting on our arse in front of the television filling our face with too much food can render the finest doctors in the land impotent. Doctors do attempt to control disease and sickness, but usually only when health has broken down. The good family doctor knows that the practice of medicine must go beyond handing out pills and giving needles. So it is with policing. Most crime is local in nature committed by – and against – locals. The most important tool in dealing with it is local knowledge.

Information – The Lifeblood of Policing

Information is the lifeblood of policing – but ordinary people have a lock on it. Surely it is self-evident that the people who know the most about crime are those who live in the neighbourhoods where most crime occurs. Yet that is where police informally mix with people the least. As proof, the evaluation of our neighbourhood foot patrols in Edmonton in 1989 revealed that motorized patrols spent only 2.4 per cent of their free time with nonpolice people, while foot patrols spent 24 per cent. Success in solving crime is directly related to the amount of time we spend with ordinary people – and away from the police culture.

Ownership: Who Paints a Rented House?

Ownership, whether it be of things, time, or destiny, is a powerful force in the human psyche. Lack of it brought down the Berlin Wall, communism, and the Ceausescus, all in a single weekend – things that the United Nations and NATO, presidents and prime ministers couldn't do over a span of forty years. When two or three people a week tried to get over the Wall, they could be shot. When a million climbed up together, its senselessness was over. A political system that ignores the elementary human issue that people want to have control over their lives will leave half of its national crop in the fields. Farmers who own their land, however humble, don't leave a grain.

There is no intellectual ownership in conventional policing. People are given functions and told how to perform them. And so, like the Soviet farm worker, they leave half their crop in the field. Mark Twain, in his own inimitable way, conveyed the idea this way: 'Almost any man worth his salt would go to war to defend his home, but no one ever heard of a man going to war for his boarding-house.'

The fundamental flaw of socialist doctrine is that it denies the human spirit. So does conventional policing. As Frederick Hertzberg of the University of Utah explained: 'The only way to motivate any person in any workplace is to give them meaningful control over it, and then get out of their way.' People must be given as much intellectual ownership of their work as possible, and then be held responsible for it.

Allegiance Must Shift from the Cloth to the Cause

This might be the toughest nut to crack, but I am convinced that no meaningful change will occur until allegiance shifts from the cloth to the cause. So many other things are tied to this single issue. In many police agencies the structure has become fractured into cliques that are much more concerned with their creature comforts than with any notion of service to the public. It needs to be said that administrators are often more concerned with coddling the troops to smooth the waves of internal dissent at the expense of putting a better product on the street. This will have to change. The conventional model, intentionally or otherwise, has fostered this 'pride in the cloth' mentality by inculcating the 'police family' mind-set. Far more attention is paid to what police wear *on* their heads than to what is *inside* them.

And so to summarize the building blocks, the urban policing model of the future must conceptualize cities as collections of villages, give ownership of individual villages to individual police officers, restructure operations around the family-doctor idea so the specialist becomes a resource to the grunt, with problem-solving as the primary goal of all. It was around these givens that our neighbourhood foot patrol was started up in April 1988.

NEIGHBOURHOOD FOOT PATROL

I was on secondment to the federal solicitor general in Ottawa as a special adviser on policing for the period 1984–6. When I returned home in November 1986, I resolved to do what I could to help change the way we carried on police business in Edmonton. At the time twenty-one constables were assigned to foot patrol in the city core, covering an area of no more than six square blocks. They were formed into squads, headquarters was home to all, and they worked in pairs. In fact, if one constable's partner did not show up for whatever reason, that individual walked with another pair, so that now they were a threesome! These people had no particular job description and did not take calls for service except as a last resort. Their main role was to fly the flag and be seen; otherwise, they could pretty well do their own thing. Of course it was considered a plum assignment – a stepping-stone to the SWAT team – and so many of our best young people worked it.

This unit was under my command, yet I was not allowed to change its role. It was clear to me that we were getting little mileage out of these people, life had become very comfortable for them, and their allegiance was clearly to the needs of the group. It would take them an hour to get out of headquarters in the morning and they would return an hour before quitting time. I presented a written plan to my chief of the day that incorporated the *givens of the work* described above. I intended to use these positions in a very different way. The plan had three components: neighbourhood foot patrol, neighbourhood storefront offices, and neighbourhood liaison committees. My intention was to assign the positions to the twenty-one neediest neighbourhoods throughout the city, wherever they may be, with individual constables assigned to each one so that ownership between the two could take root and allegiance move from the cloth to the cause. My chief disagreed and said that ownership already existed between the constables and their beats. Our definitions of ownership clashed, and so I used an example to make my point.

WHO 'OWNS' THE BIKE?

On my first day back at work after my secondment I noticed a bicycle chained to a post on 96 Street, directly in front of police headquarters. Being November, the bike was covered with snow. I checked it out. The tires were flat and it was obviously stolen or abandoned. I decided to wait and see how long it would take for someone to deal with the bike. I watched it for four months. Sometimes it was facing east, sometimes west. Sometimes it was lying down, other times it was standing against the post. Someone was touching the bike, but no one was doing anything about the problem. Every day it was necessary for these twenty-one beat constables to walk past that bike twice; going to and coming from their beats. Each must have walked past the goddam bike one hundred times – but no one did anything about it. I think I know why.

I can just see it. As each pair of constables leave 'home' to start their shift, upon confronting that confounded bike one more time, Joe thinks to himself, 'Oh what the hell, Pat will take care of it.' Of course Pat is thinking the same thing at the same time and so no one took care of the problem. Because no one constable 'owned' 96 Street, no one constable felt responsible for the bike. All could rationalize that it was someone else's problem and so the bike stayed where it was. When twenty-one people are responsible for something, no one takes ownership for it.

Why do I feel so sure about this? Because I see the same thing occur in our home every day. I have two sons; not bad kids. For years I have watched them step around, over, and sometimes through stuff that belongs to the other, but they would never think to move it. I have seen each of them wash one of two dirty dishes in the sink – because they didn't dirty the other one.

And so I was given permission to plan and implement neighbourhood foot patrol in Edmonton around that simple philosophy. We did a work-load analysis of 153,000 occurrences to determine which neighbourhoods qualified. We sought volunteers from across the organization and received forty-three. Interestingly, not one specialist volunteered. I interviewed all forty-three myself and chose those I felt were best suited to the work. We started with twenty-one beats in April 1988. One constable is assigned to each beat; they are on foot and carry pagers so that neighbourhood residents can contact them directly. Their role is clear: to take care of the policing needs of their neighbourhood themselves in the first instance whenever possible, and when necessary to call in specialized help, not only of the police service but whatever it takes to solve the problem. These constables work out of storefront offices that are staffed by citizen volunteers. They are decentralized and are not part of a specialized unit. The constables work shifts that are dictated by their work and respond to all levels of calls within their neighbourhood. The initiative has been evaluated twice: technically by the Canadian Research Institute for Law and the Family (CRILF) through funding from the federal solicitor general; and in the form of a documentary written by a local writer, Katherine Koller, as told through the eyes of the people who 'consume' and 'produce' the product, the people in the neighbourhood and the constable on the beat. Both evaluations demonstrate clearly that a common ownership does develop between neighbourhood and police officer and that, between them, they solve many more problems than conventional policing did. Both evaluations are available upon request. Today there are thirty-two neighbourhood-foot-patrol beats.

Neighbourhood foot patrol was our demonstration project to field test the philosophy of community-based policing. We learned much from it that would come in handy later. Neighbourhood foot patrol would prove to be the flagship of things to come.

A PROCESS FOR CHANGE

In June 1990, a month after his appointment, my new chief asked me to take on the job of expanding community-based policing across one of our patrol divisions. At the time I was commander of our South Division. I accepted on two conditions: that we take on the job of renovating the entire organization and that we do things my way. We agreed that I would write a detailed plan of action, spelling out what needed doing so that we were both on the same wavelength before I tackled the job.

I sequestered myself in a little office with no telephone for a month. By the end of that time I had written my plan, *A Process for Change*, which I presented it to my chief. He accepted it without change. We then presented it to our Executive Officers' Committee (EOC), and they also unanimously accepted it without change.

Put simply, the main objective of the plan is to reconstruct the Edmonton Police Service around the philosophy of community-based policing, community problem-solving being the ultimate goal. The plan has four primary components:

1 Decentralization
2 Despecialization
3 Ownership
4 New Service-Delivery System

These primary components contain numerous subcomponents. Space precludes including the fourteen-page plan in its entirety, but copies are available to anyone upon request. As I write, implementation is complete. My intention here is to explain my logic for doing what we did and to describe how we went about doing it. Plans for extensive evaluation of all components of the scheme are already under way. In that regard, the Police Executive Research Forum (PERF), Washington, DC, under a grant from the National Institute of Justice (NIJ), the research arm of the United States Department of Justice, has chosen Edmonton as one of six sites for the evaluation of community-based policing, with heavy emphasis on community involvement and problem-solving. The other five sites, all American, are Philadelphia, Las Vegas, Santa Barbara, Newport News, and Savannah. Our ultimate aim is to find a more effective way of policing contemporary society. When the evaluation results are known we are prepared to jettison or adjust, wherever and whenever necessary. What follows is a description of how we went about creating and implementing the overall plan.

First I must explain how I work. Whenever I take on a big task, the first thing I do is break it down into small manageable parts. That way, things seem to prioritize themselves and what needs doing first becomes clear. I much prefer teams to committees. I agree with what Abe Lincoln said on the subject: 'Committees of twenty cogitate plenty; committees of ten meet now and then, but most things get done by committees of one.' With committees it is never clear who is supposed to do what. Committees do not take care of the bike.

Usually, a few people will do all the talking, while a few others end up doing all the work. With teams everyone knows what they are responsible for. When an individual makes a great play, they know they alone will get the credit for it. I like it that way. On teams individuals are given *ownership* and *responsibility* for individual parts of the game plan.

Having broken the whole into individual pieces, I can then select people uniquely suited to each piece. I spoke earlier about enthusiasm, which is such an important part of any human endeavour. No matter how bright and motivated people are, they eventually lose their edge if left in the same intellectual environment for too long. Often the brightest become bored the quickest. When enthusiasm wanes, so does quality. Therefore, I believe in bringing together small teams of highly motivated people for each component of the process and giving them ownership of a piece of the action that will be completed before their enthusiasm begins to ebb. When each component is completed, I collapse that team and form another suited to the next component. This way enthusiasm is always at its peak and many people get the opportunity to strut their stuff. Also, as each collapsed team returns to the general workforce, they are now champions of the cause and can take on the cynics who are sure to surface. At the outset my chief gave me free access to choose people from anywhere in the organization to work with me. With 1400 people to choose from, lack of talent was not a problem.

What follows are the steps we went through to get to where we are today.

CORE VALUE

Whenever I take on a new project I need to have a clear understanding of the *primary* object of the exercise. What is the one thing that dominates all else? I am speaking of a core value. All successful individuals, families, and institutions seem to have one *and they never lose sight of it.* Cicero said: 'Nothing happens without a cause.' All causes have a core value to them that links function to cause. To qualify, a core value must meet three criteria: it must be *clear* in meaning, *universal* in application, and *attainable* by everyone in the organization, from chief to grunt. It must represent that which is more important than all else. Its objective is to describe the final destination for every decision and to prevent drift from that destination. Although individuals and units may take different routes, all eventually arrive at the same destination. Law enforcement is *not* a destination; it is only a stop along the way. Law enforcement is not a core value; it is a task. A core value must not be pie-in-the-sky stuff. It has to make sense to ordinary people, on their terms.

Community-based policing has been the primary goal of the Edmonton

Police Service for several years. But that phrase does not pass the crystalline test. It's too slippery. It is like a piece of abstract art; it means many things to many people. People need something with harder edges. To determine our core value we had to revisit the fundamental mandate of policing and evaluate it by contemporary Edmonton's standards. This required us to ask and answer five basic questions:

- What was the Edmonton Police Service intended to do?
- What in fact is it doing now?
- Should it be doing what it is doing now?
- What should it be doing?
- How should it do what it should be doing?

We held an EOC retreat in order to answer these questions and determine a core value that provides the answer to the last two questions. That group unanimously chose 'Committed to Community Needs' as our core value. This was then published in our bi-weekly newsletter, and improvements or refinements were solicited. When all submissions were considered 'Committed to Community Needs' was adopted as the core value of our service.

A core value doesn't mean much unless everyone and everything in the organization is evaluated against it. Only time will tell how entrenched our core value will become, but already there are significant signs that the culture of the service is shifting. If the core value achieves its mission, it will transform the reward system, which in turn will transform people's perception of how one gets ahead in the organization. There are already clear signs of a shift in career paths and a reversal of the flight-from-the-front syndrome, which saw many people fleeing patrol work for specialized inside jobs because they perceived that as the way to get ahead. I can honestly say that a new hero is emerging in the Edmonton Police Service. A significant number of people at various ranks are requesting transfer back to patrol work because they now perceive that that is where their best chances of advancement are. People in specialized units are grumbling that they are being passed over. Whereas in the past those assigned to specialized units stayed there as long as possible, many are now moving back to patrol work before their time is up. It used to be nearly impossible to get detectives to transfer voluntarily to patrol as sergeants. Now the reverse is true. I find it personally satisfying to see the stars of the future leaving inside jobs to voluntarily return to patrol. I was very proud when one of our most promising sergeants was, in turn, proud to come and tell me that he had turned down a transfer to the personnel division, a move that not too long ago would have been seen as a sure stepping stone to career progress. Perhaps the fact that we have rewritten our performance-appraisal forms and reformed the promotion process to reflect our core value has something to do with this change in attitude.

ORGANIZATIONAL RESTRUCTURING

There are far too many people in support roles in policing. The professional model is notoriously office-bound. In many organizations bureaucracy and support positions eat up two-thirds of total strength. The Edmonton Police Service grew from 40 boxes on the organization chart in 1970 to 121 in 1988. A primary aim of the process-for-change plan is to reverse that trend. As far back as 1975 the Rand study demonstrated that conventional detective work in policing is hugely ineffective. Keith Bryett (retired) of the Queensland Police Department in Brisbane, Australia, has written an insightful piece called, 'Police Specialization: A Reassessment' (1991), in which he describes the birth and growth of specialization and then demonstrates its ineffectiveness. Bryett suggests that all police officers should be in uniform – including detectives – unless they are in a covert role. I agree entirely.

A primary contributor to the growth of bureaucracy is the belief that people cannot be trusted to work on their own and so must be supervised by a higher level. In the typical agency, there will be one supervisor for every four officers. One of the lessons I learned while observing policing in Japan was that their patrol sergeants, instead of sitting in a car or office supervising the work of others, do exactly the same work as the people they are responsible for. They don't supervise – they lead, by example. As a consequence, there is far more rubber on the road and far less paperwork because the sergeants are too busy doing useful work to have time to generate paper for others.

And so the next order of business was a bureaucratic garage sale!

BUREAUCRATIC GARAGE SALE

Garage sales are very smart. They do two things: force us to clean house and get rid of junk, and provide the resources to buy new things. Garage sales force us to examine everything in the house and garage in terms of its current value, and then decide what should be kept, sold off, given away, or taken to the dump. Rarely do clothes wear out any more; they are far more likely to go out of style first. Many parts of conventional policing are just out of style. The garage-sale logic makes good sense to me and so I applied it to my work. This meant repeating the process followed in determining our core value through evaluating every unit on the organization chart according to the core value by asking the same five questions.

These questions fall into two natural categories. The first two examine the past and present. The latter three suggest directions for the future. To answer the first two, I selected five people of diverse talents from across the organization to act as analysts. We had a few 'head-banging' sessions so that we had a common understanding of what we were attempting to achieve. The analysts' task was to examine every box on the organization chart against the first two questions by researching the history of each unit and determining what it was intended to achieve at the outset. They then spent time with the people working in the unit, finding out exactly what these people were doing on a daily basis now. Each concluded their report by offering personal opinions on the future of each unit they worked on.

Armed with this data, my next step was to form an evaluation team to come up with answers to the final three questions. I selected five people for this task: four superintendents who brought with them strong backgrounds in patrol work, criminal investigation, accreditation, and personnel, and our civilian head of the fiscal and equipment division. These five were then tasked to choose one person each from anywhere across the Service to serve on the team also. In order to have an uneven number, I selected one other person. This made a total of eleven people representing, as it turned out, all ranks from constable to superintendent, as well as our top civilian manager. Intentionally, I was not a member of the evaluation team because I wanted the team to take personal ownership of the work they were about to do.

All members of the evaluation team were provided with copies of the analysts' omnibus report and given a month to study it in detail. Their task would be to answer the final three questions by applying the analysts' findings to the core value and to come forward with a universal slate of recommendations intended to restructure the Edmonton Police Service around the philosophy of community-based policing. Approval of a recommendation required seven votes rather than a mere majority. There was one final, excellent suggestion from one of our inspectors, a qualified lawyer and a well-respected person among his peers, who offered to moderate the deliberations of the evaluation team, which were guaranteed to be hot and heavy!

We sequestered ourselves in a city-owned downtown building for a week of ten-hour days so that we might feel free from the influences of headquarters. The group included the evaluation team, the analysts who would act as resource people to the team, and my project team of four. Everyone could participate at the discussion stage, but only members of the team could make recommendations and vote on them. Lunch and coffee were brought in to save time and to help us stay focused. We all felt a bit awkward on Monday morning as we struggled to start the process. The freedom for individuals to look into the bowels of the entire organization and to make sweeping recommendations for change took some getting used to. It was a new experience for all. There was no blueprint to follow because no large agency had undertaken such universal change since Wilson's time in Chicago. We had to break new ground as we went. The good news was that no one could tell us we were doing it wrong. That week was one of the most gratifying of my career. There was the expected shyness and nervousness as we got started, but I was surprised at how quickly rank was forgotten as people became caught up in the work. It was wonderful to watch these people dig into their consciences and open up with each other. I watched as individuals whom I had worked with for a quarter-century shelved personal biases and agendas, looked beyond their own careers, and began to focus on the cause of the service. There was much head-banging and many flare-ups, but by the afternoon of the first day we had broken through our inhibitions and ideas were flying all over the place.

By the end of that week, the team had put forth 164 recommendations, 132 of which received the seven votes or more necessary for approval. Collectively, the recommendations were universal and reached into every nook and cranny of the organization. If all were implemented, a deputy chief's position would disappear and Internal Affairs would be restructured, recruits would receive only half pay whilst in training and would not be sworn into office until the end of the training period, some organization-chart boxes would disappear while others would merge, and specialized units would disband while others would decentralize. The number of people reassigned from support to front-line work would increase the latter area by 30 per cent. I felt confident that the total effect of the recommendations would constitute the most significant overhaul of a large urban police agency in recent times.

The final step of the organizational restructuring called for the evaluation team to present its recommendations to the EOC, the policy-setting body for the service. This took place over a long two-day session. Of the 132 recommendations brought forward to the EOC, 112 were approved outright. The most catalytic recommendations, which would have sent out the strongest message that change was being institutionalized, were either deferred or rejected. This was unfortunate in my view. Perhaps I was expecting too much, but I felt we were being too tentative. Although the total change brought about by the 112 recommendations was considerable, I believed the timing and mood was right to do more. The composition of the EOC at the time included a new chief, two new deputies, and three new superintendents. Many members of the EOC were relatively young, with considerable personal investment in the future. At the outset of the EOC deliberations there was great enthusiasm and bravado, but people began to roll over as soon as the chief's position on individual recommendations became clear. Courage is the foremost quality that separates leaders from bureaucrats.

OMNIBUS WORK-LOAD ANALYSIS

Most police bureaucrats are consumed by the daily routine of their 'in'/'out' baskets, which keep them locked on today's problems. Not too many are up on the balcony looking down on the dance floor, aware of tomorrow's problems. Few are intimate with the *reality* of the work that drives the organization on a daily basis. Some are running blind because little evaluation is undertaken in policing to determine what works. Few agencies capture any statistics beyond those legislated by Uniform Crime Reports (UCR) requirements. Uniform Crime Reports data are worthless for tactical application. Rendered down UCR data describe only the activities of the criminal-justice system. They tell us little about our communities. They reflect only the known crime figures and reveal nothing about the vast majority of police business, which is not crime in the pure sense – the stuff the justice system never hears about.

In order to restructure policing around the realities of contemporary society, there is a great need to know what those realities are. For example, in order to institutionalize the village-in-the-city and family-doctor ideas we need to know much more about the personality of individual neighbourhoods within cities. Just as there is no single cure for disease, neither is there a solitary cure for crime. If policing is ever to progress from an incident-based to a problem-based focus, we need to know much more about what creates the need for police service by breaking down the total workload by neighbourhood and occurrence type. Only then can we begin to think about solutions.

To achieve this goal we had to break more new ground. The work-load analysis conducted in 1987 for the institution of the neighbourhood foot patrols was grid-specific. Many of these grids contained several neighbourhoods and in some cases cut across neighbourhoods. In order to implement subsequent components of the process-for-change plan, we had to find a way to do a neighbourhood-specific workload analysis. The technocrats told me this couldn't be done. They were wrong.

All workplaces have people with unique talents waiting to be discovered. Often these people are in the wrong places being forced to do the wrong things. We discovered such an individual who was able to deliver what we wanted. Constable Jody Bevan is particularly bright and enterprising. He recently returned from an unpaid leave during which he went to Germany on behalf of an Edmonton company to open up a computer-services office there. In fact, soon after his return, Jody retired to concentrate on his own computer-software company, which is thriving. (As an aside, conventional policing cannot afford to lose a Jody Bevans. We must find a way to keep such people.) Jody had been working in a technical unit for several years, but was at odds with the technocrats there. By definition I knew Jody was my man. I described to him what we had in mind. He assured me he could deliver the product with his personal equipment if we could supply him with a specific piece of equipment. We did.

We had Jody transferred to our project team. Within a month, we had the type of workload analysis we needed. We believe this model of analysis will be the norm for police agencies intent upon restructuring around community-based policing. With the cooperation of our city planning department, who provided us with city-wide neighbourhood-specific maps for the 273 neighbourhoods, we were able to reduce a database of 204,000 incidents (1990) to individual neighbourhood profiles. We could now examine each neighbourhood by the total workload generated, and then break it down by the twelve individual occurrence types described in the 'Building Blocks' section. This information equipped us to concentrate on the most needy neighbourhoods and to apply the policing strategy – for example, foot patrol, community station, traffic enforcement, undercover operation – best suited to the unique problem. Most important, this workload analysis provides the information obtained *after the investigation has been completed*, whereas UCR data represent the crime picture as reported to the police in the first instance. Research and experience demonstrate that many incidents turn out to be different from what is initially reported.

Many revelations flowed from this workload analysis that were to prove critical to subsequent components of the process-for-change plan. The analysis supports unequivocally the thesis that cities are in fact collections of distinct villages, some of which need intense police service for a variety of reasons, while others are very healthy and require little attention. Some critics claim that because people pay taxes for police services they are entitled to their slice of the pie. Well, Canada has a universal health-care system, but healthy people don't sit in doctors' offices simply because their taxes have paid for the service. A couple of specifics to make the point:

- Two neighbourhoods generated almost 24,000 occurrences between them, while six others collectively did not generate a single one.
- The same two neighbourhoods suffered 494 residential break-ins, while 18 others collectively had none.

This analysis serves two purposes. It equips management to set priorities and deploy resources effectively and it provides operational commanders with information specific to the neighbourhoods of the areas of the city for which they are responsible. Armed with this unique information we created the map room referred to earlier. It contains thirteen city-wide maps that clearly illustrate at a glance the diverse policing needs of our city. It is relatively simple to update these maps.

DECENTRALIZATION

Policing needs to radically decentralize resources and decision-making for different reasons. Our workload analysis demonstrates unequivocally that our customers and their needs are diverse. As well, cities have changed dramatically since the introduction of Wilson's centralized model. Most are massive suburban sprawls with decaying centres. The bulk of street-level crime and disorder, the stuff that fuels the fear that crime is out of control and that consumes the biggest chunk of police resources, is local in nature. It is committed by and against local residents, mainly in poorer neighbourhoods. The most effective tool in dealing with this local crime is local knowledge. The only way to get that local knowledge is to become part of neighbourhood life. Driving around in a car, no matter how frequently, might make us familiar with buildings and geography, but not with people. Technology contact must be replaced by people contact. The cars have to be parked at least some of the time and computers shut off so that people on both sides can spend time together regularly and informally. Until that happens in inner-city neighbourhoods, there is no hope of bridging the gap between the police and the residents. I am convinced that one human being could not beat another as badly as Rodney King was beaten if the people involved knew each other – even just a little bit!

INDOOR POLICING – TODAY'S TOWN SQUARE

There is another compelling reason for decentralization – the modern phenomenon of indoor life. Canadians today spend 90 per cent of their time indoors. As far back as 1988 Edmonton had more indoor shopping space than any other city in the world. *Shopping malls are the modern equivalent of the town square of yesteryear.* Indoor parking is the norm in many places. Most new residential and commercial high-rise architecture is self-contained, the aim being to meet all the needs of a captive audience under one roof. Many cities have underground transportation and most downtown high-rises in Canada and the northern states are connected by systems of pedways and tunnels.

Here is the conundrum created by this evolution. Contemporary police strategies are predicated upon the presumption that crime is a public-place event, but contemporary society spends little of its time in purely public places. Today, an infinitesimal portion of crime is committed in public places. But, while the town square was public, shopping malls are private property. As a consequence, we police *space* instead of *people*. The people are inside, while the police are outside driving around empty streets. The vast majority of people who are outside are in automobiles going from one inside place to another, and so are in little danger of being a crime victim while they are in transit. Deployed as they are, police encounter the vast majority of their customers through the medium of the automobile, but find themselves in an adversarial posture through enforcing some law related to the automobile. And so, in the typical 'law enforcement' agency, far more resources are devoted to traffic enforcement than to the causes of crime.

Thoreau said that 'man becomes a tool of his tools.' So it has come to pass in policing. Because centralization requires that all police units be in contact with headquarters, the patrol car has become the primary tool of the work. A fully equipped patrol car in Edmonton costs $35,000. The automobile is replaced every four years. Unless we can find a way to get our Chevy Caprices with their ubiquitous 'stuff' into these malls, pedways, and tunnels, we will have to park them and walk – or continue to police space, with technology contact being the dominant factor.

DESPECIALIZATION

The term 'specialist' in policing has come to mean everyone except the guy who throws the box into the truck, the grunt. In my view, specialization in policing is a cancer. It has eaten away at the front end of police work to such an extent that there are now two office jockeys for every patrol constable. Specialists spend 90 per cent of their time office-bound in headquarters, shuffling paper or talking on the telephone. One learns very little about one's city, its citizens, or its crime by sitting in headquarters. Criminals rarely show up on the third floor of headquarters!

Specialization also renders police-to-public ratios meaningless. The typical standard across North America (no one knows where it came from, by the way) to determine adequate police numbers is 1–500. This is achieved simplistically by dividing the total number of citizens by the total number of police officers. But as numerous studies have shown, many police officers have little contact with the public, make few arrests, and are not in a mode to respond to emergencies when they occur. As many as half of the total force spend of their time doing things that have nothing to do with public safety.

Consider how the shape of the typical large urban police agency has shifted over the years. A 1971 study of American cities with populations of 300,000 to 1,000,000 revealed that 86.5 per cent of sworn police personnel, excluding sergeants, were assigned to patrol operations. The organizational review conducted by my project team in 1990 revealed that, structured as we were, only 34 per cent of our sworn personnel were specifically assigned to the calls-for-service duties that the average citizen presumes nearly all police officers do. We also discovered what we called the Ghost Division. Of the 34 per cent assigned to service duties, on any given day 24 per cent will be unavailable for a variety of reasons: days off, vacation, on loan, sick, on maternity leave, and so on. Notwithstanding that there is so little rubber on the road, during 1990 those few made 85 per cent of all arrests, investigated 97 per cent of all traffic collisions (even though we have a specialized traffic section), and performed 50 per cent of all traffic enforcement. Everyone else was in some form of specialist back-up role, many of them feeding off the work of the grunts. That's far too much back-up. The typical detective, for example, will make one specialized arrest per month, and do little of anything else because it isn't his job. The indisputable fact is that specialists, like the middle managers at Citibank, contribute little to the cause because everything outside their narrow focus is someone else's job.

The most destructive element of specialization, in my view, is the perception that it leads to quicker promotion. For those aspiring to personal advancement, patrol work is looked upon as the least attractive assignment in conventional policing. Specialization causes what I referred to above as 'the flight from the front.' Here is what I mean. In 1988 there were 242 applications for transfers from patrol to five specialized areas, with no record of a single request for a transfer the other way. When we conducted our 1990 review to determine where people's heads were at, we discovered that number had grown to 389. Again, there was no record of a request to move the other way.

My personal view is that no less than 70 per cent of sworn officers should be dedicated to the front-line patrol function, where the moments of truth of policing are created. Anything less and you have too much specialization. My experience tells me that most police services are drastically overspecialized.

DIVERSIFIED SERVICE-DELIVERY SYSTEM

The medium is the message.
– Marshall McLuhan

Central to the process-for-change plan was the need for a diversified service-delivery system. I will explain why this is so, and then describe how we went about building one.

The automobile is the flagship of the conventional police agency. It dominates all else. Often more thought is given to the colour of police cars than to solving community problems. Most police officers cannot visualize police work without a police car at the centre. Invariably the front cover of the glossy annual report is emblazoned with a shiny police car, its lights flashing against a backdrop of skyscrapers. Recently I checked the front cover of six national police magazines; every one was dominated by some type of police automobile. The automobile has influenced the police psyche more than any other single thing. Because of it, low response times – to all calls for service – became the primary promise of police bureaucrats. The medium became the message. The inescapable flaw of this focus is that the officer cannot spend too much time at any single call because he has to get to the next one quickly too. What the police officer does at the call becomes secondary. Therefore being 'in service' becomes more important in the minds of bosses than being 'out of service.' 'In service' means being in the car and close to the radio and/or computer. I call this technology contact. Conversely, 'out of service' means being out of the car and away from the technology, but perhaps helping someone or just chatting with people. I call this people contact. In the police psyche, in service is good. Out of service is bad.

We need to shift priorities. With the exception of genuine emergencies, we need to concentrate less on how quickly we get somewhere and more on what we do after we have arrived. As things stand, police often create more danger on the way to a call by speeding through crowded streets than they prevent after they have arrived. Reliance on the automobile – by both the public and the police – to deliver the product must be drastically diminished. Police administrators must return the automobile to its original role – to get a person from point A to point B in order to do something there. The public must wean themselves off instant doorstep delivery and learn to access their police services in other ways.

Conventional patrol deployment is one-dimensional. Everyone is in a rapid-response mode, poised to rush with lights and sirens to the big stuff. Any unit can be dispatched to any type of call at any time. The big stuff is seen as fun, but it doesn't happen very often. The little stuff is not seen as fun, but it happens a lot. This leads to a kind of pack mentality. Have you ever seen a bunch of ducks go after a piece of bread? Often the little pieces get neglected while the pack is off chasing the rare big stuff. Genuine emergency calls are rare (about 5 per cent of the total in Edmonton), but when they do occur everyone wants to get in on the action.

There were twenty-seven police officers at the scene of the Rodney King beating on a Saturday night in a city that has the lowest police-to-public ratio of the six largest U.S. cities (Police Foundation 1986). Perhaps we are not as busy – even in the second-largest city on the continent – as we think we are. This 'hunt in packs' type of situation is not unique to Los Angeles or as rare as some of us might believe. There is a community cost to this pack mentality – and it happens in all cities. It happened in our city two years ago during a high-speed chase: notwithstanding strict, clear policy to the contrary, our own internal investigation revealed that forty-four police officers became involved in the chase at one stage or another. Many of those involved in the Los Angeles and Edmonton incidents should have been somewhere else doing something else. Many calls, perhaps even some high-priority ones, likely went unanswered as the pack stood and watched or sped through city streets. Many of those officers were out of play while their presence was needed elsewhere. This situation contributes to the feast-or-famine effect. Either you have overkill response or no one is available when life-threatening situations occur.

Also, with everyone in the same mode, waiting for the big stuff, the 'down' time between calls cannot be harnessed effectively for several reasons: (a) we don't know when it will happen; (b) we don't know how long it will last; and (c) we don't know how many people will be free. The problems with a single-dimension service delivery do not end there either. Computers in police cars have proved to be a mixed blessing. Computers gave rise to a new term in policing: 'call shopping.' These computers are a blessing to the slugs, who can now plan their day according to their personal agendas. Individuals can now bring up all outstanding calls on their computer screens and pick and choose the ones that suit them.

TELESERVE: MAIL-ORDER POLICING

'Differential response' has been a buzz-phrase for about a decade in policing. Theoretically it means using a variety of strategies to respond to various types of calls. It has become a cliché. Anywhere I have looked the concept has been reduced to either dispatching a car as soon as possible or else 'investigating' the call over the telephone. The more the volume of work grows, the more the telephone is employed. This 'solution,' commonly referred to as Teleserve, scares the hell out of me. Investigating crime over the telephone opens up a Pandora's box. Here's why.

In Edmonton in 1990, 54,000 crimes were investigated over the telephone because the complainant could not provide us with a suspect in the first instance. In these instances investigation is a misnomer. All that really happens is that a brief report is taken by telephone and the complainant is given a file number. In effect, we are asking the victims to be the investigator. If they cannot provide us with a hot lead, we are not interested in their problem. Some people see this as progressive police service; they even brag about its efficiency. They are wrong, for several reasons.

Such policy is efficient – but at the expense of effectiveness. It is a typical example of bureaucracy-based policing, because it is designed to save work for the organization at the expense of the public's interests. Such policy sends out a clear message that we will only investigate those crimes that will make us look good in UCR rankings. It also contradicts our exhortation to the public to turn to us for help, and ignores the human trauma of crime. This mind-set exemplifies why police work has ignored family violence for decades. It wasn't seen as important because we were looking at it through the eyes of male law-enforcement officers. The message received by victims is that the police (which to them represent the whole system) don't care, and so fear of crime flourishes. The police may only be interested in the big stuff, but any survey in any city consistently shows that it is the unchecked small stuff that is scaring the hell out of people (see Kelling and Wilson 1982). This approach also misses the importance of information in dealing with time. Informal neighbourhood knowledge is the key – but we can partly get it over the telephone.

There are other reasons why Teleserve is wrong-headed. When someone reports stolen property over the telephone we don't know whom we are talking to, that the property was actually stolen, that it ever existed in the first place, or that it was as valuable as reported. It is amazing how many people in Edmonton have expensive leather jackets, Alpine stereos, Ping golf clubs, and Pentax cameras!

In Edmonton, we routinely used to take theft reports of welfare money (never cheques, always cash) over the telephone. A constable in Central Communications smelled a rat, and so we did some investigating. We discovered that approximately $250,000 in such losses were being reported each month during the few days following the issuance of welfare cheques. Some people had reported multiple losses. In order to prevent such abuses, we ceased the practice of giving file numbers over the telephone and instead required the victim to report the loss in person at a community station. We were castigated in the media by various groups for being heartless to poor people. But at such times leaders hang in there and do what is right – no matter who the lobby group is.

Fraudulent insurance claims are among the fastest growing crimes in North America. They are a crime of affluence (because we have so much to insure) and cost the public billions of dollars every year. The U.S. Insurance Bureau estimates that 27 per cent of all claims are fraudulent; the Insurance Bureau of Canada puts its estimate at 20 per cent. People in the industry on both sides of the border, in private conversation, admit that the real figure is probably much higher; one estimated it to be as high as 50 per cent in some regions. Once police issue a file number, they legitimize the claim. Teleserve may be bureaucratically efficient – but it may also make us accomplices in a huge insurance scam.

Doing police work by telephone is harmful for a different reason. It eliminates the human factor; we remain anonymous to each other. The telephone enables people to say things they wouldn't have the courage to say in person, for instance, in making obscene or threatening telephone calls. It is much easier to be insulting or to lie to a faceless voice on the other end of the telephone than it is to a person standing in front of us. Also, with only a voice on the telephone by which to judge each other, our presumptions and assumptions about each other run amok. The telephone forces us to judge each other by voice alone. We can all recall occasions of complete amazement upon meeting a person we had only spoken to before by telephone. Perception and reality rarely match.

The essence of community-based policing is that the public and their police spend much more time in each other's company determining problems and discovering solutions. Conventional policing puts too much stuff between us. The two principal tools of conventional police work, the automobile and the telephone, although convenient, too often stand in the way of this coming together.

The predictability of the police workload is relatively uncontrollable. Log-jams are the norm; it is feast or famine in terms of the resources available to handle the work at any given time. These log-jams are caused by several things, all beyond the control of police managers: the time of day, day of the week, time of year, traffic volume, weather, school holidays, and special events, to name a few. If the work could be evenly distributed across the 168 hours in a week, many of our problems would disappear. But as they say in Ireland, 'that's like trying to get a drink at your own funeral.' Many of the problems facing police administrators stem from their predecessors' promise of immediate doorstep delivery on every call. Understandably, the public became accustomed to expecting no less. Those were more tranquil times, however, and the number of homes with telephones was a fraction of what it is today. But even if we could continue to meet those expectations, it would be senseless to do so. It is not necessary or sensible – and never was – for the police to drive immediately to the originating point of every call for service. There are other ways to get the policing product to market. I will illustrate how by citing recent evolutions in other service industries.

RESTAURANTS

If I want to have a salad in a restaurant I can get it in one of two ways: order off the menu or use the salad bar. Either way I gain and I lose. If I order from the menu I don't have to do any work, but I am stuck with someone else's idea of a salad in terms of composition and volume. If I use the salad bar I have to do the work, but I end up with my idea of a salad (I am grateful to 'Butch' Leonard of Harvard for this idea). Buffets are common in restaurants today. People are happy to serve themselves if they gain something by doing so.

HEALTH CARE

Doctors used to make house calls. Today, unless it is an emergency, people take themselves to the doctor and often wait two hours to be treated. To compensate there are doctors' offices everywhere, conveniently located and operated during hours that are patient-based. If a person has a medical emergency, they either call 911 for an ambulance or take themselves to an emergency ward.

MAIL DELIVERY

Universal delivery of mail to the home used to be the norm in Canada. Today we have super mailboxes. When they were announced by Canada Post several years ago, there was a strong public backlash. In fact, people adjusted to them very quickly. Now we wonder what all the fuss was about. As with the salad bar, there is good news and bad news. The bad news is that we have to walk a bit to get our mail. The good news is that we don't have to cancel our mail when we are away, we can mail letters and small parcels as we pick up our mail, thus saving a trip to the post office – and we get to meet and chat with our neighbour once in a while.

People seem to have adjusted nicely to these developments, all of which cost them something. Policing must learn from them. The delivery system of police service must evolve the same way. The time has come for people to bring their police needs to the police in appropriate circumstances. In return, the police must make it convenient for people to do so – and they must produce a better product than the one being replaced. Finally, there is a legitimate role for the telephone in the delivery of police services (for instance, in responding to information requests or making arrangements to meet), but it must be limited to a restricted role. The primary emphasis must be upon bringing the police and public face-to-face in order to work problems through together.

In Edmonton we have tried to learn from this evolution and build it into the way we deliver police services. Today, our delivery system is diversified so as to radically reduce Teleserve and to reflect the reality of the work:

- immediate response to the scene by police (life-threatening emergencies)
- response to the scene by police with short delay, e.g., 30 minutes (after-the-fact personal crimes)
- delayed response, perhaps until the next day by agreement of both parties, to the scene by police (after-the-fact property crimes)
- attendance at community stations at the convenience of the public (minor crimes or problems where attendance by police at the scene is unnecessary)
- telephone service (information requests)

In order to achieve diversification,we created an infrastructure of decentralized community police stations.

COMMUNITY POLICE STATIONS

The first step in decentralization was to establish an infrastructure of twelve community police stations. The workload analysis told us where these community stations should be located. All twelve are now in operation. They operate twelve hours a day, seven days a week. Each is staffed by two or three permanently assigned police officers and also by community volunteers who work side-by-side with the officers. When the infrastructure is completely in place, Edmontonians will be able to access their police service at four divisional stations, twelve community stations, and twenty-two neighbourhood-foot-patrol storefront beat offices.

With the infrastructure in place, people can now bring their appropriate non-emergency needs, the majority of the total, to their local police station. They can do so by either going to or telephoning the community station in the first instance, or by being advised to go there if they telephone central communications first.

DIVERSIFIED SERVICE DELIVERY – THE PROBLEM

Here is the problem we faced in Edmonton. For the past twenty years, the cry has been, 'Call the cops!' Police themselves have been exhorting the public to call them with their slightest problem. Police cars were emblazoned with telephone numbers, mountains of pamphlets have been distributed, and streets are lined with Neighbourhood Watch, Block Parents, CrimeStoppers, and CheckStop signs, all entreating people to call the telephone numbers listed below. The main thrust of conventional crime-prevention units has been to call the police every time they see something suspicious. And people have. In 1991 in Edmonton there were 586,000 telephone calls to central communications alone. We estimate there were another 200,000 to divisional, community, and storefront stations. Then there was the 'on scene' stuff. The average answer time for 911 calls was 1.5 seconds, while the average answer time for complaint-line calls was 8.7 seconds. As a consequence, 102,000 of the people who called the complaint line hung up before their call was answered. We can never know how many of these people called back on the 911 line, but it is reasonable to assume that many did. Over the years, as the number of complaint-line calls grew, so did 911 calls. In 1986, 911 calls totalled 153,000; by 1991 that figured had jumped to 260,000. According to our own research and experience only about 5 per cent of all 911 calls prove to be true emergencies after they have been investigated.

Of the 586,000 calls in 1991, a unit was dispatched in response to 168,000 (35 per cent). The average response time for service-level calls was 44 minutes. The remaining 418,000 callers were either handled over the telephone or had hung up before we could get to them. *Fifty-five thousand crimes were investigated over the phone!*

We inaugurated the new delivery system on 7 January 1992 with two stations, complete with a media blitz and numerous public presentations explaining the coming changes to the community. We also purchased a full red page in our telephone directory for easy reference to police services. The page displays a map of the city, showing clearly where all community stations are located. In order to encourage citizens to help us become more effective, we listed the telephone numbers on the red page in this order: 911, in large print, first; the community stations next by their frequency of use; and the central, non-emergency complaint line last. If people call their community station but actually need an officer at the scene, a unit can be dispatched directly from the community station.

The motto of our community stations is, 'The buck stops here.' It is the responsibility of the community-station officer to settle the matter if possible (you would be surprised at how many suspects or people with arrest warrants will voluntarily turn themselves in when telephoned by a police officer). If the community-station officer cannot complete the matter at the station, a mobile unit can do follow-up work – but responsibility for completing the case remains with the community-station officer. If the problem cannot be solved at the community station, the station officer has the authority to assign it directly to a mobile unit.

The twenty-two neighbourhood-foot-patrol officers work in close conjunction with the community stations. Where it made sense to do so, about half relocated their beat offices in the community stations. Much of the follow-up work generated by the community stations is reassigned to neighbourhood-foot-patrol officers because it originated in their neighbourhoods.

It is important to remember that our enhanced (the source telephone number is displayed on the computer screen) 911 system is untouched by these innovations. Every 911 call is answered in less than two seconds. In fact, early indications are that this system is being flushed out and purified as a result of the new delivery system.

A DIVERSIFIED DELIVERY SYSTEM – THE SOLUTION

Here are the results of the diversified delivery system. Since its inception we have been keeping daily figures on everything through our Organizational Studies Unit. What follows are the results to the end of 1993.

A total of 235,000 people *walked* into their community stations. Of the walk-ins, 40 per cent reported criminal matters and 23 per cent traffic matters. Only 6 per cent went there for information (we were worried the stations might become only curiosity pieces). Eighty per cent of the people surveyed classified their problem as routine. Eighty-seven per cent said they would have reported their problem to the police even if the station didn't exist (we were also worried that the stations might generate unnecessary or frivolous complaints). Ninety-seven per cent said they were satisfied with the time it took the officer to handle their complaint. Most important of all, 90 per cent said they would prefer to go to a community station in future rather than call the complaint line.

While the community stations were doing their work, here is the impact they had on the conventional delivery system:

- total calls into central communications dropped 34 per cent (166,000 fewer)
- total 911 calls dropped by 15 per cent (the first drop in ten years)
- average telephone answer time dropped from 81.4 to 33 seconds
- total unanswered telephone calls dropped by 61 per cent
- total dispatched calls dropped by 22 per cent (but the percentage of total incoming calls dispatched rose from 33 to 41 per cent)
- average response time to service level calls dropped by 23 percent
- crimes investigated over the telephone at central communications dropped by 79 per cent
- face-to-face encounters between police and public have increased from 155,000 to 369,000

This type of radical surgery on the delivery system is needed for urban policing to regain control of the incoming product so that emphasis can shift from response times to problem-solving. Numerous studies (Sherman 1986, Minneapolis; Braiden 1987, Edmonton) show that most calls for service come from repeat sources. Just as the neighbourhood foot patrol had demonstrated five years earlier, the officers working out of each community station very quickly develop the local knowledge so necessary to problem identification and solution. Because Mohammed is now coming to the mountain, travel time between calls is eliminated. As a result, a constable working at a community station can handle many more complaints than his mobile counterpart in the same time. Not only has personal contact between the police and public doubled, there is now also much more free time for mobile patrols to concentrate on their neighbourhood problems.

The new service delivery forces producer and consumer to come together on a regular basis in non-confrontational terms. It breaks the city into villages and allows each area to be policed according to its unique needs. A familiarity has developed that was impossible to accomplish police were relying totally on the automobile and telephone to deliver their product. Each station is partially staffed by citizen volunteers (we have a total of about 400) from the surrounding neighbourhood. Community-station officers are also volunteers permanently assigned to a particular station.

As a result of these structural changes the culture of the organization is forced to change in the same direction. Instead of trying to explain what community-based policing means to people, our new way of doing business *demonstrates* what it means. By regaining control over the volume and nature of the work, we can now see the big picture more clearly. This allows us to work smarter. It also prepares the way for installation of the final piece of the plan, a common sense of ownership between police officer and citizen.

OWNERSHIP

The Rodney King beating confirmed for me something I have long believed about policing. So many of the problems of conventional police work stem from the fact that almost every encounter between the police and public is stranger-on-stranger. When two people don't know each other, fear and suspicion is the norm. When two people do know each other, however slightly, a different chemistry kicks in. Some kind of bonding occurs. Just as we can say things to a faceless voice on the telephone we could not say in person, so too can we do things to each other as strangers that we could not do if we knew each other.

If the 1100 police officers and the 635,000 citizens of Edmonton remain strangers to each other, nothing much of substance will be accomplished. We can never get to know each other in policing until we break large cities into villages. The strategy of two police officers working together *do not increase officer safety* and has no place in community-based policing. Because of the one-dimensional conventional deployment mentality, every time a two-person unit is off at a routine call (the majority of the time) they are not in a position to help elsewhere. Also, when two friends are together they have no need of others. So it is with the two-person unit. The 'police family' mind-set sees the police as a besieged enclave within a city. This mind-set must be pried apart so that individual officers begin to identify more with their neighbourhoods and less with their own group. Until allegiance shift from the cloth to the cause, fundamental change in policing will prove elusive.

In Edmonton we are attacking the problem head-on. In the past the city was broken into patrol districts, with a mobile unit assigned to each district. These districts were purely bureaucratic entities. They ignored neighbourhood boundaries and in fact often cut through the middle of natural neighbourhoods. Also, assignment to a patrol district was temporary. The end result was that the patrol district meant little to the police manager or the grunt – and nothing to the Joe Citizen.

Today we don't bother with patrol districts. In their place we have ownership of turf. Individual patrol officers have ownership of every one of the 273 neighbourhoods in our city. Because certain neighbourhoods are less populated or troubled than others, individual officers own several. Whenever possible, calls for service are dispatched to the individual who has ownership of that neighbourhood. If that officer is off duty, calls investigated in those neighbourhoods by other officers or reported at community stations come back to the 'ownership' officer for follow-up. When these officers have down time, they spend it working on whatever the neighbourhood priorities happen to be at that time, or else doing what they can to solve the problems of their steady customers. Because of the decrease in dispatched calls brought about by our new service delivery, these officers are now assigned on average only two service calls per shift. This leaves significant time for them to concentrate on their neighbourhoods, develop local knowledge, get to know the residents and their problems, and learn where to find the resources to solve those problems.

CLEAN-UP

And so, to finish. It has taken me too long to learn what I have about policing. Those who follow must get up to speed quicker. They must not make the same mistakes as I have, but mistakes they must make as they strive to make policing community-based, and then keep it that way. In this paper, my intention has been to explain the past and provide suggestions for the future. Contemporary police officers need to understand the true mandate of their calling, learn from the past, and in the process strip away the myths that have attached themselves to the work like barnacles over the years. I have sought to ask the right questions, identify the real problems, and provide some practical answers. Above all, my goal here has been to be as honest as possible, as politely as I can, about how things look from my winejug so as to contribute uniquely to what we know about policing. There is a great need for police chiefs and overseers to think comprehensively about their work, and above all else to do what is right. Too much of what passed for innovation in the past two decades were self-serving efforts to curry favour with the public. It has given us what I call sign policing. Our streets and highways are littered with signs, each one announcing another in a series of crime-prevention programs, few of which have ever progressed beyond installation of the sign.

Quick-fix solutions are still the norm today. Policing is becoming a dumping ground for short-term, politically-correct promises made to single-issue groups for personal reasons. These promises are the same old sycophancy wrapped in a different package. I predict that these 'solutions' will create new problems. They are like the national deficit – they only delay and compound the problem. As an example, the phrase 'The police must reflect the mosaic of the community' is not a solution to the malaise that afflicts policing. It suggests that the white male is the manifestation and cause of all that is wrong in North American policing, and that if we only change in colour all will be well. Good luck, I say. When Mark Twain said the human race was flawed, he was talking about all of us. As I write, bigotry and racism are rampant across the globe. Unquestionably visible minorities and women are underrepresented in police ranks. Indeed, white-male-chauvinist thinking is at the root of our worst problems in policing, but choosing people solely because of their colour or gender is as wrong-headed as choosing people simply because they have a university degree. I know visible minority and female police officers who are as incompetent at the work as their white male brethren. The twenty-seven police officers at the scene of Rodney King's beating included African American, Latino, and female officers – and none of them did anything to stop it. *We do not need more police officers; we need more police officers with character. Their colour or gender is absolutely immaterial. Policing does not need ethnic specialists; it needs universalists.* Doctor Martin Luther King's elemental credo – that we judge all people, not by the colour of their skin, but by the content of their character – should be ours too as we work to right what is wrong with convention. Mahatma Gandhi and Doctor King – even Malcolm X – died because they were fighting for *human* rights. Because they were wise, they too discovered what Ben Franklin had two centuries before about hanging together – or separately.

There is a framed quotation on the wall in my office. It has been there for years. It sums up everything I have tried to say in this paper, and I will end with it. 'Police others as you would have others police you.'

REFERENCES

Bittner, Egon. 1974. 'Florence Nightingale in Pursuit of Willie Sutton.' In Herbert Jacob, ed., *The Potential for Reform of Criminal Justice*. Beverly Hills: Sage Publications.

Braiden, Chris. 1987. Repeat-call study of 153,000 calls for service to the Edmonton Police Service.

Bryett, Keith. 1991. 'Police Specialization: A Reassessment.' *Canadian Police College Journal* 13(4).

Houghton, James R. 1988. 'Quality in the Eye of the Beholder.' *Harvard Business Review* 66(6).

Kelling, George L., and James Q. Wilson. 1982. 'Broken Windows.' *Atlantic Monthly*, March 1982, 3.

Law Enforcement News. January 1993. Interview with Sergeant Stacey Koon, LAPD, by Marie Rosen-Simonetti.

Police Foundation. 1986. Comparison study funded by National Institute of Justice of the six largest U.S. police departments.

Schlesinger, Leonard A., and James L. Heskett. 1991. 'The Service-Driven Service Company.' *Harvard Business Review* 69(5).

Sherman, Lawrence. 1986. Repeat-call study of 323,000 calls for service to the Minneapolis Police Department.

Stuebing, William K. 1991. 'Crime Prevention.' Paper presented at Red Deer College.